Print Journalism
A critical introduction

Print Journalism: A critical introduction provides a unique and thorough insight into the skills required to work within the newspaper, magazine and online journalism industries. Among the many highlighted are:

- sourcing the news
- interviewing
- sub-editing
- feature writing and editing
- reviewing
- designing pages
- pitching features

In addition, separate chapters focus on ethics, reporting courts, covering politics and copyright whilst others look at the history of newspapers and magazines, the structure of the UK print industry (including its financial organisation) and the development of journalism education in the UK, helping to place the coverage of skills within a broader, critical context.

All contributors are experienced practising journalists as well as journalism educators from a broad range of UK universities.

Contributors: Rod Allen, Peter Cole, Martin Conboy, Chris Frost, Tony Harcup, Tim Holmes, Susan Jones, Richard Keeble, Sarah Niblock, Richard Orange, Iain Stevenson, Neil Thurman, Jane Taylor and Sharon Wheeler.

Richard Keeble is Professor of Journalism at Lincoln University and former director of undergraduate studies in the Journalism Department at City University, London. He is the author of *Ethics for Journalists* (2001) and *The Newspapers Handbook*, now in its fourth edition (2005).

Print Journalism
A critical introduction

Edited by Richard Keeble

Routledge
Taylor & Francis Group

LONDON AND NEW YORK

First published 2005
by Routledge
2 Park Square, Milton Park, Abingdon, Oxon, OX9 4RN

Simultaneously published in the USA and Canada
by Routledge
270 Madison Ave, New York, NY 10016

Routledge is an imprint of the Taylor & Francis Group

Designed and typeset in Janson and Akzidenz Grotesk by
Keystroke, Jacaranda Lodge, Wolverhampton
Printed and bound in Great Britain by
MPG Books Ltd, Bodmin

British Library Cataloguing in Publication Data
A catalogue record for this book is available from the British Library

Library of Congress Cataloging in Publication Data
A catalog record for this book has been requested
Print journalism : a critical introduction / edited by Richard Keeble.
     p. cm.
  Includes bibliographical references and index.
  1. Journalism. I. Keeble, Richard, 1948–
  PN4775.P73 2005
  070.1'7–dc22

                                            2005010422

ISBN 0–415–35881–7 (hbk)
ISBN 0–415–35882–5 (pbk)

Contents

Part III   More Key Areas: Ethics, Law, Copyright and Politics   **265**

Part IV   And Finally: An Education Overview   **315**

Contributors

Rod Allen is former Head of Journalism at City University, London. He was the publisher and editor of *Broadcast* before he joined the current affairs and features department of London Weekend Television as a producer. He subsequently became controller of international development at LWT. He has written and broadcast extensively on media topics and co-edited five volumes in the John Libbey series Current Debates in Broadcasting. Email: r.allen@city.ac.uk.

Peter Cole is Professor of Journalism at the University of Sheffield and head of the Department of Journalism Studies there. He was deputy editor of the *Guardian*, founder editor of the *Sunday Correspondent* and news review editor of *The Sunday Times*. He writes a weekly column on the media for the *Independent on Sunday* and has published academic articles and book chapters on various media issues. Email: p.g.cole@sheffield.ac.uk.

Martin Conboy is a Reader in the Department of Journalism Studies at the University of Sheffield. He has worked for many years in Germany and Britain on critical and historical approaches to the press. He is the author of *The Press and Popular Culture* (Sage 2002), *Journalism: A Critical History* (Sage 2004) and the forthcoming *Tabloid Britain: Constructing a Community Through Language* (Routledge 2005). Email: m.conboy@sheffield.ac.uk.

Chris Frost is Professor of Journalism at Liverpool John Moores University where he heads the Department of Journalism. He is the author of *Media Ethics and Self-Regulation, Reporting for Journalists* and *Designing for Newspapers and Magazines*. He was a newspaper journalist and editor for more than twenty years and is a former president of the NUJ. He is Chair of the Association for Journalism Education and Chair of the NUJ's Ethics Council. Email: c.p.frost@livjm.ac.uk.

Tony Harcup has more than twenty years' experience as a journalist and is now a senior lecturer in the Department of Journalism Studies at the University of Sheffield in the UK. He is the author of *Journalism: Principles and Practice* (Sage 2004) and has previously published research on news values, ethics and alternative media. He is currently working on a second book for Sage entitled *The Ethical Journalist*. Email: t.harcup@sheffield.ac.uk.

Tim Holmes is Course Director for the PG.Dip. in Magazine Journalism, Cardiff University. After eighteen years as a magazine journalist, editor and publisher, he was appointed to lead Cardiff's magazine diploma in 1995. His publications include 'McLuhanism, Bricolage and the Custom Motorcycle', a paper for the

ACA/PCA annual conference, 2004 and *Subediting for Journalists* (Routledge, with Wynford Hicks, 2003). Email: holmesta@cardiff.ac.uk.

Susan Jones is an honorary research fellow at City University, London. She has worked on computer-based document processing, in various ways, since 1966. For seven years she was closely involved with the Masters course in Electronic Publishing at City while her book, *Text and Context* (Springer-Verlag 1991) covered text retrieval, digital media, hypertext and markup languages.

Richard Keeble is Professor of Journalism at the University of Lincoln. Before that he taught for nineteen years at City University, London. His publications include *Secret State, Silent Press* (John Libbey 1997), *The Newspapers Handbook* (4th edn, Routledge 2005) and *Ethics for Journalists* (Routledge 2001). He is the editor of *Ethical Space: The International Journal of Communication Ethics*. Email: rkeeble@lincoln.ac.uk.

Sarah Niblock is a full-time lecturer and researcher in the Department of Journalism, City University, London. She began her career on the *Birkenhead News* and *Liverpool Echo* and has freelanced for *Company* and *Cosmopolitan* as well as national newspapers and radio. Her book, *Inside Journalism* (Blueprint), was published in 1996 and she has written widely on journalism, cultural studies and visual culture. Email: S.Niblock@city.ac.uk.

Richard Orange is a senior lecturer in journalism at the University of Lincoln and also runs a press agency, Orchard News Bureau. He has worked at the *Banbury Guardian, Staffordshire Newsletter, Cheshire Chronicle* and the *Lincolnshire Echo*. He has also edited and produced a series of travel guidebooks to Switzerland and is Press Officer of the Lincoln-based Circular Chess Society. Email: rorange@lincoln.ac.uk.

Iain Stevenson is Professor of Publishing Studies at City University. Previously he was a publishing executive with a number of international publishing companies including Longman, Macmillan, Pinter, Wiley and the Stationery Office. He has written widely on copyright, publishing history and serial publication and is currently working on a book on British publishing in the twentieth century. Email: w.i.stevenson@city.ac.uk.

Jane Taylor is Head of Journalism at the Surrey Institute of Art and Design, University College. She has a background in print journalism (the regional press and magazines, with a stint on LBC as a reporter). Her Ph.D. in creative and critical writing has been submitted. Most recent projects include papers for the *Journal of Media Practice* and guest editorship of *Pretext*. Email: jetaylor @surrart.ac.uk.

Neil Thurman is a senior lecturer in the Department of Journalism at City University, London and since 1999 he has directed the Master's Programme in Electronic Publishing. Previously, in editorial and management roles with Interactive Learning Productions, Yorkshire International Thomson Multimedia and Granada Learning, he produced more than fifteen interactive videos and multimedia CD-Roms. His research into the globalisation of journalism online and reader contributions to news web sites has been presented as far afield as South Korea and Austin, Texas. Email: neilt@soi.city.ac.uk.

Sharon Wheeler is Field Chair in Journalism and Professional Writing at the University of Gloucestershire. She has been a print journalist since 1985, covering everything from top rugby matches to flower shows. Sharon has extensive experience of feature writing, reviewing, music writing, sports reporting and production work on a range of newspapers, magazines, academic journals and web sites. She is editor of <http//www.reviewingtheevidence.com>. Email: swheeler@glos.ac.uk or shazw@hotpress.com.

Introduction

This is a unique textbook for journalism, communication and media studies students. It attempts to draw together for the first time in a single volume a wide range of the elements of print journalism. The prime focus is on the practical skills, but the treatment is always critical and placed within broader economic, historical and theoretical contexts.

Journalism education tends to get a bad press. Within the print industry, widespread scepticism persists about the value of studying the subject (paradoxically, since the vast majority of entrants are university graduates). Why bother, say, with the history of the press in the nineteenth century or explore the ideology of objectivity? Isn't it better to get stuck into the business of bashing out news stories on time – and to the right word length?

This text represents a serious and sustained response to that approach. All the contributors are journalists but they are also teaching the subject in higher education institutions across the country. And underlying all the chapters is the belief that studying journalism offers enormous practical, political, ethical, theoretical challenges and, in addition, prepares students to be reflective, critical practitioners in a range of careers.

Significantly, a lot of the contributors stress the difficulties of the tasks. Strangely, journalism and media studies are dubbed 'soft' subjects in mainstream newspapers. Yet the evidence suggests it remains extremely rare to gain a first-class honours degree in journalism (or in a degree combining journalism with another subject such as sociology, politics or English). And this is not surprising given the range of skills involved.

First, journalists need to have a deep understanding of the historical roots of the media, being able to analyse the factors impacting on the changes in technology, news values and professional routines. Martin Conboy's chapter focuses on the history of the print media in Britain, arguing both originally and persuasively that the impact of magazines on the development of newspapers has to date been inadequately acknowledged. Historians and media sociologists have tended to prioritise the role of the print media in relation to the world of politics. In contrast, Conboy highlights the ways in which the mainstream print media, with magazines at the forefront, have responded creatively over the centuries to the entertainment and lifestyle requirements of their **readerships**.

Journalism as a genre of literature only comes alive when directed at a specific target within a clearly defined market. Thus Peter Cole's chapter examines the structure of the British mainstream print industry and the organisational routines

readership number of people who read paper as opposed the number of copies sold.

at individual publications. Following on from this, Iain Stevenson, in the final 'Context' chapter, looks into the business of producing newspapers and magazines, exploring important concepts such as 'revenue streams' and 'cost management'.

Moving on to more practical matters, Sharon Wheeler and Sarah Niblock look at news writing, journalistic research techniques (with a special focus on the interview), the role of the news editor and the sub. But underpinning all of the practical tips lies an exploration by Sarah Niblock of that crucial question: what is news?

News appears 'natural' and a doddle to bash out. In fact, journalistic registers are complex: they have to be learned – and practised regularly. Capturing the main angle of event appropriate for your publication is often no simple task. Condensing it into a lively **intro** section and following that up with a tightly structured story, maybe combining **quotes**, information, **colour** and **background** is equally difficult.

Though the featurisation of news gathers pace, there is still value in examining **features** separately. Thus Jane Taylor identifies the seemingly infinite variety of genres (which often demand different writing styles, tones and research techniques) while Tony Harcup and Tim Holmes draw from their wide journalistic experiences to offer advice on pitching, feature writing and editing.

There is clearly a creative, subjective dimension to all print journalism. But it is most apparent in personal opinion columns, and reviews and tips on these are provided by Tim Holmes and Rod Allen. Newspapers and magazines are, in many ways, like people and thus they only work effectively when words and design combine to create a distinct, attractive 'identity'. Chris Frost's chapter, therefore, explores the principles of design and their applications in print publications while, at the same time, leading you confidently into that strange world of production jargon – bastard **measure**, **em**-rule, **puff**, **raster dot** and so on.

The overall impact of the Internet on the print industry – both in the UK and around the world – has been massive and, not surprisingly, all journalism courses now include online skills in core units. Thus Neil Thurman and colleagues explore the history of newspapers' uneasy, shifting relationship with the web; they offer advice on writing and designing online. And they end with an original focus, exploring blogs and wikis, both of which are throwing up important challenges to journalists' professionalism and privileged position within the public sphere.

As the debate over alleged dumbing-down, **tabloidisation**, infotainment and junk journalism reaches fever pitch, questions over legally and ethically responsible journalism, highlighted by Richard Orange, Richard Keeble and Iain Stevenson become even more important. A separate chapter on ethics is in danger of suggesting that such issues can be isolated from the practice of journalism. In fact, as a number of other writers here stress, it is impossible to engage in any form of reflective journalism without confronting ethical/political issues. Thus, the chapter has the simple ambition of highlighting a few major strategies and controversies while its questioning approach and focus on alternative media seeks to challenge the mainstream consensus and inspire responsible action.

Most beginning journalists will at some stage have to cover local politics. Investigative reporter Richard Orange does more than explain the intricacies of local government. He shows how to a curious and knowledgeable reporter seemingly dull council committee minutes can easily be excellent sources of news.

---

intro opening of news or feature story usually containing main angle. Not necessarily just single par. Also known as 'lead'. US: nose.

quote abbreviation for quotation; also when a reporter files copy over phone 'quote' then means first inverted commas. End quote marks are often known as 'unquote'.

colour section of newspaper copy focusing on descriptions or impressions. Thus a colour *feature* is one which puts emphasis on description and the subjective response of the journalist though the news element may still be strong.

background section of news or feature story carrying information which serves to contextualise main elements. Also, in computer jargon, indicates hyphenation and justification system is operating while copy is being input.

feature as distinct from news story, tends to be longer, carry more background information, colour, wider range of sources and journalist's opinion can be prominent.

measure width of a block of text measured in 12 pt ems.

em the square of the body height of the typesize. *See* mutton.

puff advert for editorial material inside a publication.

Finally Rod Allen directs a critical eye at journalism education in the UK and the many courses on offer.

Though the areas covered here are extremely broad, it is still easy to identify many which are missing. But rather than (somewhat defensively) steal the thunder of our critics, I'll stay mute and invite you to send all comments and criticisms to me at rkeeble@lincoln.ac.uk. Indeed, this entire text will only 'work' if it provokes a creative dialogue with you – its readers. All the contributors have added their email addresses to their brief biographies. So don't hesitate to respond. Over to you.

Richard Keeble
Lincoln, December 2004

raster dot   dot of ink in a screened picture that allows shades of grey to be represented with black ink.

tabloidisation   claim that media in general are following tabloid values prioritising entertainment, sensationalism and scandal above 'hard facts'.

Part I
Context

History, structure and business of print media

The print industry – yesterday, today and tomorrow

An overview

The print industry – yesterday, today, tomorrow

An overview

Martin Conboy

Newspapers and magazines share many features in their historical development. Both have needed to combine an astute understanding of readership to survive financially. Both have appreciated the need for variety and entertainment. Too often, historical surveys of journalism have focused solely on its primary political function, which is to inform the public, and have, therefore, neglected its secondary but complementary function, which is to engage with the broader lifestyle and entertainment requirements of the readership. In its secondary function, journalism has contributed enormously to a wider cultural politics. In short, journalism in both printed formats is best seen as the continuous recombination of novelty, information, opinion and entertainment.

Early periodical publications

The emergence of periodical information in print accompanied broader cultural changes already evident across much of Western Europe during the seventeenth century (Burke 1978). These involved a greater emphasis on the specifics of time and place, more interaction in literary forms between protagonists and narrative and, above all, more sense of the potential for human agency in social affairs. In its earliest forms, periodical print culture incorporated a struggle between those who wanted to control the flow of public information and those who wanted to disseminate it, whether for political or commercial purposes.

Periodical newsbooks and news sheets began to spread across the cities of Europe from 1609 and reached England in 1621 with the publication of the first *coranto* translated into English. The first dated and sequential newsbooks began to be published in England the following year. The sort of writing distinguishing newsbooks from other literary forms centred on the transitory and the contemporary. And while it foregrounded the political, it also sought to surprise and entertain. But the element of the newsbooks that distinguished them from previous forms of information was their regularity, which Sommerville has described as 'periodicity', without which no journalism industry could have developed (1996: 4). This meant that a commercial dominant was always the driving force behind innovation in print journalism, and this attracted printers and publishers to invest in it to make a profit.

After the fall of the Star Chamber on 5 July 1641, the authority of the monarch over printing in England was in tatters, and the newsbooks of the 1640s were the first publications to be able to break the taboo on reporting parliament. The first such publication was *The Heads of Severall Proceedings in this Present Parliament* from 22–29 November 1641, written by Samuel Pecke and published by John Thomas. The years of the English Civil War (1642–51) saw the birth of many techniques of modern political journalism: for instance, the planted item, the inadequately denied rumour, the inside story (Frank 1961: 54) plus, in a world of endemic parliamentary and aristocratic corruption, another staple of journalist-manufactured news, the exposé (Mendle 2001: 58).

To boost the authenticity of descriptions and reports of speeches, an early form of shorthand was developed by John Farthing that allowed varying accounts of an event to be synthesised by cross reference. From 1643 the mercuries introduced satirical writing and scurrilous innuendo about public figures and overt political propaganda in the first regular attempts to create a public forum through a consistently partisan idiom in print. Their power and reach increased as their reputation for accuracy and probity declined. The newsbooks and mercuries contained an impressive range of content from poetry to plays, which all formed part of a broad commentary on public life that was both informative and entertaining.

The period also witnessed the first experiments with advertising in periodicals. Advertising had started as a strategy by printers to use up empty space by placing announcements in their newsbooks for other publications of theirs, from books to pamphlets. But the practice soon developed a lucrative momentum of its own, enough for the publishers to be able to canvass for external advertisements to boost their revenue. It would not be long before the interdependence of advertising and news became a characteristic combination of print journalism with all the benefits and compromises this brought.

Siebert has concluded that by the time of the Commonwealth (1649–51): 'Journalism, controlled or uncontrolled, had become a permanent social and political phenomenon' (1965: 220). Readers were being targeted not only as participants in political and broader cultural life but also as consumers who could deliver profits to the printers and publishers. This meant the new medium was not solely political but part of a generic hybrid between public information source, topical entertainment, communal identity and profit that together constituted journalism.

The formation of a public sphere

By the Restoration in 1660, there was a return to central and licensed control over print journalism but, even under repressive conditions, the logic of this embryonic culture of periodical communication was to find ways of renegotiating its public presence. Harris and Lee (1978) suggest there was at this point no political or commercial drive to produce journalism for a wider audience, although there was clearly a readership for it. The scale of this potential readership was demonstrated by the wide circulation of ephemeral publications such as broadsides, chapbooks and ballads as the mainstream press was forced by legislation and the need for economic stability to concentrate on the respectable commercial classes for its constituency. Ultimately, such a division was always going to be too restrictive for the commercially orientated and generically varied practice of journalism.

The term 'newspaper' is first used in 1670, and as a specific form of print culture it begins to take on its identifiable characteristics. From the Restoration onwards, we see the historical crystallisation of the bourgeois class and its expression in print, which Habermas has identified as the public sphere (1992). The Licensing Act lapsed in 1695 not because the ruling political classes felt secure about unrestricted printing but because it could no longer be administered efficiently. Yet as the era of direct censorship and control ended, a new one began where the financial preferment of ministers played more of a role in establishing which publications would gain financial stability. First Harley and then Walpole established a system of bribes, preferential access to news and sponsorship for newspapers and periodicals that they felt presented their ministry in the best light. There was, nevertheless, a wide range of experimentation in journalistic form with the first daily newspaper, the *Daily Courant*, appearing in 1702. Barbers' shops, taverns and especially coffee shops all formed part of a spreading national network of outlets for newspapers and periodicals where people gathered informally to read, exchange opinion or catch up on the latest rumour or gossip.

The gathering reputation and impact of journalism came not through the newspapers at this point but through the literary and political periodicals of the reign of Queen Anne (1702–14). These flourished in the years between the lapsing of the Licensing Act and the imposition of Stamp Duties in 1712. During this period the main contributors to the development of journalism were Daniel Defoe's *Review*, Jonathan Swift's *Examiner* and Steele's and Addison's *Tatler* and *Spectator*. Defoe's publication was typical of the hybridity of these experimental periodicals, including an essay on foreign politics and a satirical section on contemporary affairs. It was not in any way a newspaper but more a reinvigorated form of political essay sheet with a humorous edge to some of its writing. It revived the tradition of political persuasion on many matters of economic and military policy in tightly argued, accessible prose as well as mocking the faults of other political commentators.

Richard Steele's *Tatler*, begun in 1709, was originally even more of a hybrid than Defoe's periodical. Published as a thrice weekly, like many of the newspapers of the time, it covered news for its first eighty-three editions. From 1711 Steele joined forces with Addison to produce the *Spectator* as a daily publication. Both these periodicals sought to educate the bourgeoisie in the ways of a polite society, giving advice and guidance on taste, fashion and behaviour as well as providing opinion on the latest literary productions. Thus by the end of the reign of Queen Anne, journalism had emerged as a new form of social communication that blended political with wider cultural information across a range of publications and representational styles.

The defining legislation structuring this new public sphere of information exchange came with the 1712 Stamp Act and the imposition of advertising duties, which were a shrewd combination of revenue-raising and policing. The consequence of this emergent political economy of journalism was that although newspapers and periodicals had the potential to foster radical political debate, their ownership and intended market made them inherently conservative in their world views if they were to survive politically and economically. The restrictions on the press and the effective political control exerted by Walpole did, however, meet with resistance that was to contribute to the shaping of journalism from an oppositional perspective. Essay journals that provided commentary on political affairs as well as a forum for letter writers to contribute to political debate were popular with readers and, therefore, with advertisers. The provocative 'Cato's' Letters in the *London Journal* started this trend and it was continued by *Mist's Weekly Journal, Fog's Weekly Journal* and the *Craftsman*.

Yet for all their provocative polemic it was not these essay papers that attempted to renew the coverage of parliament that had briefly flourished during the Civil War. This was reintroduced by the first named magazine, the *Gentleman's Magazine*, founded by Edward Cave in 1731. A digest of news, literary and political comment and, from May 1731, live parliamentary proceedings, this magazine certainly lived up to its motto '*E pluribus unum*' (Out of the many, comes one).

At first, the novelty of topical information had provided the impetus for the development of newspapers and other periodicals. Steadily, the range of information in circulation was growing so that by the middle of the eighteenth century gossip, shipping news, court reports, social commentary, parliamentary debate and political opinions were all well developed in the newspaper. From the 1750s John Gurney provided a newly systematised shorthand that was able to reinforce journalists' claims to eyewitness veracity (Smith 1978: 162). In addition to formal politics, the poetry, parables and epigrams that alluded to political affairs made these publications more accessible and entertaining to readers and linked them to more general enter-tainment values. Advertising became an increasing feature of newspapers throughout the eighteenth century and formed part of the wider system of intelligence, inflected towards the business and political preferences of a narrow section of society. Distinctions sometimes made between the important political content of these newspapers and their trivial and ephemeral features, including advertising, miss the point that a judicious blend of the informative and the entertaining has always been the optimal blend for a successful newspaper written for a broad readership, not just for scholars or politicians.

By the end of the century three daily London-based newspapers had begun to draw together the strands of the extended experiment in newspaper journalism into a successful format. The *Morning Chronicle*, edited by James Perry, the *Morning Post*, edited by Daniel Stuart, and *The Times* were all combining credibility, probity and financial success. The first two were demonstrating the benefits of control of the whole newspaper by one manager although this function was not described as 'editor' before 1802. From this point, the financial success of newspapers was to be exploited by owners and editors to emphasise their editorial independence from government. The rise of the leading article was a device that allowed this claim to be demonstrated on a daily basis on the important issues of the day, and increasingly newspapers sought out the best writers to articulate distinctive political and economic arguments for their readership.

As a parallel development to the prestige newspapers of the early century, the reviews, which did much to contribute to and extend intellectual bourgeois opinion, were considered 'the mandarin periodical form of the 19th century' (Shattock and Wolff 1982: 5). The Whig *Edinburgh Review* was founded in 1802 as a liberal, reformist organ and this was countered in 1809 by the Tory *Quarterly Review*, based in London. In 1817, what was to become *Blackwood's Edinburgh Magazine* was founded and a radical alternative, the *Westminster Review*, completed the picture from 1823. Later in the century, the monthlies and then the weeklies took over much of the role of the quarterlies but were aimed at a much broader readership. They fitted more easily into the commercialised environment of the late century than their high-minded and commercially restricted predecessors. The *Cornhill Magazine*

(1860), the *Fortnightly Review* (1865), the *Contemporary Review* (1866) and the *Nineteenth Century* (1877) all provided space for topics that needed more reflection and perspective than a daily could provide, together with a wider range of literary discussion for a more extended leisured class.

The defeat of a radical press

As one set of developments was moving newspapers towards commercial respectability and political independence, a long suppressed radical impulse gained renewed momentum at the start of the nineteenth century. Under the impact of social and intellectual developments linked to the American and the French Revolutions and in the wake of the unemployment and radical social upheavals of the early industrial revolution, readerships were being increasingly politicised along class lines. Newspapers and periodicals began to address their readers in one of two ways: as a market for economic purposes or as a social class for political purposes. Government fears of the impact of revolutionary ideas led them to raise the stamp duty twice between 1789 and 1797, but this merely encouraged the radicals to publish illegally and so raise their oppositional credibility with their readers.

Hollis (1970) has identified two phases to these radical publications: the first identified by an emphasis on the 'old corruption' and the second informed by much more of a socialist analysis of class politics and property. The first phase between 1815 and 1819 included the writings of Cobbett, Carlile, Wade and Wooler. This journalism, in the form of a weekly polemic, provided an organic link to their targeted readership, the working classes. Public meetings, subscriptions and boycotts of commodities all encouraged an interaction with an engaged readership. The extension to the public sphere that the radical unstamped publications provided was much more than a space for the polite exchange of political or aesthetic views, it was a crucible in which citizens could become aware of a range of alternative strategies for understanding and changing the world. This was far from the paradigm of journalism as an objective practice but very close to an ideal of journalism that offers an active community of readership in which politics and public communication combine with radical intent. This stage was suppressed in the wake of a series of repressive measures (under the name of the Six Acts) that specifically targeted the radical publications after the Peterloo massacre in 1819. The second phase in the 1830s accompanied the push towards parliamentary reform but expressed a strand of radical thinking which went beyond a mere shift in suffrage. Hetherington and O'Brien, for instance, ran unstamped publications to push for political representation from the perspective of a specifically socialist critique of property, but the reduction of stamp duty from 1836 meant that the radical press was drowned in a torrent of cheap publications aimed at the working classes.

Provincial newspapers

The lapsing of controls on the press, which saw such a prolific experimentation in the form and content of newspapers and magazines in the metropolis from the early eighteenth century, also enabled a provincial press to develop throughout Britain that was to contribute significantly over the eighteenth and nineteenth centuries to the diversity of relationships available between readers and printed news media. Initially, the spread of newspapers to the provinces was driven by the exodus of printers from the capital, looking for a more lucrative, less densely competitive environment to ply their trade. This led to early provincial newspapers being targeted at local readerships yet dominated by secondary news sources, chiefly from London. The actual local content was minimal. These newspapers experimented in presenting a variety even within this restricted early manifestation and tried serialisation of novels, local employment notices and sometimes news from overseas sources as well. Reports of local trials were some of the first indicators of a shift to a more locally based news agenda.

The intensification of the Industrial Revolution from the late eighteenth century witnessed a corresponding spread of the provincial press, especially of an urban variety. These papers played a significant part in forging the identities of these growing centres of population and economic activity. As their economic success became assured, these newspapers became more confident in supplying news of a local nature, particularly addressing local political matters. It was these newspapers that first encouraged a local electorate to demand true representation from their local MP. Local political factions throughout the country used the local press as a battleground for the hearts, minds, not to mention wallets of the local population so that the national public was increasingly complemented by a series of local publics. As their reputation grew, so too did the practice of London-based newspapers using provincial content to reinforce their claim to true national inclusiveness.

Newspapers and markets

The removal of taxes and duties on newspapers and other periodicals between 1836 and 1855 shifted the onus of control from political to commercial interests. The tradition of journalism that emerged was one that was commercially and politically incorporated and acted as a conciliatory, consensual channel between politicians and commercial interests and the press rather than as an inflammatory intervention on behalf of a radicalised people in pursuit of rights and progress. This journalism increasingly played a part in normalising the functioning of capitalism through its advertisements and the need for business capital.

Dropping taxation had made investment more attractive and paved the way for more competition between politically stable newspapers in the hands of respectable men of property. It enabled a form of journalism to become established that could act as an agent of social control (Curran 1978). Chalaby claims the modern discourse of journalism takes shape at the point when market mechanisms begin to dominate the ownership, strategies and competitive practices of public writing after 1855 (Chalaby 1998). The word 'journalism' itself also enters the language at this moment of economic liberalisation. It is used for the first time in the January edition of the *Westminster Review* 1833 and its usage came to signify the yoking of higher and lower cultural forms which in itself constituted a challenge to existing cultural distinctions (Campbell 2000: 40).

In newspaper form the first entrant into this brave new world was the *Daily Telegraph* whose arrival coincided with the final removal of taxation. This was a paper which at a penny was intended to introduce a different clientele to the daily news-paper: 'The Times, the paper for the City merchant, and the Daily Telegraph, for the clerk and the shopkeeper' (Brown 1985: 246). It brought elements of the human interest of American popular journalism, public campaigning around issues of concern to its specific readership and interviews with celebrities of the day.

The remainder of the nineteenth century saw journalism's rise to a political and social legitimacy based on the establishment of its commercial status. This journalism is best exemplified by the rise of The Times to its position of towering dominance based on its ability to enhance its political and editorial independence by investing in the latest technologies and its maintenance of hugely profitable circulation and advertising. By the end of the century the place of journalism within the political process was so well established that it could claim for itself: 'a place of power at least equal to half-a-dozen seats in parliament [. . .] and these free of the Whip, independent of the Speaker, and subject not at all to the gentlemen of the front benches' (Greenwood 1897: 704).

Technological innovation made a significant surge with the steam printing of The Times on a König Bauer press in 1814 but it continued with additions such as the telegraph and lithographic printing, as the century progressed. The private transmission of news via telegraph began in 1866. This had an impact on the very language of journalism and the development of the inverted triangle of the news story. The telegraph, together with the advanced system of shorthand introduced in 1840 by Pitman, meant there was more of a verifiable base to much reporting of news and so there was more scope to develop **angles** conforming to the particular identity of the paper. This was followed by further developments in printing and telegraphy into the 1870s including web rotary presses, the private wires and the telephone. The increased quantity and reliability of news combined with the rise in advertising from the 1880s meant journalists were able to concentrate on how the paper was put together rather than simply filling the space. Under the influence of more interventionist editors, newspapers developed identifiable **house styles**. The establishment of the Reuters News Agency ensured the supply of a steady and reliable source of news. News had always been a commodity, but it was rapidly becoming a more streamlined and capitalised commodity (Baldasty 1992: 140).

The magazine: the most fertile format

Across periods of great disparity in terms of technology, politics and economy, the periodical has provided many of the formative innovations around which the discourse of journalism has been constructed. Perhaps, to make an extravagant claim, the periodical and the magazine have been the most fertile and influential journalism format. From the Restoration, periodicals with a more serious, even self-conscious, awareness of their contribution to print culture continued to emerge, indicating the potential of such publications to contribute to journalism by disseminating general information and debate among the learned classes of society.

The *Journal des Savans* was published from January 1665 as a twelve-page weekly review of literature and ran for 250 years. A similarly highbrow venture emerged the same year with the *Acta Philosophica Societa Anglia*, from March, published by Henry Oldenburg, later renamed the *Philosophical Transactions of the Royal Society* and

---

angle   main point stressed in story usually in intro. Also known as 'hook'. US: peg.

house   media organisation. Thus in-house (meaning within particular media organisation). House organ is company's own newspaper or magazine. See also style.

style   special rules adopted by newspaper relating to spellings, punctuation and abbreviation. Often contained within style book though increasingly carried on screen. Many newspapers somehow survive without them.

concentrating on a monthly digest of scientific articles. These periodicals were preparing the ground culturally for the full development of the bourgeois public sphere in the literary journals and essay sheets of the early eighteenth century. The newspaper was simply not broad enough in its social and political ambition to serve this purpose. The magazine became so dominant that by the Victorian period Shattock and Wolff can claim it was in the periodical form that the social experience of the period was embedded (1982: xiv–xv).

The popular Sunday press drew heavily on magazine formats and was very influential in the mass-market journalism that emerged after the lifting of the final taxes in 1855 and, according to Vincent, 'in translating the category of news into a completely new category of popular leisure, coincided with the virtual disappearance of working-class politics' (1993: 252). One of the most successful blends of news and entertainment which drew upon new reprographic technologies was the *Illustrated London News* from 1842 which appeared with thirty-two woodcuts on its sixteen pages but it was the three Sunday newspapers, *Lloyd's Illustrated London Newspaper* (1842), *News of the World* (1843) and *Reynolds' Weekly Newspaper* (1850) which were to define the popular Sunday market and exert a formative influence on the rest of the landscape of popular journalism for the rest of the century and, in the case of the *News of the World*, into the twenty-first century. They all managed to construct a version of the rhetoric of 'old corruption' which sought to expose scandal in high places for the edification of their readerships without any consistent probings of the structural causes of social inequalities and appealed in so doing to the tradition of printed narratives, ballad and sensation. They combined this wide appeal with astute marketing and effective distribution on the national railway system.

As the working classes became attracted to their depoliticised, commercially orientated content, this form of periodical journalism had become 'the effective means of social control which the establishment had always hoped the popular press might be' (Berridge 1978: 256). Into the twentieth century, the popular Sunday papers still exist but with a slightly adjusted agenda. They retain their commitment to an apolitical 'old corruption' analysis that is strong on scepticism of those in power, especially politicians, but their hard-news content has given way to a celebrity-driven agenda.

Magazines: hobbies and lifestyle

A further development in print journalism that was lubricated by its increased commercial attractiveness in the second half of the nineteenth century was the rise of more specifically targeted publications. The *Field* in 1853 was the first hobby magazine and the growth of such magazines followed the familiar trend down the social classes as consumer fashions and growing affluence enabled mass markets for hobbies to develop for wider audiences. The *Shooting Times* and *Country Magazine* both make their first appearance in 1882, followed by publications such as *Amateur Gardening* and *Horse and Hound* in 1884, *Yachting World* in 1894 and the first British motoring magazine, *Autocar and Motor*, in 1895.

With the expansion of advertising, popular magazines tested markets for journalism lower down the social and financial scale and soon began mapping products onto that market. The first to try was George Newnes's *Tit-Bits*, which was the herald of the penny weeklies and the New Journalism of the 1880s. Moreover, their enormous financial success enabled Harmsworth and Pearson in particular to found the two most influential newspapers of the early twentieth century, the *Daily Mail* (1896) and the *Daily Express* (1900). *Tit-Bits* illustrated how information could be sold as entertainment. It contained no illustrations but plenty of competitions, prizes, jokes on the front page and a considerable amount of news of public affairs from a selection of sources and in a random order. It built on the well-established tradition of an intimate form of address with its readers that was such a popular feature of both radical pamphlet, women's magazines and Sunday newspapers.

Generalist magazines began their decline in the 1960s as television and then newspapers took over many aspects of their traditional role. With the growing affluence of readers and the emergence of an identifiable youth culture, new specialist periodicals emerged to define magazine journalism in terms of narrowcasting. Readers are encouraged to see themselves and their self-fulfilment as being channelled through identity and individual activity. The same trend that has seen the expansion of this market has had, as always with magazine developments, a crossover effect on the content of newspapers. The ability of such **narrowcasting** to influence the mainstream of newspaper journalism was evident in the way that the *Face* (1980), as the self-proclaimed 'style bible', had an impact not only on the magazine market for young and affluent readers but also on **broadsheet** newspapers.

The most recent development in this narrowcasting has been for magazines aimed at a general male audience, as men. Most men's magazines before the 1990s had been reserved for specific hobbies or DIY. One of the reasons why magazines for men, even in this restricted form, had been relative latecomers to the print periodical market was that the newspaper, with its sports pages, business and political news, was a medium already aimed implicitly at men for general interest. There had not been the cultural space available for the development of a parallel to the woman's magazine. That was until a new generation was launched with *Arena* in 1986, soon to be surpassed as market leader by *FHM* (1994), *Loaded* (1994) and *Maxim* (1995). Influenced as much by the market-orientated lifestyle journalism of the 1990s as by the **gonzo journalism** of the likes of Hunter S. Thompson and the continuing trend towards irony in contemporary journalism, they have been variously interpreted as providing a reaction to feminism, a bastion of newly acceptable sexism or part of an increasing crisis in masculinity (Jackson et al. 2001).

Women's magazines: making visible the invisible

Women in journalism are narrated, as so often, 'hidden from history' (Rowbothom 1996). This is ironic considering the extent to which one of the dominant trends of journalism from the middle of the nineteenth century has been the steady inclusion of styles of writing and illustration of greater interest to an idealised female reader. Women were prominent in much of printing's early history (Halascz 1997) and are only edged out of supplying a significant presence in the emergent public sphere as new controls on the ownership patterns and transformations in sex-roles along patriarchal lines favoured the capital of groups of men of property (McDowell 1998: 5). Yet despite this there was the recognition as early as 1693 that women constituted

narrowcasting targeting publication to specific groups of people such as property owners or clubbers

broadsheet large format newspaper (e.g. the *Financial Times*) in which four pages fit across the width of the press; usually considered to be of a more serious quality than a tabloid. Some former broadsheets (such as *The Times* and the *Independent*) have recently gone tabloid (though they call this format 'compact').

gonzo journalism a highly subjective genre of journalism, sometimes drug induced, pioneered by the American, Thompson (1937–2005) in the 1960s and 1970s.

an attractive market, in the form of the *Ladies' Mercury* published by a man, John Dunton. It promised to respond to 'all the most nice and curious Questions concerning Love, Marriage, Behaviour, Dress and Humour of the Female Sex, whether Virgins, Wives, or Widows' (Adburgham 1972: 26).

Richard Steele was also committed to the inclusion of women in wider intellectual and social life and his *Tatler* frequently engaged with women's issues. He included a 'Poetical Tale for Ladies' and later created Jenny Distaff as a *porte-parole* for women. However, there were occasions when women writers were able to disrupt the polite patterns of behaviour expected of them by male publishers. The *Female Tatler* from 1709 was the forum for the coarse and scurrilous Mrs Crackenthorpe, the nom de plume of Mrs Mary Delarivier Manley, who demonstrated the potential of transforming personal gossip about public affairs into political polemic of a satirical and entertaining nature.

Attempts also continued during the eighteenth century to explore the market for a wide range of publications aimed at women, most of which were committed to some form of news reporting. The high point of the essay periodical was the *Female Spectator* monthly from 1744 to 1746. Edited by Eliza Haywood, it is considered to be the first magazine for women and produced in its entirety by women (Shevelow 1989: 167). However, social attitudes led to changes in women's publishing and the more serious-minded essay periodicals were replaced by a more leisured magazine format that emphasised beauty, health, fashion, romantic fiction and correspondence.

The nineteenth century witnessed the inclusion of the family into this magazine space and as owners sought to avoid the taxation on newspapers and as newspapers themselves became better equipped to deal with public demands for news, the women's magazines gradually erased news from their pages. This, it is claimed, had the effect of institutionalising the absence of news from women's reading thereby defining, 'femininity as incompatible with engagement in public affairs' (Beetham 1996: 26). Women journalists remained restricted. Most had subservient roles on newspapers and produced the tedious stock reports characteristic of what had become known as the 'penny-a-liners', deskilled and unprofessional. Even those with more to offer had to conform to the traditional anonymity and were therefore invisible as women or sometimes 'wrote in drag' (Easley 2000: 154). Women editors and even proprietors claimed greater affinity with their female readers but this did not alter the dominant discourse which restricted women to representations of their world based on domestic identities or sentimental escapism.

The market for women's magazines grew still further in the years following the education acts of 1870 and 1871. White has registered the introduction of forty-eight new titles between 1880 and 1900 (1970: 58) all aimed at the lower end of the social spectrum and emphasising a domestic slant to their content. By 1882 the **half-tone** process had been introduced which assisted in raising the presentational standards of advertisements in women's magazines and began a more visually aware approach to the layout of newspapers, particularly the popular ones.

half-tone any rasterised picture where shades of grey are represented by different-sized dots.

Women's journalism and the New Journalism

The New Journalism of the 1880s in the *Pall Mall Gazette* and the *Star* took on many attributes that had been associated with women's journalism for over a century and made them commercially attractive to a wider and more general readership through the inclusion of more personal detail and human interest in its news. Such approaches had been identifiable in the Sunday press at least since the beginning of the century and had drawn significantly on influences from American popular journalism. But the New Journalism significantly produced this for a daily readership, borrowing from magazine and Sunday journalism their conversational tone. Salmon (2000: 29) analyses the increasingly personalised tone of this journalism as masking the lack of any real relationship with its readers. Moreover, although readers were increasingly addressed in a more personal tone about matters that touched the everyday in a banal way, they were correspondingly marginalised in these newspapers from the sort of politics that directly impacted upon their lives (Hampton 2001: 227).

The strategies adopted by the women's magazines of the late nineteenth century emphasised the appeal to an idealised women reader in the individualised tone of address, while successful newcomers such as *Good Housekeeping* (1922) and *Woman* (1937) were able to extend their editorial identity to encompass a more broadly defined social conscience for the popular women's magazine including features on topical social issues from birth control to women at work. From the 1960s an even more intensively commercialised version of lifestyle publication emerged, *Flair* (1960) and *Honey* (1961) being two of the earliest successes in this category while the introduction of the British edition of *Cosmopolitan* proved the market leader from 1972 until being taken over by *Glamour* in 2001.

Since the heyday of the 1930s and 1940s, women's magazines have retreated, in the main, from engaging with social issues. Newspapers, especially broadsheets, have also moved commercially to include more of interest to increasingly affluent and socially engaged professional women readers. Women journalists have moved from the 'velvet ghettos' (Creedon 1989) to contribute more broadly than ever before to the fullest range of print journalism. The increasing feminisation of mainstream journalism has all the characteristics of a hegemonic compromise, allowing female voices into the discourse of journalism while doing so on the terms of the dominant male perspective, particularly when they have the potential to increase profits.

The long popular century

In contrast to the New Journalism, which had challenged the more conservative newspapers with its style and address, Northcliffe, with his *Daily Mail* from 1896, 'created a popular journalism which was less interested in political and social action per se than as the means to increase circulation' (Goodbody 1985: 23). It did not sensationalise and moved to positions it was confident would gain the support of his lower-middle-class readership such as the jingoism of his coverage of the Boer War. Northcliffe's reworking of the New Journalism had an effect on the shape and content of journalism across the twentieth century, forcing other proprietors to adapt the content of their newspapers to match or improve upon the pattern he had set.

On 26 April 1900, the *Daily Express* was launched to rival the *Daily Mail* and to exploit the new market for popular daily journalism that Northcliffe had opened. The mass popular dailies were successful to the extent that they were able to integrate the tone and content of the magazines into their own pages, while remaining distinct from the magazines in their news coverage and political columns. Furthermore, the changes in typography, make-up and content made newspapers more attractive to both readers and advertisers throughout the period 1880 to 1914 and quadrupled the number of purchasers of daily newspapers (Wiener 1988: 56).

Matheson has identified the language of this journalism as being as important an indicator of the changes within journalism as its visual appeal and organisational practices. It was spread to a large extent across the spectrum, from quality to popular newspapers. This shift involved much more editorial intervention to make **copy** fit the format and style of the paper and saw a further refinement of house styles. The role of the **sub-editor** was pivotal in the creation of this new discourse in fitting the copy into a format that allowed a newspaper to be read on the move and tailoring it to fit the space available within the pictorial and advertising space (Matheson 2000: 565). Smith considers the language of this period's journalism as having undergone a fundamental change. The 'story' became the basic molecular element of journalistic reality and the distinctions of categories of news into hard and soft became reconfigured as part of its discourse (1978: 168).

The intensification of press competition

By the twentieth century, journalism had become identifiably Big Business. The cost of bringing out a new paper has been estimated as increasing from £25,000 in 1850 to £100,000 in 1870 and to £500,000 by 1900 (Lee 1976: 76–103). The leading proprietors, notably Northcliffe, Beaverbrook and Rothermere, presided over a period that continued the trends towards concentration, competition and entertainment in print media. The circulation wars triggered in the popular market in the 1920s and 1930s saw thirty newspapers close between 1921 and 1936 although the total sales of newspapers doubled (Curran and Seaton 1993). This competition led to a concentration of the market and a narrowing of political range. Sensationalism, special offers, campaigns, layout and aspects of writing style of the 1930s all contributed to the further development of the dynamics of New Journalism.

Yet beyond competition and marketing, it was the incorporation of visual elements into popular journalism that determined the most significant changes of the period. On 7 August 1933, Christiansen on the *Daily Express* produced a cleaner, better-spaced newspaper with more and bigger headlines and more **cross-heads** to break up the page. It was followed by all its rivals including the relaunched *Daily Mirror* which from 1934 under the editorial direction of Bartholomew triggered the **tabloid** revolution with its signature heavy black **bold** type for its headlines, pin-ups, youthful style, simplified language and a prominent use of pictures to reach a new readership. It redrew the map of popular journalism in print by integrating all the visual appeal of popular culture and consumerism for the first time. After the

copy   editorial material. Hard copy refers to editorial material typed on paper.

sub-editor/sub responsible for editing reporters' copy, writing headlines, captions, laying out pages etc. Stone sub makes final corrections and cuts on page proofs. US: copy editor.

cross-head   a heading placed within the body of a story; *see* side-head.

tabloid   newspaper whose pages are roughly half the size of broadsheet. All pops or popular papers are tabloids as are sections of some of the heavies. Serious tabloids exist in France (*Le Monde*, for instance) and in the USA (*Los Angeles Times*).

bold   more heavily defined version of a roman font.

war, the *Daily Mirror* soon began to climb to a pinnacle of influence in popular journalism (Engel 1996) ousting the *Daily Express* with a populist, proletarian and youthful appeal encapsulated in the slogan which ran from 11 May 1945: 'Forward with the People.'

Post-war developments

The continuing intensification of competition for circulation, advertising and profit was creating a journalism with clear political implications. This is what McManus (1994) has criticised as 'market-driven journalism'. It saw newspapers of the left of centre and the liberal tradition forced out and an increasing levelling of journalism towards a market-orientated consensus that appealed to the advertisers and economic interests of owners. Consequently, this consensus was very much to the right of the political spectrum. (Curran and Seaton 1993: 106).

Broader developments within the regular coverage of politics saw a widening of the gap between popular newspapers and the quality newspapers targeted at elite sections of society. One consequence of the restriction of political debate to a narrow range of elite broadsheets and specialised journals is that analytical, contextualised journalism becomes a source accessed only by the political and economic elites who continue to value print media for their analytical information (Dahlgren 1995: 58–9). In 1962, *The Sunday Times*'s first colour supplement continued the process of 'magazinification' in the qualities which sought to broaden their coverage while at the same time enhancing their appeal to advertisers trying to attract readers from higher income groups.

The post-war period witnessed much official concern over various aspects of newspaper journalism and there were three Royal Commissions set up to investigate it: 1947–9, 1961–2 and 1974–7. Concern may have been limited at this governmental level to structural and ethical issues but for newspapers themselves, the burning question that remains relates to their ultimate survival. Newspaper circulation, under intense competitive pressure, is in a long and downward spiral.

'Tabloidisation'

The most sustained and widespread set of debates around contemporary journalism emanate from the tabloid newspaper. The label of 'tabloidisation' is given to the trend that has seen what critics perceive to be the chief characteristics of the tabloids infecting other forms of journalism, both print and broadcast. 'Tabloidisation' may refer to an increase in news about celebrities, entertainment, lifestyle features, personal issues, an increase in sensationalism, in the use of pictures and sloganised headlines, vulgar language and a decrease in international news, public affairs news including politics, the reduction in the length of words in a story, the reduction of the complexity of language and also a convergence with agendas of popular and, in particular, television culture.

It is clearly, if nothing else, a composite 'growl list' of elements, some of which have haunted the minds of commentators on journalism over centuries. It is because of this lack of specificity that Sparks (2000) questions whether 'tabloidisation' is a useful diagnostic tool at all although he does concede that the debate itself is an indication of a specifically contemporary set of worries over the nature of journalism across media. This does not mean that it does not have implications both for journalism itself, in the alleged 'decline in standards', for example (Bromley 1998: 25), or for the political functions of journalism in a democratic system.

The 1980s saw the popular press retreat from political journalism towards an increasing dependence on sex, sensation and symbiosis with television's brand of mass popular culture. They were more dependent on circulation than advertising because of the advertisers' assessment of the income of their projected readership and this circulation was boosted by more reliance on celebrity, popular inter-textuality with other media and selective and extremely vicious partisan politics.

Broadsheet newspapers have also been enmeshed in the clustering of trends characterised as tabloidisation. The late twentieth century saw a further narrowing of ownership and the incorporation of newspapers into more broadly defined media conglomerates that have eroded the boundaries between journalism and media entertainment. To survive the intense competition, broadsheets have become heavier with more lifestyle and consumer coverage. They have increased the numbers of specialist supplements and the size and quantity of high-profile advertisements. An increasing number of their journalists are given the media star treatment with photographs accompanying their **byline** and freer rein to write from a more personalised perspective. Yet surveys consistently reveal a mistrust of journalists' veracity (Worcester 1998: 47).

byline gives name of journalist who has written article. Otherwise known as 'credit line'. Subs sometimes call it 'blame line'. When appears at end of story known as 'sign-off'.

Contemplating the future

It seems fair to assume that online journalism will come increasingly to be considered as a genre in its own right rather than as an adjunct to print, radio or television. However, we cannot consider this initial survey to be complete until we have briefly assessed what the current impact of online journalism has been on newspapers and magazines.

Broadsheets have benefited from their ability to provide what is missing in instantaneous broadcasting, a reflective and analytical mode of commentary unavailable in most other news media. They have been able to blend this with an astute deployment of Internet capacity. They can today provide quite exhaustive connections from their own archives to help readers pursue their particular interests, sometimes in considerable depth. Thus newspapers can claim to have become enabling portals, opening up from their own output into a range of parallel sources, albeit for a social range of readers as narrow as that of their hard-copy circulation.

The web sites of national and local newspapers and the publication of email addresses of prominent **columnists** allow a more in-depth and interactive engagement with contemporary journalism. The regular posting of web logs on the Internet introduces another radical and personalised slant into the news, with the diarist/journalist of the twenty-first century emerging from the observational journalistic tradition of Pepys and Dickens. Online journalism, therefore, provides a technological enhancement of narrowcasting audience appeal and diversity of content that have always formed part of the appeal of newspapers and magazines. Newspapers are at the hub of a hybrid operation that makes the whole package more

columnist journalist who provides comment in regular series of articles.

akin to an extended magazine with specialisations ranged around the core of a more general news function.

The Internet enhances this hybrid identity, and both newspapers and magazines have been quick to add it to their spectrum of services to maintain their brand appeal and to reinforce their interactivity in an age when linear modes of media reception are becoming increasingly outdated. Because of their essential political ambitions, broadsheet newspapers in particular at the start of the twenty-first century give a glimpse of a radically altered, more open-ended journalism under the influence of the Internet and its archival potential. Yet, politically, journalism's elevation of a bourgeois, capitalised identity to a hegemonic position allows little scope, currently, for alternatives within the contemporary public sphere. Contemplating the future of newspapers and magazines as part of a technologically advanced, globalised print industry may well be speculative in the extreme, yet based on their history, one may safely conclude they will need to maintain the balance between reader identification, cultural credibility and financial success to sustain their location at the centre of our cultural lives.

References

Adburgham, A. (1972) *Women in Print: Writing, Women and Women's Magazines from the Restoration to the Accession of Victoria*, London: George Allen & Unwin.

Baldasty, G.J. (1992) *The Commercialization of News in the Nineteenth Century*, Madison, Wisc.: University of Wisconsin Press.

Beetham, M. (1996) *A Magazine of her Own? Domesticity and Desire in the Women's Magazine 1800–1914*, London: Routledge.

Berridge, V. (1978) 'Popular Sunday Papers and Mid-Victorian Society', in G. Boyce, J. Curran and P. Wingate (eds), *Newspaper History from the Seventeenth Century to the Present Day*, London: Constable, 247–64.

Bromley, M. (1998) 'The "Tabloiding" of Britain: Quality Newspapers in the 1990s', in H. Stephenson and M. Bromley (eds), *Sex, Lies and Democracy*, Harlow: Addison Wesley, Longman, 25–38.

Brown, L. (1985) *Victorian News and Newspapers*, Oxford: Clarendon Press.

Burke, P. (1978) *Popular Culture in Early Modern Europe*, London: Temple Smith.

Campbell, K. (2000) 'Journalistic Discourses and Constructions of Modern Knowledge', in L. Brake, B. Bell and D. Finkelstein (eds), *Nineteenth-Century Media and Construction of Identity*, Basingstoke: Palgrave, 40–53.

Chalaby, J.K. (1998) *The Invention of Journalism*, Basingstoke: Macmillan.

Creedon, P. (1989) *Women in Mass Communication: Challenging Gender Views*, London: Sage.

Curran, J. (1978) 'The Press as an Agency of Social Control: An Historical Perspective', in G. Boyce, J. Curran and P. Wingate (eds), *Newspaper History from the Seventeenth Century to the Present Day*, London: Constable, 51–75.

Curran, J. and J. Seaton (1993) *Power Without Responsibility*, London: Routledge.

Dahlgren, P. (1995) *Television and the Public Sphere*, London: Sage.

Easley, A. (2000) 'Authorship, Gender and Power in Victorian Culture: Harriet Martineau and the Periodical Press', in L. Brake, B. Bell and D. Finkelstein (eds), *Nineteenth Century Media and the Construction of Identities*, Basingstoke: Palgrave, 154–64.

Engel, M. (1996) *Tickle the Public: One Hundred Years of the Popular Press*, London: Gollanz & Prentice-Hall.

Frank, J. (1961) *The Beginnings of the English Newspaper*, Cambridge, Mass.: Harvard University Press.

Goodbody, J. (1985) '*The Star*: Its Role in the Rise of Popular Newspapers 1888–1914', *Journal of Newspaper and Periodical History*, 1 (2): 20–9.

Greenwood, F. (1897) 'The Press and Government', *Nineteenth Century*, July: 109–18.

Habermas, J. (1992) *The Structural Transformation of the Public Sphere*, Cambridge: Polity.

Halascz, A. (1997) *The Marketplace of Print*, Cambridge: Cambridge University Press.

Hampton, M. (2001) 'Understanding Media: Theories of the Press in Britain, 1850–1914', *Media, Culture and Society*, 23 (2): 213–31.

Harris, M. and A.J. Lee (1978) *The Press in English Society from the Seventeenth to the Nineteenth Century*, London and Toronto: Associated University Presses.

Hollis, P. (1970) *The Pauper Press*, Oxford: Oxford University Press.

Jackson, P., N. Stevenson and K. Brooks (2001) *Making Sense of Men's Magazines*, Cambridge: Polity.

Lee, A.J. (1976) *The Origins of the Popular Press 1855–1914*, London: Croom Helm.

McDowell, P. (1998) *The Women of Grub Street*, Oxford: Oxford University Press.

McManus, H.R. (1994) *Market Driven Journalism: Let the Citizen Beware*, London: Sage.

Matheson, D. (2000) 'The Birth of News Discourse: Changes in News Language in British Newspapers, 1880–1930', *Media, Culture and Society*, 22 (5): 557–73.

Mendle, M. (2001) 'News and the Pamphlet Culture of Mid-Seventeenth Century England', in B. Dooley and S. Baron (eds), *The Politics of Information in Early Modern Europe*, London: Routledge, 57–79.

Rowbotham, S. (1996) *Hidden from History: 300 Years of Women's Oppression and the Fight Against It*, London: Pluto.

Salmon, R. (2000) ' "A Simulacrum of Power": Intimacy and Abstraction in the Rhetoric of the New Journalism', in L. Brake, B. Bell and D. Finkelstein (eds), *Nineteenth Century Media and the Construction of Identities*, Basingstoke: Palgrave, 27–39.

Shattock, J. (2000) 'Work for Women: Margaret Oliphant's Journalism', in L. Brake, B. Bell and D. Finkelstein (eds), *Nineteenth Century Media and the Construction of Identities*, Basingstoke: Palgrave, 165–77.

Shattock, J. and M. Wolff (1982) *The Victorian Periodical Press: Samplings and Soundings*, Leicester: Leicester University Press.

Shevelow, K. (1989) *Women and Print Culture*, London: Routledge.

Siebert, F.S. (1965) *Freedom of the Press in England 1476–1776: The Rise and Fall of Government Control*, Urbana, Ill.: Urbana University Press.

Smith, A. (1978) 'The Long Road to Objectivity and Back Again: The Kinds of Truth We Get in Journalism', in G. Boyce, J. Curran and P. Wingate (eds), *Newspaper History from the Seventeenth Century to the Present Day*, London: Constable, 153–71.

Sommerville, J. (1996) *The News Revolution*, Oxford: Oxford University Press.

Sparks, C. (2000) 'Introduction: The Panic over Tabloid News', in C. Sparks and J. Tulloch (eds), *Tabloid Tales*, Oxford: Rowman & Littlefield, 1–40.

Vincent, D. (1993) *Literacy and Popular Culture*, Cambridge: Cambridge University Press.

White, C.L. (1970) *Women's Magazines 1693–1968*, London: Michael Joseph.

Wiener, J. (ed.) (1988) *Papers for the Millions: The New Journalism in Britain 1850–1914*, Westport, Conn.: Greenwood Press.

Worcester, R.M. (1998) 'Demographics and Values: What the British Public Reads and What It Thinks about its Newspapers', in M. Bromley and H. Stephenson (eds), *Sex, Lies and Democracy*, Harlow: Addison Wesley, Longman, 111–23.

The structure of the print industry

2

The structure of the print industry

Peter Cole

SURVIVING AGAINST THE ODDS: OWNERSHIP

Definitions of journalism vary from the flip to the pompous, and the ones that matter lie between those extremes. Journalism is about finding things out and then telling other people in as interesting and accessible a way as possible. Take it a step further and journalism is about uncovering things various interested parties would prefer left undiscovered. Another popular definition says journalism is about comforting the afflicted and afflicting the comfortable. It is about finding out what is really going on. It is about holding those who wield power – political, commercial, financial, legal, social – to account, representing those over whom power is exercised. Through the access journalists are granted or gain for themselves, the powerful are kept in check, the powerless supported. Journalism, the **Fourth Estate**, thus exercises a critical role in a free society and is always checked, constrained or outlawed in undemocratic societies. Journalism is important.

None of the above definitions works for celebrity journalism, which focuses on the unworldly activities in exclusive resorts, fashionable restaurants and £1,000-a-night hotels of those who have achieved celebrity or, more often these days, thrust themselves upon it. They do not work for kiss-and-tell, Big Brother or the fictional world of the soaps, all of which are staples of many of today's newspapers and magazines. Yet all these are products of the journalistic process. Newspapers and magazines are said to exist to inform, educate and entertain, but not all do all of those things, and the balance of emphasis varies wildly.

We in Britain are print junkies. Visit the main retail outlets in high streets, stations or airports and you are lost for choice as your eye passes over shelves of publications, on newsprint or glossy or in-between paper. There are magazines with CDs attached, magazines wrapped in plastic bags, magazines about fishing, magazines about train-spotting. Every interest is catered for, from fashion to fitness, motoring to mountain biking, hi-fi to home improvement. Newspaper racks carry a range of titles in a range of sizes, with headlines ranging from the latest twist in EastEnders to the latest government policy. There is the local evening paper. There is the local weekly. There is the local advertising paper, with nothing but **classified advertising** in it. Choice is there in abundance.

Each day of the week more than 12.5 million national newspapers are sold in Britain. On Sundays around 14 million are bought. About 70 per cent of adults regularly read a national newspaper. The figure for the regional and local press is even higher, with some 85 per cent of adults reading these papers. Circulations

Fourth Estate the supposed position of the press as the fourth most powerful institution after Lords Spiritual, Lords Temporal and Commons. (Lord Macaulay: 'The gallery in which reporters sit has become a fourth estate of the realm.')

classified ad a short advertisement in a newspaper or magazine (usually in small print).

of regional and local papers total more than 40 million each week, while almost 30 million free newspapers are distributed. We are among the most avid newspaper readers in the world.

We buy magazines, too, at an astounding rate, spending £2.6 billion on consumer titles. The magazine market is in constant flux, with new titles coming on stream to fill perceived gaps. One moment it is men's monthlies, the next men's weeklies. Football magazines sit alongside *What Anything-you-care-to-name?* Magazines you never asked for come through the post, on the back of your credit card, motoring association or charity allegiance. *What's On TV* sells 1.7 million copies per **issue**, *Take a Break* 1.2 million. *Sky* magazine is sent to 6.4 million homes, *Near and Far* (for AA members) to 3 million homes. All of these are the products of journalism; journalists write them design them, edit them.

issue all copies of the day's paper and its editions.

National newspapers

The national newspaper market is heavily segmented, to the extent that using the same word, 'newspaper', to describe publications as different as, say, the *Sun* and the *Financial Times* with the same generic word is both unhelpful and inaccurate. But both are published each day and consist of words printed on newsprint (paper), so to that limited extent they are similar products. For the purposes of description, in terms of different market sectors, we tend to refer to the popular market, the mid-market and the quality market, the latter at least being a loaded term.

The tabloids

Tabloid is often used as a synonym for popular, although technically it is a description of format, or size. We would not, however, refer to the *Independent* or the small version of *The Times* as a tabloid; nor would they. Hence their use of the term '**compact**', which is less specific and thus better suits their purposes and self-image. **Red-top** is a more colloquial term for tabloid and refers to the **masthead** or title piece of papers like the *Sun*, *Mirror* and *Daily Star*. During the *Mirror*'s brief and commercially unsuccessful sortie upmarket, during the Iraq war of 2003, it removed itself from the red-top group by changing its masthead to black.

compact tabloid version of former broadsheet newspaper e.g. the *Independent*, *The Times*.

red-tops tabloid newspapers such as the *Mirror*, *Sun* and *People*, so-called because their mastheads are red.

masthead paper's title piece.

The mid-markets

Mid-market simply describes in-between. The two occupants of this sector, the *Daily Mail* and *Daily Express*, are both tabloid in format and both sell more copies than the *Daily Star*, while the *Daily Mail* has now overtaken the *Daily Mirror* in circulation. There is thus a subjective element to the descriptors, with an increasingly arbitrary hierarchy of up-marketness through the gradation from tabloid, through mid-market to quality. It was simpler when the hierarchy described both physical size and circulation, from small papers selling the most to large papers selling the least.

The qualities

The quality market also confuses. Broadsheet used to be synonymous with quality in describing market sector, and a less loaded term. But now that the *Independent* and *The Times* are tabloids/compacts that term no longer works. Terminology may be a problem but we know what we mean. But eventually the market sectors will have to be 'rebadged' by the Audit Bureau of Circulations (**ABC**), which publishes its figures under these sector headings.

ABC Audit Bureau of Circulations: organisation providing official figures for newspaper circulation.

National sales

National newspaper sales often surprise those outside the media industries. *Guardian* readers find it hard to believe that for every copy of their chosen paper sold nearly ten copies of the *Sun* cross the counter. Including the *Daily Record* in Scotland (just under half a million), the total daily sales in the popular, or tabloid, market in the middle of 2004 were a little over 6.5 million, with the *Sun* the dominant title selling 3.3 million each day.

The mid-market sale was 3.4 million, with the *Daily Mail* taking the lion's share, 2.4 million. The so-called quality sector accounted for 2.7 million, spread across six titles including the *Scotsman*. The market leader is the *Daily Telegraph*, with a sale of around 900,000. All the quality titles have a greatly enhanced sale on a Saturday. The circulation figures quoted are averages across six days.

Not content with devouring newspapers throughout the week, we have a long tradition of reading a different kind of newspaper on a Sunday. Historically Sunday was the day for the 'dirty' papers with the more salacious 'stories' of vicars up to no good and smutty court cases being enjoyed across all social divides. The *News of the World* was, and remains, the best-selling newspaper of the week (3.7 million copies), but no sector of the market is declining faster than the popular Sundays, with the *People* losing sales fastest. However, we still buy around 7.5 million popular or tabloid newspapers on a Sunday.

The mid-market (just the *Mail* and *Express*, as on weekdays) accounts for 3.3 million copies. The Sunday qualities, where broadsheets still are broadsheets, sell around 3 million copies in total, with *The Sunday Times* the dominant title, selling about half of the total.

All those figures suggest a buoyant national newspaper industry selling a staggering number of copies. Both those things are true up to a point, but it does remain an industry in decline, at least in terms of the amount of product being sold. In the glory days of the 1950s and 1960s newspapers sales were even bigger. Once the *Daily Express* sold 4 million copies a day and the *Daily Mirror* 5 million. More recently the *Sun* sold in excess of 4 million. Total sales of national newspapers are falling steadily, most notably in the tabloid sector, particularly on Sundays. But there are individual reverse trends too. The *Daily Mail* has steadily gained sale for twenty years. *The Times* has moved forward. New newspapers like the *Independent* (1986) and *Independent on Sunday* (1990) have entered the market, and while the road has not been smooth they are firmly established players.

Gloomy predictions for the future of newspapers have been made for years. They would be replaced by radio, by television and by the Internet. But it hasn't happened, and it won't for a very long time to come. Why else would rich individuals and great corporations be so keen acquire them?

National newspaper ownership

In June 2004 the *Telegraph* titles (*Daily*, *Sunday* and the weekly political magazine, the *Spectator*) were sold to the Barclay Brothers for a sum approaching £700 million. That's how desirable newspaper ownership remains. This record sum was paid for a newspaper that has steadily been losing circulation for some years. The Barclays, shrewd, low-profile businessmen based in the Channel Islands, are driven neither by vanity nor the desire to gain political influence. Their decisions are always based on the balance sheet and they clearly see a successful and profitable future for the *Telegraph* titles. They succeeded Conrad Black, the wealthy Canadian who was driven by vanity and a desire for social status and political influence.

Now only the Daily Mail Group and the *Guardian* remain in the hands of their historic owners. In the case of the *Mail* (and its much more recent *Sunday* stable mate) it is the Northcliffe/Rothermere family who have played such a major role in the development of newspapers since the nineteenth century. The *Guardian* is owned by the Scott Trust, formed by its legendary editor (of the then-*Manchester Guardian*) C.P. Scott. It acquired the *Observer* in 1993.

For the rest, the Mirror Group (with its *Daily* and *Sunday Mirrors*, as well as the *People*) has changed hands several times, mostly recently being acquired by Trinity, the largest publisher of regional newspapers in the country. The *Express* titles, once owned by that most unashamedly political of proprietors, Lord Beaverbrook, are now in the hands of Richard Desmond who built his fortune on publications that tended to be cellophane-wrapped and located on the newsagent's top shelf. The *Financial Times* is owned by the Pearson Group. The *Independent* and its *Sunday* title have moved a long way in fewer than twenty years from the dream on which it was founded, a wide range of relatively small investors securing the independence from proprietorial interference its title proclaimed. Today it is owned by Tony O'Reilly, the Irish entrepreneur with major newspaper interests in many countries.

And then there is Rupert Murdoch, the Australian turned American whose News International is responsible for the biggest-selling daily paper in the country, the *Sun*, the biggest selling Sunday, the *News of the World*, the biggest selling Sunday broadsheet, *The Sunday Times*, and the one-time 'top people's paper', *The Times*. About one third of the national newspapers sold in the UK are published by Rupert Murdoch. Table 2.1 illustrates the proportion of the market by circulation (sales) held by the big owners.

The thriving regional press

The UK has a thriving regional press with about 1,300 weekly and daily titles. Of these some 650 are distributed free, the most significant being the *Metro* titles in the big conurbations, which have proved popular and successful in recent years. Some 40 million UK adults read a regional newspaper, significantly more than read a national. The trend over the past decade or so has been for the sales of regional

Table 2.1 Proportion of market held by the big owners

Owner	Titles	% of market by circulation
News International (Murdoch)	*Times, Sun, Sunday Times, News of the World*	36.6
Express (Desmond)	*Daily Express, Daily Star, Sunday Express, Daily Star Sunday*	13.5
Trinity Mirror	*Daily Mirror, Sunday Mirror, People*	17.6
Guardian Media	*Guardian, Observer*	3.4
Pearson	*Financial Times*	1.7
Associated	*Daily Mail, Mail on Sunday*	18.8
Independent News and Media (O'Reilly)	*Independent, Independent on Sunday*	2.0
Barclay Brothers (Telegraph)	*Daily Telegraph, Sunday Telegraph*	6.5

morning and evening daily newspapers to decline. There are nineteen paid-for regional mornings and seventy-five evenings. The top-selling morning papers, the *Eastern Daily Press* based in Norwich and the *Yorkshire Post* based in Leeds, sell a little above and a little below 70,000 respectively. The top-selling evenings are the *Express and Star* in the West Midlands and the *Manchester Evening News*, both selling around 170,000.

Various factors have contributed to the steady fall in circulations. The decline of manufacturing industry has meant fewer factory workers making their way to the bus home and buying the evening paper on the way (those still working in factories use a car). The growth in other sources of news – radio and television – has made the evening paper less relevant. And earlier **deadlines** – most evening newspapers are at best lunchtime **editions** – have made the news less up to date. Regional morning papers, of which there are few, suffer from finding it difficult to provide value for money in competition with national newspapers that have grown enormously in size and the number of sections they provide, particularly in the quality sector. Another factor must surely be cost-cutting by the big owners.

deadline time by which copy is expected to be submitted.

edition specific version of a publication. Editions can be published for a specific day or a specific time of day or place.

The strength of the weeklies

The success story of recent years has been the local weekly paper, with about half of the 520 or so paid-for weeklies gaining circulation. With the urbanisation of society and the increasing anonymity this drives, there has developed a search for community. Dormitory village life is one manifestation of this, the rich buying second homes or commuting from their so-called 'villages' to the big city. But in towns across the country, people refer to local communities, and local papers reinforce the sense of community.

'Small is beautiful' is a term successfully exploited by a publisher called Ray Tindle whose newspaper interests were once concentrated in Guildford and Farnham, wealthy Surrey towns. Having sold his *Surrey Advertiser* group to the *Guardian*'s regional arm, he concentrated on buying tiny, 'parish-pump' newspapers up and down the country. Tindle believes in all the old values of local newspapers, reporting the fêtes and the flower shows, making sure as many names as possible appear in the paper each week. His enterprise, based on small newspapers with small circulations, often well under 10,000, has been enormously successful.

One notch up the scale, the weekly titles owned by the big publishers have enjoyed similar success, both in terms of sales and profitability. Concentrating on local news and championing small communities, they have maintained or increased sale as the evening papers in the bigger towns and cities have suffered. With no pressure to cover other than local news, with their captive local marketplace for advertising, of services, retailing, entertainment, births, marriages and deaths, they have a defined and coherent agenda. They can run pictures of babies, school classes, weddings, sports days, dance festivals, dinners and dog shows, knowing that every face and every name is a reader, with plenty of relations to buy a copy too.

These local papers also know that every planning decision, every traffic-calming measure, every parking development, every new supermarket or corner-shop closure is controversial, a story, and sales. This is a very pure form of journalism, and a training ground for good journalists who go on to bigger things.

Local newspapers have one other big advantage in they that tend to have a monopoly over local news. Television seldom gets more local than regional, although there are plans for local television stations across the country. Certainly the technology is available for distributing such services. Local radio stations tend to be music driven, with a very limited news service that cannot compete with the local paper.

Regional press ownership

The regional press landscape has changed dramatically over recent years, with huge shifts in ownership and concentration into the hands of a few huge publishers. The age of the independent publisher is almost gone, and today the largest twenty regional publishers account for 85 per cent of all regional titles and 96 per cent of total weekly circulation. In reality the situation is starker than that, with the big four dominating the marketplace as a result of recent merger and acquisition.

The biggest is Trinity Mirror with 235 titles in all sectors of the regional market selling or distributing a total of 15.6 million copies. It dominates Wales, Merseyside, Newcastle, Birmingham and swathes of London. While the pessimists were saying the regional press was dying and some publishers were selling out, Trinity was relentlessly buying – one of its biggest regional acquisitions was Thomson Regional Newspapers in 1995 for more than £300 million.

Gannett, the huge American publisher, is the second largest through its British arm, Newsquest. Its big acquisition was Westminster Press in 1996 for £305 million from Pearson, the publisher of the *Financial Times*. Newsquest titles are spread around the country, from York and Bradford to Glasgow and Southampton. In all there are 215 titles, and 10.6 million copies are sold or distributed each week.

Northcliffe, the Daily Mail Group's regional operation, is one of the few that has not changed hands. It is the third largest group owning 110 titles and selling or distributing 9.1 million copies a week. The highly successful *Metro* series of free daily papers, found on buses, trains and trams in big conurbations such as London, Manchester and Newcastle, are in the same family but are published by Associated Newspapers rather than Northcliffe. Nearly 6.5 million copies of *Metro* are distributed around the country each week. The *Metro* series alone makes Associated the fifth largest regional publisher.

Above them in fourth place is Johnston Press, accounting for 8.4 million copies a week, through 241 titles. Johnston grew first as a publisher of weekly titles, initially in Scotland and then around the country. Its leap into the big league came in two stages. In 1996 it bought Emap for £211 million, and then in 2002 it bought Regional Independent Media (RIM) for £560 million. RIM itself was a venture capital purchase four years earlier of United Provincial Newspapers (UPN), the regional arm of the Express group.

In the space of seven years the regional press landscape had changed and what the Americans call 'corporate newspapering' was in control. Those who had taken strategic decisions to move out of regional newspapers – Westminster Press, Thomson, UPN, Emap – on the basis that they could not see a future in the regional press, certainly did lucrative deals but were wrong to write off regional newspaper publishing. The new owners are doing very well, and if they are managing decline the returns remain good.

THE WELL-OILED MACHINE: ORGANISATION OF NEWSPAPERS AND MAGAZINES

While newspapers are unlike other products, they are still the result of a manufacturing process. Journalists hate to be reminded of this, but need to be from time to time. Businesses that make repeated losses tend to go out of business. Of course newspapers are not like fridges, cars, clothes or toothpaste. They have characters and souls. They are about ideas and flair and creativity. They can influence events, change views, right wrongs, make readers laugh or cry. Toothpaste, by and large, does not achieve any of these things.

So while there is the editorial operation, the generation and presentation of what goes in the newspaper, what the reader looks at and reads, there is a substantial infrastructure supporting that core activity. Like any business a newspaper will have a management structure made up of the people who run the business, hopefully effectively and efficiently. These people will, in the main, not be journalists, although in some organisations the editor of the newspaper will play a role in management, perhaps sitting on the board.

Marketing, accounts and personnel

There will be the usual departments like accounts and personnel. Marketing departments have developed and become much more important in recent years. Current thinking sees newspapers as brands, and brands are there to be exploited by marketing people. Newspaper titles are as familiar to the public as Coca-Cola or Cadbury, and they have the added ingredient that they are intellectual brands. The *Guardian* and the *Sun* are known not simply as newspapers but as certain kinds of newspapers. They represent something. Their names can be attached to lectures or calendars, to events or spin-off products. Publishers spend a lot of time thinking about these matters.

Printing: a core business

There are non-editorial departments more central to the core business. Newspapers have to be printed. Printing is a complicated and costly technological process. Setting up new printing plants will cost tens of millions of pounds. Presses have to be run and maintained so that the newspaper you buy is of high quality with good colour registration and clear print.

The paper on which the publication is printed has to be bought and its quality maintained. This is a crucial cost of newspapers and publishers spend a lot of time doing deals over newsprint, as the paper is called. And of course it is consumed at a rate. The presses roll every night for a daily paper and only so much can be stored. The delivery flow has to be managed carefully.

Distribution and advertising

Newspapers must be distributed. Britain is unique with its flourishing national press, a consequence of a small land mass and a large population and also historically for its comprehensive rail network, which for many decades allowed newspapers to be printed in London and distributed by rail every night to every corner of the country.

Costs and the deterioration of the railways put an end to that in the 1980s when Rupert Murdoch, having revolutionised production with the introduction of new technology in his Wapping plant, then revolutionised distribution by using his own transport company TNT to truck newspapers round the country. The use of printing presses, sometimes subcontracted from other publishers, in various regional centres, with pages being first faxed and then electronically transmitted to satellite printers, reduced distribution problems and dependence on London printing presses.

The other department central to a newspaper publishing operation is advertising. There are two sources of revenue for newspapers: the first comes from the cover price, what a reader pays to buy a newspaper; the other is advertising revenue, what advertisers pay to place an advertisement in the paper. In the case of free newspapers, like *Metro* and free weeklies, advertising is the only source of revenue. What publishers can charge for advertising is determined by circulation, how many copies are sold or, in the case of free newspapers, guaranteed to be distributed, and by the kind of audience reached. When publishers talk about the number of AB readers they have, they are describing the socio-economic classification of their readers, their disposable income and lifestyle: how much money they might have to spend and what they might spend it on.

There are two kinds of advertising: display and classified. **Display advertising** is placed on editorial pages or, in the case of full-page ads, beside editorial pages, and

display ads large advertisements usually containing illustrations and appearing on editorial pages. Advertising department will organise distribution of ads throughout the newspaper which is usually indicated on a dummy handed to subs before layout begins.

is bought by manufacturers or retailers of products or providers of services. Such advertising includes cars, electrical goods, mobile telephones and savings or investment products. **Classified advertising**, so described because it is arranged in labelled sections, includes jobs and property. The *Guardian* is a good example of a national newspaper that has been very successful in the classified advertising market, building sections like Media, Education and Society around its dominance of jobs advertising in those particular areas.

classified ad a short advertisement in a newspaper or magazine (usually in small print).

So advertising departments are vital and employ large staffs whose job it is to 'sell space'. Editorial staff think that advertising uses valuable space which could be better used for the words they write. Advertising staff know that without them there is no space at all and no newspaper. The twain seldom meet, metaphorically or actually.

Modern newspapers are large and unwieldy beasts, particularly those at the upper end of the market. Think of a Saturday *Times*, *Telegraph*, *Guardian*, *Independent* or *Financial Times*. There are as many words in these editions as half a novel, more in the case of many novels. Even Monday to Friday papers these days are pretty bulky. To produce these every day, on time, with no empty space, with quality content, up to date with the news and properly designed is an extraordinary feat of organisation. However long you have been in the business it strikes you as little short of miraculous that it happens at all, let alone every day.

It depends on a well-oiled machine, clear and decisive decision taking, good leadership at every level and enormous professional ability right across the editorial department. National newspapers employ large editorial staffs – 400 in some cases, although papers with limited resources like the *Independent* have far fewer. Behind those whose words and pictures appear in the paper lie many more engaged in the organisation and production of the paper.

National papers (and the bigger regionals) are organised on a departmental structure. There will be departments, with editors in charge, responsible for home, international, business and sports news. There will be a features department, subdivided into general features, arts, columns and opinion, leaders, **listings**, travel. Somebody is responsible for items of vital importance to many readers like the weather, the crossword and the cartoons. Such structures vary a little from paper to paper but they are fundamentally similar. Those with many sections, such as the Saturday papers listed above and many of the Sunday papers, may have separate editors for each section. Some papers have an editor solely responsible for the Saturday edition. There will be a pictures department. Then there will be the production operations, with groups of sub-editors responsible for copy-editing (checking and honing the stories or features produced by the writing journalists), page design, formatting and headline writing.

listings lists usually of entertainment events giving basic information: times, venue, phone numbers and so on.

Editorial executives

At the top of the organisational structure are various editorial executives without specific departmental responsibility, or responsible for a range of departments. These will be assistant editors, a deputy editor and the editor. The roles of these journalists are to look across the whole paper, to think of its balance of tone and content, to be the mechanism or conduit that ensures that one hand does know what the other is doing, that ensures the absence of duplication or omission. And, of course, to take the big decisions, ultimately the editor's, about what goes in and what is left out, the priority given to various elements within the paper in terms of the size and prominence of individual articles, the amount of space allocated to different sections of the paper.

The sharp end of such decisions is the front page. Which story will 'lead' the paper (dominate the front page)? Which other stories will appear on the front? Which picture will be used? What items inside the paper, or in other sections, will be trailed or flagged or cross-referenced from the front page?

Spotlight on home news

Let us take one particular department to describe how the news-gathering operation works, home news. It is run by a news editor sitting at a news **desk** surrounded by a team of people carrying out general and specific news-desk roles. The overall responsibility is to provide coverage – stories – of the domestic news of the day. Decisions must be made about what is to be covered, how it is to be covered, who is to cover it, by what time, at what length. Judgments will be made about how important the story is and how prominently it is likely to be displayed in the paper.

Forward planning is vital, knowing in advance what is scheduled to happen so that, where possible, decisions can be taken in advance about whether an event will be covered and how it will be covered. Plans can always be changed in the light of the circumstances on the day. Planning for the predictable allows space for dealing with the unpredictable. Much news is predictable. We know when particular criminal trials will take place, when prime minister's questions and specific debates take place in parliament, when certain conferences occur, reports are published, awards are presented, television series begin, by-elections take place, books are published, major sporting events occur, anniversaries happen and a thousand other things, from school terms starting to budgets being presented, from company annual meetings to film premieres. All these are in the diary, predictable.

The news desk will balance stories it would like to have staff cover against number of available reporters, will assign stories and brief reporters. It will take them off stories if potentially more important or interesting stories emerge. News comes in from a variety of sources: the Press Association, the national news **agency**, provides a constant feed from all over the country; organisations issue **press releases** and statements; public relations people contact news desks, as do members of the public and, on occasion, whistle-blowers. Information comes from the emergency services, from **freelance correspondents**, through the post. It comes from other publications, magazines, specialist journals. News desks monitor radio and television. News comes from ideas or observations or **contacts** of the newspaper's own staff. And news happens: bombs, floods, motorway pile-ups, murders, arrests, sackings, promotions, marriages and separations. One way or another the newspaper always gets to hear.

Home news departments contain specialist journalists, correspondents responsible for a particular area, such as health, education, politics, local government, show business,

desks departments of newspapers: thus news desk, features desk.

agency main news agencies are the PA, Reuters, Agence France Presse, Itar-Tass, Associated Press. Also a large number of smaller agencies serving specialist and general fields. Copy known as wire copy. See also **snap**.

press release announcement made by organisation specially for use by media (not necessarily just press).

freelance journalist contributing to several media outlets and not on permanent staff of any one organisation. See also **stringer**. US: freelancer.

correspondent usually refers to journalist working in specialist area – e.g. defence, transport – or abroad, e.g. Cairo correspondent.

contact journalist's source.

continued

environment, arts news or transport. News editors expect these correspondents to be abreast of everything happening in their patches, to have contacts and sources who will tip them off about anything interesting that is happening. Correspondents are expected to bring in stories, to tell news desks what is happening, not wait to be told themselves. To a certain extent they self-edit. (For more on the role of news editor see Chapter 8.)

The conference

conference meeting of editorial staff to discuss previous issues and plan future ones.

The **conference** is the forum for the exchange of information across departments and to senior executives up to the editor. Most national newspapers will have two main conferences a day, with a number of smaller functional conferences taking place throughout the day. Earlier in the day there will be more discussion of coverage, in which views are expressed, the tone set. Later, when so much more is known about what has happened and what is on offer, it is a question of taking decisions about the shape of the next day's paper.

Newspapers depend on both effective teamwork and individual performance, on creative ideas and imaginative implementation. Egos abound, but the most effective control is the clock. Happily argument and disagreement must always be cut off by the deadline; the paper has to come out. So there are many voices but ultimately one decisive voice; several possible main stories but ultimately the page one **lead**; many ways of constructing a story but only one published version. And tomorrow is always another day.

lead The main story on the page. Could also mean the story's intro.

The role of reporters

The pace of a local paper is very different from a national, but the workload is equally intense. Reporting staffs are usually very small and reporters tend to be young and inexperienced, embarking on their careers. They are forced to learn a lot in a short time. Resources are such that the local-paper reporters undertake a very pure and basic form of journalism: they have to find out what is going on. They have to make the calls, to the police, fire and ambulance. They have to build contacts all over their circulation area, know the gossips, know who has influence. They have to read the council agendas, the parish magazines, the planning applications.

They have to talk to the local councillors, the school governors, the chamber of commerce, the probation officers. They have to use their eyes as they walk around town, notice the traffic jams and the building being demolished. They have to talk to neighbourhood-watch organisers, leaders of pressure groups. They have to read noticeboards and become aware of campaigns and protests. And usually the local reporter has to write more stories in a day than a national newspaper reporter does in a week.

Magazines and newspapers: not really a world apart

Most newspaper reporters see magazines as a world apart, a different business. They are both right and wrong and more wrong than right. Apart from the obvious similarity that both newspapers and magazines are made up of printed words and pictures on a page, the connections between the two are many and growing. Reporters who see their role as turning over stones, **digging** out the truth from those with something to hide, covering action from wars to pub brawls and shedding light on the activities of the rich and powerful, seldom stop to acknowledge what a large proportion of their newspapers do something very different.

dig to do deep research.

The growth of what has become known as lifestyle journalism has brought the subject matter of magazines into newspapers. Most newspapers regularly feature health and fitness, food and drink, fashion, property and home improvement, children and education, computers and gaming, gardening and relationships (for which read sex and infidelity, advice from **agony aunts**, finding your man or woman, keeping your man or woman, getting rid of your man or woman).

agony aunt woman offering advice to people who write to newspapers with personal or emotional problems. Agony uncle is the male equivalent, but not many of these around.

Until the advent of electronic technology for newspaper production, the Wapping revolution (with the shift of Murdoch's titles away from Fleet Street) and the huge reduction, in some cases elimination, of the power of the print unions, newspapers were constrained in size. A broadsheet quality daily newspaper often contained just sixteen pages, the tabloids the small format equivalent of that. One of the products of the technological and industrial change was a huge increase in pagination with added sections each day and many added sections on Saturdays and Sundays. News could not expand to fill papers ten and more times bigger than their predecessors, so there was a huge expansion in what could be described as features or reader services.

Until then, newspapers had no space for listings. If you lived in the capital and wanted to know what to do or where to go you bought *Time Out*, which listed everything available. There were equivalents in other big cities. Newspapers moved in and started to provide listings. If you wanted to know what was on television you bought *Radio Times* or *TV Times*, magazines that had a monopoly over advance TV programming. After dealing with the copyright issues the newspapers starting producing their own TV listings guides for the week ahead, in magazine format.

'Free' magazines were added to newspapers – pioneered by *The Sunday Times* and now taken up by almost all, in various formats and on various styles of paper. *The Sunday Times* now provides its original magazine plus *Style*, *Culture* and frequent one-off specials. The *Observer* produces specialist magazines on sport, food and music on a rotating basis. And at the other end of the market the *Mirror* has produced a pocket sized *3 AM Girls* magazine. The purist reporters should look around their own newspapers if they think magazines have not influenced them.

The rise and rise of celebrity journalism

The influence goes further though, right into the main body of the paper where magazine ideas and approaches now feature strongly. The changing 'news' agenda has helped to bring this about. The rise and rise of celebrity journalism, where the lives and times of the rich and famous and not so famous have seemingly engrossed the nation, has meant that newspapers, particularly at the popular end of the market, have had to borrow ideas and often material from magazines. The relationships between the *Mail* and *Hello!* and between the *Express* and *OK!* are obvious examples. But more subtly the human interest approach of women's weekly magazines like *Take A Break* and *Woman* have been increasingly copied by newspapers.

It is seen in the employment of magazine journalists by newspapers and the buying by newspapers of magazine features. Newspaper news and features editors would be failing in their jobs if they did not keep abreast of what is going on in the magazine world. What successful magazines have always been good at are marketing and market research, targeting, reader awareness and presentation. All these words and concepts are now the everyday currency of newspapers too, and they have never been ashamed to pilfer good ideas.

So while the newspaper and magazine approaches and disciplines have areas where there is no overlap, there are plenty where the overlap is considerable. Both depend for their success on ideas and flair. Both depend on deep knowledge of their target audiences, although newspapers will target a much broader audience than most magazines, which seek out and aim to occupy a niche. Magazines, in the main, have less of a sense of history and longevity. Publishers are ruthless in killing titles they feel have nowhere to go and put huge energy and resource into identifying and exploiting new market opportunities.

Newspapers use the tools of market research, surveys and focus groups to develop their titles and their editorial content through knowledge of their readers' likes and dislikes, their changing lives and priorities. Because newspapers come and go very rarely, they have long histories, characters and titles that resonate down the decades. Magazine publishers react to fad and changing fashion, always seeing potential for a new title. Surfing has taken off in Britain. So have surfing magazines.

Football moved upmarket from its traditional male, cloth-cap image. Intellectualised by Nick Hornby and others, it spawned thinking people's magazines like *When Saturday Comes* and *Four Four Two*. Men did not read lifestyle magazines; they read magazines about their interests – cars, music, hi-fi. But then came *FHM* and *GQ* and men did read lifestyle magazines. And the newspapers noticed and thought about it, and it influenced them.

The magazine industry

The magazine industry is dominated by big players: IPC, recently bought by Time Warner, Emap, Bauer, National Magazine, Condé Nast. The BBC is now a significant player. There are plenty of smaller players, but only the big companies have the resources to make the investment and take the risks success demands.

The industry is conventionally seen as divided between consumer magazines, business-to-business (B2B) or trade magazines and customer magazines. 'Consumer magazines' essentially covers all the magazines we see on the racks of newsagents. B2B magazines are trade magazines, read by professionals in the field covered. Customer magazines are used by companies to support and enhance their brands. They are usually produced under contract and distributed free to customers. They may come from supermarkets like Asda, credit-card companies like American Express, campaigning or preservation organisations like the National Trust.

The consumer magazine sector is divided into very many subgroups, for example: TV guides, sports, news and current affairs, music, motoring and women's interests. ABC (Audit Bureau of Circulations) figures are provided in this way, although amalgamations show that the best selling paid-for consumer magazines are *What's On TV*, *Take A Break* and *Radio Times*, all selling more than 1 million copies, *What's On TV* selling over 1.6 million. It is interesting to note that all the women's weeklies, as well as *Take A Break*, *Woman's Own*, *Bella*, *Best*, all sell more than 400,000 copies. That is more than the *Guardian* or the *Independent*. Of the newer titles the celebrity magazine *Heat* sells 550,000 copies. And of the magazines you feel have always been around, *Good Housekeeping* sells 400,000 copies a month.

The structure of magazines

Magazine publishers have the same corporate components as those described for the newspaper industry, except that they will subcontract more activities, most importantly printing. But marketing and promotion, advertising sales and distribution are every bit as important as for newspapers.

Editorial departments differ to a certain extent, with a much greater reliance on freelance writers than is the case on newspapers, although in those areas where newspapers undertake magazine-like activities they too will use freelance writers.

Editors

Magazines are run by editors whose careers are often insecure and whose reputation is dependent on the success of the last title they ran. Magazine editors must be creative, inspirational and capable of binding teams together and creating atmospheres where ideas are the main currency. Magazines cannot depend on events happening; they have to make them happen. Equally editors have to be down to earth and organised, understanding the production and the scheduling of its different stages. The monthly magazine editor must have a curious body clock, feeling in the mood for Christmas in September when the seasonal issues are being prepared and feeling like a summer holiday in December. Above all she or he must know and understand the readers.

Features desks

Features desks generate ideas, conceptualise, commission writers (which depends on knowing who out there is both good and reliable). They edit **copy**, working on it to ensure it fits both the concept and the page.

copy editorial material. Hard copy refers to editorial material typed on paper.

Art desks

The art desk, run by an art director, is crucial on a magazine, where design is often as important as content and part of the targeting process. A magazine cannot be at the forefront of popular culture if it looks dull and unimaginative. Again reader awareness is vital. Magazines are often redesigned to maintain their cutting edge, but once a design is set, part of the job of the art director is to ensure that it is faithfully followed. Templates are often employed to deliver this consistency of 'look'.

Picture desks

The picture desk is also a key part of a magazine. It depends on the magazine, of course, but celebrity magazines must have up-to-date and preferably exclusive pictures of their subjects, and freelance photographers will be constantly trying to sell pictures to magazines. Picture researchers are employed to search picture libraries for the right picture to set off a feature. The picture desk will always work closely with the art desk. All the specialist consumer magazines will have their different emphases. There are people out there who specialise in photographing amplifiers or *boeuf bourguignon*, a salmon leaping or a mountain bike crashing.

Fashion magazines are, of course, dependent on their fashion teams, dealing with the fashion designers and retailers, setting up models and locations for photo shoots, dealing with the magazine's designers and picture desks about the most suitable photographers for the look they are trying to produce.

At the core – the conference

At the core of the magazine, just as at the core of the newspaper, is the conference where ideas are exchanged, concepts developed, plans made. There will be the show-offs and the luvvies, the argumentative and the quietly thoughtful. But none of these egos would produce a magazine if they were not underpinned by talent and professionalism. The success of the creative people in editorial will determine the success of the magazine.

Sources and further reading

Curran, J. and J. Seaton (2003) *Power Without Responsibility: The Press, Broadcasting and New Media in Britain*, 6th edn, London: Routledge.

Engel, M. (1996) *Tickle the Public: One Hundred Years of the Popular Press*, London: Victor Gollancz.

Franklin, B. (1997) *Newszak and News Media*, London: Arnold.

Franklin, B. (2004) *Packaging Politics: Political Communications in Britain's Media Democracy*, 2nd edn, London: Arnold.

Franklin, B. (2005) 'McJournalism: The Local Press and the Mcdonaldization Thesis', *Journalism: Critical Issues*, Maidenhead: Open University Press: 137–150.

Franklin, B. and D. Murphy (1991) *What's News? The Market, Politics and the Local Press*, London: Routledge.

—— (1998) *Making the Local News: Local Journalism in Context*, London: Routledge.

Horrie, C. (2004) *Tabloid Nation: From the Birth of the Daily Mirror to the Death of the Tabloid*, London: André Deutsch.

Greenslade, R. (2003) *Press Gang*, London: Macmillan.

Keeble, R. (2001) *The Newspapers Handbook*, 3rd edn, London: Routledge.

McKay, J. (2001) *The Magazines Handbook*, 2nd edn, London: Routledge.

McNair, B. (2003) *News and Journalism in the UK*, 4th edn, London: Routledge.

Ponsford, D. (2004a) 'Regional Press Topples BBC in Trust Survey', *Press Gazette*, 23 September.

Ponsford, D. (2004b) 'We're All Doomed . . .', *Press Gazette*, 22 October.

Sarikakis, K. (2004) *British Media in a Global Era*, London: Arnold.

Stokes, J. and A. Reading (1999) *The Media in Britain: Current Debates and Developments*, Basingstoke: Macmillan.

Tunstall, J. (1996) *Newspaper Power: The New National Press in Britain*, Oxford: Clarendon Press.

Williams, K. (1998) *Get Me a Murder a Day! A History of Mass Communication in Britain*, London: Arnold.

Web sites

Audit Bureau of Circulations: <http//www.abc.org.uk>.

Johnston Press: <http//www.johnstonpress.co.uk>.

Newsquest: <http//www.newsquest.co.uk>.

Media Guardian: <http://media.guardian.co.uk>.

Newspaper Society: <http//www.newspapersoc.org.uk>.

Northcliffe: <http//www.thisisnorthcliffe.co.uk>.

Periodical Publishers Association: <http//www.ppa.co.uk>.

Trinity Mirror: <http//www.trinitymirror.com>.

Press Gazette: <http//www.pressgazette.co.uk>.

Profits and the public interest

3

The business of newspapers and magazines

Profits and the public interest

The business of newspapers and magazines

Iain Stevenson

All newspapers and magazines exist within a business framework. Even a simple news sheet produced on a home computer involves costs which must be recouped by payment. The purpose of this chapter is to sketch out the business structures of newspapers and magazines and to introduce some of the key concepts working journalists should understand in their daily life. References will be made to specific publications and to the special aspects of periodical publishing that distinguish it from other forms of business. While in many ways publishing businesses behave like any other commercial organisations by seeking to maximise profits while minimising costs, as in so many other of its aspects, the newspaper and magazine business is like no other and many of its business practices are unique or unusual.

A little history

Newspapers and magazines in a real sense owe their origins to business imperatives. The earliest newspapers (such as the *Daily Courant* of 1702) were primarily carriers of business intelligence for merchants and traders and justified their relatively high prices by the value of the information they provided to their business-oriented readers. Similarly, many early magazines specialised in fields such as agriculture and manufacturing and were of interest primarily to those carrying on business. Only after the abolition of the stamp tax on newsprint (1855) and the expansion of literacy following the Education Acts of 1870 did newspapers and magazines become 'general' and news as we now recognise it emerge (see Chapters 1 and 4).

This led to publications becoming major businesses in their own right rather than mainly the servants of business. From the beginning of the twentieth century, newspapers developed as powerful business empires led by astute, expansion-minded 'press barons' such as Alfred Harmsworth, Viscount Northcliffe (1865–1922) of the *Daily Mail*, William Aitken, Lord Beaverbrook (1879–1964) of the *Daily Express*, Sir Edward Hulton (1869–1925) of the *Daily Sketch* and *Evening Standard*, and Robert Maxwell (1923–1991) of the *Daily Mirror*. But although these men wielded great economic and political power, their companies were often inefficient, poorly run, hobbled by the so-called 'Spanish practices' of high-cost, in-house printing and expensive distribution.

After the 'Wapping Revolution' of the middle 1980s, pioneered by Eddie Shah of the short-lived *Today*, Rupert Murdoch of News International (*Sun*, *The Times*, *The Sunday Times*) made use of new technology such as direct inputting to cut costs and increase efficiency. As a result, the business structure of newspaper and periodical publishing companies became leaner with traditional demarcations between jobs disappearing and more flexibility in roles emerging. The methods used to achieve this may at the time have appeared brutal and divisive, but it can be argued such radical business 're-engineering', as it is termed by management consultants, was necessary to ensure business survival.

Today, newspapers and magazines, although not without business problems and challenges, tend to be parts of diversified international media groups owned by financial institutions and investors rather than the personal fiefdoms of the swashbuckling proprietors of Fleet Street legend. They are much less colourful but certainly much more business-like.

Some definitions

Before looking at business structures and practices, it is important to understand some key business and financial terms:

Revenue (or *turnover*) is the total amount of income generated by the business activities of an organisation.

Costs are the amount of money required to generate the revenue. They are often divided into 'direct' (printing, paper, distribution) or 'indirect' costs (buildings, wages, fixed equipment), but in this industry a better way of looking at them is as 'variable' costs (those which change depending on how much business you are doing) and 'fixed' costs (those which you incur simply by existing and which do not vary depending on how much business you do). Fixed costs are often referred to as 'overheads' and the 'cost base' and their size and tendency to enlarge is the main focus of concern of business managers.

Profit or *earnings* is the difference between revenue and costs and is often divided into 'gross' profit (which is revenue minus direct or variable costs only) or 'net' profit which is gross profit minus the overhead. The *gross profit* (or GP) is often used as a headline figure to compare the performance of a company with others in the same sector but the *net profit* (or NP) is the key measure of a company's individual success or lack or it. Profit (or loss) is usually given in money terms but the margin is the profit expressed in percentages of revenue. Gross margins for publishing businesses are generally in the 35 to 65 per cent range and net margins are in the 0 to 15 per cent range. Usually a company achieving 'double digit' (i.e. more than 10 per cent net margin) is felt to be doing well. A currently fashionable way of describing a company's profitability is EBITDA (Earnings Before Interest, Tax, Depreciation and Amortisation) which is roughly but not exactly equivalent to net margin and is felt by analysts to be a precise measure of a company's financial performance.

Capital is the amount of money put into a company to enable it to set up and continue business. It is provided by *shareholders*, who are allocated shares in the business representing the money they have staked. Until the shares are sold, shareholders are entitled to a regular allocation of the profits decided by the company's directors. A share has two values, the face value, which usually remains fixed and is the basis on which the profit share (or dividend) is calculated, and the quoted value. This is the price at which the share can be bought or sold on the Stock Exchange and it varies depending on general financial conditions and specifically

continued

the performance of the company and its dividend 'yield' (the amount of money shareholders receive for their investment relative to its cost). The primary duty of company directors is to look after the interests of their shareholders, the ultimate owners of the business, and in particular to protect 'shareholder value'. This is a complicated concept that includes not only the current trading value of the shares but also their potential for growth and the real value of the assets owned and created by the company.

Most shareholders are today large financial institutions like pension or insurance companies, fund managers or banks who generally will invest or not on purely financial criteria. But many media organisations have substantial shareholders who will take other factors than yield or return into account, such as the social importance of a publication or even its prestige. For established businesses, an increase in capital is achieved by asking the existing shareholders to buy more shares ('a *rights issue*') or by asking venture capitalists, who are firms (usually branches of banks) to put up new money to expand the business in exchange for shares (which generally have some kind of preferential payout mechanism) or to fund a new '*start-up*' either within an existing business or independently. Apart from profit reinvested (which is at the discretion of the directors), 'shareholder funds' are the only source of money to develop and maintain a business.

Cash flow is particularly vital in a business like publishing. It is 'the cash that comes into the business and stays in the business'. With a product as perishable as news and information which can experience peaks and troughs in revenue out of kilter with costs, it is very important for managers to understand exactly when money is coming in and going out. The conventional reporting cycle of a business is one year at the end of which directors will produce annual reports in the form of a *profit and loss account* (P and L) and a balance sheet. The P and L reports the aggregate totals for the year of revenue, costs and profits, while the balance sheet details assets, creditors and debtors. They are essentially accumulative and static and can mask weaknesses in the dynamics of a company's trading that managers need to be aware of. For instance, a publishing company can possess a business which is 'seasonally loaded' like a holiday magazine where the revenue from sales, advertising and other sources can all come in a short period while the costs, particularly overheads, are more evenly spread. Unless cash-flow projections (usually on a monthly basis) are made and controlled, a business like this could appear profitable on an annual basis but be facing shortfalls of cash at particular times. These shortfalls could force it to borrow (thus raising costs because of interest charges) or even limit its activities because it has no cash available at the time it needs it.

The financial management of a business is a complex activity that demands specialist knowledge and skills. Most working journalists (even if they work in the business press) do not aspire to take these roles on: nevertheless, business imperatives will determine what they can and cannot do. They will also shape their career paths and materially affect their well-being, job satisfaction and rewards. Understanding the simple concepts outlined above will enable you to understand how these forces work and their impact.

The key players

To provide a business profile of the newspaper and magazine industry, I have selected several key players. To find out more about these or other companies in the industry, use one of the many business-information web sites available such as <http//www.hoovers.com>.

Newspaper and magazine publishers vary in scale from enormous multinational conglomerates to small single-title companies or family-owned concerns. Here the focus is on the former but many of the latter are interesting and make significant contributions in business and journalistic terms. The revenue, profit and employment figures quoted for each company are rounded from a recent typical financial year, usually 2003. For more recent and detailed information, consult the individual company's most recent annual report, usually available on its web site.

News Corporation plc is a subsidiary of the global News International Group of which the Australian Murdoch family, headed by Rupert Murdoch, are major (but by no means majority) shareholders. The global company has interests in many media, radio, satellite and terrestrial television, book publishing, the Internet and e-commerce as well as newspapers and magazines. Its annual turnover is about £15,000 million and it posts a profit of about £900 million. It employs 37,000 people worldwide. In the UK, it owns the national newspapers, the *Sun*, the *News of the World*, *The Times* and *The Sunday Times* although these are relatively small elements of its overall business.

The Daily Mail and General Trust has interests both in national and regional newspapers. It owns the *Daily Mail*, the *Mail on Sunday* and the London *Evening Standard* as well as more than 100 regional and local titles. It has been notably successful with the launch and development of the 'free-sheet' *Metro* (see below), a saddle-stitched, full-colour tabloid distributed free to commuters in London and other major British cities. It also has a substantial interest in Euromoney Publications, which specialises in business and financial magazines as well as e-commerce and broadcasting activities. Its revenue is about £2,400 million per year with a profit of £70 million and almost 19,000 employees. More than 60 per cent of the shares are owned by Viscount (Vere) Rothermere, a direct descendant of Alfred Harmsworth.

Trinity Mirror plc is a relative latecomer to national newspaper ownership. Building its business in regional papers such as the *Birmingham Evening Mail* and the *Liverpool Echo*, it acquired the Mirror Group in 1999 with the national tabloids the *Daily Mirror*, the Sunday *People* and their Scottish equivalents, the *Daily Record* and *Sunday Mail*. It also publishes specialist sporting papers like the *Racing Post*. Its foray into the national arena has not been notably successful, and while Trinity regional papers remain strong, it faces problems with its national titles. Its annual turnover is about £1,200 million but in 2002 it showed a loss of about £20 million. It employs about 11,500 people but these numbers are quickly dropping as it endeavours to cut its cost base.

At the time of writing, the American Hollinger International Inc. of Chicago is extricating itself from British newspaper ownership with the sale of its *Daily Telegraph* and *Sunday Telegraph* titles and the magazine the *Spectator* to the Barclay Brothers, who already own the *Scotsman* and the weekly, *The Business*. Hollinger in its homeland owns twenty-three major newspapers and more than 250 other publications, but it is embroiled in legal action against its former chairman, Conrad Black. With sales of $1,000 million, it posted a recent loss of $238 million and its future stature as a newspaper publisher outside the USA seems uncertain.

The ownership and business objectives of the Guardian Media Group (GMG) are distinct from other major newspaper owners. GMG is a private company completely owned by the Scott Trust that exists to protect and support the editorial objectives of the titles it owns. This means the company is more or less immune from takeover and can probably take a longer view on investment and its return than other publishers. As well as the national broadsheet daily, the *Guardian* and the Sunday *Observer*, it publishes two leading regional evening papers, the *Manchester Evening News* and the *Reading Evening Post*. It also has extensive interests in local radio, magazines and e-commerce. Its web site, Guardian Unlimited (www.guardian.co.uk) has been developed as one of the most extensive and widely used newspaper sites. With sales of about £300 million, just over 3,000 employees and profits of £26 million it is one of the most secure, efficient and coherent major newspaper publishers.

The Irish Independent News and Media plc (INM) publishes the *Irish Independent* broadsheet and the Dublin *Evening Herald*, as well as 165 other titles in Ireland, South Africa, Britain and Australia. Its main British title is the *Independent*, which remains the weakest in circulation terms of the national broadsheets as well as the most recently founded. Launched in 1986 by Andreas Whittam Smith and a group of journalists from the Telegraph group, it was intended as a serious, centre-ground newspaper free from the perceived editorial interference of the proprietors of *The Times* and *Telegraph*. It has undergone many vicissitudes and changes of ownership, but in the present group, under the energetic chairmanship of Tony O'Reilly, it has achieved a measure of success and stability. It has been noted for its distinctive approach to design and layout, especially its innovative use of editorial photography. In 2004, it dramatically launched a new 'compact' (tabloid format) edition in the London region to appeal to commuters and this has resulted in increased circulation. This prompted *The Times* to follow suit and the other broad-sheets are contemplating similar format changes. With around 11,000 employees, INM has annual revenue of about 1,600 million euros with a net profit of only 35 million euros.

Among national newspaper publishers, Pearson plc has only a small market share with one specialist daily the *Financial Times (FT)* and a 50 per cent share in the weekly news magazine, *The Economist*. With its extensive transatlantic interests in educational publishing, Internet and other media producing an annual revenue of more than $7,000 million but with a net profit of less than $100 million, it has long been predicted that Pearson will leave newspapers and magazines altogether. The recent track record of the *Financial Times* has not been good and it has suffered from a severe drop in advertising revenue, particularly recruitment in the financial sector, which previously bolstered its profits. Nevertheless, Chief Executive Marjorie Scardino has been strong in her support of the title and has expressed her belief in the value of the *FT* as a global brand (see below).

The national newspaper titles published by Northern and Shell plc have also faced problems. This privately owned publisher was founded by Richard Desmond, and its original stock in trade was 'adult' top-shelf soft-porn magazines. It entered newspaper ownership in November 2000 with the purchase of the declining, mid-market tabloids, the *Daily* and *Sunday Express*, as well as the then-struggling 'red-top', the *Daily Star*. It also launched the celebrity glossy magazine *OK!* and a Sunday edition of the *Star*, both of which have been notably successful. The *Daily Star* has also staged a remarkable turnaround and alone among the tabloids has increased circulation. Desmond has sought, with a view to floating his company on the Stock Exchange (selling shares to outside investors), to reposition by disposing of almost all his 'adult' publications (although he retains a soft-porn TV channel), but he has been unable to stem circulation decline in the *Express* titles (though the *Star* ones are showing significant increases). Markedly smaller than its competitors with a turnover of about £50 million and an annual profit of about £1.4 million, it is, however, notably efficient with just over 200 employees.

The purchase of the Express group brought Desmond a 50 per cent share with the Telegraph group of the state-of-the-art production plant at West Ferry in London's Docklands where the vast majority of all newspapers destined to be sold in the south of England are printed, including those published by other groups, like the *Guardian* and the *Financial Times*. According to the agreement between the operators, should either partner be sold, the other could buy the remaining half share at advantageous terms. Most observers thought Desmond would seize this opportunity to dominate newspaper printing by exercising this right following the sale of Hollinger's interests to the Barclay brothers. Surprisingly, in August 2004, Desmond reached an agreement with Sir Frederick Barclay to continue to operate West Ferry as before and not exercise the option to purchase the *Telegraph*'s share.

Away from Fleet Street there are two major players in local and regional newspapers that are impressive in their performance. The Edinburgh-based Johnston Press owns more than 240 local titles (mainly small-town weekly papers) published in Scotland, northern and midland England and East Anglia. Decidedly non-metropolitan in its outlook, it currently turns over about £550 million with net profits exceeding £100 million, which have themselves grown more than 50 per cent in three years.

Newsquest is owned by the American newspaper giant Gannett and publishes more than 300 regional papers throughout the UK with a combined circulation of 11 million (which is more than the sale of all national newspapers). These include the *Lancashire Evening Telegraph* and the *Northern Echo*. It has been particularly active in web-site and e-commerce development, although its print titles tend to reflect traditional values and local news values. With 9,300 employees it generates revenue of over £600 million and has more than doubled in size since 1997.

In magazine publishing, the leading company is IPC Group Ltd, a subsidiary of the American media group Time Warner. It has a stable of more than eighty magazines concentrating in the consumer market with a number of leading titles, many of which are strong brands in the sector, like *NME (New Musical Express)*, *Decanter*, *Horse and Hound* and *Loaded*. Its position has been challenged by Peterborough-based Emap (East Midlands Allied Press) which has been active in launching new titles, revamping established ones and gaining market share in both the consumer and specialist markets. It publishes some 150 titles, including *FHM*, *Heat* and *Smash Hits!* and also has interests in exhibitions and radio. With revenue exceeding £1,100 million and more than 5,000 employees, its net profit is just over £100 million.

Another major magazine publisher is the American company Condé Nast, which is a subsidiary of the newspaper publisher Advance Publications Inc., owned by the brothers Si and Donald Newhouse. It publishes famous international titles at the top end of the market such as *Vogue*, *GQ* and *Vanity Fair*, which can be profitable but are also susceptible to fluctuations in advertising. A similar European magazine publisher is the French Hâchette Filipacchi Médias (HFM), a subsidiary of the giant and diverse Lagardère group whose interests cover not only media but also defence and aerospace. Its flagship title *Elle* is a strong, upmarket title in the female fashion and cosmetic sector but again vulnerable to volatile and unpredictable shifts in the prestige advertising on which it depends.

Markets and publishing models

Like any other products, newspapers and magazines depend on satisfying market demand. Market analysis and market planning are complex subjects but a simple and useful way of thinking about markets is to consider the three 'P's: product, price and position. These characteristics allow periodical publishers to visualise with some degree of sophistication how what they publish fits into their desired target market and how it is faring against competitor titles.

Product is the basic 'proposition' offered by the publisher to its current and potential readers. Journalists would argue that the content of the publication is the most important product element but many other factors like design, image of the publication and its readers' self image, 'extras' like cover-mounts and readers' events are all part of the product mix. The most essential characteristic of the product mix is its perishability. Newspapers have a shelf-life of between half a day and a week, magazines a week to a couple of months. The product, therefore, has to renew itself continually since an out-of-date product is worthless, except to librarians and historians. The renewal process is generally evolutionary, and most publications change slowly in response to changes in the market, but occasionally dramatic changes become necessary to revamp the offering totally. This is usually in response to a slide in circulation or the arrival of a competitor, but sometimes is due to changes in fashion. Such 'relaunches' which involve normally a complete design make-over, a radical revision of content and the 'refreshment' of editorial structure are more common with magazines than newspapers, but the recent launch of the 'compact' *Independent* and the typographic and structural refounding of the *Guardian* in the early 1990s are examples. Relaunches are not without risk as they sometimes seek new readers while ignoring the existing ones and can be costly. The investment involved, of course, has to be recouped by increased revenues but the history of periodicals is littered with examples of relaunches that have actually harmed or even wiped out the publication.

Price might be felt to be a simple equation between costs and revenues, but the determination of a publication's selling price is actually a much more complex and dynamic process. The price charged to the consumer has to figure not only the costs of producing the publication, other revenue streams such as advertising (see below) and distribution costs (including discounts to wholesalers and retailers), but other factors such as the costs of unsold copies, promotional copies, the perceived value of the publication to its readers and most crucially the price structure of competitors.

Economists tend to think of publications as being moderately 'inelastic' in price. In other words, demand does not necessarily change if the price is changed. But many newspaper publishers behave as if high price elasticity is a key factor. During the 1990s the *Sun* conducted an aggressive price war against its red-top tabloid competitors by undercutting their news-stand price. While this temporarily increased the *Sun*'s circulation, there is evidence that such tactics caused long-term damage to the entire red-top market. It certainly had a deleterious effect on News International's profitability. This was a short-term tactic to increase market share at the expense of the longer-term strategic objective of maximising profitability.

The importance of position

Position is arguably the most important factor in determining a publication's success. Each publication has a defined target constituency of readers on whose information, entertainment and cultural needs it must satisfy. Newspapers are usually divided into 'upmarket' (usually broad sheets like the *Guardian* and the *Daily Telegraph* with educated, mid- to high-income professional readers); 'mid-market' (once broadsheet, now tabloid, like the *Daily Mail*, with a mid-managerial, middlebrow and middle-class readership) and 'red-top' (tabloid with a blue-collar readership interested in sport, celebrity, television and scandal). These crude divisions are largely caricatures, and the 'reader demographic' of each category is in reality much more mixed with red-tops providing much serious political coverage while broadsheets/compacts indulge in show-biz and celebrity reportage. Nevertheless they do provide a useful thumbnail analysis of each title's market position.

The market positioning of magazines is much more precise and focused than newspapers. General news magazines like *Time* and *Oggi* which are major elements in the periodical market in the United States and continental Europe have never, at least until recently, been successfully established in the UK, with the last example, *Now!*, the brainchild of Sir James Goldsmith lasting barely two years before collapsing in April 1981. Most magazines serve specialist demographics defined by professional, leisure, age cohort, gender or information-need characters.

The art of keeping in touch with and reflecting the needs of target demographics is a preoccupation of magazine editors and publishers. Competition can be fierce in these arenas particularly if market analysis reveals a tempting new demographic. The recent head-to head launch by Emap and IPC of two new titles, *Zoo* and *Nuts* aimed at males aged sixteen to twenty-four who do not otherwise read magazines involved television advertising, events, giveaways and reputed launch costs of £8 million.

The models adopted by publishers to reach their markets also determine their business approaches. All newspapers and many magazines follow the 'retail consumer' model which means that they are distributed to readers via the wholesale and retail news trade and are purchased individually as they are published. While many purchasers are regular and reliable customers, this approach involves a lengthy 'supply chain' at each stage of which a cut of the cover price is taken, thereby reducing the final revenue the publisher receives. It also incurs a certain amount of risk, as the publisher has to estimate how many copies to print.

Publishing: the specialist way

In specialist magazine publishing, the emphasis is on subscription-selling where the customer pays before the publisher produces the publication and incurs costs. This not only has the benefit of improving cash flow but also reduces risk. Specialist publishing, which in its most rarefied form is the publication of scientific journals by companies like Elsevier and Springer, is very profitable and much less risky, although it has recently come under challenge from electronic forms of publishing. A middle-ground model between retail–consumer and subscription–specialist is the recently developed model of B2B (business to business) and B2C (business to consumer) formats where magazines and newsletters cater for specific professional and specialist information needs aimed at carefully targeted readerships.

These are often 'closed circulation' where the demographic is narrowly defined and readers who do not fit the desired profile are rigorously excluded. They are often sold at a subsidised subscription rate and even free, the costs being completely met by advertising. Variations of this kind of publication are the in-house magazines produced for customers (B2C) of supermarkets, chain stores and airlines. These are produced as complete magazine packages for the sponsoring company by contract publishing houses of which the leading example is John Brown Citrus Publishing Ltd.

Revenue streams and cost management

Circulation revenue is the principal source of income for newspapers and magazines. In the consumer market, for every pound handed over by a customer, about 45 pence is received by the publisher, out of which they have to pay printing and paper costs as well as editorial, contribution, overhead and management costs. The remainder is claimed at various points in the supply chain by news-trade distribution and wholesale and retail newsagents. As circulation increases, these 'marginal costs' are spread over more copies. At certain points they can increase more than proportionately but, of course, as circulation decreases, costs decrease less and each individual sale costs more.

While most publishers plan to increase circulation, the strategy to do so can be complex and there has to be a very careful analysis of the costs involved. As we have seen, pricing strategy can be a big part of circulation management, with temporary price reductions and special offers being used to bolster circulation and enhance market share. The job of the circulation manager and his or her staff is to ensure that the existing channels to market are maintained and kept free, to negotiate and manage special deals with distributors and the newsagency trade and to develop new ways of selling more copies.

In the UK where retail and wholesale newsagency is dominated by one major organisation, W.H. Smith and Company, which has been undergoing its own well-publicised business problems, the circulation development role has particular difficulties. The main one, particularly in the magazine sector, is retail visibility. To ensure a title is displayed prominently, or even at all, at the point of sale in a newsagent requires constant activity and promotion. Newsagents and publishers make use of sales data provided by the independent ABC to monitor how titles are selling. Those that under-perform are mercilessly culled by retailers and lose their shelf space, which, of course, will compound their problems. Among the incentives used to boost circulation, enhanced discount and special deals for retailers, special offers, cover-mounts and relaunches for consumers are used by publishers, all of which increase costs and reduce profitability.

Although circulation revenue is vital, few publications could survive on this stream alone. A few ethically led, politically leftist or specialist publications eschew advertising, but for most the income from the sale of advertisements is an essential component of income. There is in the consumer market a direct link between circulation and advertising revenue since generally speaking the more copies a publication sells, the more it can charge for advertising space. Advertisers use ABC figures as a rough guide to the value of a publication as a vehicle for their announcements, but many other factors are relevant, including readership profile, geographical coverage, prestige and life of each issue.

The importance of advertising

Advertising is categorised as 'classified' (for example, recruitment, real estate), 'display' (announcements distinct by their design from editorial copy) or '**advertorial**' (where advertising masquerades as an editorial feature). The basic rates for advertising space are published on the publication's 'rate card' and these are consolidated for the entire industry in the reference work BRAD (British Rate and Data) which is used by advertising agencies and contractors to book space on behalf of their clients.

advertorial where distinction between editorial and advertising becomes blurred.

In practice, rate-card charges are only guidelines and advertising rates are infinitely flexible depending on whether the advertiser commits to a series, whether space is taken in sister titles, how close the publication is to press date and what the advertising department's targets and bonuses are. Most advertising sales staff are remunerated on performance so are incentivised to achieve as much turnover as possible. This sometimes leads to conflict with editorial staff as advertising sales staff may seek to gain extra space to sell by 'bumping' editorial copy. The publisher or managing editor, who is the executive responsible for the overall financial performance of the title (and to whom the editor and advertising manager will report), will adjudicate on such disputes, and it has to be said that advertising almost invariably wins.

Classified advertising, although relatively unglamorous, has been the most spectacular success story of periodical advertising. Many newspapers have developed specialities in classified recruitment that reflects their readership profiles and generates large revenues. For example, the *Guardian* publishes large supplements carrying media, IT and public-sector jobs while senior corporate management vacancies are the province of *The Sunday Times*. An interesting development of daily press recruitment advertising has been the republication of weekly ads in a special 'jobs' Saturday supplement that allows job hunters to browse and gives advertisers a second bite. This enables both higher rates to be charged and the advertising to be seen as a reader service.

In the local press, classified advertising, particularly recruitment, real estate, household and personal services, even 'lonely hearts' and contact columns, has expanded enormously and consistently even when the economy has fluctuated. It is advertising growth that has largely contributed to the success of Johnston Press and Newsquest. In many local weekly papers it is not uncommon for more than 100 pages of classified advertising to be carried. It should always be remembered, however, that ultimately classified advertising is vulnerable to the health of the economy. When the housing and job markets are buoyant it will flourish but it can disappear suddenly (and disastrously for the financial health of the publication) if conditions reverse. The recent troubles of the *Financial Times* are mainly attributable to the drying up of recruitment advertising in the financial sector.

The free-sheet phenomenon

Indeed, in many publications, advertising is actually part of the editorial offering. Magazines in the female fashion and cosmetic sector carry prestige advertising which appeals as much to their readers as the features, while most specialist publications are bought as much for their **ad** content as their editorial.

ad   abbreviation for advertisement.

Some publications depend entirely on advertising revenue for their income and are published as 'free-sheets'. A particularly innovative and successful example is *Metro* from the *Daily Mail* stable. First published in London and aimed at commuters, it is made available free to be picked up at railway, underground and bus stations. *Metro* is a tabloid, full-colour paper, unusually saddle-stitched, reputedly as a condition of distribution to prevent loose pages littering tube lines. It tends to be discarded quickly after reading so its readership per copy tends to be much higher than conventional newspapers. Editorially, it is compiled cheaply making use of syndicated and agency copy and recycled features. It carries no **opinion pieces** and takes no editorial line. It employs the minimum number of editorial staff and although the balance between ads and copy is carefully adjusted so that the former never appears to dominate the latter, it has proved itself a successful advertising medium that can charge premium rates. It incurs minimal distribution costs and for journalists it represents a rather frightening glimpse at a future where their copy simply exists as a frame on which to hang advertising. Nevertheless, *Metro* flourishes and is published in several regional editions for larger British cities (although without much local modification or specific content). For many young professionals, it is, perhaps worryingly, the only newspaper they regularly read.

opinion piece   article in which journalist expresses overt opinion.

Ethics and 'advertorials'

The increasing popularity of 'advertorials' also poses professional dilemmas for journalists. These are paid-for features which masquerade as editorial copy but which in reality are intended simply to promote products. In style, they are written to match editorial copy with bylines and typographic congruence with editorial pages. Sometimes headed '**advertising feature**' (but sometimes not) they would not normally fool critical readers as to their purpose but to the unwary they may be confused with genuine, independently written articles. Journalists may feel that to contribute such material compromises their integrity and independence but they may come under pressure from their employers to do so. They are particularly common in consumer publications in the food, household and travel sectors and these forms of covert advertising are likely to increase in the future.

advertising feature   editorial feature produced to support an advertisement or series of advertisements.

Other revenue streams include licensing, in which fees are paid for the republication of articles elsewhere, the running of exhibitions and events (particularly in the magazine sector) and the development of 'masthead brands' in which the publication title is related to other products and services (the *Financial Times* has explicitly sought to develop its brand in this way). Many publications provide 'off the page' ordering services for goods such as books and recordings or services like holidays and while these were originally conceived primarily as reader services they do afford useful commission income.

The problems of going electronic

The most problematic revenue stream is that associated with electronic publications. Most newspapers and magazines maintain web sites that provide generally full-text articles from the publication as well as additional features like links, archiving and additional material not published in print. Some newspaper sites, particularly Guardian Unlimited and Electronic Telegraph are particularly extensive with high functionality and readerships many times that of their parent print publications. While these sites have undoubted benefits in increasing the publication's visibility and global reach, they do have a problem in that the culture of the World Wide Web makes it difficult for them to enforce a charging mechanism that defrays the cost of providing them let alone being a source of profit.

Effectively the electronic versions of newspapers (less so for magazines) are being subsidised by the paid-for print versions and, apart from the minimal income from pop-up and banner advertising, are drains on a title's revenue rather than a contributor. Many attempts have been made to establish paid-for electronic newspapers, but they have generally not succeeded, even in specialist areas such as the financial press where they might be expected to do well. Most publishers are persisting with electronic developments and they probably have no choice. But unless a charging model emerges that users will accept then, in business terms, newspaper and magazine web sites cost a great more to run than they yield.

Gazing into the future

Predicting the future of newspapers and magazines involves interpreting complex and contradictory trends. Sales of national newspapers are generally in decline although local papers show growth. There are more magazine titles published than ever before but new launches have recently been fewer and are probably balanced out by closures. Readership (measured by the National Readership Survey) is increasing but from fewer purchased copies. Advertising is currently healthy but volatile and there are signs that recruitment advertising is migrating from print to the web.

New technologies, particularly the wider adoption of broadband and mobile telephone developments, offer both threats and opportunities. Print delivery of information remains flexible and popular, but there are concerns that it may not be the medium of first choice of new generations. The general business environment with low interest rates, nearly full employment and low inflation is benign but could quickly change. What is certain is that the publishing industry will survive by adopting creative and innovative solutions to the deceptively simple business of delivering news, entertainment, discussion and diversion to an information-hungry public.

Further reading

Greenslade, R. (2003) *Press Gang: The True Story of How Papers Make Profits From Propaganda*, London: Macmillan.
Niblock, S. (1995) *Inside Journalism*, London: Routledge.
Woll T. (1999) *Publishing for Profit*, London: Kogan Page.

Part II

Practice

Sourcing, news, features, comment, reviews, production and going online

'Get me a great quote'

Sourcing and research

4

'Get me a great quote'

Sourcing and research

Sharon Wheeler

scoop exclusive.

If you have always assumed that journalists hang around in pubs and then come out with front-page **scoops**, think again! There's far more to finding news than getting your round of drinks in and nattering to the regulars. But then again there is a grain of truth in the old tale – and for a very good reason. Wherever you find people, you will find stories, be it pubs, sports centres or the supermarket queue.

Making contacts

contacts book
pocket-sized booklet
carried by reporter
listing contact details of
sources.

News happens wherever there are people. It comes from formal sources such as police, fire, ambulance and coastguard, from businesses and other organisations and from the less formal setting of clubs and societies. It comes, too, from individuals with a good story to tell. All journalists keep a **contacts book** – and guard it with their life. It's an indexed address book with names, phone numbers (home, work and mobile) and email addresses of useful people they have come across in their work. A bulging contacts book, updated regularly, is a journalist's lifeline. If you decide to keep your contacts book on your computer or notepad, back it up regularly – there are plenty of true horror stories around about journalists losing a career's-worth of contacts when the computer crashes.

tip-off information
supplied to media by
member of the public.

Contacts provide a journalist with **tip-offs** on potential stories, background information on stories and also quotes. Not every contact will provide all of these all of the time. Some will be people you talk to daily, others weekly, whilst others might be casual acquaintances who provide occasional tip-offs. Journalists get into the habit of checking with their contacts regularly, even if only for a casual chat.

Getting to know the key people in an area should be one of the first tasks for a journalist new to a patch. Spending some time either visiting or phoning can pay off later when a story is at stake. Getting into the habit of phoning – and visiting in person – at about the same time where possible is a valuable routine, as is knowing when not to pester someone. You won't get a scoop every time, and it can take up to eighteen months to really get your face known in an area, but gradually contacts will learn to trust you.

Potential contacts include:

- emergency services
- MPs and their agents
- other political people – both councillors and officers

- people from pressure groups and charities
- business people
- union leaders
- headteachers
- religious leaders
- community leaders: people from ethnic groups, gay and lesbian groups, housing associations, groups for people with disabilities, neighbourhood watch
- chairs of clubs and societies
- shopkeepers
- sportspeople
- voluntary organisations
- people special to your patch (armed services, lifeboat, lifeguard, harbourmaster, university experts).

This list is broad but many papers interpret it narrowly. For example, few papers cover sport for the disabled, unless a competitor happens to have been selected for the Paralympics – and even then the story will more than likely concentrate on the person's bravery rather than their sporting ability. And when it comes to religious leaders, it's almost certain that the only ones getting a look-in on a regular basis are Protestant and Catholic clergy. Some urban papers have made attempts to widen the net by employing reporters of African or Asian descent, many of them also speaking Urdu, Punjabi or Hindi, to work with different communities.

Finding news

Stories come about through a variety of different sources. You'll deal with a great many routine jobs in the office which may produce copy, such as sorting through the mail, scanning through stories sent in from correspondents, reading that day's newspapers (including your own – always read the adverts and letters page, where you will often pick up ideas for stories), checking web sites and monitoring TV and radio stations and agency copy, such as the Press Association.

Stories will come via the office **diary** where the news editor allocates jobs that are known about in advance, such as meetings or court appearances, to various reporters. You may follow up a story in a press release or answer the phone when someone contacts the paper directly with a story. Or you may pick up a tip-off about a story from a friend or acquaintance, or through phone calls to contacts. Reporters who bring in an endless stream of what are known as off-diary stories are highly prized.

diary day-by-day listing of events to cover.

Whichever publication they are on, journalists gather news in a similar fashion. They do 'the calls' – checking in regularly with the emergency services. They speak to councillors, business people and leading sportspeople on a regular basis. If you analysed a local paper over the course of a week, though, you would almost certainly find that the stories are coming from the same few sources. Certain organisations and sections of the community are rarely represented in routine '**ring-arounds**': gay and lesbian groups, community groups, racial groups and most organisations representing people with disabilities only get a look-in when a story is reactive. That is, they are asked to comment on stories but are rarely given the chance to generate their own proactive copy.

ring-around story based on series of telephone calls.

Researching a story

The importance of solid and accurate research and meticulous recording of information cannot be emphasised enough. Once a newspaper – or a journalist – gains a reputation for inaccuracy or sloppy research, it can be very difficult to regain that good name.

Before you can write a story, you have to substantiate it – that is, 'stand it up'. This means doing some checking to verify that what you have been told is true. Some stories you can take on trust: you assume that the flower-show results you have been given are true, as are the details about a school rugby tour to Canada. But a tip-off about sabotage at that flower show or the claim that two of the rugby players are being sent home early from the tour for drug-taking need careful checking as printing inaccurate information could land the paper in legal difficulties.

Tracking down the relevant person to interview can often take longer than actually conducting the interview. If it's a member of the public you are trying to track down, ask around. For instance, most news reporters dread the budget, as it means finding case studies in strict categories such as single mum, married twenty-somethings who earn under £25,000, a forty-something divorcee and a retired couple. Friends and acquaintances can be invaluable when it comes to suggesting people to chat to. Avoid, though, interviewing a family member or friend for a piece, as there is likely to be a conflict of interest and potential rows when you print something they don't like. If they tip you off about a story, get them to suggest a friend or a colleague you can talk to.

Much information can be gained simply by phoning relevant people. If it's someone in an organisation, start at the top and move lower if necessary. Stories need authority, so in most cases you need to go for the managing director of a company and not the tea lady. That's not to say that the tea lady is not a good source of what's going on – very likely she knows far more about what's happening on the shop floor than the managing director does – but she does not have the authority of a title, the overview or the perceived expertise to comment to the media.

A large number of companies or organisations have press officers who are the first port of call for the media. Some are happy to allow reporters access to relevant members of staff once they have ascertained what the story is; others insist all information is channelled through them. The advantage is that the reporter will almost always come away with a quote. The disadvantage is that it may be bland, the same as that given to every other paper and only what the company wants the paper to know.

As a general rule, if you are dealing with a fairly big organisation, ask the switchboard if there is a press office. If there isn't one, ask to be put through to whoever deals with press enquiries or has specialist knowledge of the area you are enquiring about. And it's always worth politely pushing PR people to let you talk directly to the person with the information.

Advising on researching a story is like the proverbial piece of string; the flower show results will necessitate a quick call to the organiser whilst an in-depth series of stories on council corruption will require weeks or months of painstaking behind-the-scenes research before the story gets anywhere near the paper. And though you can do without an expert's view on the flower show – unless you have been sent to cover the huge annual Chelsea Flower Show – you will need several for the corruption story.

Reporters soon become adept at tracking down experts in various fields. On a local level find out who the key players are in a range of organisations. If they cannot help you, ask them to suggest someone who can. Start collecting names, numbers and email addresses of people in national organisations, businesses, charities, pressure groups and specialist organisations. You never know when you might need them. Always scour through newsletters, magazines and web sites for useful contact names. Save the clubs and societies guide that's published annually in many towns and cities. Never throw away a press release until you've noted down the contact details. The story in the press release might be useless, but the contacts may come in useful later.

Reference books

It's worth starting to build your own library rather than relying on what your newspaper or magazine has tucked away. Some newspapers have good libraries with a range of up-to-date reference material; others have a dog-eared dictionary and an out-of-date *Who's Who*. Aside from the obvious ones like a dictionary, encyclopaedia and a decent set of maps of your area, the *Oxford Dictionary of Writers and Editors* and the *Guardian Media Directory* are essentials. Make friends with the staff in your local library – aside from knowing exactly where to find information, they will also be able to point you towards weighty tomes like *Who's Who* and the *Encyclopædia Britannica*. If you are a specialist reporter, start to acquire useful reference books within your area – annual handbooks are essential if you're a sports reporter, whilst the *Rough Guides* to the different genres are useful for those covering music.

Cuttings libraries

Any newspaper or magazine of any size has its own **cuttings** library. Traditionally these were presided over by a librarian and contained shelves and shelves of bulging envelopes or folders full of articles and photographs cut from each copy of the paper and filed for future reference. Now, in the days of electronic resources, most publications will have online libraries where judicious use of keywords will bring up past stories on relevant people, issues and organisations.

Whereas previously journalists could only check cuttings from their own newspaper or from sister publications in the same group, the Internet has widened the net considerably. So a journalist researching a story on bullying in schools can easily track down background information – both official and otherwise – from other publications, official web sites and even personal live-journals or weblogs.

cuttings stories cut from newspapers or magazines; 'cuttings job' is an article based on cuttings; also known as 'clips' or 'clippings'.

The Internet

The Internet has had probably the most significant influence on people's lives over the past few years. For journalists, it has brought information that might previously have taken days or weeks to gather so much closer. But it also has its shortcomings and can lead to some pretty sloppy journalism. There are a host of good books that will talk you through the best way to find what you want in cyberspace.

Start bookmarking useful sites in your favourites folder and check the sites regularly. Official sites are essential but you will also pick up useful material from those run by amateurs and enthusiasts. Sign up for email discussion lists on areas of interest to you (Yahoogroups and Smartgroups are among the main providers). Browse newsgroups and message boards to keep your finger on what's happening. Also put your name down for email newsletters. You will end up deleting a large number of them as thinly veiled advertising but some are excellent, newsy and a good source of potential stories.

The Internet has obvious shortcomings, though, when it comes to verifying information. You have no proof that the person you are chatting to online or via email is who they say they are. Some suggestions for dealing with this issue are discussed in the interviewing section (Chapter 5).

Computer-Assisted Reporting (CAR) seems to be the latest in-phrase in the US and you may hear it mentioned in the UK. It covers collecting data online and manipulating it in **databases**. At the moment it's less of an issue in the UK, mainly because access to official information here is a long way behind the USA.

database storage of electronically accessible data.

Naming the names

Newspapers insist on names, as they add authority, veracity and depth to a story. You are, thankfully, less likely to get away with that infuriating magazine feature approach of 'my friend Sue' where the cynical among us wonder if Sue really does exist! And asking for sources' names is some defence against being fed false information, although newspapers need to remain vigilant here that a person is who they say they are. And they need to cross-check with different sources if there is the slightest doubt. Where possible, quote a named person. Managing Director Jane Smith looks far more authoritative than simply quoting a company spokeswoman. Some companies, particularly those with press offices, though, will insist on the latter and you will have to live with that.

There are occasions, however, when people will legitimately ask you to keep their names out of the paper even though they are happy to be interviewed. These might include someone talking about gangs terrorising a housing estate who is worried about reprisals, or a whistle-blower who wants to go public on dodgy dealings in a business or organisation. It's a matter of professional pride to journalists that they do not reveal their sources – reporters have faced legal action for refusing to name sources. Bill Goodwin, a reporter on *Engineer* magazine, was ordered by a court in 1990 to reveal his source on a story he had written. He eventually took the case to the European Court, which ruled in 1993 in his favour, stating that the UK courts' views were incompatible with the right to freedom of expression.

The Dr David Kelly/Andrew Gilligan case in the lead-up to the US/UK invasion of Iraq in 2003 raises another important issue – that of single-source stories. BBC radio reporter Gilligan's interview with the weapons expert, who later committed suicide, is an excellent example of a senior and respected expert providing an off-the-record briefing for a journalist. In an ideal world – one with flexible deadlines

– journalists would ensure they had all information verified by a second source. But realistically reporters, news editors and editors are likely to assess each case on its merits – and depending on the seniority of the expert quoted.

The *Guardian*'s media commentator, Roy Greenslade (23 February 2004), conducted a survey after the Kelly affair and found a large number of anonymous source stories in the home, business and foreign pages of national newspapers on one day (16 February 2004). He said:

> What is clear from a survey of a single day's newspapers [. . .] is that the custom of using anonymous sources in a variety of guises – insiders, onlookers, analysts, observers, friends – has not changed since Gilligan's report. Unnamed sources giving unattributable briefings remain a key component of the art of storytelling. Without them, many of the stories listed in our chart [. . .] would be less balanced and certainly less factual. In one instance – a page three article in the *Sun* about Liz Hurley – the story would not have been published at all, since the whole of it rests on the claims made by 'a friend'. Our list does not include unnamed spokespeople who are specifically linked to companies, organisations or branches of government. It is presumed that they are official corporate affairs executives, PRs or in the case, for example, of 'a Home Office spokesman', an official with the right to speak to the press.

On and off the record

Before too long you will be faced with the problem of an interviewee telling you that the interview is/was **off the record** – meaning you cannot use what they say in print. As a general rule, do not break the confidence unless you are prepared to take the consequences. You may get a story in the short term but in the long term you will lose people's trust and cooperation. And while that might not seem important if you are working on a big newspaper and don't think you are likely to encounter the person again, it could be the kiss of death for a journalist on a local newspaper where the circle of contacts is so much smaller. Also, it is poor professional practice.

There are several ways to approach the on- or off-the-record issue. Bear in mind that the matter will not arise in most everyday stories – people will look at you most strangely if you ask whether the flower-show results are on or off the record. It's best, too, in most cases to let the interviewee take the initiative and insist on an interview being off the record; if you put the idea into people's heads, they may well then have second thoughts about what they are going to say.

The best options tend to be:

● Establish ground rules at the start.
● If they say something contentious during the interview, check you can quote them.
● If they say an interview is off the record, try – gently – to persuade them otherwise.
● If they persist, agree what can be used – they might be happy for part of the interview to be **on the record**.

off the record when statements are made not for publication but for background only. Information derived from comments should in no way be traceable back to source.

on the record when there are no restrictions on reporting what is said.

- Reluctantly – and depending on its strength – make the story unattributable; i.e. use the information but without the person's name. Phrases like 'it is understood that . . .' come in useful here.
- Find another source for the story – your coy interviewee may be able to suggest someone.

Sources and further reading

Bell, E. and C. Alden (eds) (2003) *The Guardian Media Directory 2004*, London: Atlantic Books.

Buckley, P. and D. Clark (2004) *The Rough Guide to the Internet*, London: Rough Guides.

Keeble, R. (2005) *The Newspapers Handbook*, 4th edn, London: Routledge.

Northmore, D. (1996) *Lifting the Lid: A Guide to Investigative Research*, London: Cassell.

Randall, D. (2000) *The Universal Journalist*, London: Pluto.

The dos and don'ts of interviewing

5

The dos and don'ts of interviewing

Sharon Wheeler

Interviewing isn't simply a matter of wandering along, flipping open a notebook and scribbling a few notes, or slapping a tape recorder down on the table and staring off into the horizon as the interviewee obligingly drops nuggets of information into your lap unprompted. In fact, it's a difficult skill that needs hours (some may even say years) of practice.

Most people don't meet a journalist from one week's end to the next, so whilst they may be more than happy to talk to you, they don't know exactly what you want and need from them. And naturally there will be the times when you are trying to persuade someone who really doesn't want to talk to you that it is in their interest to do so. To interview well you need tact, almost endless patience, courtesy, a bit of amateur psychology, an ability to listen (even when you are stupendously bored and wish you were anywhere but there) and an unquenchable interest in people.

Conducting the interview

It goes without saying that if you have made an appointment to interview someone, you should keep it unless there is a very good reason. Wherever possible, it makes sense to fix a time for an interview – it formalises the arrangement in the interviewee's mind. It will also give them time to mull over what they need to tell you, to make their own preparations and to sort out any paperwork that may prove useful in telling their story. Of course, there will be times when you either cannot make an appointment or want to catch someone off guard, but for most routine stories, an appointment is good manners.

It's worth bearing in mind than many people's views on journalists may have been coloured by the rather unflattering portrayal of reporters in TV shows. So some thought about what you wear for the interview and how you conduct yourself may pay off in the long run. Clothes that look good on a club dancefloor do not transfer well to formal interviews with members of parliament, business leaders or grieving families, whilst T-shirts and badges showing political allegiance are not appropriate either. Keep your private life to yourself.

The opening words

The first thing to do, once you arrive, is to introduce yourself and your newspaper, magazine or web site clearly. Bear in mind that newspapers in an area often have very similar names so you do not want to be mistaken for the opposition. Remind the interviewee why you have come to interview them. First they may be busy people with a lot on their minds, second they may well be involved in a number of big issues that have attracted press interest. Some people will find the use of the word 'interview' rather intimidating and formal so suggesting having a chat often gets better results.

All reporters need to develop small talk – and to know when to use it. A busy council leader may want to cut straight to the chase, but a person less used to being interviewed may be put at their ease by a friendly, relaxed observation about how well England played last night or how lousy the traffic in town is at the moment. A reporter needs to cultivate a pleasant, polite exterior – and to stick to it, even in the face of provocation from aggressive interviewees. And learning to look interested, even when you're hearing someone's family history from the year dot, is also an essential skill.

People used to talking to journalists will not bat an eyelid when you produce your notebook, but others often find it intimidating when you start writing in mysterious hieroglyphics. A good way is often to produce your notebook as the interview starts and to make a self-deprecating comment along the lines of 'Let me just jot down what we talk about so I'll remember it all later.'

To note or tape – or both?

At some stage in your career you will be faced with the decision as to whether to use a notebook or a tape recorder. For most experienced reporters, the former is generally preferable, especially if you have persevered and achieved the 100 words-per-minute shorthand goal necessary to gain the National Council for the Training of Journalists' certificate, the NCE. Notebooks can go anywhere with you, including courts and council meetings, and don't run out of batteries or get knocked off tables during a media scrum.

But there are times, particularly when conducting long feature interviews, when not having to scribble frantically and being able to maintain constant eye contact with the interviewee is a distinct advantage. Both shorthand notes and tape recordings will need transcribing as soon as possible after the interview. Bear in mind that the latter takes much longer to transcribe as you will have to stop and replay sections frequently. Both notebooks and tapes must be kept for a year after the publication of the article in case of legal action.

A good, accurate shorthand note of an interview will always be recognised in court and as a defence in disagreements over misquoting. *The Times* reporter Matt Dickinson certainly found it a godsend following his interview with then England football manager Glenn Hoddle in 1999. Hoddle had said that disabled people were paying for sins in a previous life, but claimed later he had been misquoted. *The Times* assistant editor (sport) Keith Blackmore said at the time: 'Of course we stand by what was written. It was Glenn Hoddle who actually rang Matt Dickinson for the interview. It lasted about 25 minutes over the phone, and although there is no tape of the interview we have a perfectly good verbatim record of what was said.' See <http://archives.tcm.ie/irishexaminer/1999/02/01/phead.htm>.

If you do decide to rely on a tape recorder, always take a notebook along as well in case the batteries fail or the person you are interviewing declines to be recorded. Notebooks are, of course, invaluable for jotting down impressions during an interview; you can hardly lean over to the tape recorder and observe that the interviewee looks shifty and is fidgeting in their seat when you are asking the difficult questions.

Establishing the facts

The first thing to bear in mind whilst interviewing is that you must be prepared to ask lots of questions. Everything you need to know will not be dropped into your lap in the first five minutes in a neatly wrapped parcel. The people you will be talking to will not normally know what you are looking for, so it's up to you to elicit the information with carefully thought-out questions. Lynn Barber, an award-winning feature writer on a number of national newspapers, advises (1991):

> Good interviewing is about listening rather than asking questions – listening for what they don't say as much as what they do, listening for what they say glibly and what they say awkwardly, listening for the 'charged' bits that touch an emotional nerve. Clever questions, in my view, are a waste of time; the really clever question is the shortest one that will elicit the longest answer – in practice, usually 'why?'

You'll need to develop the ability to ask open-ended questions that will lead to full answers; asking someone 'Were you pleased when he was sacked' will gain a different – and not very helpful – response than if you had asked 'What did you feel like when he was sacked?' Closed questions that produce yes/no answers are not generally helpful since they will not give you anything to quote in a story. And negative questions, for example, 'I don't suppose you could tell me . . .', are also likely to elicit the answer 'No'. As a general rule, prefacing a question with 'who', 'why', 'what', 'when', 'where' or 'how' will give you a much better chance of receiving a full answer – and these helpful little words cover most bases for finding out what you need to know.

Before you get too far into an interview, take some time to find out the person you are interviewing's personal details. That way you have all the key information in case an interview is terminated early for whatever reason. Newspaper news editors tend to get twitchy if you don't return with full names, ages, addresses and people's occupations. Ensure, too, that you check spellings of names and places – the man's name 'Dennis' can also be spelled 'Denis' and 'Denys'. And place names are a notorious trap for unsuspecting journalists new to an area – there's a place called Mildenhall in both Suffolk and Wiltshire, but in the latter it's pronounced 'Minall'.

Including this information helps to pinpoint the person for your readers and also builds up a picture of the interviewee. It also helps to avoid confusion so that the reader knows that the J. Smith who has absconded with the stamp club's funds is forty-year-old Jeremy and not his eighty-year-old neighbour John. Be sensible about whom you ask, though – you don't need to ask a police press officer how old they are or where they live.

FACTS CHECKLIST

Name: First name is vital. Newspapers do not accept Mr A. Bloggs in print.

Address: Check house number and always keep a note of it, but not all papers use it for security reasons. Include road name, suburb (if appropriate) and town or city in your story.

Age: This adds to the overall picture of the person you are interviewing. It's more interesting to know that someone doing a parachute jump is sixty-five as opposed to twenty-five years old.

Job: Again, this helps build up a picture of the person. A high-flying barrister wandering around a car-boot sale looking for bargains could be an intriguing person to interview for your feature on these events.

Keeping control

Once the interview is underway, it's vital for you, as interviewer, to keep a firm hand on it. Clarify vague answers as you go along and do not be afraid to push politely for more details if needed – 'I just need to get this straight in my head' is a good explanation for this. Don't stick rigidly to your list of questions. Listen for clues from the interviewee and be prepared to follow these if they look like yielding useful information. Let people talk, too, as frequent interruptions will break their train of thought and can reduce nervous interviewees to monosyllables. But also be prepared to nudge wafflers back on track with comments such as 'that's very useful, but I'd like to ask you about'.

On the whole, journalists will tell you that people are surprisingly cooperative with them and will help them if they can. But you cannot insist that anyone speaks to you, and before too long you will encounter someone who is either nervous and inarticulate or downright uncooperative.

For the former, keep the questions simple and avoid yes/no answers. Be patient with the person and coax them along. They will probably need more interjections from you than usual in an interview: 'Tell me a bit about . . .' or 'Did that happen before or after?' You can also use silences to your advantage as well since most people, after a while, will feel they have to talk to fill the silence.

For the latter, it's absolutely vital to go into the interview as well prepared as you can and to keep your cool, even in the face of rudeness from the interviewee. Keep a note of all the questions you ask and keep putting the questions, even if you're not getting answers back; no comments can be extremely revealing. Keep a careful shorthand note or tape of the conversation and report all threats or potential trouble to the news editor or editor.

Some interviewees like playing hard to get so there will be times when you call on that amateur psychology and massage their egos by telling them how much it will help your story if they give their side. And even though you can't make anyone speak to you, you can point out that this is their chance to put across their side of the story. If this doesn't work, tell them the story is being used anyway.

Closing the interview

Finishing an interview isn't a matter of just snapping your notebook closed, bidding the interviewee a swift farewell and then rushing back to the office to type up your story. The closing few minutes of an interview can be used to make sure you have covered all bases. A useful final question is often something along the lines of 'Is there anything else you think I should know?' Don't rely on this as a substitute for sloppy or lazy interviewing but as a backstop in case a nervous or unsure interviewee spots a gap to tell you the piece of information they have been sitting on all through the interview. Nine times out of time you will probably get the response 'No, I don't think so.' The one occasion where someone drops a wonderful story angle in your lap makes it worth asking the question.

It's always worth using the end of the interview as an opportunity to recap on any parts of the conversation that you weren't clear on, or where you thought the interviewee was struggling for some reason. Don't assume you will be able to contact the person again later – you might be on a tight deadline or they are just about to leave for a trip of a lifetime around the world.

That said, make sure you exchange contact details with the person. Leave them your business card or name and phone number and make sure you take all possible phone numbers and email addresses for them in case you need to contact them again – and write that information straight into your contacts book. Ask them, too, where they will be for the rest of the day in case you do need to get back to them. Bear in mind that impressions count for a lot so thank the interviewee for their time and leave them with a good impression of you.

As you are leaving, watch out for two questions that reporters dislike having to handle: 'When will the story be used?' and 'Can I see your story before it goes into the paper?' The short answers are 'I can't promise anything' and 'No'. The best way of letting people down gently is to tell them that it's not up to you when and if a story is used, as that is the editor's decision and that it's also not the newspaper's policy to show people stories in advance of them being published.

You can also sweeten the pill by saying you will double-check with them if there is anything you are not clear about before submitting the story. The only time it may be permissible to show an interviewee a story in advance is if it's a complex technical story; in that case it's usual to allow them to correct matters of accuracy only. In the high-flying world of glossy magazines, many celebrities demand **copy approval** after an interview. In this case you go with your publication's policy.

copy approval
person allowed to see and approve copy before publication.

Telephone interviews

The myth that reporters spend all their time out of the office on jobs is, regretfully, just that. A high proportion of stories are gathered over the telephone and while most of the interviewing rules apply, there are various other factors to be taken into consideration.

When you interview someone face to face, you pick up on body language. That advantage is missing from phone, fax and email interviews. And there's always the risk of misunderstanding or not having the person's undivided attention when you aren't talking to them in person. Some people simply do not feel comfortable with these electronic methods of communication and while they might be perfectly friendly and chatty in person, they become mistrustful and monosyllabic over the phone. And most people find it much easier to slam the phone down on someone than to shut a door in their face.

The best approach to telephone interviews is to be clear, concise and focused. Ensure at the outset that you are talking to the correct person – the danger with phone interviews can be getting passed all round the building. Explain clearly what you want and aim to sound bright, friendly and alert. It may sound obvious, but ensure you are speaking into the mouthpiece. Instead of wedging the receiver on your shoulder, try to obtain a hands-free headset. Listen to the other person's tone of voice carefully and clarify quickly if there is any confusion. Where possible, pick your time sensibly before phoning. Unless it is a big story you are unlikely to be popular if you telephone people very early in the morning or late at night.

It's worth doing a little more preparation with phone interviews – it will almost certainly save you time in the long run. People generally will not want to give lots of background on the telephone, so do as much homework as you can, or ask them to email you background documents that might help if you are working on a long and complex story. Keep your questions brief and focused, as it's easy for both sides to lose the thread over the telephone. And try to avoid long pauses. Whilst they might work to your advantage face to face, they might well have the opposite effect over the telephone and you may find yourself listening to the dialling tone.

Listen carefully to what the other person is saying and if you think they are joking or being ironic, check. And bear in mind that certain letters sound very similar, so mishearings are more than possible on a crackly line – the person you thought was called Nick may turn out to be called Mick. If in doubt, check, check and check again.

Email and fax interviews: for and against

Email interviews are now much more common given the Internet explosion. And while they may be invaluable when it comes to reaching someone on the other side of the world, they also bring with them their own shortcomings. As with phone interviews, you are missing out on the interviewee's body language. And, more importantly, you can't always guarantee that the person you are emailing is who they say they are. So you must expect to do a certain amount of checking up, although even this will not always be foolproof.

If the email comes from a recognised organisation, this is fair enough. But individuals' addresses are more problematic so you may have to do some digging on other Internet sites or by talking to experts or acquaintances to see if they can verify that the person is who they say they are. If possible, try to phone the person once as a way of checking up on facts supplied. But at some point you may have to take the person on trust and go with the story – it will often depend on the strength of the individual story.

The advantage of email is that you will always have a copy of the correspondence, which makes quoting and checking back on what was said so much easier. And while you may be time-limited in a face-to-face interview, people often don't mind chatting by email, as it can be done in between other things.

Fax interviews are less common, but they can be a very good way of contacting difficult-to-reach people. They're also a useful way of conducting certain formulaic interviews, namely the questionnaire-style ones.

Press conferences

A press conference is a formal event where information is passed on to journalists from across print, broadcast and online media – they range from police conferences appealing for information in a murder hunt to football clubs introducing their new signing. Most have some kind of statement read out at the beginning, which tells you what the organiser's news angle is. This is not necessarily your news angle. There may well be several speakers and they may take questions at the end, although you cannot rely on this.

Always remember that press conferences are stage-managed events, and that the news the organisation wants you to know is not necessarily the only or the best angle. The advantage of press conferences is that you will almost always come away with a story of some kind and that it's a good chance to make some contacts and get your face known. The disadvantage is that you might not know in advance what the press conference is about, which makes doing some research before you go tricky. And, of course, it's very difficult to get an **exclusive** from a press conference since everyone is being fed the same line.

exclusive story supposedly unique carried by newspaper. System becomes devalued when attached to stories too frequently or when the same story is carried in other newspapers (as often happens).

There are some ways round the problems. Always try to secure a separate interview with the speaker(s) afterwards, although you cannot rely on this happening. Make sure before and after the press conference that you speak to interested parties. If the press conference is being organised by a business, you may be able to talk to contacts at the company who can tip you off about what the story is. Remember: keep digging and asking questions.

Check the names and titles of speakers before the event starts and also ask if there will be a chance for a separate interview afterwards. If you're going to use a tape recorder, put it on the speaker's table – but sit near the front so you can see if the tape runs out or if it gets knocked over and the recording button goes off. Always have a notebook and pen with you as back-up.

Once the press conference starts, listen carefully and pay attention. Jot down questions asked as well as answers so that you are reminded what was said when you come to write up. It's normal practice – and good manners – to raise your hand when you want to ask a question. When you are picked, give your name and paper before asking the question. You will have to make a decision at some stage if you have a very good question that no one else has asked. If you know you will get an interview with one of the people afterwards, save it. Otherwise, you will have to smile through clenched teeth while everyone else benefits from your good idea.

And there may be an issue over asking a controversial question, especially if it's one likely to bring the occasion to a premature halt with someone storming out. If you're going to ask it, weigh up when best to use it: too early and the press conference may end abruptly, too late and the event will be curtailed before you get to ask your question. Treat the speakers with courtesy. Don't be afraid to push for answers – asking the same question in a slightly different way sometimes works – and don't let them dodge questions, particularly if you get the feeling they're trying to hide something. Be persistent, but not rude.

After the press conference has finished, hang around for a while if you can. You should talk to as many people as possible, as they are a captive audience – you don't want to have to chase them on the phone later. If there is lunch or coffee after, it's a good opportunity for networking and making contacts.

When you get back to the office, sift through your notes. Is there an unusual angle or follow-up that other journalists missed? Is there a better angle than the one you were fed at the press conference? You don't necessarily have to go with the story the organisers were trying to foist on you. Phone around other interested parties for comments so that you have as well-rounded a story as possible.

That willingness to go the extra mile and to come up with fresh and interesting people to be interviewed will benefit you as a journalist and, armed with the skills talked about in this chapter, will help turn you into an employable reporter.

Sources and further reading

Adams, S. with W. Hicks (2001) *Interviewing for Journalists*, London: Routledge.

Barker, D. (1998) *The Craft of the Media Interview*, London: Hale.

Barber, L. (1991) 'How *Does* Lynn Barber Do It?' *Independent on Sunday*, 24 February.

—— (1999) 'The Art of the Interview', in S. Glover (ed.) *Secrets of the Press: Journalists on Journalism*, London: Allen Lane/Penguin: 196–205.

Harcup, T. (2004) *Journalism Principles and Practice*, London: Sage.

Practice and theory

What is news?

6

Practice and theory

What is news?

Sarah Niblock

Having a news instinct – a 'nose for news' as it is sometimes referred to – is considered an essential requirement for any journalist. Job advertisements for reporters frequently spell out the need for prospective candidates to have a knack for spotting a good story. Being able to unearth fascinating and stimulating ideas for coverage is vital to ensure that news is never old, stale or, worst of all, plain boring.

If you listen to the way experienced editors discuss the day's affairs, you get the impression that news judgment is gut instinct – so you either have it or you don't. That might explain why senior journalists who work in newsrooms day in and day out seem to be able to make important decisions in an instant about what stories will make the front page and what will be dropped (or '**spiked**' in the jargon).

spike to reject copy or other information (e.g. press release). Derived from old metal spike which stood on wooden base on which subs would stick unwanted material. Had advantage over 'binning' since material was accessible so long as it remained on spike.

But when you take journalists out of the newsroom and ask them to stand back from what they do, to reflect on their daily routines, news instinct may not be the unique and innate quality it seems to be at first glance. Everyone who has a role to play in the editorial production of news, whether for magazines or newspapers, must acquire a strong sense of the type of stories their publication thrives upon.

Unsurprisingly, new recruits are frequently put to the test at interviews with the question: 'Have you got any good story ideas for us?' Spotting strong potential news stories is, indeed, a rare and prized talent but it is generally acknowledged to be a learned skill, honed by studying the press, talking to journalism colleagues and by immersing yourself in the 'thick' of newsroom life.

This chapter will examine the most abiding definitions of what makes news. It is noteworthy that these definitions, known as 'news values' or 'news-selection criteria' by academics, are rarely uttered by professional journalists who, on the whole, prefer to go about their daily operation in a more hands-on way. Staffers on a busy news desk, where phones are ringing and screens are flashing, do not evaluate stories against a given tick-list of standards. Instead, they use their news 'feelers' as their yardstick for measuring the worth of incoming material. Having worked in the environment over time, they internalise the ideals and aspirations of their news organisation and can apply them swiftly and confidently.

While journalists, readers and academics might disagree over their validity and emphasis, there is no doubt that news values are ever present and precisely applied by news teams to ensure the continued readability and credibility of their publication. It is helpful to start by looking at the fundamental definitions of news in our culture, before going on to examine their application and adaptation in the context of the fast-paced, highly competitive journalism environment of today.

New(s)

The origins of the word 'news' lie in the Latin term *nova*, which means 'new things'. The first three letters spell out the freshness and originality that underline all accounts of newsworthiness. The *Concise Oxford English Dictionary* defines 'news' as 'newly received or noteworthy information, especially about recent events', again emphasising the topicality of the revelation. So, to put at its simplest, news is a record of the latest events, incidents and developments that in some way touch on the lives of a newspaper's or magazine's readers.

The second half of that last sentence is important. There are many times more new events circulating than any newspaper or magazine could ever print. So it has to select those items that will have the most interest to its target audience. Some news stories will directly affect readers' day-to-day existence, such as worrying new crime statistics for home-owners or attractive new tax incentives for business leaders. Others will touch on readers' hearts and imaginations such as eyewitness accounts of a humanitarian crisis in another country, or how an individual overcame all odds to achieve success. As a record of change, news must reflect the diverse array of events, issues and interests that make up the everyday, whether for millions of readers of a best-selling national tabloid or for the few thousand who turn to a weekly business magazine for the freshest insights into their industry.

There is an additional word we must put next to 'news' to help us comprehend its remarkable and arresting characteristics – and that word is 'story'. It is the selection and retelling of a happening that makes it become news. Or, as Phillip Knightley (2000: 38), the veteran reporter and author of a seminal text on the history of war correspondents, wrote: 'the most elementary qualification of a good reporter: the ability to recognise what is news.' The journalist acts as a storyteller, re-presenting the facts and also prioritising the most recent and attention-grabbing elements. So a fundamental definition of news must be its delivery – news is a packaging of new and relevant facts in a particularly readable order and language that makes it both informative and interesting.

Given the quantity of material with potential for coverage that pours into newsrooms daily, every event reported in newspapers and magazines has gone through a gate-keeping process. Maybe a dozen other stories were rejected in favour of the one chosen. The news values employed in this selection process are partly determined by the intrinsic newsworthiness of the story itself, that is just how eye-catching and attention-grabbing the event depicted will be on the page. But the news in magazines and newspapers is not homogenous. For instance, on a Sunday, it is rare to find more than two national newspapers running the same front-page story. Each title tries to be different and stand out from the others to attract its own very loyal readership.

So, if we take 'unusual people' as an intrinsic news value, a tabloid may apply much greater weight to a story about a particular celebrity than a broadsheet because of each newspaper's extrinsic values. These will include factors such as how celebrity-focused the newspaper's approach is, how picture-led the production design is or simply how many news pages are available.

But it must be stressed that no journalist follows a set list of news values posted on the office noticeboard. Reporters and news editors are united by their keen sense of what makes news and what their editor-in-chief is looking for. Studies have shown that all experienced journalists will tend to rank news stories in a similar manner, with those stories matching the greatest number of news-value criteria being highest on the list.

Exploring the meaning of news values

A seminal study of what makes news was undertaken by a pair of Scandinavian researchers, Johan Galtung and Mari Holmboe Ruge (1965) in the mid-1960s. They identified twelve recurring factors in news stories which they felt indicated a pattern of predictability to what events and issues are most likely to be reported. Here is a list of their criteria and a summary of their meaning:

- Frequency: how close a story happens to the moment of publication.
- Threshold: the level the event must reach in terms of scale for it to stand out.
- Unambiguity: the story should be clearly understood.
- Meaningfulness: the story should be relevant to the readers' frame of reference.
- Consonance: the build-up to an expected event.
- Unexpectedness: how unpredictable an event is.
- Continuity: a big story will remain in the news for days or weeks.
- Composition: a story may be selected because it helps balance the other stories.
- Reference to elite nations: some places are covered more than others.
- Reference to elite people: events affecting famous people.
- Reference to persons: news that has a human focus.
- Reference to something negative; bad news usually contains more of the above criteria than good news.

Galtung and Ruge's formulations have not gone uncontested. One critique of their general validity is that their sample consisted of just four days' coverage of a war. Another view is that their study reveals more about how the events were framed than why they were chosen in the first place. According to Allan Bell (1991), for instance, it is clear that we need to know much more about the context in which stories are selected so that we can better understand the production and branding processes that determine the overall feel of the paper or magazine.

Intrinsic news values

These news values are the in-built characteristics of an event or an issue that appeal to the consensus views and values of the culture the readers inhabit. These most closely resemble Galtung and Ruge's list as they represent inherent values within events:

Impact

Information has impact if it affects a lot of people, particularly if those people constitute the publication's readership. This news value can be roughly divided into two sub-sections, scale and impression. *Scale* explains why major disasters, big company closures or significant scientific breakthroughs get onto the front pages. Large-scale stories contain high figures, such as death tolls, redundancies or money. Stories whose impact is to leave an *impression* may not involve large numbers but may attract a strong emotional response from readers. News of a hit-and-run death, for example, is met with anger and sadness from all in society regardless of their background.

Newness

Stories must be contemporaneous if they are to achieve prominence. There is no point reporting yesterday's news in print today when your readers may already be well-briefed by broadcast and other media or, in a worst case scenario, your rivals. Newness will vary depending on the individual news cycle of the output. So anything that has happened since last Wednesday may be fine in a local weekly newspaper, though the reporters should always check they have included the latest developments before going to press.

By contrast, a regional evening newspaper, which may produce five editions per day, will seek to update and reangle each story with each new publication. Even though monthly consumer-magazine news pages can be produced three months ahead of publication, the words 'latest' and 'new' will be stamped throughout their text to lend the stories pace and immediacy. Journalists are quick to point out that it is not so much the recentness of the events that make them newsworthy but how close their revelation is to the moment of publication.

Exclusivity

It is frequently overlooked in accounts of news making that the most prized stories tend to be exclusives. When a paper or magazine has 'scooped' its rivals, the story will be given maximum prominence as it attracts more readers. Being the first to 'break' a story is highly celebrated. Even when the story is known to other journalists, each paper will be in hot pursuit of a new twist to lend their coverage authority over their competitors.

Unusual people

It is a familiar journalistic mantra that news is about people rather than things. As a society we place tremendous importance on the integrity of human existence, which means that stories involving the most vulnerable people attract most coverage. Street robbery of an elderly woman will be considered news while the same assault on a middle-aged man, though disturbing, would not have such impact for readers. Children are unusual in the same way.

There is nothing new in the press's interest in celebrities, but what has changed in recent years is the concentration on their failures and foibles to show how like the rest of us they are. Consequently, if a famous person falls over in the street and is caught on camera it has every chance of making the headlines while the same event involving a stranger would not. The emphasis on the human aspect of stories is important in all types of publication.

Conflict

This value is clearly prominent in the coverage of wars but the term also accounts for the popular recurrence of reports of disagreements in many areas of public life, from trade disputes to mud-slinging in the House of Commons. Conflict is dramatic in all walks of life and it is a key role of journalism to report debate and to invite witnesses – the public – to form an opinion for one side or the other. It is a unique feature of the British news media that they will use the language of the battlefield to headline relatively innocuous, non-combative conflicts, such as pensioners 'attacking' food packagers or chocolate firms 'axing' the nation's favourite bar.

Unpredictable

A motorist once called a national news desk to say a small private aircraft *nearly* had to make an emergency landing on a motorway. It was a busy news day and, weighing up the other available stories, the news editor spiked the item saying 'nearly isn't news'. Unpredictable events, such as natural or man-made disasters, are more likely to make good copy because of the effect they elicit from readers.

Every journalist is searching for the story that can make a reader think 'Wow' or 'Fancy that!' such as when reporters warned of a Brussels-sprout shortage one Christmas. The news media like nothing more than to surprise. In a survey of 300 leading US journalists conducted by the Columbia Journalism Review, 84 per cent said they felt a story would not be covered if it were 'important but dull' (Preston 2000).

Talking points

Journalists working for tabloid-style popular publications will frequently make a point of listening to radio phone-in programmes for a sense of the main conversation topics of the day. More value is given to stories that relate to issues or events in the current spotlight than to issues they care less about or which may have been overtaken by events. For example, as each winter brings sudden heavy snowfall or flooding, its aftermath will be dominated by coverage of clean-up operations. The follow-up story must move things forward as it is no use simply repeating yesterday's news. The follow-up story has to add to or extend yesterday's coverage with a news development.

Geography/proximity

Where the event takes place is a vital factor in determining whether it will be covered. Is the location relevant to the publication's readership? An accident in Birmingham is not going to be of interest to readers in Edinburgh unless a local person is among the casualties. Similarly, the readers of a magazine devoted to rare antiques will not be impressed with news on car boot sales.

Events which take place in cultures or contexts that are very different from that of the publication's target readership will not be seen as meaningful and will not be followed up. That is not to say journalists will ignore major incidents outside their own terrain. For example, journalists working in many types of sector would examine the impact of a breach of security in one region from their target readers' perspective.

Accessibility

If an event or issue is too complicated to unravel, it is more likely to be spiked in favour of one that is easy to understand. According to Stephen Glover, founding editor of the *Independent on Sunday* and Fleet Street columnist, 'journalists are here to explain, to make some sense of a world that is growing more mind-boggling by the minute' (1999: xiii).

Readers must be able to grasp the full meaning of an event within the first few words or they may switch off. This is why complicated political or social issues are more the preserve of specialist journals and books where there is space to unpack concepts. Newspapers and magazines aim to give the reader news they can comprehend quickly on the train to work or at the breakfast table. One criticism of newspaper coverage of wars is that it devotes little if any time to explaining the historical context of the battle. Editors maintain it is not their job to do so and that they only have space for reportage and commentary about the latest developments

In the context of today's fast-paced and competitive journalism industry, contemporary definitions of what makes news depend not only on the intrinsic impact of the story's content. Of equal and, in some cases, even greater prominence in the journalist's mind is the ever-present extrinsic 'brand' identity of their title. The style, tone and target-readership determine which stories are going 'feel' right for that publication and its audience. Your local free-distribution paper will have different values from a national daily. Specialist business magazines will each have a different agenda from the commerce pages of a broadsheet newspaper. All titles have their own version of a 'good story', which is owned and internalised by their staff.

Extrinsic news values

These values are not as easily accounted for in theoretical analyses of news since they relate closely to journalists' experience of the process of selection rather than a study of the final products.

Brand identity

Journalists need to choose their stories according to their knowledge of their publication's implied reader. To attract and maintain brand loyalty and leadership, publishers invest greatly in market research to identify not only potential readers' preferences but also details about how much they earn, what types of jobs they have and what their leisure activities are. Reporters and editors have to become quickly aware of their publication's target readers and choose stories that will appeal to them.

Competition

As we have seen, newspapers and magazines aim to be first with the news but face stiff competition from one another and from other media, especially broadcasting and the Internet. Journalists have a keen eye on their rivals, which may cause last-minute changes to the news agenda. For instance, a regional evening paper's news desk will respond instantly if local radio reports a 'breaking' story, not only to keep up with the broadcasters but also to ensure they beat tomorrow morning's nationals.

Competition from rival news outlets is another reason why newspapers in particular ensure they cover major predictable stories, or 'diary' events, as well as seeking exclusives. Each title aims to report on a product launch, May Day march, or murder case in a 'better' way than its rivals, when they know that readers may be tempted away to another title.

Production values

Available space, time and even budget constraints are extrinsic factors that have a direct impact on what makes news. The number of available news pages will vary from edition to edition, partly according to the amount of advertising sold. As a result, a potential page lead may be cut to a one-paragraph 'news in brief' or even spiked when space is at a premium. If a reasonable story arrives on the news desk minus a picture, it may be spiked, while a weaker story with a striking accompanying photograph may make it to Page 1. Deadlines and lack of money can prohibit journalists from pursuing leads: stories that will take the journalist away from other duties have to be potentially excellent to warrant the expense, and some titles simply cannot afford to fund time-consuming investigations.

Conclusion: why is it always a bad news day?

This list of intrinsic and extrinsic news values is far from exhaustive. Nonetheless, it is frequently observed that journalists seem almost obsessed with the negative, the gloomy and the downright sad. If the measure of newsworthiness is a story's ability to encapsulate as many of the values listed above as possible, it is unsurprising that tragedies, conflicts and unsavoury revelations are going to be in the spotlight of public concern. However, journalists are much less concerned. According to them, the best stories are the ones we've not read yet.

Further reading

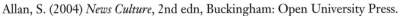

Allan, S. (2004) *News Culture*, 2nd edn, Buckingham: Open University Press.

Bell, A. (1991) *The Language of News Media*, Oxford: Blackwell.

Ferguson, R. (2004) *The Media in Question*, London: Arnold.

Fuller, J. (1997) *News Values: Ideas for an Information Age*, Chicago, Ill.: University of Chicago Press.

Galtung, J. and M.H. Ruge (1965) 'The Structure of Foreign News: The Presentation of Congo, Cuba and Cyprus Crises in Four Norwegian Newspapers', *Journal of International Peace Research* 1: 64–90.

Gans, H. (1979) *Deciding What's News*, Constable: London.

Glover, S. (1999) 'Introduction', in S. Glover (ed.) *Secrets of the Press: Journalists on Journalism*, London: Allen Lane/Penguin, pp. vii–xiv.

Harcup, T. (2003) *Journalism: Principles and Practice*, London: Sage.

Knightley, P. (2000) *The First Casualty: The War Correspondent as Hero and Myth Maker from the Crimea to Kosovo*, London: Prion Books.

Macdonald, M. (2003) *Exploring Media Discourse*, London: Arnold.

Preston, P. (2000) 'Why Papers Won't Say Our Freedom Is in Peril', *Guardian*, 11 June.

Tumber, H. (1999) *News: A Reader*, Oxford: Oxford University Press.

Williams, K. (2003) *Understanding Media Theory*, London: Arnold.

Beyond the inverted pyramid

7

Developing news-writing skills

Beyond the inverted pyramid

Developing news-writing skills

Sharon Wheeler

News writing is a totally artificial form of writing that many people try to emulate but few manage successfully; parodies of tabloid writing in novels, for example, rarely hit the mark. Writers think that the 'gay naked vicar in mercy dash to Palace to save the Queen' is an easy formula to ape. It isn't. News writing bears next to no resemblance to report writing, essay writing or letters to friends and relatives. Instead, it's a form in which a great deal of factual information is packed into a very short space. It's also a much-maligned form showing, at its best, authority, power, wit and verve.

hard news news focusing on who, what, where, when, why, based on factual detail and quotes and containing little description, journalist comment or analysis.

soft news light news story that can be more colourful, witty and commenty than hard news.

You will see **hard news** and **soft news** bandied about as terms. Hard news is the bread and butter of the paper and involves important stories that affect people's lives, such as crime and politics, whilst soft news is the fluffier end of things, with the focus on celebrities and lightweight stories. In some ways it's a false distinction since all news should win its place on merit. News is people and they should have a starring role, whether the story is about a murder or a charity walk.

Aspects of news

News stories are instantly recognisable as news

profile picture in words which usually focuses on an individual but organisations, cars, horses, a building, and so on can be profiled.

Features, comment and sport belong elsewhere in the paper. So the first example is a classic news intro; the second is the sort of teaser intro you might see on a **profile** on the features pages.

> News: A cricket-loving teenager from Coventry has been named as Britain's youngest millionaire.

> Feature: Geeky and monosyllabic, Britain's youngest millionaire seems more interested in how many test-match hundreds Ian Botham made than in discussing his fortune.

News stories are instantly comprehensible

They pitch the reader straight into the action.

> OK: Police have launched a murder hunt after a wife found her husband dead in the bath.

> Not OK: It was a fine, sunny day in suburban Gornal as happily married Ethel Scroggins returned home from her weekly shopping trip to Tesco.

News stories are simple, crisp and direct

A good news story gets straight to the point and does not use inverted sentences.

> OK: A jilted lover electrified his rival's car in an attempt to gain revenge.

> Not OK: Because he wanted to get revenge, a jilted lover electrified his rival's car.

News stories are dramatic and attention-grabbing

You have a matter of seconds to lure a reader into your story, so make the most of them.

> OK: A madman with an axe terrorised a Birmingham housing estate last night.

> Not OK: After an incident on a Birmingham housing estate last night, residents finally decided to call the police.

News is factual

Comment by the reporter is avoided: experts' views are the ones of interest and must be sourced clearly.

> OK: The government's decision to introduce student loans is a disaster, a top university vice-chancellor claimed last night.

> Not OK: The government's decision to introduce student loans is a disaster.

News should be balanced

Facts need to be substantiated ('stood up'). Put points of dispute to each party, then quote each side even-handedly.

OK: Residents say teenagers belonging to the youth club are responsible for the vandalism. But youngsters claim the problems are being caused by gangs from other estates in the city.

Not OK: Teenagers from the youth club are responsible for vandalism on a housing estate.

News answers the key questions

Who, why, what, when, where and how will cover all bases. Formulating your questions with these words will generally gain you the information you require for your story:

- Who was involved in the train crash?
- Why were two trains coming in opposite directions down a stretch of single track?
- What steps are being taken to stop this happening again?
- When did the accident occur?
- Where were you when the crash happened?
- How did you feel afterwards?

News should adhere to the KISS theory

This is rendered either as Keep It Simple, Stupid or Keep It Simple and Straightforward. Whichever, the same principle applies – never over-complicate news stories.

Writing intros

The introduction (intro) is the first paragraph of a story and it's an attention-grabbing device. It highlights either the most dramatic, important, interesting or unusual part of the story. Intros tend to be contrived – they don't begin at the beginning but, instead, pull out the most dramatic, exciting, important or unusual part of the story. A well-constructed story will later explain, justify and expand on the intro.

The intro is said to be the hardest part of the story to get right as so much depends on it. You may find sometimes that you don't even write the intro first. If you are having problems, construct the rest of the story, then write or **rewrite** the first par (paragraph). You have only a handful of words to play with – fifteen to thirty are about right – so each word must count. Keeping one idea to a sentence and one sentence to an intro is generally the best approach. Here are a couple of intros from the *Wexford People* (23 April 1997) and the *Birmingham Evening Mail* (26 November 1992) where there's far too much going on:

rewrite to use information provided in story but compose it in completely new language. Known as 'rewrite job'.

A man who lost part of his middle finger when it was sliced off by a windscreen-wiper blade on the homecoming bus carrying the 1996 All-Ireland senior hurling championship was given the benefit of the Probation Act when he appeared at Gorey District Court on Friday.

A Birmingham father chased away a city teenager who saw the man's daughter attacking a fourteen-year-old girl who was later stabbed to death, it was alleged in court.

If you've overloaded your intro, look again: splitting a complicated intro down the middle will generally give you your second **par**. Or, as with these two examples, fillet out information that can be moved further down the story. When you are working on the intro, try the trick of summing up the story in a sentence: it often gives you a possible opening. And if the intro makes sense without the rest of the story, chances are you are on the right track.

par, para
abbreviation for
paragraph.

Identify what the best angle of the story is or look for a word or phrase that signals what is intro material. And now's the time to get personal, as names sell papers, so aim to get a real person in the intro where you can. Finding a named person who has been waiting nine months for a hip-replacement operation is much more powerful than a vague intro about hospital waiting lists. Getting a famous person into an intro, as the *Independent* (29 July 2004) did here in a story about an arts studio under threat, is also good practice:

> An arts charity that has helped the careers of successful British artists, including Rachel Whiteread, Antony Gormley and Julian Opie, is under threat following pressure to build a government city academy on the site.

But you may need to apply the so-what test; if the person isn't famous you might want to save the name for the second paragraph. Summarise people's titles, then spell out in full further down. The reason Arthur Scargill was always referred to as 'miners' boss' was because he was the President of the National Union of Mineworkers. And that lengthy title isn't what you would call snappy intro material. Place names, too, may be better further down, as they often slow up the action and also discourage people who are not from that area from reading on.

It's vital in intro writing to get the chronology clear in your mind. If you are not clear what happened, the reader will not have a clue. And keep an eye on the tenses: dramatic present tense ('has' or 'is') and future tense ('will', throwing the story forward) often work better than the past tense (for example 'criticised'). But if you use the latter, ensure it's not dated nor confusing.

Try to start the intro with a strong word: 'angry residents' or 'forgotten football star' start with a punch. Avoid, if you can, beginning with a number (it can look clumsy written out in words and is also problematic for page layout where drop capitals are used), a quote (too disorientating for the reader who has no idea who is talking) or 'yesterday'/'today'/'tomorrow' (rarely the point of the story).

As with any newspaper writing, knowing your market is essential. A double entendre intro may be fine for the *Sun*, but *Financial Times* readers won't be so keen. It's always a useful exercise to see how different newspapers treat the same story. In the following example, a story on research into how museum exhibits are being eroded by the human fart, the *Mirror* (26 November 1990) goes for a nudge, nudge, wink, wink approach, whilst the *Observer* (25 November 1990) offers a more languid play on words:

If you're planning to feast your eyes on Britain's art treasures, give the baked beans a miss. (*Mirror*)

Investigators have finally got wind of the source of a mysterious pollutant that is damaging priceless works of art. And they have sniffed out the culprits – the very people who come to admire the treasures. (*Observer*)

Delayed drop intros

off-beat   unusual story
often with a humorous
twist.

These create suspense by delaying the point of a story. It's generally an inappropriate technique on hard-news stories, but can be used sparingly on **off-beat**/humorous soft news, some human interest stories and atmospheric stories. Bear in mind, incidentally, that you can create a slight delay in an intro with dash or three dots '. . .' and then hit the reader with a sting in the tail. Here's how the *Daily Telegraph* (14 October 1997) and the *Daily Mail* (14 October 1997) approached a story about a man whose new toupee was blown away by a gust of wind while he waited at a bus stop:

The news intro
A balding bachelor is in dispute with a wigmaker after his made-to-measure toupee was blown away the first time he went out in it. (*Daily Telegraph*)

The delayed drop intro
For balding bachelor John Surtees it was a return to the golden age of his youth. (*Daily Mail*)

The twelve-point plan for intros

1. Fifteen to thirty words.
2. Direct, simple, uncomplicated.
3. Highlights a key part of the story.
4. Concentrates on just one idea; answering questions comes later.
5. Needs some identification; origins, sequence, names come later.
6. Should not be obscure.
7. Avoid abbreviations; general reference often best.
8. Don't start with a quote.
9. Don't start with a number.
10. Don't begin with time or place.
11. Ban jargon and officialese.
12. Don't invert: put the point of the sentence first.

After the intro: structuring the story

As a general rule, you will need to shape the information you have gleaned into an intro, followed by explanatory and amplifying material, with background or secondary material included towards the end. Arranging the information in some sort of order before you start to write is useful – some people find scribbling down key words or bullet points helps speed up the writing process. What you are looking for is dramatic, new or urgent information to lead on. Then the other key facts have to be filtered through the story. Look at how the *Gloucestershire Echo* (6 February 2003) structures a long front-page story:

Jacko's not so wacko, says Oliver

Former child star Mark Lester has launched a passionate defence of his close friend Michael Jackson.

Jackson has gone into hiding today after a TV documentary made him out to be a bad father.

But Mark, the star of *Oliver* who lives in Cheltenham, says viewers got a distorted view of Jackson's life.

He said he would happily trust his own children with the singer and allow them to sleep in his bed.

'He's a fantastic person and the programme was totally unfair,' said Mark. In the ITV interview shown on Monday, Jackson said he had let a 12-year-old boy sleep in his room. His admission has outraged some children's charities. Today Mark, who has four children Lucy, 11, Harriet, nine, Olivia, seven and Felix, three, said: 'If Michael wanted them to stay over, I'd be delighted for them to go and sleep in his room. I'd have no problem. I know him, it makes me so angry that this has been suggested. Reporter Martin Bashir made it seem seedy.'

Mark has been friends with the megastar for 25 years.

This is a long story for a tabloid local paper – forty-eight paragraphs starting as the front page lead and then turning on to page 3. Aside from showing how an international story can be localised and how regional papers do make frequent use of celebrities in their area (Mark Lester is a frequent visitor to *Echo* pages), it also provides the reporter with a challenge when it comes to handling a great deal of material.

A lot of information is packed into the nine paragraphs quoted above – we learn that Lester is a former child star, that he is a friend of superstar Michael Jackson, that he has four children of his own, and that Jackson has been the subject of a controversial documentary on TV. There are also three quotes, including the very powerful one where Lester says he would allow his children to sleep in Jackson's bed.

The rest of the story is very quotes-heavy, but they provide a new – and exclusive – angle on both the documentary and other controversies surrounding Jackson. There are twenty-one paragraphs of Lester responding to each of the allegations made about the star in the ITV programme. The next seven paragraphs recap how the pair met and also remind readers of Lester's claim to fame: he had the lead role in the film version of *Oliver*. Six paragraphs then provide Lester's angle on an older story where Jackson dangled his baby out of a hotel bedroom in Berlin. The final five paragraphs mention when the documentary is to be screened in the US, closing with quotes from Jackson's London-based representative.

The story fits neatly into the **inverted pyramid** structure, the time-honoured way of writing news stories where the juicy stuff is up top and the copy tapers down to less important information at the bottom. The rationale for pyramid structure is

inverted pyramid traditional representation of news stories (with main point at start and information declining in news value thereafter and ending with short background). Tends to oversimplify structure of news story. Better to imagine series of inverted pyramids within an overall large pyramid.

that it makes cutting so much easier for a sub-editor who might be faced with trimming back the story. Some stories finish with a sting in the tail that cannot really be cut but news generally works best when it's top-loaded. Here the reporter keeps a firm hand on the structure of the copy but allows Lester to speak for himself. In the *Echo* story, tagged as an exclusive, the reporter keeps a firm hand on the structure of the copy, but allows Lester to speak for himself.

Further tips on how to write well

Good journalists have the enviable ability of being able to boil down complex issues into easily accessible stories where not a word is wasted. They never assume that the reader knows everything and will ensure that past history is recapped briefly and put into today's context. They will also have weeded out clichés and jargon from what they have been told – the reader wants to know that a family in a burning flat was rescued by firefighters using a turntable ladder, rather than hear the usual fire brigade-speak about 'three appliances attending an incident'.

Well-written news stories will be in the active voice and will focus in on specifics – readers are nosy and want to know exactly how many people were sacked from a firm for sending smutty emails, or how many people will lose their jobs when a factory shuts.

News stories reflect the ever-changing nature of the English language, so slang, plays on words (puns) based on popular culture and nicknames do not look out of place. And while tabloids in particular will happily play around with news form, mobile-phone texting and email language are not appropriate for everyday stories.

Well-written news stories are vigorous and fluent, with a sense of vitality and energy. The *Independent*'s front page on the day the 9/11 Commission reported on the September 2001 attacks (23 July 2003) was an example of accessible reporting. Under the headline: 'The system was blinking red', it reported:

> A blue riband commission delivered a blistering indictment of America's failure to prevent the September 2001 terrorist attacks yesterday.
>
> Concluding that the attacks were 'a shock, not a surprise', it detailed a litany of intelligence failures to act upon the 'drumbeat' of warnings that al-Qa'ida was planning a 'spectacular' attack on American soil.
>
> As early as 23 March 2001, the National Security Adviser, Condoleezza Rice, was warned that al-Qa'ida cells were in the US and that terrorists might use a truck bomb in Washington.
>
> US intelligence agencies warned of 'something very, very, very big'. 'The system was blinking red,' CIA director George Tenet said. But the information pointed to an attack outside the US.
>
> In May the FBI had warned of plans to launch attacks on London, Boston and New York. By late August a report, 'Islamic Extremist Learns to Fly', had landed on Mr Tenet's desk and the CIA warned the Paris embassy of 'subjects involved in suspicious 747 flight training'.
>
> The commission issued recommendations for reform of the country's intelligence structure yesterday but warned that further and probably deadlier attacks were to be expected.

Setting aside some rather messy partial quoting (see later), these first six paragraphs of a twenty-one-para story deliver succinctly the findings of a 567-page report. The excellent first paragraph pulls the reader in with the use of words and phrases such as 'blue riband commission', 'blistering indictment' and 'failure'. And this authoritative front-page lead is accompanied by an accessible bullet-point list of twenty-three key warnings that were missed. Lists, graphics and maps are classic ways in which newspapers can aid readers' understanding of complex issues.

For a radically different but equally accessible news story, take the *Sun*'s angle on British Telecom being forced to change one of their prerecorded announcers because customers complained about the woman's Birmingham accent (19 November 1994):

**Orl the
loins are
bizzai
roight
now . . .**

Yowl never believe this, roight, but BT got in a bit of a fix when they picked some Brummie bird to make pre-recorded messages.

Quoite frankly, they wuz inundated with irate members of the public who claimed they couldn't make out a word of what she was cowin' well on about.

The poor girl, a BT office worker in Birmingham, must have been chuffed to bits when she was picked to say: 'This izz the international service. Ploys hold the loine. An operator will be with you shortloi.'

And: 'This izz the international operator service. All our operators are bizzai at present. Ploys try later.'

But punters, specially them what were calling from foreign parts loike, said they couldn't understand a word.

You could not approach most stories this way, but these opening pars prove to be lively, memorable and witty – and a good example of tightly structured news writing. It's a relaxed bit of storytelling, as if being told over a pint in the pub.

Choosing your words

Tabloid or broadsheet, all stories should aim for absolute clarity – and that means short, simple sentences. Fifteen to twenty words for tabloid sentences and thirty to thirty-five for broadsheets/compacts are a fairly reliable indicator. One thought to a sentence is the best rule of thumb for news writing, and you can take that one step further and keep paragraphs short and sharp as well. In tabloids you'll generally see one sentence to a paragraph, both for reasons of clarity and for appearance on the page. Broadsheets/compacts are more likely to have two or three-sentence paragraphs, again with design factors in mind.

People tend to read newspapers on buses or trains or over a cup of coffee and a biscuit, so their attention span may be short or their reading disturbed. A writer may only have a few seconds to hook a reader so the story must grab them from the start.

Facts, narrative and quotes need to be woven through the story in a logical order. Copy needs to flow fluently so words such as 'and', 'meanwhile' and 'now' are useful for launching the next paragraph. Sentences should be short, crisp and grammatical.

The rules of quoting

Good quotes are the icing on a story. Take these four from a story headlined 'Girl, 9, suspended for refusing to play football' from the web site Ananova (15 March 2001). All are gifts for a reporter who simply has to transcribe them into the story and let them speak for themselves:

> Mr Martin, 49, a building firm owner, told the *Daily Mail*: 'Rebecca has refused to play football because she feels it is a sport for boys and it is a thuggish game. My wife and I think she could be scarred later in life.
>
> 'It is also played by people are who are of a slightly different disposition from me and my family. They are yobbish.'
>
> Mrs Martin added: 'I don't think it is suitable for ladies to play football. Little girls should play tennis or netball.'
>
> Headteacher Frances Hartley said: 'Rebecca's parents said they did not want her to do football because it is played by uneducated northern yobs.'

Quotes add punch, authority and colour to a story, bring the reader into direct contact with the newsmaker and provide variety and a change of pace within the copy. Ideally there should be a good balance of direct quotes, reported speech and narrative. Direct quotes are, as they sound, an exact reproduction of what someone said to you, housed inside quotation marks.

Reported speech lacks quote marks and is useful as a variation, or where you need to paraphrase a hefty quote, or where you simply didn't secure that good a quote from someone and need to give a flavour of what they said. Journalists quickly develop an ear for what's a good quote; if what's said is newsworthy, striking, interesting, unusual, controversial or sums up the situation, then quote it.

- Aim for 100 per cent accuracy. This is non-negotiable. Always keep notes of what's been said – they are your only defence. If you can't do shorthand, invest in a hand-held tape recorder.
- Always make it clear who is speaking. Never leave any doubt in the reader's mind. If there's more than one person being quoted in the story, ensure you have attributed clearly. Longer quotes may need to run over several paragraphs.
- Note where the speech marks go. For instance: Journalism lecturer Sharon Wheeler said: 'If you can't pick a juicy quote, you'll struggle as a journalist. But don't panic – it's a skill that comes with practice. Keep at it and you'll soon develop an ear for what's worth using.'
- Don't run on quotes that come from different parts of an interview. Note the introduction of the second quote.

> Angry resident Enid Smith said: 'Our lives are being made a misery by these kids hanging around, revving up their motorbikes and swearing at anyone who asks them to stop.' She added:

'We've complained to the council and the police on numerous occasions, but no one seems to care.'

- Partial quotes are best restricted to intros. This is where clarification may be needed, but ask yourself if it's clear who's speaking and whether you actually need them. Aim to quote fully where possible. For instance:

  Journalism lecturer Sharon Wheeler criticised students for 'sitting around in workshops staring out of the window'.

- Single quote marks are used to quote inside a quote. They are also used to avoid confusion, especially in controversial stories. For instance:

  Angry neighbour Agnes Jones said: 'Mr Shufflebottom jumped up and down on the spot and yelled, "I'll see you in court".'

- In news copy, using 'said' is generally best. 'Claimed' and 'alleged' can add strength (and can be crucial in court reports). 'Chortled', 'opined' and 'stated' are ones to avoid.
- Never invent or tamper with quotes. This is dishonest at best and legally unsafe at worst.

And finally . . .

A lot of journalists will claim that news writing can't be taught – you can either do it or you can't. It's certainly true that some people have a natural aptitude for it, but like all forms of writing, constant practice, reading every paper and magazine you can lay your hands on and really soaking up how the professionals do it will give you more than a fighting chance of mastering the skill.

Further reading

Evans, H. (2000) *Essential English for Journalists, Editors and Writers*, London: Pimlico.

Hicks, W. (2001) *English for Journalists*, 2nd edn, London: Routledge.

Hicks, W. with S. Adams and H. Gilbert (1999) *Writing for Journalists*, London: Routledge.

Keeble, R. (2005) *The Newspapers Handbook*, 4th edn, London: Routledge.

Randall, D. (2000) *The Universal Journalist*, London: Pluto.

Staying calm under pressure

8

The role of the news editor

Staying calm under pressure

The role of the news editor

Sarah Niblock

It has been said that all of us are editors, whether or not we work in a news medium. We edit how we live our lives and how we communicate with others. We edit by making choices and decisions. News editing is also about making choices, such as selecting the best stories to cover and the best words to write them with. News editing is an exacting and demanding task. But it is also a human and subjective skill that is shaped and informed by personal as well as broader professional factors.

Readers of magazines and newspapers want to be kept informed of the latest events and issues that affect their lives yet do not wish to wade through the hundreds of stories available each day to get to the facts they need. It is not just a question of selecting what stories may be of interest, it is how to angle and package those selected events to ensure they grab readers' attention and make them read to the very end.

The amount of time each reader has available to spend on news each day is limited and many other activities compete for that space. Crucial decisions have to be made on what to present, in what order and in what way. Therefore, it requires seasoned understanding and expertise on the news editor's part to judge how the article relates to the readership. The role of the news editor, then, is to examine the news for a given day or week and to try to draw out the meaning in it – that is, to understand not only what it is about but also to relate it to the context of the newspaper or magazine's target audience. Is it of high interest currently? Does it provide new information? Is it entertaining?

Routine tasks of the news editor

It is the primary role of the news editor to coordinate the activities of all the reporters who work for the title. This involves keeping in touch with the progress of stories journalists have been assigned by the news desk and discussing ideas generated by reporters. As deadlines approach, the news editor must ensure each essential story is delivered on time so that it can be checked carefully before sending it to the sub-editors. The news editor has a list of who is working on what and reporters may be taken off a less urgent story if a bigger event 'breaks'. They must ensure that everything the newspaper or magazine should be covering is being covered so that there are no gaps.

Their tasks will vary from publication to publication but will typically include:

- scanning a broad range of electronic sources, such as wires and broadcast media for possible stories
- briefing reporters on new stories
- commissioning copy from freelance reporters
- reading incoming copy, checking and querying with reporters where necessary
- rewriting or **renosing** copy where necessary
- briefing the production desk on an incoming story
- ensuring a steady flow of news items are sent to the production desk to avoid logjams
- managing timeline of news gathering to ensure deadlines are met
- attending and briefing senior editorial staff at news conference
- acting as a conduit between the public and the reporters, which may include dealing with complaints.

> **renose**   to change the angle of a story.

On some publications, the news editor's role can encompass other responsibilities, including:

- managing a budget
- carrying out staff management functions, such as appraisals
- working as a reporter
- working as a sub-editor and page designer
- talking about current stories to other media such as radio and television.

A typical eight- to ten-hour shift will begin with the news editor reading the latest publications relevant to their field, especially their own publication and those of their rivals. In a twenty-four hour operation, the news editor role may be undertaken by up to three staff on a shift basis and the outgoing staff will do a handover to the incoming news editor. This will consist of a verbal and written briefing on what stories are being covered and what stage in production they are at.

The news desk: the operation's command centre

The news editor has a leadership role over the news desk, which is the command centre of the publication's news operation. If it is a large publication, the news editor may be assisted by a deputy news editor and, as is commonly the case in evening regional and national newspapers, an assistant news editor. Physically, the news desk is located in a central, accessible position, often between the news reporters and sub-editors. The news editor will normally have several telephone lines at their disposal, plus a couple of television screens, radios and computers. News-desk computers allow staff to read and edit incoming copy from reporters, **freelances** and news agencies such as Press Association. They can also email, conduct web-based research and send edited text to the production desk.

> **freelance** journalist contributing to several media outlets and not on permanent staff of any one organisation. See also **stringer**. US: freelancer.

News editors do not work in isolation. They spend a good part of their time discussing what stories are being followed up with the editor and other members of the editorial team. In this way, they can formulate strategies for writing and packaging the stories in a manner appropriate to the publication's style and readership. A single story may be reported in several ways – the secret is to find the correct approach for the target audience. Is the angle selected going to grab the attention of readers or would an alternative lead be better?

This will be debated at some length in the daily news conference attended by the editor and other senior editorial staff. Before each news conference, the news editor compiles a list of the stories being followed up so they can be discussed in the meeting. News editors also have to be aware of the feedback from letters, emails, telephone calls to the editor, comments from colleagues, focus-group surveys and hard evidence such as sales when a particular headline is run. It tends to be the case that if a news editor does not receive complaints, they can assume things are going well!

What skills are needed to be a news editor?

Given their myriad responsibilities, news editors have to be seasoned, experienced journalists. They will usually have worked their way up from trainee or junior reporter to senior reporter and then chief reporter either on their current publication or elsewhere over a number of years. This way, they will have accumulated considerable experience both in news judgment and in the careful human skills required in handling a dynamic team – and a demanding readership – under pressure.

Many highly trained and distinguished journalists steer clear of this role mainly because the dual requirements of split-second news judgment and managerial flair! At any single deadline, they may be gently coaxing a flummoxed reporter to complete a complex story while simultaneously staving off the demands of a frazzled sub-editor anxious to put the page to press. Throughout this high-octane moment, the wires are buzzing, the telephones ringing and the editor is hovering – needing a quick chat about a forthcoming meeting.

Unsurprisingly, news editors should be unflappable, good-humoured and well organised. Tasks have to be prioritised in a split second when so many are vying for their attention. News editors must be quietly self-assured to maintain the confidence of their team while never too arrogant to ask questions and seek advice or a second opinion.

In addition to their personnel attributes, news editors must have an advanced knowledge of all aspects of the news-making process including writing, reporting and also design and production. News making is a team effort of which news gathering is just one part and the news editor plays a central role in keeping the machinery of journalism functioning well. They do this best by having a good working knowledge of the diverse jobs in the production cycle and being able to speak their different languages.

The role of the news editor

As has been shown, the job of a news editor is about making choices and not only about what stories to follow up. They also have an important guiding role in choosing the right words, the best sentence structure, the best approach, the best ethical strategies and the best angle for their readers. On a practical level, this is done through asking questions of the stories they encounter at each stage of the news cycle, from when an event first happens to just before the story is put on the page.

Is this the news the reader wants?

One of the most fundamental skills of a good news editor is the ability to put his- or herself inside the reader's head. With possibly hundreds of stories available from a broad range of sources, the news editor plays a primary role in sifting the wheat from the chaff. Their guiding principle is to know what will grab the reader's attention. It is a common misapprehension that news editing is a process of selection. In reality it is about rejection, 'killing' stories that do not fit with the publication's locality, identity or tone. Not even everything reporters have written that day or week will automatically get into print. That too will be whittled down to the best stories, based on achieving a good balance and variety on the pages.

News editors will be tuned into current talking points and will be on the look-out not only for routine events but also exclusives that mark out their pages as unique in comparison with their rivals. This may mean trying to find an issue they can campaign on or striving to secure a sought-after exclusive interview with a big name. In short, the news editor will not only be identifying good ideas but guiding and pushing their team to strive for the best coverage and so make their title stand head and shoulders above their competitors.

Paul Webster, deputy editor (news) of the *Observer*, a UK Sunday broadsheet:

News editing on Sunday newspapers is different from the daily papers in that you have a lot of time thinking of ideas but then a relatively short, concentrated time putting them to page. We look ahead because Sunday papers try to be agenda-setting. We like to think of ourselves as setting up the issues that will be important in the week ahead, things that will survive the daily coverage.

People who lead busy lives aren't going to have time to wade through endless mounds of newsprint during the week. What will remain from this week that will be alive at the weekend? What's going to become important? It's always rewarding as a news editor when a piece you've selected and run with gets echoed throughout the following days and is picked up by other media.

There's no such thing as the classic *Observer* story. Historically it was felt our preoccupation was with the poor and with social injustice. However, society has changed. Our readership spans the entire political spectrum. We are anxious to attract a younger audience and more female readers so we need to choose stories that appeal to a very wide range of people – from the young metropolitan reader who likes music to the Middle England couple.

As one of the editors, I have to look at reporting and presenting news in different ways to ensure we meet the interests of readers whatever their age, location or interests. We can do this partly through **editionalising**, but also by making sure we include diverse case studies from around the country in our stories.

editionalising
publishing more than one edition on any day to take in breaking news

---

continued

Broadsheet news editors are keen to encourage the personality of the writer to come through, so we are much less rigid in the way we edit copy than the dailies. You don't want a sausage factory. News editing here is a team decision, with a group of executives talking through various ways of covering the issues and events, with our editor making the ultimate decisions.

Headlines, pictures and stories get moved around a lot in the final stages of preparation on Saturday. Because of our timescale – most of our news selection, writing and editing happens on Friday and Saturday – we have the great advantage of being able to stand back from the subject during the week, to enable us to provide readers with much more reflective, in-depth account.

Does the story contain any 'holes'?

As experienced reporters themselves, news editors should be able to spot ambiguities and omissions in an instant. Did the reporter ask all the important questions or will the article raise more questions that it answers? For example, if a reporter has been to interview police about a factory fire in which several people have been injured, it would be a glaring omission not to ask how many people have been hurt and to which hospital they have been taken.

It would be second nature to most reporters to ask those questions. But if the factory is known to have been criticised by Health and Safety inspectors for careless storage of flammable liquids a year ago, it would be a hole in the story if the reporter had not quizzed the owners about their safety record. The experienced, seasoned eye of the news editor can negotiate the twists and turns of each story and guide the reporter towards comprehensive coverage.

Is it accurate?

The news editor will continuously query the facts contained within a story with the reporter to ensure absolute accuracy. Accuracy is not only for legal and ethical reasons (see below), but also to protect the integrity of the newspaper and the reporting team. It is a fundamental responsibility to check and double-check facts to maintain the trust of the readership and their sources. The news editor will be searching to ensure consistency in the use of figures, spelling of names and addresses and asking the reporter to double-check them with their notes.

If the news editor has any doubts, they will check themselves in a number of ways. For instance, they will most likely have the newspaper's archive of previous stories at their fingertips, electronically stored. Or they will simply pick up the telephone and check. Either way, they will be seeking to ensure the story has an accurate foundation in fact so that it stands up to scrutiny.

Is it written properly?

While the precision fine-tuning of news is the responsibility of the subs desk, the news editor must also be able to correct stories without recourse to dictionaries or stylebooks, though they will stress the importance of looking things up if in any doubt. News editors lead their reporting team's sense of tone and style, shaping introductions, debating choice of vocabulary and aiding the consistency of tone.

On a practical level, if reporters are pulled up on sloppy grammar or non-adherence to house style, this saves unnecessary wastage of subs' time. By casting a fresh eye over a reporter's story, the news editor can help rewrite a garbled sentence or sharpen a buried angle. Seasoned reporters look back on their first news editors as teachers, so the role has to be undertaken with patience as well as firmness.

Branwell Johnson, former news editor and editor for national weekly B2B magazines (now news editor on Marketing News web site www.mad.co.uk):

While news editor on *Video Trade Weekly* (1990–2) and later as editor on weekly trade magazine *View* (1993–2000) I had responsibility for overseeing the news pages while also sourcing and writing many of the stories myself. I had to ensure a steady copy flow to production and ensure each page carried a balance of stories about people, products, marketing and company acquisitions and mergers. You cannot have a page filled with the same type of stories.

The typical weekly editorial structure of business magazines is based on news meetings on Monday and Tuesday mornings. Reporters pitched their stories to give me an idea of what leads had potential to be developed. Some were obvious diary stories but there was a strong emphasis on finding exclusives – competition in the trade press is just as fierce as in consumer publications.

As the news editor I made suggestions on how stories could be stood up or strengthened – providing contacts and alternative sources – and kept an overview on how stories were developing with one eye on page deadlines. Reporters were expected to provide pictures or picture ideas and liaise with the library.

Although the editor had final say about placements and headlines on *VTW* I prioritised layout order and was expected to change or pull stories right up until **deadline** to ensure the strongest copy. The pace could be frantic in the last half hour with last-ditch efforts to confirm story leads and late-breaking stories appearing. I remember when the Dunblane shootings in 1996 happened having to chase Warner Home Video who were about to release the film *Natural Born Killers* to see if it would be pulled.

Specialist titles require a combination of traditional reporting and news editing skills together with a depth of knowledge about the sector. As I was dealing with companies in a volatile market it was vital to keep abreast of the company law and procedures surrounding receivership, administration and mergers. Reporters were encouraged to be able to interpret financial data and look at profit and loss sheets to identify trends in an instant. Working in the trade sector also means throwing yourself into all opportunities to meet decision-makers, executives and useful contacts so out-of-hours networking at conferences, presentations and other events is paramount.

> **deadline** time by which copy is expected to be submitted.

How can we make this story even better?

With the stories being covered, the news editor must ask what would make for a more exciting and engaging article for the reader? Does it need a particular approach? What format will do the best job at imparting the information to their target reader? For instance, sometimes stories containing lots of technical details work better when supplemented with sidebars or **fact boxes** with specific information.

fact box list of facts (boxed) relating to story. Useful way of creating visual and copy variety on page.

Competing with other visual media, newspapers and magazines have become aware of the benefits of illustrating their coverage to maximise their impact. The news editor will alert the picture desk at the earliest opportunity if an image is required and, with the reporter, will brief them on the story's content and any particularly desirable shots.

Is it legal and ethical?

As well as making decisions and taking charge, the news editor must also ask questions, especially when the legality or fairness of a story is in doubt. Does the story unfairly criticise someone without giving them an opportunity to defend themselves? Have the details overstepped boundaries of taste and decency? Breaching ethical guidelines and legal codes can have huge consequences not only for the reputation of the paper but also for journalism as a whole. They can also prove costly. News editors are always scrutinising stories, anticipating legal and ethical pitfalls and guiding their reporters on best practice.

As the laws affecting the media change over time, news editors are required to keep abreast of those developments through research and by attending regular refresher courses. Through following legal cases and their outcomes, news editors are aware of the possible consequences of running sensitive stories. But they will often aim to push the boundaries of codes and policies as far as possible within safe parameters. In order to do this, they will work in close liaison with their publication's lawyer when potential pitfalls arise.

Running stories, especially those where police are hunting criminals, can change radically over a short period of time. News editors must always check, for instance, whether suspects have been charged with an offence before they go to press. Because of strict reporting restrictions, this can mean a front-page **splash** has to be replaced at the last moment.

splash lead news story on front page.

If a news editor is managing a young team, they will often be called upon to give advice to junior staff on approaching sensitive stories. If a reporter has to call at the home of someone who is recently bereaved, for instance, they have to abide by ethical guidelines to try to ensure they do not intrude on grief whilst still obtaining the facts and quotes their news desk needs. The news editor's personal experience of difficult stories can help their reporters navigate these issues successfully.

Is there a good balance of stories on each page?

Newspapers cannot be full of sensational exposés of life on drug estates, nor can they have page after page of life on a catwalk. Likewise, magazines cannot focus purely on product sales and ignore **human-interest stories**. They have to be very carefully organised from first to last page to ensure balance. A news editor has to be good at saying 'no' to stories that do not fit with their market.

This can be very hard when faced with events and issues that would seem to merit extensive coverage, for example social issues such as homelessness and student debt. But if the story has no new eye-catching angle, it can end up being repetitive and dull, however worthy. News editors know that readers need to be 'entertained'. That does not necessarily mean they must be made to laugh, but they should be stimulated. News pages need to contain a variety of topics and moods to reflect the kaleidoscopic nature of life.

For some publications, this might mean ensuring that coverage is not too focused on one or other part of the country or on one or other specific sector or community. In taking the overview, the news editor of a national newspaper may suggest getting a quote from someone in Manchester because all the other spokespeople are from London.

human-interest story
story focusing on success, failures, tragedies, emotional or sexual histories of people, eliminating or marginalising more abstract and deeper cultural, economic, political, class-based factors.

The bigger picture: other news-editor functions

News editing is no longer a discreet, clear-cut role in the context of multi-skilling and digital news gathering. There are innumerable other functions that connect to the overall success of the title, not just the news operation. For instance, news and features on magazines and newspapers are no longer strictly separate departments and formats. News has become more featurised to give readers more context to stories than broadcast and online media while features are much more responsive to everyday news items. News editors will be in close touch with the features desk, tipping them off on current stories to inspire background articles that give breadth and depth to their own pithier coverage.

However successful they are, newspapers and magazines will face criticism from time to time and news editors are often the first port of call for readers raising concerns. This is not always unwelcome. If a news team makes mistakes, it is a problem that must be quickly rectified. However, news editors enjoy nothing more than when a story provokes a major response or public debate. It shows they are performing their function as a watchdog in their community or sector and brings much-needed publicity to their title.

In many cases, the news editor often has a very public role and may be called upon by journalists in other media to discuss their stories. For instance, the news editor of a nursing magazine may be asked by a national newspaper to comment on the latest job satisfaction survey in that sector. Or a news editor in Wales may be asked to describe the scene of a crime to the listeners of a radio station.

No newsroom is identical to the next so there may be many variations on the themes identified here. But every news editor will agree that they can never know what the next day has in store.

Further reading

Fishman, M. (1980) *Manufacturing the News*, Austin, Tex. and London: University of Texas Press.

Hodgson, F.W. (1993) *Subediting: Handbook of Modern Newspaper Editing and Production*, London: Focal Press.

Niblock, S. (1996) *Inside Journalism*, London: Blueprint.

Rudin, R. and T. Ibbotson (2002) *Introduction to Journalism: Essential Techniques and Background Knowledge*, Oxford: Focal Press.

Shoemaker, P.J. (1991) *Gatekeeping*, London: Sage.

News subbing simplified

9

News subbing simplified

Sharon Wheeler

Don't let anyone tell you sub-editors (subs for short) are failed journalists. They are, in fact, a pivotal part of any newspaper or magazine. They are the people who ensure the paper actually hits the streets and that the writers' copy is in pristine condition. They are almost always experienced journalists who have worked as reporters themselves and therefore know the pitfalls and requirements.

Not only do they turn reporters' raw copy into the finished product you see in the publication, they also write headlines and **captions**. On many papers the old distinction between page planners and down-table subs is disappearing, to be replaced by computer-literate page editors who either design the pages or work to a template, as well as dealing with the text.

caption words accompanying picture or graphic.

The basic skills

Sub-editors need a number of skills, but the most pressing are:

- a heightened sense of news values
- attention to detail
- a cool head under pressure
- an ability to work fast and accurately
- an ability to see the wood from the trees
- a way with words
- good general knowledge
- a good knowledge of the law as it applies to print publications.

Dealing with raw copy

Once a reporter has written a story, it will go to the news desk and from there to the subs' desk. On larger papers there may be a copy-taster whose job it is to assess the strength of all stories; otherwise the chief sub or their deputy will do this. The story will then be picked up by a page-editor or sub.

They will check the story flow to see if it makes sense. Reporters, who can become too close to a story, may think they understand what's going on. A sub will check for lack of clarity, confusion and gaps. If any facts are missing, the sub will ask for more information to be obtained from sources or clarification from the reporter on what was meant. Subs will also double-check spelling, grammar and punctuation. Not all copy that comes into a newspaper is written by professionals – and the latter can and do make mistakes, even in the days of computer spell-checkers.

Keeping it in style

One of a sub's key jobs is to ensure copy conforms to house style – the newspaper's own rules on certain spellings and matters of punctuation which ensure consistency across the paper. Each editor will have their own likes and dislikes, so certain words are often banned. I worked for a paper which insisted on 'gaol' rather than 'jail' and on another where neither 'kids' nor 'Xmas' were allowed, which proved to be a challenge when it came to writing single-**column** tabloid headlines about schools or the festive season. Most publications have their own style book, ranging from a couple of A4 sheets stapled together to bound booklets. Some of these, including those of *The Times* (Austin 2003) and *The Economist* (2003), have been published. The *Guardian*'s (<http://www.guardian.co.uk/styleguide/0,5817,184913,00.html>) and *The Times*'s (<http://www.timeson-line.co.uk/section/0,,2941,00.html>) are available online.

column vertical section of article appearing on page. Also known as 'leg'.

Cutting to length

When it comes to story length, the news desk may have been vague with the reporter, saying airily: 'Give it what you think it's worth.' By the time the story arrives at the subs' desk, several big stories may have broken and what looked like a good page 5 lead several hours ago could end up being relegated to four pars on page 22. So the sub must cut the story to length. This isn't always as straightforward as it may seem; if the reporter has conformed to the inverted pyramid structure, then the sub's job may well be virtually done for them as they cut extraneous matter from the bottom. Otherwise, they may be forced to **rewrite** and **rejig** to retain the sense of the story.

Cutting stories isn't always as easy as it sounds, particularly if the reporter has structured it in a particularly intricate way. Most news stories can be cut from the bottom where, if the reporter has done their job properly, the least important information will have been included. Otherwise, a sub must ensure that cuts do not interfere with the flow or leave out vital facts. Each story needs to be treated on its merits, but it's always worth seeing if a quote or two can be cut, or whether an extra person can be lost if the reporter has spoken to several people.

What a sub should never do, though, is to cut a balancing quote from someone giving the other side of the argument. If a story is only a couple of lines too long, you can often 'lose a word'. This means trimming odd words from sentences to try to remove one- or two-word lines. The word 'that' is often a good candidate for the chop. The joys of on-screen subbing make it very easy for subs to spot **widows** and **orphans** – lone sentences or single words floating at the top of a column – and to cut accordingly.

rewrite to use information provided in story but compose it in completely new language. Known as 'rewrite job'.

rejig/rehash rearrangement of copy provided by reporter usually by sub-editor to produce a better structured piece.

widow short line left at top of column.

orphan short line left at foot of column.

Finding the best intro angle

A good sub will have a sharp eye for the best angle in a story – a seemingly minor point buried two thirds of the way down may well end up being intro material. Sub-editors who work frequently with agency copy, such as that from Press Association (PA) or Reuters, will be well used to conjuring up snappy new intros, preferably with a local angle. After all, nothing looks worse to an editor than the same agency story appearing word for word in competitors' newspapers.

Checking for legal accuracy

Subs, too, must be bang up to date on their media law. Reporters – and not just inexperienced trainees – may have inadvertently left legally unsafe references in their copy, so it is up to the sub to spot and remedy these. (See Chapter 22.)

To rewrite or rejig?

Rewriting copy needs careful thought. It's bad for reporters' morale if rewrites are done just for the sake of it. They should only be done if the story can genuinely be improved. Rather than a complete rewrite, it may be possible simply to tweak and adjust copy. And rewriting carries its own dangers – mainly that of Chinese whispers. An incorrect keyboard keystroke can mean a wrongly spelled name goes down for evermore in the annals of the newspaper's history as all stories are stored in the online cuttings library. Quotes, too, are a danger area, with the potential for lazy or inaccurate paraphrasing. As with reporting, great care needs to be taken when it comes to shortening quotes. As a general rule of thumb, don't tamper with them.

The most common reasons for rewrites tend to be poor intros or badly structured copy. With the former, it's often a matter of rejigging or rewriting the intro and then leaving the rest of the story as it is. The existing intro may be overloaded or unclear or the reporter may simply not have plumped for the best or most unusual angle of the story. Many papers, quite rightly, demand the personalised angle for stories. So if a reporter has presented a 'catch-all' intro, this could well be prime material for a rewrite and to pull a real person up into the intro.

On most newspapers, you simply will not have time to print out copy and to work on paper – and in any case it is far better to ensure you can work on screen against the clock. But if you have a more leisurely deadline or are working on a long and complex story, it may help to print out the copy and keep it beside you so you can refer to it as you work. This is particularly useful when it comes to working on **running stories**, which will be discussed later. A printout of the original is always useful, too, for a last-minute check through to ensure that names have been transcribed accurately.

running story story which runs or develops over a number of editions or days.

'Marking up'

Before a story can be happily consigned to the pages, though, there is another important task for the sub to perform. They will need to 'mark up' the typesetting instructions so that the computer knows what typesizes and typefaces are required for body type, headlines, bylines and captions. In these high-tech computer days, this coding is often applied by simply pressing a function button on the keyboard. But on some publications the sub will need to type in the instructions, so an eagle eye is needed to ensure that the story appears in 8 pt type and not 80 pt.

A sub-editing checklist

Intro

- Is it snappy?
- Does it grab the reader?
- Does it make sense?
- Is it up to date?
- Is it a readable length?

Structure

- Does the story back up the intro?
- Does the story unfold logically?
- Are there any obvious gaps?
- Are quotes used sensibly?
- Are there any unnecessary repetitions?
- Check key facts aren't left until last

Language

- Is the story in house style?
- Are all the acronyms explained?
- Cut out waffle/clichés
- Don't overload sentences with subordinate clauses

Quotes

- Are they worth using?
- Is it obvious who said what?
- Are they in readable chunks?
- Is the punctuation correct?
- Don't alter without a good reason

Editionalising copy

Most papers of any size have different editions – these may be based either on time or on geographical location. So subs can expect to have to rewrite or tweak stories, either for new developments or simply to make the article more relevant to a slightly different audience. Newspaper readers can be rather parochial, so big morning and evening papers are likely to be multi-edition and to involve fairly substantial page changes between editions to cater for both breaking and regional news. The sub may need to alter a story for a later edition – either to add new information, or to renose for a different edition.

Running stories

Running stories are one of the biggest challenges for both sub-editors and reporters. They are a report of an ongoing event, such as a major disaster, a lengthy court case or a sports match. Front-page news such as the 11 September 2001 attacks on the World Trade Center, Princess Diana's funeral, the Hillsborough football stadium disaster and the Ladbroke Grove train crash are all examples of big stories that unfolded rapidly over the course of several hours.

The information and copy arrives in different 'takes' – often from different sources – and has to be pieced together gradually. It will be altered or added to as the event runs its course. Each edition of the paper must contain as complete, up-to-date and self-contained a version as possible – and there may not be much time to reshuffle between editions as deadlines come thick and fast on big multi-edition papers. A decision may be made to allocate one sub-editor to deal with all the copy as it comes in.

One of the challenges is dealing with the information that may flow in from a variety of sources. These may include:

- staff reporters
- freelance/agency copy
- phone calls from eyewitnesses/those involved
- emergency services statements
- background information from library/Internet.

Dealing with the story

If you are working on a Saturday sports paper or a Sunday paper, dealing with copy from a football match, for example, is relatively straightforward as information is most likely to be filed at set times: team details at the start; scorers and sendings off as they happen; an update at quarter time; more copy at half-time; an addition at three-quarter time and the main story after the final whistle. The sub editor will hope the reporter has done much of the reshuffling in the latter, but they may need to fillet the earlier copy for run-of-play details to add to after-match quotes from players and managers.

Disaster stories, though, are hugely more complex. Later information is often more important and a sub will have to keep a keen eye on strong angles to ensure the key facts are pulled up to the top. It's important to keep checking for good angles, strong quotes, must-have information and discrepancies (such as death tolls).

Running stories are best structured as building blocks, with like information kept with like. Writing in the past tense and about completed situations is much the safest approach – otherwise the story may look stale when people read it. Writing: 'After three hours, the fire was still out of control' is fine; 'Firemen still have not got the fire under control after three hours' isn't.

Keeping the **body** of the story as constant as possible and changing the intro and first few paragraphs is a useful way of keeping a story under control for different editions. Consider using a summary lead above the detailed story as this often avoids lots of reshuffling. This follows on from the attention-grabbing first paragraph and works like an extended intro of perhaps three paragraphs or longer. It tells the story in a nutshell and is a highly condensed version of the whole story. The detailed story can then fill in details of what happened and quote heroes, experts and eyewitnesses. If it's written on the building-block principle by grouping information in sections or themes, it's easy for the sub to cut and paste or to drop chunks as new facts emerge.

One of the most difficult parts of dealing with a running story where information is pouring in from all sides is actually keeping track of what you have. Checklists become invaluable, as you can mark off what's been covered and what needs to be included.

body   copy following intro.

The danger areas

Watch for discrepancies in casualties, as emergency services may be giving out conflicting information. Keep a running total and cross-check frequently. By the same token, double-check the spellings of names and make sure facts tally. Keep an eye open for corrections coming through – reporters will be writing copy under pressure and in the heat of the moment mistakes will inevitably be made. It's worth keeping a list of file names or **catchlines** so stories can be pulled back quickly.

The temptation with a big story is to try to cram everything in. The chances are that a page or more in the paper will have been given over to the event, so there will be a number of angles being covered elsewhere. Don't overload a story – keep it straightforward and if fellow subs are working on the other stories, check frequently with them as to what's going where so that information isn't duplicated or the same words used in headlines.

Don't jump to conclusions or apportion blame: inquests and/or court cases may follow.

catchline   name used to identify a story, usually single word which is typed in right-hand corner of every page. Now more likely to be called the filename. Sub-editor will tend to use this word to identify story on layout. US: slug.

Headlines

What's the best headline you remember from a newspaper? Chances are it's from a tabloid, be it the surreal FREDDIE STARR ATE MY HAMSTER (13 March 1986) or the jingoistic STICK IT UP YOUR JUNTA (20 April 1982) and GOTCHA! (4 May 1982) or the smutty IT'S PADDY PANTSDOWN (6 February 1992), all from the *Sun*. Headlines are shop-window advertising to entice the reader into a story. Sadly, few people remember a well-turned intro!

The point of a headline is to tell the story and sell the story both accurately and succinctly. They need to be legally safe and free from ambiguity. News headlines in most cases are both objective and balanced, with opinions and statements attributed clearly. Headlines on comment pieces are another matter altogether, where an attention-grabbing inflammatory headline is guaranteed to get people reading. And beware, too, the bad-taste factor – *The Sun's* SHIP SHIP HOORAY on the story announcing that mass murderer Harold Shipman had committed suicide and BONKERS BRUNO heading the story that former boxer Frank Bruno had mental-health problems were both roundly criticised.

A headline has a matter of seconds to catch a browsing reader's eye, so they need to be crisp, unstuffy and instantly understandable. A headline such as MORE BEAT OFFICERS IN COUNTY (Ceefax, 10 July 2004) needs reading several times before the meaning is totally clear. My first thought was that it was obviously a violent place to be a police officer. In fact, reading a headline aloud as you write it is often a good way of avoiding ambiguity.

There's a very good reason why headlines need to use short, snappy words. Not only do they read crisply but they also look good to the eye on a newspaper page. Headlines tend to have accumulated their own brand of shorthand – you'll see a plethora of 'bids', 'slashing', 'rapping', 'dashing', 'quizzing' and 'probing', particularly in tabloid headlines. They are used so often because they fit the narrow measures of tabloid single columns, but they are also in danger of becoming a cliché, so it's worth spending a bit of extra time trying to find an alternative.

What to focus on

Sometimes a headline angle will leap out at you as soon as you read the story. Some years ago a sports editor used a fairly dull story on the Varsity cricket match between Oxford and Cambridge being ruined by rain, simply because he liked my instinctive headline, RAINY DAY BLUES. But if you're scratching your head over a headline, the following may give you some guidance:

1. **Names:** Personalise where possible. SHEARER TO QUIT tells you more than STAR TO QUIT.
2. **Quotes:** Select key point and make that the focus of your headline. I THOUGHT I WAS GOING TO DIE SAYS JANE is preferable to MISSING WOMAN'S NIGHTMARE ORDEAL.
3. **Look ahead:** Papers report news, not history, so you should try to throw the headline forward. ROONEY TO MISS FRENCH CLASH is more topical than ROONEY INJURED IN UNITED DEFEAT.
4. **Main angle:** Don't be obscure. You can often get away with more oblique teaser headlines in features, but for news it's much safer to concentrate on the obvious angle.
5. **Word play and puns:** Readers will remember a witty headline, but don't overdo the puns or make the word play too obscure. And always work on the assumption that people have dirty minds or will pick up double meanings you didn't intend!

LABOUR TURN TO CRIME AS A POTENTIAL VOTE WINNER is likely to have readers speculating as to what lengths party members will go to ensure election victory.

Headline language

Tabloid headlines are friends with everyone – they use first names and nicknames freely and will assume their readers know who Posh, Becks, Gazza and Cherie are. There's often a 'nudge, nudge, wink, wink' playfulness as well, with lots of puns and plays on words. Slang finds its way into headlines very rapidly. German tennis star Boris Becker asked plaintively at a Wimbledon press conference what bonking meant after seeing himself referred to as Bonking Boris in a tabloid headline.

Broadsheet headlines tend to be rather more staid and to reflect the story more closely, as the sub-editors on papers such as the *Guardian* and *Daily Telegraph* have more words to play around with. You will still spot plays on words, but they are unlikely to be as 'in your face' as tabloid front-page screamers. As always, knowing the publication's audience and its house style is essential.

Constructing a headline

Write headlines in the active voice, rather than the passive: DOG IS BITTEN BY MAN would be far less effective than MAN BITES DOG. And they need to be positive, rather than negative. The following may be an apocryphal story, but you get the point:

> Claud Cockburn claimed to have won a competition among sub-editors on *The Times* for the dullest headline: 'Small earthquake in Chile. Not many dead.' Many have since tried, without success, to trace the original.

The headline needs to contain – or imply – a verb. Forms of 'to be' are best omitted – you'll get more impact without 'is'/'are' slowing you down. The exceptions here are label-type headlines where you only have space for a couple of words. And watch out for bad line breaks, especially on front-page stories near what's called the fold (go into a newsagent's shop and see how newspapers are folded in display stands) to avoid something like:

LIBERALS CALL FOR SEX
EDUCATION IN SCHOOLS

Punctuate sparingly in headlines – and bear in mind the following:

? answer questions, don't ask them
! ration them
' ' attribute to avoid confusion
– OK as a pause
, avoid if possible
. never

point unit of typographical measurement. Approximately 72 pt to the inch or 0.01383'.

deck often used to mean the number of lines in a heading. Is, strictly, the number of headings.

strapline heading placed over another heading or headings.

upper case capital letters when used alongside small (*lowercase*) letters. When just capital letters are used (as in headlines) they are known as *caps*.

nibs short news stories.

Headlines must fit the given space and must be a good, readable shape. It's all too easy to tweak typesizes on the computer, and some newspapers have rules about the number of **point** sizes you can drop a headline. If you cannot get an exact fit on each line, go for an egg-timer shape with the top and bottom lines full out. Certain shapes, such as an L shape, look awful and are difficult to read. If there's a strapline or subdeck, write these after the main **deck** and don't use the same words. A **strapline** goes above the main headline and a subdeck below it.

Tabloids write a lot of their headlines in capitals. Otherwise what's called **upper and lower case** is used – they use capitals where appropriate, such as on names and places: 'Headlines are written like this, says Sharon' *not* 'Headlines Are Written Like This, Says Sharon'.

Finally, don't overstate the case and throw in lots of over-used words such as 'lashes', 'flays' and 'slashes', or pepper the page with exclamation marks to show the reader how witty a headline is. A good headline doesn't need any dressing up.

Caption writing

Caption writing is an overlooked art. A witty caption can lift a fairly average picture into something the reader has enjoyed looking at. One of the most entertaining accounts of caption-writing appears in Leslie Sellers' wonderfully eccentric *The Simple Subs Books* – now sadly out of print, but worth trying to track down either online or through second-hand bookshops. Sellers comments (1985: 110): 'The good caption writer is rare and therefore prized. There are many subs who can competently handle a running story, or knock up a passable page lead from a PA law report, or do a crisp **nibs** column: but there are far fewer who can create a superb caption.'

The worst thing a caption writer can do is to state the obvious. The caption needs to reflect what's in the photo, but to give it a twist so that it is (as appropriate) original, imaginative, eye-catching, informative and witty. 'Blowing their own trumpets . . . Cheltenham brass band display the panache that has won them a national award' is much more appealing than 'Musicians celebrate their brass band win'.

You'll encounter several kinds of captions:

1. Caption story: several lines, or, occasionally, several paragraphs.
2. A caption, generally beneath the picture, which supplements the story.
3. A self-contained brief caption with no story – found on an outstanding/unusual picture.
4. Caption written into story: 'England fly half Jonny Wilkinson, pictured left'.

Numbers 1 to 3 give you the chance to be creative. You can use a lead-in phrase, often playing on words. You should not repeat either the headline or the intro but instead relate the picture to the story. If you've got a number of photos to caption for the same story, you might be able to link them – for example, a series of Jonny Wilkinson practising his place-kicking might be sequenced 'GOING . . . ' 'GOING . . .' and 'GONE'. And watch your tenses. It's generally safer to caption in the present tense, but if you do have to use the past tense, be consistent within the caption.

You might not be the sub dealing with the actual mechanics of **cropping** and sizing the photo, but double-check that you are captioning what's actually in the picture and not the earlier version with an extra person to one side. And if you can, check that pictures haven't got muddled on the page – one of the perennial nightmares is to discover that a picture of the Queen is captioned instead as England rugby captain Martin Johnson and vice versa.

crop   to select an area of a picture for publication.

If you're writing a caption for a single-column head and shoulders picture, the usual convention is to use either just the person's name, or the name followed by one word relating to the person out of the story. If it's the latter, choose a lively word: 'Wheeler . . . happy' or 'Blair . . . livid'.

Finally, I can't improve on Sellers' example (Sellers 1985: 124–5) of a picture of lots of buses bringing churchgoers to an Easter conference in South Africa. His suggestion is: 'DROPPING IN FOR A HYMN AND A PRAYER . . . Heaven's eye view of just some of the buses that carried the faithful yesterday.' As the man says: 'You could set that to music and play it on your harp.'

Further reading

Austin, T. (ed.) (2003) *The Times Style and Usage Guide*, London: Collins.
The Economist (2003) *The Economist Style Guide*, London: Economist Books.
Hicks, W. and T. Holmes (2002) *Subediting for Journalists*, London: Routledge.
Hodgson, F.W. (1998) *New Subediting*, Oxford: Focal.
Quinn, S. (2001) *Digital Sub-Editing and Design*, Oxford: Focal.
Sellers, L. (1985) *The Simple Subs Book*, Oxford: Pergamon.

What makes a good feature?

The different genres

10

What makes a good feature?

The different genres

Jane Taylor

Getting to grips with genres

The term 'genre' can be applied both to versions (news, features) and types (fashion, music) of journalism. As Fredric Jameson writes (2000: 268): 'Genres are essentially literary institutions, or social contracts between a writer and a specific public, whose function is to specify the proper use of a particular cultural artifact.' And he cautions that it is 'the generic contract and institution itself which, along with so many other institutions and traditional practices, falls casualty to the gradual penetration of a market system and a money economy'. Named genres are a useful way of identifying aspects of features as well as the kind of expectations brought by readers to them: it follows that the closer the match between the two, the more successful the feature is likely to be.

Feature writers are those journalists who are most likely to rough up the page a little, disturbing it with an additional turn at the end of the news story by digging deeper, or at a tangent to the news. Given more space than the news writer, they are able to raise questions about the way we live and perform; they may campaign with conviction, entertain with wit and verve, shock, explain, reveal, respond, caution, inspire, inform, enlighten. To understand feature writing as a genre in itself – spawning a number of subgenres that may help to identify why this or that feature works – it is offered here within an overarching framework relating to:

- publication
- subject matter
- approach and purpose
- narrative strategies.

The marketplace for features

No journalism can exist without the marketplace and its constraints. As specific markets within the publishing industry give rise to the concept of journalism itself supporting a number of genres, so a published feature needs to conform to the requirements of the features genre – this is what makes it marketable. There are caveats to this, though, indicating that any notion of genres producing maps or blueprints for feature writers that merely have to be filled with customised content is simplistic and may be misleading. First, far from being formulaic, it is the feature, rather than the news report, that offers journalists some opportunities of taking liberties with form. Second, genres themselves are subject to fluctuating social, political and cultural emphases: they tend to arise in line with developments and fashions in publishing and their boundaries mutate as they increase in number to meet ever more precise niche demands of the moment.

However, we need to be clear that in talking about feature genres we are talking about categories reflective of mass culture rather than (strictly) literary genres. But since it is in the feature that journalism is permitted to perform across a broad spectrum, with subjectivity at one end and objectivity at the other, I shall be examining some aspects of how the literary can both influence and infiltrate feature reportage to positive advantage.

Yet more tensions arise within this: however 'sub-literary' a form journalism itself may be deemed, however compromised by the commodification of the marketplace, the best and ground-breaking features certainly possess the power to challenge received ideas and even act as catalysts of change. It is because of the feature writer's (inner) creativeness in the framing of an original idea and his or her (rational) tenacity to probe and discover facts that good feature writing can be usefully located within the concept, and the dictates, of genre. These, then, are some of the dynamics that make feature writing such an exciting, interesting and challenging business, despite its essential market-drivenness.

Like a punter at Ascot or Newmarket, the feature writer first has to study the form, and a number of first-class directories, listing newspapers and magazines by category, area and contact (available in libraries and brought out annually) provide an overview and details of what is out there.[1] In a nutshell, features are mainly published in national, regional and local newspapers and in magazines (consumer, B2B and customer).[2] The magazine industry alone offers some 8,000 titles covering a huge variety of interests, as diverse as *Asphalt Now* (professional), *Asthma News* (health), *Enjoy Jersey Magazine* (regional), *Popular Patchwork* (craft), *FourFourTwo* (sport) and *The Banker* (business). Each has a precisely defined readership determined, to a very large extent, by advertisers seeking likely buyers for their goods and services. For any features section, it is the delivery of readers to lucrative advertisers that keeps the publication afloat, which is where genre identification (in the sense of leading writers to an understanding of the nature of their market and so helping deliver readers to advertisers) comes in.

Specialist features

In terms of feature genres, it is useful to identify some of the key 'specialist' genres – sometimes written by those with a primary area of expertise but more often than not by chameleon journalists with a special interest in the field and willing to act as informed conduits and demystifiers. For instance, notice the current proliferation of popular health magazines, drawing upon specialist medical knowledge and making it accessible to a wide readership.[3] Around each specialist genre a number of conventions (not necessarily fixed but on the whole transparent) have accrued by which the writer may be guided in order to produce a viable, marketable piece.

Travel features are a case in point. There are two markets here: one associated with tourism, foregrounding, often in a themed context, the 'time out' benefits of visiting other places: cost and mode of travel, hotels and entertainment features; the other with a more documentary approach to exploring particular landscapes and cultures. *The Sunday Times* series 'Authors in the Front Line' yields vivid insights into life in, say, war-torn Chad (see A.A. Gill, 11 July 2004). There is no doubt that the very best travel journalism in the latter category qualifies as literary journalism, with William Fiennes, Martha Gellhorn, George Orwell and William Dalrymple exemplars of the genre.

But how do travel writers pierce the veil of their own cultural assumptions to report accurately from hugely different places around the world? It seems there is always one Big Question like this that can be extrapolated from the set conventions and expectations of a specialism. The following questions illustrate just how closely specialist feature writers are invisibly, silently pursued by wider, often frighteningly securely embedded agendas that are reflective of prevailing currents of political, economic, social or cultural thought.

For instance:

- How does the sports writer avoid fermenting unnecessary xenophobia?
- How does the food writer avoid creating unnecessary scaremongering?[4]
- How does the science writer ensure that a proper range of experts are quoted on controversial subjects?[5]
- How do writers of political conviction take steps to avoid selecting evidence to fit their case?
- How do writers on traumatic events (such as war) avoid the temptation to impose themselves on victims?[6]
- How does the interviewer eliminate preconceptions for a rounded and fair representation of a person?
- How do journalists under cover avoid setting up artificial honey traps, for the sake of the story?

And so on. In each of these instances there is at least one serious ethical consideration that may be expected to recur, given the nature of the specialism, and become a defining element of the genre.

Topics

As an addendum to this, in terms of subject matter as opposed to specialism, it should be noted that genre boundaries tend to blur when the influence of current news begins to infiltrate even specialist feature pages. Most months, there are one or two topics that are so keenly felt that they may penetrate the glass ceiling of genre itself. These are generally the big, rolling issues that touch readers' everyday lives or imagination in one way or another, making them hungry for information, case studies and comment. Such topics reach out to readers sensitised to the kind of background hysteria emitted by cumulative news coverage, which can result in a sense of gathering panic penetrating mass readerships, whether moral at base and vulnerable to prejudice or largely self-preservational.

In recent years, crises around mad cow disease (BSE), HIV, asylum seekers, paedophilia, Ecstasy and working wives have all yielded rich material for feature writers to tackle in a number of ways. Sometimes a topic penetrates the collective psyche in such a way that *most* special-interest groups seem to be touched by it at some deep, human level. For example, a very cursory scan of publications in July 2004 quickly produced a number of features on suicide bombers in a range of publications aimed at men, young girls and working women.[7]

Distinctive journalistic fields

In this section, I want to turn away from the market and briefly consider feature genres in terms of particular conventions of journalistic writing. By doing this we can begin to distinguish matters of style and structure. The terms used below, unlike the commonly accepted descriptions of specialist features just discussed, are specifically journalistic but applied to the kind of approach a topic might lend itself to. And often there is a choice: the best and the hungriest feature writers are continually on the look-out for 'spin-off' opportunities, chances to make the same material, differently presented, work for different markets.

These distinctive 'journalistic fields' are a useful way of mentally previewing the end product (the completed feature) and to some extent they may act as a guide for the writer towards his or her adoption of appropriate techniques for getting there. The following genres will be readily identifiable in any newspaper or magazine which publishes features so the following is a succinct snapshot, for easy reference, beginning with the 'hardest' (most immediate, reality-based, fact-dependent) and moving to the 'softer' end (most introspective, observant, personal).

News feature

Essentially, this is the name given to an up-to-the-minute response to a news item or issue, amplifying it with analysis, background detail, interviews, comment. If it is a big issue, it will follow a particular (hopefully original) angle on that issue and may produce additional facts boxes and other page paraphernalia to enrich and deepen the reading.

Backgrounder

This type of feature takes a longer view, often digging down into the origins of an issue (which readers may have lost sight of in the flurry of news reporting) and plumbing relevant historical concerns. Equally, it may present the evolution of, say, a business, a product, or a scandal. Like the news feature, it may set out a controversial matter over which sides are clearly gathering force in an attempt to summarise or elicit a range of standpoints.

backgrounder feature exploring the background to main story in the news.

Investigative feature

This is a form of reporting that concerns itself with the public interest, in the sense that it is overtly in pursuit of wrongdoing, whether this is moral, financial or political.

It demands huge persistence, risk analysis, the will to probe and the acuity to find out exactly where, and whom, to question. This is sometimes done by teams of journalists, especially for scandals like Thalidomide and Watergate, two causes célèbres of this particular genre.[8]

Profile

People, places, organisations, goods . . . all may be profiled although the first two are the most ubiquitous. A good profile will use sensitive background research and carefully worked-out interviewing techniques in order to fulfil the expectations of readerships seeking something of the full flavour of the subject and its context. Profiles may be written up as emerging stories in a continuous narrative style, but people profiles are increasingly presented – especially in busy, genre-specific contexts – in strict question-and-answer formats, drawing attention to a one-dimensional response for quick, focused, assimilation.[9]

Editorial

leader   the editorial comment.

This is the genre of **leader** articles in broadsheet newspapers where a viewpoint is legitimately taken, which is indeed the point of the exercise. This will not be personal to the journalist writing it but a reflection of the editorial/proprietorial stance on an issue of the day. The case for this is presented and argued with economy, though bombast is not unknown (it is routine in tabloid leaders, whose rhetoric derives from simple wordplay, frequently taking a didactic and over-simplifying stance to the issue).

Human interest

The angle here and the whole thrust of the piece, whatever the topic, is on the experience of people involved in the story: suffering, triumphing over adversity, achieving, getting caught up in disasters, grieving, arguing for change. Sometimes their stories are told by the journalist with frequent quotes from the subject. Often such interviews are rendered entirely in the first person, shaped by the writer's perspicacious questioning and narrative sensibility.

Fly on the wall

This is also called 'going undercover', or (to use a term from sociology) 'participant-observation'. Spectacular results can be provided by devoting swathes of time to such operations by a feature writer (or team of writers) although increasingly fewer print markets will sustain the cost of this, particularly since television tends to produce a more exciting display of the operation (the sight of Roger Cook being attacked with a baseball bat on Central TV's *The Cook Report* remains oddly compelling).

Eyewitness

For drama, insight, empathy and a fully sensuous appeal, the **eyewitness report** may be delivered by a journalist on the spot (for example, in war zones). But equally it could be a result of conscientious, in-depth interviewing, after which the writer may put all or large parts of the experience in the words of the beholder for dramatic effect and a sense of first-hand authenticity (see also 'human interest', above).

The purpose of identifying these fields is that it alerts the writer more accurately to the market-sensitive potential of a putative feature. Thus, given an insight into breast cancer, a feature writer might ask, Which publication would be more likely to take, say, an investigative piece on hospitals with low survival rates? Which would respond to a profile of a Macmillan nurse? Which to a backgrounder on the myths and the science of treatments? And so on. Also, the approaches listed above are all, with their areas of exclusion as well as their particular conventions, at the same time material-sensitive, pointing towards the fact that material gathered for certain topics at the same time tends to suggest itself for some publications more than others.

eyewitness reporting presence of reporter at news event can provide unique opportunities for descriptive writing.

Distinctive functional fields

In this section, I want to briefly introduce four further genres, each indicative of the broad purpose of the type of journalism it describes. These four 'functional fields' stand out in sharp contrast to each other (although there will be areas of overlap). From the point of view of both a feature writer about to start putting his or her piece together and, at the reception end, the commissioning editor, it is useful to be able to form an idea of what will be the main thrust of the feature. For the former, it will flag up points of style and structure, while for the latter it is useful to see at a glance how, and where, in the publication such a piece may be placed. They are:

- information-based journalism
- opinion-making journalism
- entertainment journalism
- literary journalism.

Information

It may seem a truism, but a vast amount of what we could call the worthy backbone of all journalistic copy is to do with producing information, contributing not just to the knowledge economy we live in but also to the everyday development of our perceptions, outlook on life, lifestyle, social and professional relations, skills, plus that whole cabinet of curiosities which contains 'general awareness'. Here, we can make a distinction between the work of specific B2B titles or customer magazines addressing precisely defined professions, crafts or trade groups and those leisure magazines (whether, for example, they focus on a sport, a locality or a type of cultural activity) as well as the named pages in newspapers which cater for aspirational free-time pursuits. While the former are likely to use a form of discourse and vocabulary which speaks to those in the know, legitimately making assumptions about their level of knowledge, the challenge for the latter is the degree of their awareness of the conceptual level and interest potential of a readership which is likely to lack the cohesiveness of a special-interest group.

Opinion-making

These are likely to be features with attitude, whether they represent individual convictions or campaigns, and may tackle difficult and often seemingly intractable issues. Michael Ignatieff is one writer who, through the Balkans conflict in particular (1997), has made the case for a journalism that increasingly deals with new varieties of conflict flowing from globalism (whether in the form of direct action by pressure groups, outright war or internecine struggles played out on smaller stages). These activities, relentlessly reported on news pages, produce rich reflective and investigative material for the feature writer.

The problem for journalists covering conflict issues becomes how to avoid 'the narcissism of minor difference' (Ignatieff 1997: 55) in favour of maintaining the scope of the bigger picture. Covering issues that emerge from racial, national and local conflict – attempting to uncover their dynamics, talking to key political players as well as ordinary casualties of history – then places the postmodern journalist in the role of 'moral witness', operating within a media industry obliged to adopt new roles as 'sentinels of moral engagement' between factions (Plaisance 2002: 205 and 206). Such 'engagements' take place all the time and it is easy for readers in western democracies who are used to seeing diversity of opinions being expressed to take them for granted.

A modest but useful example of this appears in the *New Statesman* of 28 June 2004 via two quite separate features, unheralded by the publication and so feeding seamlessly into the multifarious flow of opinion throughout the issue. First is the cover story, 'A Dangerous Time to be a Jew' by Simon Sebag Montefiore. But then this is directly countered a number of pages further on by investigative reporter John Pilger who uses his regular column to discuss the ramifications of an alleged pro-Israeli bias in UK television news reports.

Entertainment

By contrast, it has to be said that much of today's journalism, including some of the best, aims, whether overtly or subliminally, to entertain: just consider the number of columns where journalists with a 'name' and well-known people (who are often ghost-written) speak their minds. It is not surprising this is on the increase given that reading magazine and newspaper features tends to be a leisure activity – and given the media's crucial role in creating and sustaining celebrities. Such features are so powerful (in terms of cover sales) as well as pervasive (in terms of column inches) reminding us that celebrities are a prime vehicle for the expression of popular culture.

Even the apparently vacuous, famous-for-being-famous have great news value and appeal both to readers and editors because, as P. David Marshall argues (2001: x), 'the celebrity as public individual who participates openly as a marketable commodity serves as a powerful type of legitimation of the political economic model of exchange and value [. . .] and extends that model to include the individual'. Moreover, although 'entertainment' journalism covers a far broader field and purpose than celebrity interviews, we should bear in mind that 'celebrity status also confers on the person a certain discursive power: within society, the celebrity is a voice above others, a voice that is channeled into the media systems as being legitimately significant' (Marshall 2001: x).

The profile writer, Lynn Barber, known for her skillful and incisive interview technique when profiling celebrities, reminds us of the two-way traffic of this sort of journalism, despite its essential lightness: 'The people I interview are not novices. They know the media game' (Barber 1999: ix–x). Despite the implications of such a potentially collusive form of journalism, she warns: 'I don't believe there is any ethical problem about interviewing, but I think there can be a behavioural one for some beginner journalists' (Barber 1999: xiii).[10]

Literary journalism

I have left this category to last, not because of residual criticism (mostly from hard-news writers and only in the UK) that such a term is oxymoronic and that any characteristics of literature do not properly belong in journalism. Nor do I wish to suggest that this is a preferred mode for feature writing – far from it – or that it represents the pinnacle of writerly achievement in journalism (though it often does). It is for two other reasons.

First, in this genre of journalism (also lately referred to as 'creative non-fiction') it is possible to trace the genealogy of a certain sort of journalism style. As such, it offers alternative techniques for feature writers in their negotiations with the world around them, encouraging an open mind and a degree of lateral thinking when working on an idea. Next, it is within this type of journalism that we can pinpoint aspects of narrative that either exemplify or give grounds for what must always be necessarily curtailed opportunities for journalistic experimentation (curtailed, that is, because of the nature of journalism as opposed to fiction).

What is 'literary journalism'? In a nutshell, it is a form of writing (often conversational, autobiographical or confessional) that is aware of the potency of borrowing techniques from fiction in order to get to the heart of the matter.[11] It is journalism which:

- often investigates ordinary events, celebrating their specialness with an original and unexpected angle;
- adopts an intimate voice which might be informal, frank, or ironic;
- takes a disengaged and mobile stance from which readers can be addressed directly;
- mixes primary narrative with tales and digressions to amplify and reframe events.[12]

The contesting of objectivity as the exclusive purpose of journalism does not automatically mean the licence to rant, to become polemical, self-indulgent, an intrusive 'I'. Lorna Sage, in her foreword to *Journalism, Literature and Modernity*

(Campbell 2000: ix) takes this particular argument a step further when she writes: 'Journalism, chatty and informal as it sometimes sounds, in fact depends on a degree of distance, alienation even, of author from audience. It inserts itself between writer and reader, locates that gap and makes it wider.' In other words, literary journalism is 'the sort of non-fiction in which arts of style and narrative construction long associated with fiction help pierce to the quick of what's happening – the essence of journalism' (Sims and Kramer 1995: foreword). Sustained examples of literary journalism can be found regularly in publications such as the *London Review of Books* and the *Guardian*, (the national newspaper that offers comprehensive feature coverage, daily).[13]

Conclusions

Feature writing is that most fluid of journalistic forms which is why it is useful to make a prism of its genres like this, however condensed. Allusions to the constraints of publication have been placed against the freedom to choose a subject, a choice of ways to proceed and a choice of writing styles and conventions. The horizontal and vertical scope of the genres described here (considered broadly across categories of journalism and hinting at depth when referring to techniques) is necessarily abbreviated and should be read as a starter in a rich field of further reading – of what is out there daily, weekly, monthly and quarterly in terms of mass-market publications and in those books and journals which aim to open the door on debates about what journalism is and what it does.

Notes

1. I have found the most useful and comprehensive of these to be *Willings Press Guide*, the *Guardian Media Directory*, *Brad* and the *Writers' and Artists' Yearbook*.
2. Consumer magazines are those that deal with leisure, entertainment and matters of general consumption, for example *Marie-Claire*, *The Economist*, *TV Times*, *Autocar*. B2B cater for business and professionals: *Press Gazette*, *Nursing Times*, *Construction News*, *Farmers Weekly*. Customer magazines are in-house publications produced specifically for clients: for example, the *AA Magazine*.
3. Books are beginning to appear which address 'cross-over' writers, i.e. professionals in other fields who want to try journalism. See T. Albert (1993) for a guide to how to write medical journalism.
4. *The Sunday Times* magazine, of 4 July 2004, is a case in point with a child wearing a gas mask on a cover titled: 'Toxic Families'.
5. See, for example, Rob Edwards, *New Scientist*, 26 June 2004, discussing the protocols of scientists' bylines on material written by others.
6. H. Himmelstein and E. Faithorn (2002: 545) discuss the journalistic propriety of such interviews, reflecting that: 'While many potential interviewees may indeed want to tell their stories to the world, in the immediate aftermath of a catastrophic event they may not at that moment be capable of a rational recounting of the event.' This is also taken up by both the NUJ and Press Complaints Commission in their codes of conduct.

7. For example: 'Living with the Enemy', *Esquire*, July 2004; 'I survived a suicide bombing', *ElleGirl*, July 2004 and 'I am a suicide bomber', *Marie Claire*, July 2004.
8. Note the '-gate' suffix is now routinely used for major investigative stories, e.g. Irangate and even Cheriegate. It began with Watergate, the Democratic Party's headquarters in Washington that was broken into by Republican spies in June 1972, the subject of a famous exposé by two American journalists, Carl Bernstein and Bob Woodward of the *Washington Post*. The most famous British example of sustained investigative journalism challenging the multinational drug company producing Thalidomide, shown to cause birth abnormalities, was performed by *The Sunday Times'* Insight team.
9. Almost every newspaper or consumer magazine will yield examples of Q and A responses to single issues, for example attitudes to location, music, relationships, mode of travel, food or first love.
10. The behaviour to which she refers is the young journalist's tendency towards being star-struck on early assignments, leading to faux-empathy in which the inexperienced interviewer tries posturing a 'relationship' with the interviewee, which Barber does not recommend (Barber 1999: xiii).
11. At a slight tangent to journalism, but a wonderful model for feature writers of taut, personal writing, I offer three recent memoirs: Mantel 2004, Morrison 1998 and Sage 2001.
12. This is condensed and adapted from the far more comprehensive list provided by Mark Kramer in the foreword to *Literary Journalism* (Sims and Kramer 1995).
13. Also, as illustrations of a tangential, sometimes delightfully idiosyncratic approach to events and experiences, try the following, each from *Granta*, the monthly magazine which each decade publishes its list of 'Britain's best young writers': 'The Smoking Diaries', by Simon Gray, in 'Life's Like That', *Granta* 82 and Ryszard Kapuscinski's hilarious, occasionally surreal and troubling (1998) *The Soccer War*, London: Granta Books.

References

Albert, T. (1993) *Medical Journalism: The Writer's Guide*, Oxford: Radcliffe Medical Press.

Barber, L. (1999) *Demon Barber*, Harmondsworth: Penguin.

Himmelstein, H. and E. Faithorn (2002) 'Eyewitness to Disaster: How Journalists Cope with the Psychological Stress Inherent in Reporting Traumatic Events', *Journalism Studies*, 3 (4) November: 537–56.

Ignatieff, M. (1997) *The Warrior's Honour: Ethnic War and the Modern Conscience*, New York: Henry Holt & Company.

Jameson, F. (2000) 'The Political Unconscious: Narrative as a Socially Symbolic Act', in M. McQuillan (ed.) *The Narrative Reader*, London: Routledge.

Mantel, H. (2004) *Giving up the Ghost*, London: Harper Perennial Books.

Marshall, P.D. (2001) *Celebrity and Power*, Minneapolis, Minn.: University of Minnesota Press.

Morrison, B. (1998) *And When did you Last See Your Father?* London: Granta Books.

Plaisance, P. (2002) 'The Journalist As Moral Witness: Michael Ignatieff's Pluralistic Philosophy for a Global Media Culture', *Journalism: Theory, Practice and Criticism*, 3 (2): 205–22.

Sage, L. (2000) 'Foreword' in K. Campbell (ed.) *Journalism, Literature and Modernity*, Edinburgh: Edinburgh University Press.

Sage, L. (2001) *Bad Blood*, London: Fourth Estate.

Sims, N. and M. Kramer (eds) (1995) *Literary Journalism: A New Collection of the Best American Nonfiction*, New York: Ballantine.

The right idea at the right time

11

Pitching the feature

The right idea at the right time

Pitching the feature

Tony Harcup

This chapter covers the identification of appropriate outlets for different feature ideas and how to present feature ideas to commissioning editors in a professional manner. It deals with issues such as how to communicate with different publications (and sections within publications), how to interest them in ideas without giving too much away and how to respond to rejection. The chapter suggests that before **pitching** an idea, journalists should first identify the audience, style and interests of particular newspapers and magazines and then establish why the idea is right for this particular publication at this particular time.

pitching proposing story idea to newspaper/magazine

Advice is given on how ideas may be conveyed succinctly to busy commissioning editors and there is discussion of the advantages and disadvantages of approaching editors via telephone, email, in writing and in person. The tone of the chapter is open rather than prescriptive, recognising the diversity of publications and approaches within the marketplace. However, suggestions for good practice are offered and journalists are warned against promising more than can be delivered. Advice is also offered on the importance of agreeing the word length and deadline (and fee if appropriate). The chapter encourages both lateral thinking and critical reflection and includes suggestions for further reading.

Making a pitch

Anybody serious about becoming a journalist should not need long to discover it is not quite the glamorous lifestyle of legend. A couple of weeks' work experience in your local newsroom should be enough to show you that, like genius, journalism is one part inspiration to 99 parts perspiration. But, assuming you are competent at putting in the latter, it is the former that will mark you out from the crowd.

Most journalists can do an adequate job when handed a story; rather fewer seem able to bring in ideas themselves. Yet, as freelance journalist Dan Roberts (2004) points out: 'The thing to remember is that ideas are the lifeblood of this industry. The right idea, no matter who it's from, will receive positive attention from the most hard-bitten features editor.'

This chapter is addressed to people pitching ideas on a freelance basis, but the advice can be adapted by staff journalists who wish to pitch ideas to editors of different sections on their own publication. Whether freelance or staff, if you can regularly come up with your own ideas – and suggest fresh approaches to familiar stories – then you will quickly become known in the trade as a 'self-starter' who does not need spoon-feeding. As such, you need never be short of work.

Coming up with a good idea is not enough on its own, however. You have to communicate (or pitch, in the jargon) the idea to a commissioning editor. Hopefully they will like the idea, ask you to write it and even offer to pay you. Getting a commission is the appropriate moment to punch the air and shout 'Woo-hoo!' . . . but only after putting the phone down in a calm and professional manner.

It may be useful at this stage to show you an actual pitch. Here is an email I recently sent to the features editor of *Press Gazette*, the journalists' weekly trade magazine:

> Julie, would you be interested in a **thinkpiece** from me discussing why we always seem so keen on bad news/tragedy stories? I know it's not exactly a new topic but I think it's always of interest and that I could say something fresh that is both provocative and entertaining. It's prompted by the newspaper my postgraduate journalism students produce – which is absolutely full of deaths and tragedies, etc. – so it could include some discussion of what we should be teaching trainee journalists about what makes a good story, etc. I think it could make a lively piece for your Analysis slot. Interested? Best wishes, Tony Harcup.

thinkpiece analytical article

I do not quote this as a perfect example or as an approach that would work in all circumstances, but because it illustrates many of the points made in this chapter.

The first thing to note is that it did not come out of nowhere. I have read *Press Gazette* for decades and have contributed the occasional piece over many years, so I know them and they know me. The informal tone is therefore appropriate. The opening sentence contains the pitch in essence, suggesting both the topic (bad news) and the style (thinkpiece). It also makes clear that I am proposing to write it myself rather than simply suggesting an idea. I then pre-empt the most likely objection (it's old hat) by suggesting a new approach based on something specific within my own experience (the students' newspaper).

In the process, I indicate why I am qualified to write it (I teach journalism and they are my students). I use words (fresh, provocative, entertaining, lively) designed both to give a flavour of the piece and to push the right buttons with the features editor. I imply that the idea would be of particular interest to more than one section of the magazine's readers (working journalists and those involved in journalism training). Finally, I suggest an appropriate slot (Analysis), showing I've done my homework and making the editor's job easier. It did the trick – I got the commission.

The perfect pitch

The perfect pitch is the one that gains the commission. But what is commissioned will vary from publication to publication and from features editor to features editor. That's what makes it perfect: it has to be right for them at that moment, not a general idea gently reheated for the umpteenth time.

It never fails to amaze me that some wannabe journalists think they can impress an editor with their journalistic prowess despite giving the impression they have never actually read the newspaper or magazine in question. Shaun Phillips, features director of *Esquire* magazine, says: 'I get lots of generic pitches that don't consider the magazine's content. The best pitches are from people who have a specific slot in mind for the feature' (quoted in Roberts 2004). Wrongly targeted pitches are infuriating for editors since the subtext implies the journalist is either lazy, stupid or, more likely, both. You will have far more chance of success if you pitch an idea with the relevant publication specifically in mind and, even if you are unsuccessful in the short term, you may have a potentially receptive ear for future proposals.

The right idea at the right time

The first step to help you come up with an appropriate idea is to survey the market. Familiarise yourself with as many different newspapers and magazines as you can. National, regional, specialist, general, frothy, serious . . . read 'em all. Most publications have their own web sites which range from the useful to the useless, but you are more likely to get a sense of the character of a title by looking at the printed rather than electronic version. If you cannot afford to buy them, why not browse in a bigger newsagent or bookshop? Then go to libraries, both town and university, which usually have selections of the latest periodicals. Incidentally, don't bother with academic journals: they don't pay, hardly anybody actually reads them and they won't want your feature anyway.

Do think beyond the obvious, though. Most journalists work for titles you have probably never heard of, and virtually any subject imaginable – from accounting to zebras – will have at least one magazine devoted to it. Check out as many as you can to get a feel for both style and content.

When you have identified a suitable publication for your initial advances, try to locate the most likely section of that newspaper or magazine which may well have its own commissioning editor. If you happen to know somebody already working there, even in a different department, that could be a lucky break. Not only could they suggest the right person to contact but you could also use the line 'so-and-so suggested you might be interested in . . .' to give your idea some reflected kudos. (Of course, if so-and-so is regarded as a waste of space, then dropping their name will do you no favours: err on the side of caution.)

Find out the name of the features or section editor by looking in media directories such as *Benn's*, *Pims* or *Willings* in reference libraries. (The annual *Guardian Media Directory* is both handier and more affordable, although it has fewer details on each publication.) You can also look on publications' own web sites. Make a careful note of job titles and do not confuse an assistant editor (who may be able to commission you) with an editorial assistant (who may be much nicer but will not have a budget).

When you have identified the best person to approach, make sure you write down the correct spelling of their name. You won't win any prizes for getting such details right, but you will certainly earn a bad mark by getting them wrong. Finally, it is safest to assume that the person named has probably changed job since the information was published so double-check by ringing the company first and asking the switchboard whether the name you have is still correct. A little politeness goes a long way in this business.

Now you are ready to make your pitch. But how? If you ask half a dozen journalists how they go about it, you will get at least half a dozen different answers.

Making contact

Unless your idea has a very short shelf-life, I would not advise making initial contact by phone. You might have prepared yourself for the pitch but you have no idea what the person you are calling may have been doing before you rang – even assuming you get through. If you ring up and try to pitch an idea when they are busy thinking about something else or waiting for another call, then you will be ploughing a furrow on infertile land. The phone is vital for news, of course, but for features I have found it more fruitful to make initial contact in writing or email so that the commissioning editor can feel in control when considering the idea.

Successful feature writer Helen Carroll also favours the electronic route for an initial approach. 'Email is a useful tool for outlining ideas to commissioning editors, though you may have to follow it up with a phone call the following day,' she says. If you phone after having sent an email or letter, the features editor should already have some idea of what you are talking about and will therefore be less likely to feel ambushed or irritated by your call.

If you are using email, ensure you have a sensible email address for professional purposes. Unless you are pitching to the *Sunday Sport* your email is unlikely to be looked at, let alone taken seriously, if it comes from randyandy@something or thesexyone@other. And, just because email is a less formal medium than the traditional letter, it does not mean that errors of spelling and grammar somehow do not matter. They will be noticed – if not by you, then by the commissioning editor – and they will not impress. Nor will littering your email with exclamation marks (!), which are the mark of the amateur!!!!

Experienced freelance Chris Wheal warns that, in any event, emails may not always get through. 'Often people get so many emails, especially on the nationals, they don't take the time to read them,' he says. 'People like the details in emails but you need to phone and warn them that the email is coming so they watch out for it. Or even use the post, because your good idea may not even be spotted.'

It can be a fine line between being persistent and being a pain, so learn when to persevere and when to back off. And remember your manners. If you are writing to somebody you don't know, don't call them by their first name. Don't call people 'mate' on the phone, either. And 'Dear sir or madam' is a complete no-no. After all, if you cannot be bothered to find out their name, why should they be bothered to read your pitch?

Andrew Bibby, another successful freelance journalist, points out that you will need to develop (at least) one approach for publications that have never heard of you and another for those that have already used your work. He explains his modus operandi when it comes to the former: 'First, find out the name of the relevant commissioning editor, for the appropriate section of the paper or magazine. Ring them – persevere if you don't initially get through – and very briefly introduce yourself and explain the idea. Try to get the commission over the phone, but – assuming this isn't possible and/or they're wavering – offer to follow up with an email. Email immediately with a very brief outline. Then, if there is no reply, ring again after a few days.'

For contacting editors who know him, Andrew tends to use email these days. The fact that they recognise his name means they will be likely to read something from him even when their email inbox is overflowing with unread messages. 'It can sometimes be useful to offer two or even three ideas, on the basis that at least one is likely to appeal,' he adds.

How much information do you need to give? Like so much in journalism, this isn't rocket science – unless you are pitching to an aeronautics magazine, of course. It is something far more complicated: a combination of intuition, common sense and learning from trial and error. Freelance Christine Morgan says: 'In my pitches, I try to give just enough detail to get them interested. Some feature editors like lots of information, others don't. You get to know what works with experience' (quoted in Roberts 2004).

Don't forget that you are selling your journalistic nous and skills as well as the idea itself so don't undersell yourself. If you can legitimately call yourself a freelance journalist rather than a student, then do so. If you have a particular expertise or personal involvement relevant to the topic, then say so. If you have recently had an impressive-looking piece published elsewhere that gives a good example of what you can do, then let them know and offer to supply a cutting or web address.

Why, why, why?

For initial pitches, focus on the three whys. Why this idea, why this publication and why me to write it? Work out the answers, then come up with the most succinct way of expressing them. If you can't convince yourself, you're unlikely to convince an editor.

'Keep outlines brief and punchy', advises Helen. 'Don't give too much detail in the outline as commissioning editors are less likely to plough their way through it.' Andrew agrees with keeping it short and sweet: 'One paragraph, and make the piece sound interesting and intriguing.' On the other hand, Chris feels that a bit more detail can pay dividends: 'Just an idea is rarely enough, you need to have done a little research or have some basic fact – or, even better, a case study – in the bag to win them over and show you are serious.'

Of course, you don't want to give away so much information that your ideas and contacts can simply be stolen. But nor do you want to give the impression that you think anybody you are pitching to is the sort of rogue who would steal the ideas of a novice.

Features rely far more than do most news stories on presentation and illustration. Therefore, if you have an idea for how your feature might be presented, or what pictures could go with it, don't be afraid to say how you visualise it. Even if the idea is not quite right, it shows that you have thought about it, and it might spark off other ideas that could encourage the editor to pick up on your proposal.

Ideas often develop and change during the conversation between the person doing the pitching and the person at the other end. Most of us cannot afford to be too precious and so are willing to negotiate. You may think your idea is already perfect, but an editor might like to hack it about or tweak it a little to come up with something different. There's always the chance their idea is better than the original, of course – it does happen – but even if it isn't, remember that he or she is the editor and you aren't (yet). You can either do it their way or take your chances by offering the original idea elsewhere. However, do not offer more-or-less the same feature to more than one publication at the same time. I made that mistake once and my ears still ring at the thought of the abusive phone call I received as a result. It was a fair point, well made.

Most important of all, if you want to establish and then maintain any sort of credibility as a journalist, you should ensure you never promise more than you can deliver. You may have the bright idea of interviewing the latest triple-A-list celeb about their biggest secrets but there's no point in pitching the idea unless you have worked out how you are going to get access to the star in question. Never exaggerate the strength of a story to win a commission. If you do, you will either look foolish when you deliver the copy or – far worse – you may be tempted to exaggerate the story itself. Promise only what you know you can deliver and what you know to be true.

It is not usually a good idea to write a feature first and then try to hawk it around afterwards. It gives an unprofessional impression, both because the feature will not have been written in the style of a particular publication and because it suggests you are a bit, well, desperate.

Andrew's golden rule is to only ever write on commission. 'This is, I know, difficult when you're starting out. So the amended rule is as follows: don't ever submit material **on spec**, it's highly unlikely to be used. Even for speculative stuff, always make contact first, preferably by phone, or alternatively by email, so that at least your name is known and likely to be recognised. The fallback, if no commission is forthcoming, is to get them to agree that they'll look at the piece if you send it in. Once you've submitted it, you then have the excuse to ring up subsequently.'

> **on spec**
> uncommissioned article submitted voluntarily to media.

Dealing with rejection

You'll also have to prepare yourself for that most common of all experiences: rejection. As Roberts (2004) advises: 'You must develop a rhino-like skin pretty quickly, as emails go ignored and ideas that took days to research are rejected with a five-word reply.' Five words? Two are more common: 'No thanks.' Or, worse, no reply at all; then, if you chase it up, you may eventually be told by somebody who clearly has not read it that your piece was not quite right for them.

Don't take it to heart. And don't burn your bridges. You may have made a useful contact that will ensure the next pitch gets a hearing. And, with a bit of lateral thinking, you may be able to tweak the original idea and make a pitch to a rival publication.

You can learn from the experience of even an unsuccessful pitch. 'I'm still working on my pitching technique,' says Christine Morgan. 'I don't think you can ever perfect it, because editorial directions keep changing [. . .] You'll always get rejections, but I never take them personally. For every five ideas I pitch, if I get one commission I'm happy.' (quoted in Roberts 2004). The strike rate of somebody just starting out is likely to be less than one in five. So, if you can't take rejection, it's time to consider another career.

Clinching the deal

Just as occasional sporting highs can seem even better if you support a team that usually disappoints – bear with me, I know what I'm talking about here – so all the character-building rejections you get will only make it more pleasurable when somebody eventually says 'Yes'. Before doing a lap of honour around your bedroom, try to contain your excitement long enough to clarify the details of the commission.

The National Union of Journalists (NUJ 2004: 7), which offers useful advice as well as representation to its freelance members, suggests you ensure you know the following:

- The name and position of the person commissioning you.
- What you have agreed to do, how many words.
- How you will deliver the copy: **hard copy**, disk, email (text or Word attachment) and so on.
- When is the deadline?
- How much will you be paid?
- What expenses will be paid if any?
- Do you need to send an invoice and, if so, to whom?

hard copy copy typed on sheets of paper (usually A4 size). Each page is known as a folio.

I usually make it a rule never to trust anybody whose desk is too tidy, but you will need to maintain some sense of order to keep a note of all the above details. You will find it useful to maintain some rudimentary files and to keep your contacts book up to date, adding details of section heads and commissioning editors as you go along. If you have more than one commission at once, keep handy a list of jobs with their word limits and deadlines. The publication is your client and you are a supplier of a professional service, so try to act like it.

'As soon as you have agreed to carry out a piece of work and have accepted the terms and fee offered to you, you have a contract with your client,' points out the NUJ. Some journalists insist on agreeing commissions in writing. 'A written contract is no more legally binding than an oral agreement, but it is useful proof that a contract was entered into should they refuse to pay you.' (NUJ 2004: 6). The union also provides advice on copyright issues such as whether you will be paid extra if your article is also put on a web site or syndicated to other publications.

Concerns about copyright and contracts are likely to seem a million miles away from the experience of most people wanting to break into journalism, who would be willing to pay in blood for the buzz of seeing their byline in print. But, however pathetically grateful you are that somebody is willing to publish your work, it is important that you conduct yourself in a professional manner and deliver what you have promised, when you have promised it. That will make the next pitch more likely to be successful.

The personal touch

To help establish and maintain your reputation, you may also consider the benefits of pressing the flesh. Andrew recalls that, in his early days, he would often arrange to make personal visits to meet commissioning editors. Putting a face to a name is useful in itself. It will also give you a clearer picture of what they are looking for and give them a better idea of who you are and what you can offer.

Chris suggests taking this further. He is unapologetic about using the language of the sales rep when advising people who are just starting out as freelance journalists: 'Network, go to press events, to drinks parties and awards and meet people working for the publications. Then buy the commissioning editors drinks and even take them out for lunch. That way, when you phone or email or write or text them, they will know who you are and at least give your idea the time of day. Pitching cold is the hardest thing to do, so I always suggest I meet them and buy them a drink or lunch. They are usually so shocked that a freelance is prepared to pay, they fall over backwards. But a long-term relationship always pays dividends.'

Further reading

In addition to reading as many newspapers and magazines as you can get your hands on, you will find useful introductions to the newspaper and magazine industries respectively in Keeble (2001) and McKay (2000). Alden (2004) is a goldmine of media information and contacts. *Press Gazette* will keep you up to speed about new publications and the comings and goings of editors and also includes informative features about various aspects of journalism. Finally, the NUJ (2004) offers advice on fees, expenses and copyright issues.

Acknowledgement

All quotes from Andrew Bibby, Helen Carroll and Chris Wheal are taken from interviews with the author, for which many thanks. Thanks also to Bethany Bolton and Terry Wragg who read a draft of this chapter.

References

Alden, C. (2004) *Guardian Media Directory 2005*, London: Guardian Books.
Keeble, R. (2005) *The Newspapers Handbook*, 4th edn, London: Routledge.
McKay, J. (2000) *The Magazines Handbook*, London: Routledge.
NUJ (2004) *Freelance Fees Guide 2003–4*, London: National Union of Journalists.
Roberts, D. (2004) 'The Knights' Tales', *Press Gazette*, 21 May: 18–9.

Doing it in style

Feature writing

12

Doing it in style

Feature writing

Tony Harcup

pay-off last par with twist or flourish.

This chapter explains how feature writing differs from hard news. It includes discussion of the importance of both the intro and the **pay-off** and also covers the roles played within features by quotes, facts, anecdotes, colour, opinion, analysis, description and context. The importance of using language and style appropriate to the publication and to the subject matter is also addressed. The chapter goes on to introduce ways in which the above elements can be woven into a readable whole, including the use of linking words and phrases.

The tone is open rather than prescriptive, recognising the diversity of publications that exist and the range of different approaches taken by journalists. The point is made that features tend to be longer than news stories and tend to use more sources, background and context. Journalists working on features may have greater freedom to experiment and introduce their own voice and experiences into the piece. In discussing these issues, the chapter encourages critical reflection. Suggestions for further reading are also offered.

Features: more than just smart writing

Features are as often defined by reference to what they *not* – hard news – as to what they *are*. They come in all shapes and sizes, and virtually anything you can think of could be turned into the subject of a feature. There are fewer rules in writing features than in writing news although features tend to be longer than news stories and to use more sources, background and context. Not always, though. Some features rely heavily on the personal experience or opinions of the writer. As with so much in the world of journalism, the best way of learning about feature writing is to read and write lots of features and encourage other people to read and comment on your features. As national newspaper journalist David Randall (2000: 141) comments: 'Writing is like a muscle, it will be a lot stronger if you exercise it every day.'

You may like to imagine yourself as a writer who has more in common with the literary greats than with the grubby hacks who get their hands dirty with hard news, but features are journalism, not literature. It follows, therefore, that feature writers are reporters too. You are unlikely to emerge on the scene as a brilliant feature writer if you have not also gained at least some experience in gathering facts and writing news.

Randall (2000: 193–4) criticises those who guard the border between the land of facts (news) and the supposedly fact-free swamp of features:

It produces narrow thinking which can restrict coverage of news to conventional subjects and puts writing it into the unimaginative straitjacket of a formula. With features, it encourages the insidious idea that normal standards of precision and thorough research don't apply and that they can be a kind of low-fact product [. . .] The opposite, of course, is the case. Most news pages could benefit from a greater sense of adventure and a more flexible approach to stories. Similarly, most features sections cry out for sharper research and less indulgent writing. There is no great divide between news and features. Best to think of it all as reporting.

We do not have to go all the way with Randall in blurring the distinction between news and features to acknowledge that the latter should be about something more than smart writing. If feature writers are reporters too, that means getting the basics right: checking facts, words and spellings and attributing sources. That's good journalism.

Turning research into copy

Whereas news stories tend to follow a rather formulaic approach – pushing the crucial points up front into the intro, then assembling the remaining information in diminishing order of importance – features have a far greater variety of styles. Features may have fewer hard and fast rules but Melvin Mencher (2003: 194) offers the following suggestions:

- Show people doing things.
- Let them talk.
- Underwrite: let the action and the dialogue carry the piece.
- Keep the piece moving.

If you bear that in mind as you write your feature – and as you read it back to yourself, more of which below – you won't go far wrong.

Journalists working on features often have greater freedom to experiment and to introduce their own voice and experiences into the piece, but only up to a point. Just as a hired gunslinger shoots whom he is paid to shoot, feature writers learn to write what their editor wants. Experienced journalist Chris Wheal points out that feature writing, even for a freelance, 'does not mean writing in your own unique style'. Rather, it means 'writing in the style the editor wants, to the deadline the editor sets, using the contacts the editor approves of and coming to the conclusion the editor is happy to publish'.

Even within such constraints, however, features typically give journalists the opportunity to get stuck in to a topic. As Richard Keeble (2001: 194) notes, features 'tend to contain more comment, analysis, colour, background and a greater diversity of sources than news stories and explore a larger number of issues at greater depth'. The idea of creating all that from the jumble of notes gathered while researching the subject might seem rather daunting at first, but the more you do it the better you will get at it. As Randall (2000: 141) explains:

[The] way you progress and develop whatever talent you have is to write hundreds and hundreds of stories and make mistakes. You leave vital things out and put irrelevancies in, write half the piece, then realise it is going wrong and have to start again, write clumsily, pompously or stiffly, turn in work that is confusing or trite, and commit to paper or screen whole paragraphs so silly that if you had to speak them, your voice would trail off in embarrassment mid-sentence. Now for the good news. After a while, by hanging around a good newspaper and listening, by reading, studying the good and the bad and being your own sharpest critic, you begin to see a way. There will still be times when you take a long time to get a story to work, but by and large, the more you write, the more fluently you write.

Getting started

Once you have done your research and established what the focus of the story is, and how you are going to tell it, the rest should begin to fall into place. Sally Adams (1999: 74) suggests that, before you start writing, you ask yourself the following questions.

- What's the most startling fact you have discovered?
- What's the best anecdote unearthed?
- What's the most astonishing quote?
- What's the most surprising event?
- What's the item with the greatest 'Hey, did you know that?' factor?

The answers should suggest an appropriate way in to the feature. There will be many potential entry points. For example, each year for the past decade I have been commissioned to write a feature about house prices for a glossy local lifestyle magazine. It is not really a subject to set my heart racing with excitement and the brief is the same every year: say something (anything) about trends in the local property market and accompany it with a chart showing examples of what you can get with your money.

A flick through the cuttings suggests some of the different ways of entering what is essentially the same subject. First, there was a focus on the elusive 'feel-good factor' that affected house prices, with an intro based on Chancellor Kenneth Clarke's oft-repeated promise that the property market of the mid-1990s was about to recover. Then there was a focus on the recovery itself, with an intro about the housing market having turned more corners than Theseus in the Labyrinth (geddit?). Another focus was the developing trend towards city-centre living, with an intro about one of the leading estate agents receiving lots of funny looks when he first suggested the city centre as a residential location.

There was the one focusing on the way tiny back-to-back houses were being snapped up by singleton young professionals that allowed me to construct an intro recalling a scene in an old Alan Bennett play about the last back-to-back home being preserved in a museum (with Mam and Dad still living in it, of course). Several features focused on particular locations or housing developments, including one on the site of a demolished block of flats that had once been the scene of a TV sitcom starring Diana Dors, and there were also 'progress report' style pieces with intros based on the opinions of house buyers or estate agents. A more recent focus was on the difficulties facing first-time buyers in 2004 with an intro blaming it all on former Prime Minister Margaret Thatcher (well, it was the twenty-fifth anniversary of her coming to power).

My brief was specific in that the features had to be a certain length, cover the local property market, include an updated guide to prices and conform to the house style. But the brief was relaxed in that I was not expected to follow a particular line or interview certain people 'suggested' by the editor. When writing up your feature, though, you should refer back to the brief agreed with your editor. If your subsequent research has suggested an angle significantly different from the brief, then it would be better to check if the new approach is acceptable before investing too much time in writing something that will not be used.

Structuring your feature

Good features have a beginning, a middle and an end. Features should also have a theme, an idea, something to say. And, as indicated above, a focus. The focus might be on an individual – looking at events through their eyes – or on a group, a community, an event, a location, something, anything. Deciding on a focus should make it easier to think of an intro, although sometimes it works the other way around.

The intro

The feature intro, also known as the lead, is a slippery customer compared with its more straightforward hard news counterpart. There are many different styles of intro and the main consideration is, what works? The intro might draw us in, intrigue us, startle us, tease us, it might even bash us around the head. The single most important function of the intro is to make the reader want to read on. In the process, the intro might make it clear what the article is about. But, then again, it might not. If you go through as many newspapers and magazines as you can, paying particular attention to feature intros, you will get some idea of the variety of possible approaches. You will also see how frequently the intro will focus on something very specific – a comment, a look, a thought, a phone call, a memory, a journey, an arrival, a view – some tiny detail that paints the little rather than the big picture.

Although features tend to be longer than news stories, it does not necessarily follow that a feature has to be one long chunk of text. Sometimes that will be appropriate but the subject might also lend itself to being broken into several related articles, possibly giving different people's perspectives or telling specific stories. Other structural devices worth considering are:

- fact boxes summarising key points
- lists or charts that may illustrate part of the story
- chronologies to help the reader understand at a glance what happened when
- quote boxes to summarise who says what in an entertaining and easily digestible way

sidebars short stories
printed alongside
longer article providing
additional, contrasting
or late-breaking items.

● boxes or **sidebars** containing expert advice on the issue or details of where to get further information.

Look and learn how these and other techniques are used in various newspapers and magazines and think about what might be appropriate for your feature.

The substance of the piece

The content and structure of a feature will vary depending on the subject matter, style of the publication, perceived interests of the readers, intentions of the writer and on the time and energy available for research. But, just as a top-class cook cannot make a great dish from poor-quality raw materials, even a brilliant writer needs the right ingredients to create a satisfying feature article. Features typically comprise some or all of the following:

● facts
● quotes
● description
● anecdotes
● opinions
● analysis.

The above should not be thought of as discrete elements as they often overlap. Facts, for example, may be included within description or analysis, while direct quotes may be used to give opinions or to tell anecdotes. As Tolstoy explained, commenting on *War and Peace:* 'I don't tell; I don't explain. I show; I let my characters talk for me' (cited in Mencher 2003: 155). If we take the above elements in turn, we will see what he means.

Facts

Facts are an essential ingredient of journalism and features are no exception. Facts will distinguish your work from that of the fiction writer and the bar-room philosopher alike. Different subjects lend themselves to different treatments. When you have a large number of facts to include (prices, percentages, sales, dates, chemicals, results, rulings, whatever) you may wish to make the feature more readable by including them at appropriate points throughout the text rather than in indigestible chunks. Alternatively, you might consider creating a separate fact box.

Quotes

Quotes can bring writing to life by injecting authority, drama or powerful expression into the piece, thereby allowing your characters to talk for you. Think carefully which bits of your research to quote and which bits to translate into your own words, as the simple facts of a story do not normally need to be told through direct quotes.

Profiles of individuals usually contain a greater number of quotes, helping us glean something of the subject's voice and character.

Description

Good feature writers take a leaf out of Tolstoy's book and aim to show rather than tell. That means description. Let the reader see what you are seeing, hear what you are hearing and smell what you are smelling – with specific details rather than vague generalisations – and you will make your story come alive.

Anecdotes

Anecdotes are stories – in our context, they are stories within stories. They may amuse, entertain, inform or even shock. Anecdotes can help us understand how people felt or reacted at a particular time, tell us something about the human condition and, by revealing a succession of small pictures painted in sufficient detail, they can help show the larger canvas. Not least among your considerations, interesting anecdotes may also keep somebody reading.

Opinions

Features usually contain more opinion than do news articles, often from a greater variety of sources that go well beyond the traditional 'both sides' of a story. Some publications will expect you to include your own opinion, others certainly will not. Again, study the style of the newspaper or magazine before you submit.

Analysis

It may be appropriate to go beyond reporting opinions to include some analysis or a range of different analyses. This may be provided by experts who have conducted relevant research but it may also be provided by 'ordinary' people with direct knowledge or involvement. As with opinion, some editors may expect your feature to offer your own analysis of a topic and others will not, so make sure you know what is required. Either way, the purpose of analysis is to take journalism beyond simple reportage, beyond showing us what is going on to help us understand it.

Pay-off

And then there's the ending, known as the 'pay-off' because it rewards the reader for sticking with you. Whereas news stories often end on one of the least important pieces of information – and can frequently be cut from the bottom without losing anything vital – features tend to have a more rounded ending. This can take the form of a summary, twist, quote or a return to the scene of the intro. Most importantly, the ending should not give the impression the writer has run out of steam or, even worse, lost interest.

Doing it in style

Experienced journalists cannot stress often enough that, as freelance Andrew Bibby says, 'you must know the publication you're writing for'. He means *really* know it. Feature writer Helen Carroll agrees: 'Really familiarise yourself with the style by reading lots of features in that newspaper or magazine, and then write it in the appropriate style. Don't overwrite.' Here are some useful questions on style:

- Does the newspaper or magazine tend to run features in present tense or past tense?
- Can you say 'I'?
- Does it favour a self-deprecating style of writing, more of a know-it-all tone, or neither?
- Will you need to explain some basics to readers or can you take them as read?
- Should the paragraphs all be short – and how short?
- For quotes, do they like you to name the speaker before or after the quote, or in the middle?
- Should you cap up Internet or not?
- How do they abbreviate Councillor – Coun or Cllr?

If you are writing for a publication that produces its own style guide – the *Guardian*, *The Times* and *The Economist* all publish theirs as books – you will find most such answers (plus many more) contained within. In addition, you must read and absorb the newspaper or magazine itself.

Familiarising yourself with a publication's style does not mean copying its existing feature writers. You are not a robot and you should find your own voice. But editors will expect you to use a language and style appropriate to the publication, its readers and to the subject matter.

The substance of the feature – that is, the results of your research including interviews – must be woven into a readable whole. The finished product has also been likened to a mosaic. To deconstruct this process, take a feature from your target publication and go through it to identify and analyse the different elements outlined earlier – intro, facts, quotes, description, anecdotes, opinion, analysis, pay-off. Then note how one point is made to refer to another by the use of linking words and phrases (transitions). Highlight or circle such transitions – which can be as simple as 'and', 'but' or 'also' – and note how they are used to make the feature flow smoothly. As Mencher (2003: 169) points out: 'Transitions are the mortar that holds the story together so that the story is a single unit.' Without that mortar, the feature will collapse into a mere heap of words.

Reading it through

You must read your copy to check your English; you cannot rely on a computer spell-checker which will not know if you want to check, cheque or even Czech your spelling. Too many people seem to think that using a dictionary while writing is beneath them, rather like using an indicator while driving. Say it loud: I use a dictionary and I'm proud.

Checking should go beyond spellings and misplaced apostrophes, though. Feature writer Debbie Cenziper (cited in Mencher 2003: 210) always reads her features three times before submitting them:

- First, to check the rhythm and flow of the story.
- Second, to check if she has been fair to the people interviewed or written about.
- Third, to check all the facts.

This highlights that it is useful to look for different things when you read your work through. I read my features many more than three times during the writing process and I invariably find something that can be improved or removed. I also find it useful, when time permits, to get somebody else to read my copy. Not necessarily another journalist – in fact, preferably *not* a journalist – but somebody who can genuinely approach it as a reader and who will give you some honest feedback. You may complain that they fell asleep after two pages or that they misunderstood your clever prose but, if they did, then the chances are that other readers will respond in a similar way.

Always keep in mind you are writing not for yourself, nor for other journalists but for your readers. As Sally Adams (1999: 71) emphasises:

> The best way to ensure a feature flows smoothly from start to finish is to turn yourself into the reader and, while writing, to keep going back to the top and reading it right through to yourself – as though for the first time – to check that nothing is ambiguous or mystifying, that sentences are not too long and that the rhythm is right. To do this, you should sound the words, albeit silently, in your head. And re-read not just once or twice, but every time you pause, whether it's to check a fact, answer the phone or stare out of the window.

So, an awful lot of work can go into making a feature effortless to read, but that is no excuse to deliver your work late. The secret of a long and successful career is simple, according to freelance Christine Morgan (cited in Roberts 2004): 'Always deliver what they want, stick to the brief and never miss a deadline.'

Improving your writing

Having delivered your copy on time you may have thought that was that. And it may be. But don't be surprised if the features editor comes back to you with a query or a suggestion for changing the piece in some way. Such after-sales care is all part of the service and the process can be useful if you go into it with an open mind. Similarly, when your feature appears in print, read the published version and note what changes, for good or ill, have been made to your copy by the subs.

Chris Wheal offers the following advice for improving your feature writing skills: 'Get a job, get paid to write to someone else's rules. Move jobs and learn to write to another editor's rules. Go on as many training courses as you can and especially ones where your copy is ripped apart by more experienced journalists or even your peers. Take all the criticisms seriously and try to learn from them.'

The more experience you gain, the more you will be able to criticise your own and others' work. Never forget that you can improve your journalism not only by writing as much as possible but also by reading widely. Read as many articles as you can – different styles, different publications, alternative media, overseas newspapers – and absorb, critique and engage with them. Before long *you* might be the one to whom others turn and ask: 'How do I get started with this feature?'

Further reading

Adams (1999) and Keeble (2001) both usefully deconstruct a number of feature articles. Randall (2000) emphasises the importance of, and gives advice on, good reporting and good writing. For a US perspective on features as well as news, see Mencher (2003). Harcup (2004) includes a discussion of the principles and practice of feature writing, with plenty of examples of intros and more, as well as a style guide. Detailed help with spelling and grammar can be found in Evans (2000) and Hicks (1998) while Truss (2003) provides an entertaining romp through the vagaries of punctuation.

Acknowledgement

All quotes from Andrew Bibby, Helen Carroll and Chris Wheal are taken from interviews with the author, for which many thanks. Thanks also to Bethany Bolton and Terry Wragg who read a draft of this chapter.

References

Adams, S. (1999) 'Writing Features', in W. Hicks with S. Adams and H. Gilbert, *Writing for Journalists*, London: Routledge, pp. 47–98.

Evans, H. (2000) *Essential English for Journalists, Editors and Writers*, London: Pimlico.

Harcup, T. (2004) *Journalism: Principles and Practice*, London: Sage.

Hicks, W. (1998) *English for Journalists*, London: Routledge.

Keeble, R. (2005) *The Newspapers Handbook*, 4th edn, London: Routledge.

Mencher, M. (2003) *News Reporting and Writing*, New York: McGraw Hill.

Randall, D. (2000) *The Universal Journalist*, London: Pluto.

Roberts, D. (2004) 'The Knights' Tales', *Press Gazette* 21 May: 18–19.

Truss, L. (2003) *Eats, Shoots & Leaves: The Zero Tolerance Approach to Punctuation*, London: Profile.

Facing the challenge of
feature editing

13

Facing the challenge of feature editing

Tim Holmes

In an ideal world no feature should need editing. The commissioning brief would have been so clear, the writer so able, the production planning so exemplary that exactly the right number of words, written in exactly the right tone, covering exactly the right ground would have been delivered on time, to fit exactly into the layout, which would fit exactly into the overall scheme of that issue.

Now, from the list above, spot all the things that can go wrong. If it's only one or two, it will probably be OK; if it's more there will be trouble. Rather than trying to shut the sub's table door after the copy has bolted, it is easier to regard the process of editing a feature as something that starts long before the first keystroke is made. Feature editing can thus be divided into three major subsections: pre-copy, copy and post-copy (a useful fourth addition to the process is post-issue). The frequency and production schedules will vary enormously (daily, weekly, monthly, quarterly) but the principles are standard.

PRE-COPY EDITING

Planning

Planning is not just something that happens. It must, in fact, be a regular part of any publication's schedule. This is stating the obvious but planning must not be left only to the editor and executives or section heads; it must work its way down so that even **casuals** are clued in to what is going on.

casual journalist employed by newspaper/magazine on a temporary basis. Since it is cheaper for employers, numbers are growing.

Flexibility is an important element. Print publishing is a fast-moving environment and when a major story breaks a newspaper's plan can be turned on its head in an instant. In these circumstances the organisation which a good planning structure provides should mean that everyone can be kept informed of developments.

On a newspaper, features are as likely to be changed as anything else, but there may be sections which are unaffected by the news agenda, although really big stories may take pages from everywhere. It is quite common for gardening, motoring, property and suchlike to be printed in sections that go to press before the main body of the newspaper, and only an event on the scale of 9/11 will affect them.

Magazines, with the exception of news weeklies (and news-influenced weeklies such as the latest generation of women's magazines like *Closer*), enjoy a much more stable production period, although editorial pages may appear or disappear with the fortunes of the advertising sales department.

The issue

Features should be carefully planned for every issue of a publication. Often such planning will reflect a specific theme (say, Being European), a time of year (spring), an annual occurrence (Remembrance Sunday), a climactic event (World Cup final), or any number of awareness days, weeks or months.

A good place to locate suitable themes is a well-kept diary from which it will be possible to predict everything from National No Smoking Week to the final day of the Olympic Games, along with any specific local occurrences, events or commemorations. Luxuriously appointed publications may have someone (or a department) whose job it is to maintain such a diary and feed the various departments with relevant snippets; less well-endowed titles will have to rely on someone adding this responsibility to their other tasks.

Finding a topical theme is only the beginning. It may well give you a subject for features which impart a timely feeling to the publication (one indicator of good journalism) but there are a lot more decisions to make.

Pre-production

How long will the feature be? How will it be presented? What illustrations will it have? Some of these questions may already have answers. If all features in your publication run to 800 words, are laid out over three columns on a right-hand page with one photograph and a **pull quote** there's nothing more to be said. On the other hand, perhaps you just hand the copy over to the art editor or a layout sub and it will magically appear on a finished page.

> pull quote short extract from news or feature set in larger type as part of page design.

It is much better for the features editor to be more involved in the full creative process. A feature is not like news. It is a form which asks the reader to make more of a commitment, and it is a good idea to make every feature as inviting as possible. The days of newspapers and magazines being able to hand down information or instruction to a band of devoted readers with time to spare before getting dressed for dinner disappeared more than 100 years ago. Research by publishing companies shows that readers are becoming increasingly fickle about what they read and what commitment they are prepared to make, even to magazines and newspapers they enjoy.

Most readers want information to be delivered quickly and efficiently. In magazine features this often manifests itself in lists, bullet points and summarising box-outs. One of the extra dimensions British editors have brought to American magazines (for example, Ed Needham at *Rolling Stone*) is a snappier approach to the presentation of feature material. This does not always go down well in a culture used to long articles but it is a practice of which everyone involved in features should be aware.

Even *Word* magazine, which was founded at least partly on the editorial team's increasing disillusion with the **soundbite** culture of current periodical publishing (the magazine's original strapline was: 'At last, something to read'), uses a mix-and-match variety of presentational formats. Long, conventionally written and structured prose articles sit alongside list-type how-tos or encyclopedia-style glossaries of modern life.

> soundbite short, pithy quote used by journalists. First coined by US radio and television journalists in the late 1960s.

It pays the features editor, therefore, to have considered the format of any given article before it has been written. It is your job to bring readers to the table and once there to encourage them to stick around for your all-you-can-eat buffet.

Here it is worth restating the point that 'writing' and 'journalism' are not synonymous. Some magazines (Condé Nast's *Traveller*, for example) may hire writers to undertake an assignment for them (let's say sending Louis de Bernières to explore the Greek islands). In this case the author and the subject matter will be somehow matched and the magazine will, all being well, get a characteristically written essay from a famous name.

Most journalism is not like that. A features editor (or commissioning editor) will hire a journalist to fulfil a specific brief and that brief can be very tight. Obvious inclusions are the length and the deadline, but you can specify the format, the tone of voice and the breadth of coverage.

Picking a writer

Having worked out the form and format, the editor should be able to match commission to writer. Sometimes this will be the nearest available body, in which case the briefing document needs to be especially detailed, but on other occasions the features editor may be able to consult his or her contacts book for details of free-lances and their specialities, strengths and weaknesses. There is nothing underhand in this; some people are better at doing X than Y and it is as wasteful as it is pointless to get a superbly gifted prose stylist to compile a bulleted list of the twenty best diet tips.

This is one reason why it is so difficult for a new freelance to get a break. The people with commissions to offer want to make their working lives as smooth as possible and taking on an untried contributor adds an element of risk. On the other hand, always farming stuff out to old So-and-so risks getting the publication into a rut. If there is one thing readers like less than innovation for its own sake (or sometimes just any innovation at all) it is complete predictability. The moral is that features editors should be prepared to take the occasional risk if they want to bring new blood into their pages.

Commissioning brief

The commissioning brief can be as informal as a shout across the office or as formal as a closely written guide to the format, style, tone and content of the piece. The first option has the advantage of immediacy and simplicity of execution and the drawback of radical misunderstanding; the second has the disadvantages of taking some time to draw up and possibly offending the writer, but the advantage of clear criteria.

Any given editor's position on the scale of uptightness will depend principally on the individual's personality, experience and relationship with the journalist being commissioned. Variables in human nature make it difficult for a features editor, especially someone new to a job, to know how and where to pitch requests. Advice which has lasted down the ages – for better or worse – is to make your presence felt strongly to start with and then ease up. But no matter how a brief is pitched, it *must* include the following parameters:

- the topic
- the particular angle (this can be discussed or even defined with the writer)
- points which definitely must be covered
- points which should be omitted (if any)
- special people to contact (if any)
- whether you need pictures supplied or sourced (for example, portraits or snapshots for human interest stories)
- the overall length
- the format
- the tone of voice
- illustration or photographic requirements
- the deadline
- what to do in an emergency.

The contributor, especially if freelance, will probably have a list of questions too. These may include the rate of pay, claimable expenses (telephone calls, travel), kill fee (the payment, even if the piece is not used), settlement date and clarification of who will own the copyright. You need to know your company's policy on all these matters plus syndication, international rights and digital reproduction.

HANDLING COPY

Hurrah! The copy has come, it's on time and it looks about the right length. Now the editing work can begin in earnest. This stage of the process can be divided into checking that the feature:

- deals with the right topic from the right angle
- is the right length
- uses the right style
- will make sense to your publication's readers
- is as readable as possible
- is totally accurate
- contains no legal problems.

These checks can be made in three sweeps – an initial read-through, correcting the copy, then blending the copy into the layout. On a daily newspaper all three processes might have to be undertaken more or less simultaneously, while a monthly magazine's production schedule should allow more time.

Right topic, right angle

First, make sure the subject has been dealt with as requested. The features editor must have a sound grasp of what the commission was and how this feature is planned to fit into the issue as a whole. This is the basis on which to make judgments about quality and appropriateness.

If the brief has not been followed, you can be angry but that will not get you very far; you can decide there and then never to use that writer again, but that does not fill your page. So you must quickly see whether the piece is salvageable or whether you must pull a rabbit out of the hat. If the writer has taken completely the wrong tack life becomes more difficult, but mistakes in formatting (you asked for a paragraphed list, you get continuous prose) may be easier to resolve.

Right length

pagination
arrangement and
number of pages in
publication.

In some desperate circumstances this may be the only thing you care about. Perhaps it should be first on this list, but plans and **paginations** change, so even if the writer has delivered the right number of words it may now be necessary to cut or add material. Your initial negotiations with the writer may have covered this possibility; if they didn't, be prepared to haggle again.

Right style

Style is one of journalism's slippery words. On the one hand it means 'house style' and on the other it means 'writing style'. The features editor has to deal with both. Magazines and newspapers have house styles to keep the use of language consistent. A comprehensive guide will cover matters large and small; from whether to use 'meter' or 'metre, to 'the subtle distinctions between . . . modal verbs' (*Guardian* Style Guide: M) Having a firm grasp of your publication's style for alternate spellings, usage and points of punctuation is essential for fast and accurate editing.

Then there is the writer's style. Perhaps you picked someone for their brand of prose, in which case you probably got what you asked for. But perhaps your brief specified a light-hearted, casual tone and what has been delivered is dark and gloomy. Perhaps you particularly requested a jargon-free piece and it has come in full of incomprehensible terms. Do you run with what you have, or do you change it?

There is no simple answer. It will depend on how much time is available, your relationship with the writer and other factors. The point is that you have to decide quickly.

Right for your readers

demographics
specific characteristics.

Heat and the *Spectator* are both weeklies, excellent in their fields. But a feature written for one would stick out a mile in the other, not just because of the subject matter but also because of the tone and style of writing. The **demographics** of the respective readerships are miles apart and even if they overlapped, most readers would not want the magazines to converge.

To revert to the previous point about style, how can you know if the writer has used too much jargon or not explained something clearly enough? The answer lies in your understanding of the readership and how much grounding they are likely to have in a subject. Without that knowledge you cannot decide whether copy needs to be mildly cleared up or radically overhauled.

Reads right

Why has *Eats, Shoots & Leaves* been such a success? Grammarians have been banging on about declining standards of punctuation for decades but somehow Lynne Truss (2003) hit the right nerve at the right time. Perhaps people have always wanted to know how to use a comma properly but have been put off by formal textbooks; perhaps the whole phenomenon is a repeat of Stephen Hawking's *A Brief History of Time*, the most widely bought and least widely read science book ever.

One of the reasons may be that readers can tell something is not well written but lack the analytical ability to say why. The majority will not have been taught how to punctuate or spell, how to construct sentences or build paragraphs and pre-Truss may not even have known that they did not know. Punctuation is an extremely important factor in determining the readability of a piece of writing, but it is far from the only one. If it is important for an editor to be able to recognise good writing, it is even more important to be able to see the problems with poor writing and most important of all to know how to fix them.

Often, the readability of a feature comes down to three major elements – the overall structure, the flow within the structure and the format.

Structure

A poorly structured feature will never work properly. An editor faced with this problem has four possible courses of action:

1. Give the work back to the writer with some very specific advice (pro: less work for the editor; con: writer may feel highly insecure).
2. Do a complete rewrite (pro: editor gets the desired result; con: lots more work).
3. Farm out a rewrite in house (pro: less work but more immediate control; con: writer may object forcibly).
4. Scrap the feature and replace it with something else (pro: may be less hassle in the short term; con: will almost certainly be more hassle in the long run). (For standard advice on structure see Hay 1990: Chapter 6.)

Flow

Getting a feature to flow well is more of a technical skill, and it really is one which any half-decent writer should have the hang of. Nevertheless, if an editor finds that copy has a sound structure but tends to bump along, bringing the reader up short time and again it is probably the way in which paragraphs have been linked.

Although it is the soundest of advice that a paragraph should contain a single unit of thought (see, for example, Strunk and White 1999: Chapter 3), creating a satisfying read depends on those units flowing from one thought to the next. At the very least, follow Sally Adams's advice (1999: 72) and 'try to ensure the first sentence of each paragraph gives some clue to what the par's about'.

Format

Structure has been the backbone of the traditional continuous prose feature but format has become increasingly important over the past few years. As stated earlier, readers appear less willing to sift through copy to find information and if a feature, or a series of features, does not seem to be working, the editor should think about overall presentation.

Getting it right

Like 'style', 'accuracy' covers a large amount of ground. There is the basic accuracy of factual correctness. You might have used this writer precisely because of his or her knowledge of the subject, in which case a certain amount of trust is needed; if you are not familiar with the finer details of quantum mechanics you will have to rely on the writer.

There is accuracy of language as dealt with above. If there are names that you recognise are they accurately and correctly spelt? If you do not recognise them, do you need to check them and if so how? The same goes for more general information. If you have doubts about something, do not assume the writer is correct, check. A good set of reference books should be part of every editor's armoury (see Hicks and Holmes 2002: 153).

Much can be checked online but remember that in cyberspace there is probably more dis- and misinformation than anything else. The trick is to find and verify information quickly. Books like *The Internet Handbook for Writers, Researchers and Journalists* by Mary McGuire et al. (2000) or Randy Reddick and Elliot King's *The Online Journ@list* (2001) are useful guides.

Legally right

standfirst text intended to be read between headline and story which can elaborate on point made in headline, add new one or raise questions which will be answered in story (a teaser). Sometimes contains byline. Helps provide reader with a 'guiding hand' into reading large slice of copy – thus mainly used for features and occasionally long news stories. Also known as the 'sell'.

Every journalist should be aware of the legal rights and duties imposed on the media, but a features editor must know more about the law than the writers he or she commissions. An editor can land a publication in hot water by not picking up allegations in copy or by changing copy so it becomes defamatory. Editors involved in production can create libellous headlines, **standfirsts**, or even captions.

The editor should, however, have ready access to legal opinion. There should be someone to call or consult before publishing a contentious feature, or after receiving a threat of action. The size of operation has nothing to do with it – any publication, even the smallest hobby magazine, can find itself on the wrong end of a legal action. Even more than knowing the law, therefore, the features editor should know where and how to seek advice.

It is characteristic of English and Scottish laws to evolve with judgments (privacy laws are a particular case in point) and the features editor is well advised to keep abreast of developments.

Copy correcting

If your first read-through was just for sense, now is the time to check and correct. A disastrous piece will be evident very quickly, but the second reading can be used to highlight areas to look into or which need minor repairs. This is where a slight element of ethics enters into consideration, namely, the rights of the author.

Most journalists are aware of and comfortable with the pact they enter when they submit a piece. When copy goes into the editing process it becomes, by and large, subject to the needs of the publication as a whole. Cuts, even major cuts as long as they maintain sense, are probably OK, especially if the writer will get paid for the amount commissioned rather than the amount used. There may be grumbles, but it's all part of the game.

Things get more tricky when it comes to rewriting, however, and the features editor needs to make some hard decisions. Do you negotiate with the writer over this or just do it? The course of action taken will depend largely on your relationship (or your contract) with the writer.

Some publications, specialist magazines particularly, rely on contributors with expertise and high-level contacts but who are not necessarily good writers. Often they will submit copy which contains real insights or exclusive interviews but which is almost impossible to read. The features editor should establish right from the start that the copy will be rewritten but the writer's intentions and material will be respected.

Generally, this kind of situation settles down to a kind of symbiosis and it is not unknown for such contributors to be grateful for the final results – especially if they go on to win awards or sell their work in other markets. There will always, unfortunately, be writers who cavil over every cut or improvement and there is not much the features editor can do except bear it or find another contributor.

Whatever such writers believe, editors do not change copy for no reason, or at least they should not. Basic correction of factual error, spelling or grammar are easy to explain but it may be harder to justify altering a feature's format or structure. Instead of asking 'Why not change this?', make your guiding question 'Why change this?'. But if you make a change for sound and necessary reasons, stand up for yourself if the writer makes a fuss.

POST-COPY

Once the copy has been processed and passed to layout, further changes may still be necessary.

Fitting to layout

Assuming there has been a good level of collaboration between editorial and art departments and if everything goes as planned, it should only be necessary to make very small changes once a feature has been laid out. This might come down to adding or subtracting a line or two, or getting widows to turn (see Hicks and Holmes 2002: Chapters 5 and 9).

If the pagination has undergone a major revision, the situation may call for more radical surgery. And you may have to return to negotiating with the writer.

New elements

Maybe the feature looks a bit bare; maybe the subject needs more explanation than originally envisaged; perhaps the art editor just wants to break things up a bit. Usually this means sidebars and box-outs – and more decisions. Can you derive the data from the main copy without cannibalising it, will you have to do more research or will you ask the writer to provide new copy?

pix   journalese for pictures/photographs (singular: pic).

And don't forget captions. If the contributor has provided original **pix**, make sure you know exactly what and whom they show.

Post-issue

The features editor's role should not end when the issue goes to print. An important part of the whole process is to analyse the results, swiftly if needs be but as carefully as possible. Examine whether each feature works, both in itself and within the overall scheme. See what could have been better or different, and try to take lessons on for the next round of work.

References

Adams, S. (1999) 'Writing Features', in W. Hicks with S. Adams and H. Gilbert (eds), *Writing for Journalists*, London: Routledge: 47–98.

Guardian (2004) *Guardian Style Guide*. Available online at <http://www.guardian. co.uk/styleguide>, accessed 5 August 2004.

Hay, V. (1990) *The Essential Feature*, New York: Columbia University Press.

Hicks, W. and T. Holmes (2002) *Subediting for Journalists*, London: Routledge.

McGuire M. et al. (2000) *The Internet Handbook for Writers, Researchers and Journalists*, London: Guilford Press.

Reddick, R. and King, E. (2001) *The Online Journ@list: Using the Internet and Other Electronic Resources*, 3rd edn, Fort Worth, Texas: Harcourt College Publishers.

Strunk Jr., W. and E.B. White (1999) *The Elements of Style*, 4th edn, London: Longmans.

Truss, L. (2003) *Eats, Shoots & Leaves: The Zero Toleration Approach to Punctuation*, London: Profile Books.

Creating identities, building communities

14

Why comment?

Creating identities, building communities

Why comment?

Tim Holmes

There is only one First Rule of Journalism. Giles Coren (son of a journalist, brother of a journalist) pointed out in *The Times* (26 June 2004: 27) that no matter how many different pieces of advice the tiro is given by his or her elders and betters, each one is the First Rule of Journalism. There is no Second Rule, probably because it would contradict the first; journalism is not the most consistent of occupations.

For similar reasons, it is only possible to have one Revealing Quote about journalism at a time. Nicholas Tomalin's apophthegm about rat-like cunning and literary ability is an example, but is it supported or contradicted by Cyril Connolly's observation that 'Literature is the art of writing something that will be read twice; journalism what will be read once'? Or Oscar Wilde's 'But what is the difference between literature and journalism? Journalism is unreadable and literature is not read. That is all'?

For the purpose of analysing journalistic comment and opinion, however, one Revealing Quote stands head and shoulders above the rest. It is C.P. Scott's much-repeated dictum that 'Comment is free, but facts are sacred', along with its not so frequently seen rider: 'The voice of opponents no less than that of friends has a right to be heard.' But if we take Scott's Revealing Quote and apply it in reverse, perhaps we can begin to see why comment and opinion pieces are important for newspapers and magazines: 'Facts are sacred but comment is free. The voice of friends much more than that of opponents has a right to be heard.'

If facts truly are sacred, then they are serious and not to be taken light-heartedly. A journalist faithfully following Scott's words would balance every story, counter-weight every point in favour of a certain position with an equally convincing point against. In a culture used to more rough and tumble in its print media this would lead to an unaccustomed blandness. A totally unopinionated publication would be a turn-off for readers and a nightmare for proprietors in the commercial world of sales figures, advertising rates, the **Drudge Report** and **Popbitch**.

So that doesn't happen. Newspapers, magazines and web sites all thrive on building communities, and communities cluster around attitudes and points of view, prejudices and preferences. Among the more established and 'respectable' publications, C.P. Scott's words are acknowledged as an ideal, nods are made in their direction with the inclusion of contrary points of view, quotes which express opposition, but for all that any publication's standpoint can quickly be ascertained – there is often a long history of support for one political leaning or another, and the selection and presentation of news is more than a giveaway.

Drudge Report US gossip web site run by Matt Drudge which controversially first exposed the President Clinton/Monica Lewinsky scandal in January 1998.

Popbitch www.popbitch.com web site focusing on satirical celebrity gossip.

But if you really want to know where a publication's heart lies, look at the columns of comment and opinion. Because of that vestige of respect for ideals of fairness and balance expressed by Scott, these are the places where newspapers and magazines can let rip.

Comment pieces must be easy to identify and publications have developed a number of conventions to assist the search. Among these, newspapers may run pages which are literally headed 'Comment'; anything in a section containing the word 'Review' can be assumed to be largely opinion based; magazines and newspapers clearly attribute columns of opinion to particular writers, usually with a photograph of the author to reinforce and authenticate the point.

In newspapers these pages tend to be clustered around the letters and editorial sections – which is entirely appropriate as both are pure opinion, one the official voice of the reader (as mediated by editorial staff), the other the official voice of the paper. Some papers, such as the *Financial Times*, also run clearly identified comment or opinion pieces next to news items. The intention is to aid interpretation, but it is interpretation within the context of the paper's standpoint.

Magazines often aggregate opinion columns (including the editor's letter) at the front end, although there is frequently a column as the last page of each issue. Thus no matter which end a reader (or potential reader) starts flicking through there is material to establish the tone of the title.

The five purposes of comment

Comment, as an editorial category, cannot be pinned down to a single definition beyond the fact that it is one person's or entity's point of view. A practical **taxonomy** of comment might include the following categories, each of which has its own rationale:

taxonomy breakdown of an issue into groups, categories or listings.

1. community building
2. commercial advantage
3. elite reinforcement of preferred message
4. oppositional viewpoint
5. unofficial extension of predominant ideology.

Community building

It is well documented that newspaper readerships have been, generally speaking, in decline for some time. Much research has gone into the reasons for this, but our concern here is what newspapers have done to try to counter it. And a major answer has been the 'magazinification' of newspapers. Media analysts have identified the increased pagination given over to features, a greater focus on personalities (either reports on or writings by), a 'feminisation' of news and the inclusion of more comment and opinion as distinguishing characteristics of this process. But this is to mistake the result for the process, the outcome for the objective – and the objective, both in theory and practice, is to build a community.

The news industry and its practitioners traditionally fight shy of anything that can be labelled 'theory', preferring to rely on time-honoured traditions and practice-based craft which is best learned on the job. Undoubtedly there is a rational basis for this since experience – in any job, and if reflected on – tends to improve performance. But this in itself helps to reinforce the point Richard Keeble has made so succinctly: 'all practice is based, consciously or unconsciously, on theory' (Keeble 1998: ix).

The identification of community has been, consciously or unconsciously, the theoretical basis of news gathering and reporting for as long as that process has existed: the fifteenth-century 'newsdealers' mentioned by Habermas (1989: 16) were servicing a community: the community of merchants and traders. Trainee journalists on local papers are instructed in the art of nursing a '**patch**', usually a local government ward, which is as close to hanging around the parish pump as it is possible to get.

patch geographic area of special interest.

So when the Thomson Foundation teaches that news serves either geographical communities or communities of interest, it is proposing a sound theory, one which would be accepted by any journalist or publisher and which has guided many journalists in developing countries.

Local newspapers (and regional magazines) have a clearly delineated geographical community to serve, but national newspapers face the problem of locating readers within much broader boundaries. The *Scotsman* may be able to get away with appealing to a specific nationality but there would not be the remotest chance of success for a paper called the *Great Briton*, or even the *Englishman*. National newspapers must look at the second element of the Thomson Foundation's theory and find a community of interest to serve, and the obvious place to look for lessons in how to do so is the periodical industry.

Ever since 1693, when John Dunton identified the market for a title aimed specifically at women (White 1970: 23), magazines have flourished on building communities around particular interests and offering particular approaches to those interests. This can be illustrated clearly by taking celebrity magazines as an example. First there was *Hello!* which offered a rather staid, reverential look at the doings of an elite social group; then there was *OK!* which extended the demographic range of those being written about and offered a more racy take on events; finally along came *Heat* which focused on pop celebrities and wrote about them in a supposedly irreverent manner.

Each magazine has its aficionados, each has extended the market sector, and they can only coexist because each has a different reader proposition. (The example above is a gross oversimplification, but contains enough truth to make the point.)

This is what national newspapers have attempted to do, with greater or lesser degrees of success. The example always trotted out is the *Daily Mail* which identified a middle-class, middle-England (and largely politically conservative and female) readership inadequately served by other papers. Under Sir David English (1971–92) and then Paul Dacre (1992–present), the *Daily Mail* has relentlessly built a community by focusing on specific political and social issues and by clever use of in-paper supplements which used tightly focused features and clear, well-targeted analysis.

Community-building comment does not have to be about weighty or 'significant' issues. Newspapers and especially their supplements and magazines are littered with columns by those with whom readers may be assumed to share socio-cultural characteristics. This might be characterised as 'stage of life' comment, with the writers chosen for their proximity to the core reader's age, class and lifestyle. Bringing up children, living in the country, finding the right house to move to, deciding where to invest an annuity are all grist to these various mills. Whether it is Phil Hogan's weekly expatiations on the trials of everyday life for a young bourgeois family in the *Observer* magazine or Jane Shilling in *The Times* mapping modern womanhood, the intention is to create a sense of identification or shared aspiration.

This will only work, of course, if the core reader the publisher seeks to attract and the actual core reader are identical. Peregrine Worsthorne identified the problems of mismatch in a piece about how the *Daily Telegraph* could restore its fortunes by (among other things) changing the columnists, many of whom, he claimed, were appointed because their political views agreed with those espoused by former proprietor Conrad Black. After noting that Black's wife Barbara Amiel ('the worst of the lot') had already gone, he continued (2004):

> But there are plenty of others, like Janet Daley and Mark Steyn, still left sending out signals quite alien to the English ear, not so much because of the views expressed but because of the strident tone adopted to express those views – tone that may go down a storm in the *Daily Mail* but sounds desperately out of tune in the *Daily Telegraph*.

Worsthorne may have a particular axe to grind (he served with distinction under the *Telegraph*'s previous owners and was sacked in 1997) but he identifies an important point: for both newspapers and magazines, the tone of the writing is as important as the content when it comes to community-building comment.

Commercial advantage

The term 'community', in this context, should not be thought to have any altruistic basis; it is a commercial concept not a social ideal. Such comment pieces as discussed above may, however, be presented within a naturalistic framework which makes them seem like everyday discourse. This renders them more powerful as a method of conveying the publication's chosen message because, as John Hartley has noted: 'The ideological productivity of naturalisation is that circumstances and meanings that are socially, historically and culturally determined (and hence open to change) are "experienced" as natural – that is, inevitable, timeless, universal, genetic (and hence unarguable)' (quoted in O'Sullivan et al. 1994: 198).

More obviously commercial are the commentators hired for their expertise – the star columnist or the notorious columnist. Because they are taken on for particular knowledge or experience, such individuals are often to be found within specialised sections of newspapers such as sport or motoring (magazines, being specialised already, would only employ experts or contrarians).

'Big' Ron Atkinson is, or was, an example of the specialised commentator. Having been a successful football manager, he found further fame as a television pundit for ITV, and as a result was taken on by the *Guardian*'s sport section to write Big Ron's Chalkboard in which he analysed and explained tactics and manoeuvres. (Of course, this adoption of a proletarian expert by a bourgeois newspaper is itself an example of the way a professed love of football has become naturalised within the bourgeoisie.)

Big Ron's reign lasted until 20 April 2004 when he voiced his entirely unmediated, racist thoughts before engaging his brain during a live television broadcast (see <http://football.guardian.co.uk/News_Story,0,1563,1200319,00.html> for details). What he said was completely at odds with the ethos of the *Guardian*'s community and he resigned, his place at the chalkboard filled by another former footballer-turned-television-broadcaster, Andy Gray, of Sky Sports.

For an example of the notorious commentator we can look at *Inside Edge*, launched in March 2004. It is a magazine aimed at the gambling community and its launch editor James Hipwell is not entirely uncontroversial himself, being one of the two City Slickers sacked from the *Daily Mirror* in February 2000 for dealing in shares they had tipped. Writing about the new magazine for the *Independent*, David Hellier noted that football journalist Rob Shepherd had just been hired to write a column. The twist was that Shepherd had recently served a fourteen-month jail sentence for violent conduct. Hellier (2004) continued: 'Patrick Hannon, a media consultant, says that *Inside Edge* needs to differentiate itself from daily newspapers and specialist publications in order to succeed. The hiring of well-known and even controversial columnists is one of the ways of doing this'.

Elite reinforcement of preferred message

What the *Sun* says, goes. Or at least it might help things along a little. 'The *Sun* Says' is that paper's strapline for its editorial column and as such carries the preferred message of the UK's best-selling newspaper. As Stephen Glover has pointed out (1999: 292): 'Even a silly leader is imbued with some significance unless it is so bone-headed as to invite derision. The *Sun* is read by 10 million people a day, and so its leaders are considered rather important.' A newspaper's leader is its consolidated opinion, it 'carries the authority of the paper' (1999: 292), and it did so just as powerfully, perhaps more so, 150 years ago. This was one of Anthony Trollope's targets in *The Warden*, published in 1855: 'One of Trollope's special dislikes was the apparently tyrannical power of the press – and *The Times* in particular – over political opinion in the country' (Trollope 1980: xvi).

Trollope disguises *The Times* lightly as the *Jupiter* and, in noting the effect upon an individual (the eponymous warden, Mr Harding) of the massed weight of the paper's opinion, he makes a point very similar to Glover's (Trollope 1980: 91):

> They say that eighty thousand copies of the *Jupiter* are sold daily, and that each copy is read by five persons at the least. Four hundred thousand readers then would hear this accusation against him; four hundred thousand hearts would swell with indignation at the griping injustice, the barefaced robbery of the warden of Barchester Hospital!

Perhaps things were different in Trollope's day but Stephen Glover, despite emphasising the importance of editorial leaders, draws on his own experience to lift the curtain on the methods of their production (1999: 289):

I had found myself writing editorials for the *Daily Telegraph* on all manner of things about which I often knew absolutely nothing [. . .] if you were asked to produce you had only a couple of hours to acquaint yourself with the latest developments in Central America, or to work out why the government was right (or, as it might be, wrong) to raise interest rates.

Contrast this with Freddie Hodgson's advice to aspirant leader writers in his classic *Modern Newspaper Practice* (1996: 75): 'The job demands a clear head, an informed background and an ability to mould a few words into a piece of incisive, persuasive prose. The writer must feel strongly about a subject to cast a special light upon it.'

Whether deeply felt or rapidly concocted, comment in the form of a newspaper editorial is precisely the opposite of what Klancher (1987: 23) identifies as the 'democratic and communal' writing found in eighteenth-century periodicals; it is, instead, 'dictatorial discourse cast down from the pulpit . . . sermonic'. Leaders (or editorials) allow a newspaper to preach from an elite position; the paper's preferred interpretation of events can be stated canonically.

It is not too far-fetched to draw parallels here with the ways in which men and women consumed newspapers in the nineteenth century. As Martyn Lyons states (1999: 320): 'When the two genders came together as readers, the woman was often in a position of tutelage to the male. In some Catholic families, women were forbidden to read the newspaper. More frequently, a male would read it aloud. This was a task which sometimes implied a moral superiority and a duty to select or censor material.'

In the hands of a magisterial columnist of this type, the reader becomes like the nineteenth-century housewife, obliged (so the writer imagines) to consume the unpalatable but redeeming truth, even if that truth is rendered in somewhat partial terms. For as John Bold declares in *The Warden:* 'What is any newspaper article but an expression of the views taken by one side?' (Trollope 1980: 204).

Oppositional viewpoint (licensed contradiction)

Sometimes, however, a newspaper may wish to be seen to encourage debate and hires columnists who are licensed to disagree with the editorial line. Culturally this establishes a tone of diversity, and commercially it hedges its bets with the readership. The publication is able to broaden the range of opinions it can express, without institutionally committing itself to a point of view.

This was exemplified clearly in the *Daily Express* during the run-up to expansion of the EU membership (1 May 2004). On 28 April the paper's front page ran screaming headlines about a new flood of immigrants about to swamp Great Britain. Meanwhile, inside Carol Sarler used her column to declare that she was not worried about the particular situation or about immigration in general.

Another great example came from the busy pen of Boris Johnson in the *Daily Telegraph* of 24 July 2003 (archived at <http//www.telegraph.co.uk/opinion/main. jhtml?xml=/opinion/2003/07/24/do2402.xml>), in which he disagreed not just with his fellow columnists but also the paper's whole editorial stance on the BBC–Gilligan affair. Used in this way, comment pieces can be a means of provoking readers into responding – writing to and thus interacting with the publication.

As Hodgson says (1996: 47): 'Feedback in the form of letters is one of the signs of the success of such a column', and even though such letters may be critical, they contribute to the fostering of a bond with the paper or magazine: if you care enough to write, you care enough. Examples of this can be found everywhere but one of the foremost practitioners of the art was Julie Burchill when she was writing for the *Guardian* magazine.

'Unofficial' extension of predominant ideology (licensed prejudice)

At its best the practice of including comment pieces allows, say, a right-wing paper to run a piece which is written from an opposing political stance, or vice versa. On the other hand, comment pieces allow a publication to run articles which express more extreme versions of its own ideology; they often give free rein to the wilder opinions which some of that publication's readers may harbour but rarely see expressed.

One thinks, for example, of Lynda Lee-Potter, whose mean and spiteful attitude to practically everything (including her criticism of Mo Mowlam, then suffering from a brain tumour, as looking like a Geordie trucker) plays to an important faction of *Daily Mail* readers – so important that she was 'believed by her employers to be a rare exception' to the rule that people do not actually buy papers for the columnists alone (Glover 1999: 295). But as Bernard Shrimsley has observed, 'columnists flourish on newspapers that flourish. And not the other way round' (Shrimsley 2003: 24; see also <http://www.bjr.org.uk/data/2003/n04_wilby.htm>).

On the other hand, if any commentator or columnist is seen to go too far for any reason, the axe can be wielded quickly but often not quietly; after all the paper needs to be seen to be taking action. This happened to John MacLeod in 2002 when the Scottish broadsheet, the *Herald*, dismissed him for writing a 'robust moral essay on the Soham murders [. . .] The duty editor loved it. The *Herald* ran the column without the slightest change. Then it sacked me'.

According to MacLeod's description of himself, he is 'a Highlander, a sincere Calvinist. My worldview was founded on Scotland's historic faith and written from my home on the isle of Harris. The column spoke for a Scotland dear to thousands'. His mistake, it seems, was to suggest that the parents of Holly Wells and Jessica Chapman might have precluded their daughters' murders by properly observing the Lord's day, keeping the girls at home. (MacLeod's side of this story can be read in full at <http://media.guardian.co.uk/mediaguardian/story,0,7558,788305,00.html>).

Sometimes comment in a newspaper can affect a media pundit's other activities. Andrew Gilligan lost his job at the BBC largely because of his departure from an agreed script for the infamous 6.07 a.m. **two-way** with John Humphrys on 29 May 2003, but his column in the *Mail on Sunday* enlarging on his doubts about Alastair Campbell's role in amending the dossier on weapons of mass destruction did not help. Chat-show host Robert Kilroy-Silk lost his television job in January 2004 because of anti-Arab comments published (twice) in his *Sunday Express* column.

two-way broadcast discussion between studio anchor/ newsreader and reporter.

Thus, like many things in journalism, comment has a double life. On the one hand it is a means of providing balance, allowing the voice of opponents to be heard and on the other a way to reinforce and deepen the readership's prejudices, making sure that friends have the final word.

A final thought: really, why comment?

Young people do not seem to like newspapers. National Readership Survey figures show that between 2002 and 2003 there was a 7.5 per cent decline in sales to the fifteen- to twenty-four-year-old demographic (Webdale 2004) and Don Tapscott may be able to say why. Tapscott is an expert on what he has called the Net-Generation (N-Gen), children who were between the ages of four and twenty-two in 1999 when he published *Growing Up Digital*. These children are the offspring of the baby boomers and what television was to their parents, so digital communications are to N-Geners.

But there has been a paradigm shift. Until now, communication has been broadcast and unidirectional, from the few to the many, hierarchical, The Voice of the Editor. But digital systems have allowed and encouraged a two-way process. Tapscott's research indicates strongly that 'For the first time ever, children are taking control of critical elements of a communications revolution' (Tapscott 1999: 182). He found children were beginning to question assumptions which had previously gone unchallenged – indeed, were technologically unchallengeable.

One of the distinguishing features of digital communication is the ability for everyone to join in a discussion on a more or less equal footing (even allowing for the new forms of hierarchy which develop). There is great diversity of opinion regarding all things and constant opportunities for participants to present their views. Tapscott sees this as leading to a generation which increasingly questions the implicit values contained in information: 'This process is contributing to the relentless breakdown of the notion of authority and experience-driven hierarchies. Increasingly, young people are the masters of the interactive environment and of their own fate in it' (Tapscott 1999: 185).

In other words, N-Geners do not want editorials, they want a chatroom, a forum, bulletin boards, the ability to blog. They do want information, but they have developed a new set of critical skills with which to evaluate data found on the Internet. Some of what Tapscott describes could be applied to any generational break – Jerry Rubin's Yippies told the children of the 1960s never to trust anyone over the age of forty – but when allied to the new means of communication it does seem to mean something more.

Information used to be scarce, and even when it got less scarce it was hard to access or drill down into; now it is not. Newspapers used to see themselves as gate-keepers or, more recently, filters, but Tapscott's N-Geners seem more than happy to search for hours, or combine in networks of trusted suppliers of information (which is pretty much what blogging is). There is no need for a Leader: they can make up their own minds; there is no need for official comment: the world is awash with it.

So, really, why comment? It's not just a waste of space, it might even be a positive turn-off for the very demographic every publication wants to attract.

References

Coren, G. (2004) 'Don't Ask Me What the Second Rule of Hackery Is', *The Times* 26 June: 27.

Glover, S. (1999) 'What Columnists Are Good For', in *Secrets of the Press: Journalists on Journalism*, London: Penguin: 289–98.

Habermas, J. (1989) *The Structural Transformation of the Public Sphere: An Inquiry into a Category of Bourgeois Society*, trans. Thomas Burger, Cambridge: Polity Press.

Hellier, D. (2004) 'Been Inside? You're Hired', *Independent Review*, 18 May: 11.

Hodgson, F.W. (1996) *Modern Newspaper Practice: A Primer on the Press*, 4th edn, Oxford: Focal Press.

Keeble, R. (1998) *The Newspapers Handbook*, 2nd edn, London: Routledge.

Klancher, J.P. (1987) *The Making of English Reading Audiences, 1790–1832*, Madison, Wisc.: University of Wisconsin Press.

Lyons, M. (1999) 'New Readers in the Nineteenth Century', in G. Cavallo and R. Chartier (eds), *A History of Reading in the West*, Cambridge: Polity Press.

O'Sullivan, T., J. Hartley, D. Saunders, M. Montgomery and J. Fiske (1994) *Key Concepts in Communication and Cultural Studies*, 2nd edn, London and New York: Routledge.

Shrimsley, B. (2003) 'Columns! the Good, the Bad, the Best', *British Journalism Review*, 14 (3). Available online at <http://www.bjr.org.uk/data/2003/n04_shrimsley.htm>, accessed 12 July 2004.

Tapscott, D. (1999) *Growing Up Digital: The Rise of the Net Generation*, Maidenhead: McGraw-Hill.

Trollope, A. (1980) *The Warden*, edited by D. Skilton, Oxford: Oxford University Press.

Webdale, J. (2004) 'Downloading with the Kids', *Media Guardian*, 26 July: 36.

White, C. (1970) *Women's Magazines 1693–1968*, London: Joseph.

Worsthorne, P. (2004) 'Bring Back the Dull Days', *Independent Review*, 22 June: 8.

Getting personal

15

How to write comment

Getting personal

How to write comment

Tim Holmes

Writing comment is easy. Ask yourself what you think about a subject and write it down. Job done. Now ask yourself another question. When was the last time you read a leading article all the way through? Or even started one?

Spilling out opinions may well be easy, but getting people to read them is much more difficult. Just as being a 'journalist' is not the same thing as being a 'writer', so writing opinion for a newspaper, magazine or web site is not the same as tipping your mind out and keying in the content. That may be acceptable in a student paper but it won't take you far on, say, the *Maidenhead Advertiser*.

To understand clearly why it won't do and to find the principles on which to construct a guide to writing comment, it is necessary to re-examine some basics of journalism and consider the role of the journalist as commentator.

It is a cardinal rule that personal opinions should not be allowed to obtrude on factual reporting. This principle can be found expressed almost anywhere journalism is discussed – but as far as print journalism goes, there is no law against it. Nor is it directly prohibited in either of the two major codes of conduct by which print journalists in the UK are meant to abide. The National Union of Journalists and the Press Complaints Commission place similar clauses as the third in their respective lists: 'A journalist shall strive to ensure that the information he/she disseminates is fair and accurate, avoid the expression of comment and conjecture as established fact and falsification by distortion, selection or misrepresentation' (NUJ Code of Conduct); 'The press, whilst free to be partisan, must distinguish clearly between comment, conjecture and fact' (PCC Code of Practice).

Australian journalists clearly do not need to be reminded so prominently; their Society of Professional Journalists puts 'Analysis and commentary should be labelled and not misrepresent fact or context' sixteenth in its code of thirty-two clauses.

Yet although great emphasis has traditionally been placed on the need to separate fact and opinion, it is also widely recognised that no such thing is really possible. 'All news is subjective,' declares Richard Keeble (1998: 257). 'You cannot escape your own preconceptions,' says Lynette Sheridan Burns (2002: 113). 'Objectivity is not totally achievable,' echoes John Wilson (1996: 46).

According to John Lloyd, editor of the *FT Magazine* and author of *What the Media Are Doing to Our Politics* (2004a), this relativism has eaten away at reliable journalism. He argues: 'The division between news and comment has tended to erode and the habit of comment has become general [. . .] The line between fact and comment is gone' (Lloyd 2004b).

Some of this is undoubtedly because legal judgments have shifted the lines of acceptability between fact and comment. In a useful *Press Gazette* article, Cleland Thom rounded up judgments which have 'given the press more room for manoeuvre in the tricky area of what is fact and what is comment', although he made the point strongly that comment must be based firmly on fact. To this end he quoted media lawyer Jonathan Crusher: 'There is always the danger of ignoring the need for a basis of fact. It is essential to ensure that the reader has enough of the facts, upon which the comment is based, to make their own mind up' (Thom 2004).

But even though the law may seem to favour journalism in many of these cases, something happened on 29 May 2003 which led to a re-evaluation of the boundaries between fact and comment. When Andrew Gilligan broadcast his report about Downing Street's dossier on weapons of mass destruction in Iraq, he set off a train of events which culminated in his own resignation (along with those of the BBC's chairman and director general), the Phillis Report into political communications, the Hutton Inquiry (in which internal procedures in the BBC, Downing Street and the security services were laid open to public scrutiny as never before), the Butler Inquiry into the quality and interpretation of UK security information – and the BBC's own Neil Report.

Gilligan's mistake was to broadcast as fact a matter of opinion. He thought his source (Dr David Kelly) had implied that one element of the dossier (the '45 minute' clause) was made more prominent by the government than its basis in security intelligence warranted.

Although the subsequent Hutton Report was widely held, in the words of Alan Watkins (2004), to treat the BBC 'in terms appropriate to a fraudulent company promoter at Southwark Crown Court; while the Government was let off, not even with a caution, but more with an apology for having taken up so much of its members' valuable time', the BBC had to be seen to take action.

One upshot was the Neil Report which, in essence, advocated a back-to-basics approach to journalism, under five main headings:

1. Truth and Accuracy
2. Serving the Public Interest
3. Impartiality and Diversity of Opinion
4. Independence
5. Accountability.

Under the third heading, the second clause reads: 'BBC journalists will report the facts first, understand and explain their context, provide professional judgments where appropriate, but never promote their own personal opinions' (Neil 2004: 7). The report also recommended the establishment of an academy at which staff – even senior staff – would receive a version of lifelong learning.

What would such an academy, were it to concern itself with print, have to say about journalists writing opinion? A good beginning would be to identify the different forms of this kind of writing. Basically there are two, the leading article (editorial) and the column. As the **leader** is the more ostensibly significant, it makes a good place to start.

leader   the editorial comment.

Leading articles: the voice of the publication

Leading articles are the voice of the publication and are crucial to what Jeremy Tunstall called policy-making, although the 'notion that policy appears, or can appear, only in "leaders" is too naive to require discussion' (1971: 46).

Thus the first thing any leader writer hoping to succeed needs to know, before even knowing the topic of the article, is the policy of the publication. As the transmission of this policy is 'performed in the columns of the paper itself' (Tunstall 1971: 46), we could all make a pretty good stab at guessing a national newspaper's likely stance on any given subject, but the place where it will be thrashed out for sure is the editorial conference. Once that is clear, there are six obligations which a leader writer must fulfil.

Get a topic

Leaders are journalism and journalism is about news, not history. There must be a strong and relevant news peg on which to hang the leading article, otherwise why should anyone be interested in reading it? In a national newspaper this may mean commenting on an event of national importance or interest. A local newspaper may give a local interpretation to the same event, or perhaps focus on something with a provenance much closer to home. The editor's message in consumer magazines frequently focuses almost entirely on the content of the current issue, although these are usually 'timely' in some way (perhaps seasonal, perhaps focusing on a major commercial launch or development in the subject area). A political, financial or business title is much more likely to express its opinion of a major occurrence or development as it affects the target readership's interests.

Frequency of publication will have a bearing on the topic chosen. A daily can cover rapidly changing situations, a weekly will have to be careful to chose subjects with more of a shelf-life, while fortnightlies and monthlies will depend more on having a good diary of forthcoming events.

Get the facts

At the conference (or in the commission) the subjects will be decided and the writing allocated. Leader writers may be specialists who can write from a position of established knowledge or **generalists** who will almost certainly have to bone up on the topic pretty sharpish. Steven Glover makes the process sound a bit of a lark (see Chapter 14) but leader writers on influential publications will be expected to have a sound grasp on the facts. Finding the facts is an excellent first move.

generalist non-specialist reporter. News teams tend to be mixes of generalists and specialists.

In a piece written for the US-based ethics centre, the Poynter Institute, about effective editorials, Chip Scanlan quotes Michael Gartner of the *Ames Daily Tribune*: 'A lot of editorial writers try to get by on their writing or their outrage, and not on their reporting. That just doesn't work. You've got to have facts. In an article, you use them to inform. In an editorial, you use facts to persuade' (Scanlan 2004).

Gathering the facts means more than just summing up the current situation, however. Background knowledge of how it was reached is important, as is a clear understanding of opposing points of view. And, of course, the writer has to understand all the nuances and technicalities of an issue so, if necessary, seek help and remember another old journalistic maxim – there is no such thing as a stupid question, only stupid answers.

Get to the point

Once you have the facts, use them to determine the point of your editorial. As Mike Jacobs, another of the contributors to Scanlan's editorial-fest, says: 'You need to have a point and you need to get to it immediately' (Scanlan 2004). The general direction which the leader will take should be clear following the conference but, like any other piece of journalism, the sharper the angle the better it will work. If necessary, summarise the point in a single sentence, tape it above the keyboard and refer to it constantly to make sure you stay on track.

Get a structure

All good writing is underpinned by a strong structure and journalism thrives on careful structuring. As leaders are news, of a sort, the standard pyramid would work but there are two formats which can be highly effective for editorials – the Six Step Structure and the Four Step Structure, described in that order.

1. Intro: even the greenest journalist should be familiar with the need for a striking intro. Exact details will vary according to the story, but it could be the clear statement of an arresting fact, a laugh-out-loud **punchline** (remember that you are not doing a comedy routine here, get your best shot in first) or an intriguing promise. Whatever the actual words are they have to capture the reader's attention immediately.

   > punchline   main point of story. Thus 'punchy' means story has a strong news *angle*.

2. Explanation: once you have that interest you have to work hard to keep it as you start to explain the issue. This must be both as full as necessary and as clear as possible. Background research will have revealed the necessary points and an analysis of these facts into what Rudyard Kipling called the 'six serving men' (Who, What, Where, When, Why and How) should identify the most important elements and the relationship between them. At the risk of repeating myself, it is essential that you understand thoroughly what you are writing about. If there is anything which does not seem to make sense or which needs more research, get the answers now. Misunderstanding and uncertainty transmit themselves very readily, and as award-winning leader writer John Fensterwald of the *Concord Monitor* noted: 'At the first obtuse fact and boring tangent, readers will ditch [you]' (Scanlan 2004).

3. Summarise opposition: if you have done a good job above, it should be an easy matter to present the arguments which opponents have made. Again, this assumes that you have a good grasp of what those arguments are and why some people might find them persuasive. It is important to give a good account of the opposition because if their position is weak why bother even to consider it?

4. Refute opposition: make your counter-arguments, keeping to the point, avoiding tangents and obfuscation. If you have done the preparation this section should

write itself. Do not be afraid to concede opposition points which seem valid – you want to appear rational, not bigoted.

5. More reasons to refute: there's no need to go on and on, but this is the place to reinforce your primary arguments with evidence from analogous situations. You can also deploy secondary arguments but the golden rule is still to stick to the point, so do not wander off down whimsical byways.

6. **Outro**: this subsection can include your proposed solutions, set the reader a challenge or simply finish with a flourish.

outro final section of a feature.

If six steps seem too many, or space is very tight, try the four-step plan, which in its baldest form runs thus:

1. State your opinion (this will include a statement of the issue or problem).
2. Give the reasons for your opinion.
3. Cite facts that support your opinion.
4. Suggest ways of dealing with the issue or problem.

Get a taxonomy

Whichever plan you chose, leader columns fall into four distinct types:

1. Argument or persuasion

- Take a clear stance on an issue of moment: 'The government of Blogistan must not be allowed to get away with offering world citizens freedom of expression.'
- Attempt to convert the reader to the same way of thinking: 'Any right-thinking person can see that this will lead to total democratic transparency.'
- Propose a solution or course of action: 'Send a gunboat.'

2. Information or interpretation

- Identify significant phenomena: 'Lots of people are "blogging".'
- Explain the significance of an occurrence or situation: 'This means their thoughts are available to a wide audience and may be transmitted rapidly.'
- Offer background information: '"Blogging" started in 2002. You can have a go by logging on to <http//www.blogist.an>.'

3. Appreciation

- Praise an organisation, person or event: 'Blogist.an, the online company which provides free blogging facilities, has made the world a better place.'
- Justify the commendation: 'Without it, world peace would not have been possible.'

4. Entertainment

- May treat a serious subject light-heartedly with the intention of defusing it, or satirically with the intention of improving it: 'Our friends at the *Daily Getsmuchworse* have got themselves into something of a lather over what they quaintly refer to as "blogging". They are twits.'
- May focus on a humorous subject: 'Blogging – we're all at it you know, missus.'

How to write opinion columns

Columnists are hired largely to do what I suggested you should not do at the start of this section – tip their minds out and write it all down. The difference is that their minds are generally well-attuned to the task; they have to be amusing, provocative or informative on a regular basis, preferably every time they write, in fact.

It is a universal axiom of journalism that you have to know who you are writing for, and this is doubly true of columns. There is no pressing reason for anyone to read a column. It is not news, it is unlikely to contain life-changing information, it will not feature in exam questions. However, if the columnist can make readers laugh or splutter with indignation or believe that they have picked up a handy nugget of knowledge, the job has been done well.

After being voted greatest living columnist by readers of the *British Journalism Review*, Keith Waterhouse (2004: 10) wrote about his favourite columnists. The attributes he thought they shared were:

- abiding curiosity about the world
- forcefully held and expressed views
- a healthy scepticism (not cynicism)
- a well-stocked mind
- the ability to write about everything and nothing.

One other interesting point he made was that once it has become established, a column takes on a life of its own, 'it can be whatever it wishes to be, until its supposed controller is fired, expires or is **poached**' (Waterhouse 2004). Looked at another way, this seems to imply that a columnist is restricted by the persona which he or she adopts.

poached when a staff member is lured to a rival publication (usually with the bait of a higher salary and or fancier title).

This hypothesis can be tested by thinking about the columnists which Waterhouse mentions: if you have read their work at all you will probably remember just one outstanding characteristic, be it bitterness, intellectual flair, humour or a cussed resistance to accepted modes of thought (see also Glover 1999). Imagine, for instance, the collected *Sun* columns of Richard Littlejohn (is it really possible for one man to be so indignant about so many things for so long?) or the much-praised Alan Watkins of the *Observer* (well-informed he may be about both rugby and politics but how long would it be before one's eyelids began to droop in the face of such orotund rhetoric?).

Once a columnist has established his or her persona, that is what the editor will want. If rivals come a-poaching, they are not going to be looking for a new start – they want the old stuff and rich seams of it.

It could well be this gap between appearance and reality which caused Peter Wilby, then editor of the *New Statesman*, to discover that 'it is not unusual for editors to be vaguely disgruntled with and uneasy about a columnist that everyone admires . . . [star columnists] nearly always disappoint' (Wilby 2000).

Waterhouse and Bernard Shrimsley, whose *British Journalism Review* piece kicked off the search for the greatest columnists living and dead, both make the point that an instantly recognisable style is very important. 'A style so recognisable that it doesn't really need a byline' (Waterhouse 2004); someone who can 'weave words so distinctively that they hardly need to sign their pieces' (Shrimsley 2003). Even the swiftest of glances through a small selection of publications will reveal the variety of styles, and any would-be columnist had better be prepared to put in time cultivating a characteristic way of writing. Spelling and grammar are just the beginning.

If we take the advice of the columnar advocates Glover, Shrimsley and Waterhouse, a column can be about anything and it can be written in any style. Like most of the folklore of journalism this only takes the apprentice so far, and it might be helpful to add a smattering of empirically derived theoretical supposition to the anecdotal evidence.

The four categories of columns

Just as there are distinct types of leader (see above), so there are four categories of column – reasoned argument, knee-jerk reaction, deliberate provocation and pure entertainment.

1. Reasoned argument

This may or may not convince but it is a highly disciplined form of writing, almost like an essay, based on evidence or rational interpretation of facts. The writer needs to have a good understanding of the target reader and a clearly expressed message. It could be Simon Jenkins making an elegant argument in *The Times;* it could be Mary Citizen in the local paper putting the case for a speed camera outside a school. Exemplary practitioners: Jonathan Steele (*Guardian*), Donald MacIntyre (*Independent*), Mary Riddell (*Observer*), David Hepworth (*Word* magazine).

2. Knee-jerk reaction

Columns of this type pander to the basest instincts of a readership. To be successful they require a keen understanding of the audience's hopes and fears. This is an intellectually lazy form of writing, although it requires some skill to fill the word count entertainingly. It also requires a deep well of prejudice (real or assumed), the professionalism of a comedian (able to perform even if you don't feel like it) and the ability to keep up a consistent front. It could be Richard Littlejohn 'not making it up' or it could be *Max Power* calling for all speed cameras to be blown up. Exemplary practitioners: Simon Heffer (*Daily Mail*), Janet Daley (*Daily Telegraph*), Paul Johnson (*Spectator*), Dominik Diamond (*Daily Star*).

3. Deliberate provocation

Writing which tries to push readers into a reaction – good for letters to the editor, good for building a 'community of opposition' and probably good for encouraging readers to return, if only to check out what ridiculous thing that silly person has got to say. However, such columnists run the risk of going a provocation too far and alienating readers completely, in which case they may face the fate of John MacLeod (see Chapter 14). Exemplary practitioners: Julie Burchill (currently *The Times* but famously in the *Guardian*), Jeremy Clarkson (*Sun* and *Top Gear*), Tony Parsons (*Daily Mirror*), Zoe Williams (*Guardian*).

4. Entertainment

Ostensibly a skewed look at life or a straightish look at a lifestyle, at their best these columns can help to shed light on important issues by approaching them from a new angle or making fun of them. Sometimes the jolt of recognition puts life's little problems into perspective. When they work well, entertaining columns can be a pleasant and sometimes instructive way for readers to occupy five minutes which might otherwise be spent staring into space. On an off day, staring into space is the better option.

One element to watch out for in this category is the camouflaged Reasoned Argument. Some of Boris Johnson's work for the *Daily Telegraph* slots firmly into this subsection. Exemplary practitioners: Miles Kington (*Independent*), Deborah Ross (*Independent*), Allan Jones (*Uncut* magazine), Mark Thomas (*New Statesman*).

Specialist columns

Keith Waterhouse (2004: 34) dismisses cookery and gardening writers, theatre critics, book-reviewers and gossipmongers as not 'columnists within the meaning of the act'. His word is usually taken as gospel on matters relating to newspapers, but it is a fact that many people are able to use their specialised knowledge to get work published in newspapers and magazines. Most 'how to get into journalism' books or articles at some point suggest leveraging existing skills and knowledge to become a regular contributor to *Stamp Monthly* or the *Kitchen Garden* or the equivalent sections in a newspaper, perhaps developing a reputation locally before trying for a national.

Even if we accept Waterhouse's ruling, it still leaves financial, political and sporting writers, to name but a few; these are surely comrades in the struggle who would be recognised by the brotherhood and sisterhood of Fleet Street. Their work can quite easily be categorised according to the schema above. They need access to serious contacts to make their work worthwhile and often their thirst for alcoholic beverages is prodigious. The difference, perhaps, is that such columnists have come up through the rank and file of journalism before finding a place in the limelight. Many of them are still working as high-end reporters and use columns to differentiate between opinion derived from their grasp of the facts and revealing those facts in their reporting, or to add value to their insider knowledge.

Sometimes that added value can be worth a surprising amount, especially if it is in a culturally significant area. Could even the great *Daily Mirror* columnist of the

1950s, William Connor (better known as 'Cassandra') have foreseen that contributors to gossipy show-biz columns would end up running the newspaper he loved? Only if he had predicted the rise and rise of celebrity journalism, which is why Piers Morgan (1995–2004) and Richard Wallace became editor of the *Mirror* one after the other. You couldn't make it up.

References

Glover, S. (1999) 'What Columnists Are For', in S. Glover (ed.) *Secrets of the Press: Journalists on Journalism*, London: Allen Lane/Penguin, pp. 289–98.

Keeble, R. (1998) *The Newspapers Handbook*, 2nd edn, London: Routledge.

Lloyd, J. (2004a) *What the Media are Doing to our Politics*, London: Constable & Robinson.

Lloyd, J. (2004b) 'Who Really Runs the Country?' *Media Guardian*, 21 June 20: 8.

Neil, R. (2004) *The Neil Report*. Available online at <http//www.bbc.co.uk/info/policies>, accessed 28 July 2004

Scanlan, C. (2004) 'Lessons Learned: Exploring the Process of Award-Winning Editorial Writing'. Available online at <http//www.poynter.org/content/content_ print.asp?id=66362&custom=>, accessed 14 July 2004.

Sheridan Burns, L. (2002) *Understanding Journalism*, London: Sage.

Shrimsley, B. (2003) 'Columns! the Good, the Bad, the Best', *British Journalism Review*, 14 (3): 23–30. Available online at <http://www.bjr.org.uk/data/2003/n03_shrimsley.htm>, accessed 12 July 2004.

Thom, C. (2004) 'Fair Comment', *Press Gazette*, 9 April: 20.

Tunstall, J. (1971) *Journalists At Work*, London: Constable.

Waterhouse, K. (2004) 'Those I Have Loved – and Loathed', *British Journalism Review*, 15 (1): 7–12.

Watkins, A. (2004) 'So What Are We to Make of Lord Butler?', *Independent on Sunday*, 11 July: 25.

Wilby, P. (2000) 'Why I Fell Out with the Prince of Columnists', *British Journalism Review*, 11 (4): 63–6. Available online at <http://www.bjr.org.uk/data/2000/n04_wilby.htm>, accessed 12 July 2004.

Wilson, J. (1996) *Understanding Journalism: A Guide to Issues*, London: Routledge.

The art of reviewing

16

The art of reviewing

Rod Allen

The job of the reviewer

François Truffaut, the great French film director and critic, said, 'Anyone can be a film critic' (Truffaut 1980: 8). But he added that 'no artist ever accepts the critic's role on a profound level' (1980: 11). Nathan Cohen, Canada's most famous newspaper drama critic, asserted that the work of the critic 'is to present his opinions entertainingly and clearly, within the limits of the paper he works for' (Seiler 2001). These remarks suggest the three principles on which reviewing is generally based.

1. Reviewers operate on behalf of the reader, listener or viewer rather than the producers of the material reviewed.
2. Reviewers work within the context of the market served by the medium in which they appear (thus a review in *Socialist Worker* will be very different from one in *Loaded*).
3. Reviewers are explicitly required to deliver their personal opinions within a clearly defined framework.

The need to operate on behalf of the reader, listener or viewer rather than on behalf of the producers of the material reviewed emphasises the reviewer's function as a sampler of the cultural work under review and as a delegate of his or her audience. Only if the critic is strongly established as an authority in his or her field does his or her opinion count for itself. Clive Barnes in the *New York Times* of the 1960s and 1970s, Dilys Powell in *The Sunday Times* (1939–1976) and Kenneth Tynan when he was writing for the *Observer* (1950–1963); (see Lahr 2001) are among those critics whose broad body of work and critical stance were read as arbiters of popular taste.

Nevertheless, it has to be borne in mind that the power of the reviewer to influence her or his readers in a local magazine or newspaper can be quite substantial; and with that power comes some responsibility to ensure that reviews are written fairly and with the interests of the reader in the reviewer's mind at all times.

It is also clear that the context of the market within which the reviewer is operating is important. Although there are as many critical mindsets as there are readers or viewers of a given newspaper or programme, publishers can and should make assumptions about the nature of their audience and those assumptions go to make up the broad editorial framework of the publication. Accordingly, judgments are made about the cultural tastes of readers, listeners or viewers which provide the framework within which the reviewer operates.

In a local newspaper, the cultural glue which unites the audience is precisely the locality within which they live. A review of a local amateur theatrical performance may be the more interesting for mention of as many local inhabitants as possible. The nature of the interpretation will be of lesser interest to readers. Contributors to a national television programme on a 'minority' channel like Channel Four in the UK can assume some prior knowledge of cultural matters and an interest in 'high' culture on the part of viewers. Readers of the *Daily Express* will probably be more interested in the star names appearing in a show being reviewed.

Most of the assumptions under which various publications operate are unspoken while others are obvious, but a journalist starting out as a reviewer, however modest, would do well to think about the framework under which she or he will be operating before turning in copy.

Clearly if the reviewer does have a degree in English literature she or he will know a great deal more about theatrical forms than most of the readers; on the other hand, care must be taken not to be too simplistic or to appear patronising to the audience. In the evaluative phase of the review, however, it should be clear that the opinion being delivered is informed and considered and not merely based on instinct or gut reaction. An important part of the reviewing task is to offer the reader a way of judging her or his tastes against the reviewer's own, so it is legitimate and useful to write something like 'I am not keen on science fiction myself, but if you like it then this film is as good an example of sci-fi as you are likely to see'.

Bear in mind that readers are anxious for guidance – unless they are the producers of the work under review, their main reason for reading the review is to evaluate whether they would like to see the film or play, or buy the book. Or they may simply want to read an engaging, informative, well-composed (maybe even witty) piece of writing.

The review's three phases

In one sense, reviewing is everybody's second job. Taxi drivers and hairdressers will willingly express their opinions of last night's television to anyone who will listen. But the reviewer's task is to express her or his opinion in such a way that it is useful and usable to her or his audience, not only in working out whether the event is worth attending, but also in helping the audience to enjoy and understand the work on offer. And the writing should be of a sufficient quality and colour in itself to attract attention.

Martin and Jacobus (1997: 50–9) suggest there should be three phases to the work of the critic writing in a popular medium: these comprise first the descriptive phase, second the interpretive phase, and third the evaluative phase.

In the descriptive phase, the reviewer's job is to focus on the form of the review's subject, placing it in the context of the current cultural *zeitgeist* – establishing its genre and style. Readers will also welcome some information about the creator and interpreters of the work (if a film, the director and actors; if a book, the author). In the interpretive phase, the reviewer uses her or his knowledge of the differing forms of culture to explain the content to the reader, perhaps detailing some of the plot of a film. In the evaluative phase, at its simplest, the reviewer makes a recommendation about the work, or at least enables readers to make a judgment about what they

zeitgeist spirit of the age.

would think of it measured alongside what they know about the world view of the reviewer.

Although this three-part structure may seem restrictive or prescriptive, it is nevertheless followed broadly by most reviewers. Consider, for example, this brief review of the film *King Arthur* by Dave Cowan which appeared in *Time Out* on 28 July 2004:

'King Arthur'
Dir: Antoine Fuqua, US/Ireland

On paper, the story of King Arthur is a gift to film-makers eager to mine the mystery, heroism and bloodlust of the distant past, while also avoiding attack from historical purists. The Arthurian legend, which has been retold countless times, from Thomas Mallory's fifteenth-century epic poem *Morte d'Arthur* to Disney's 1963 animated movie *The Sword in the Stone*, has no basis in historical fact whatsoever. The character of Arthur, however, is now a ready-made, all-conquering medieval folk hero.

Surprisingly, producer Jerry Bruckheimer (*Black Hawk Down, Pirates of the Caribbean*) and director Antoine Fuqua (*Training Day*) have ditched much of the familiar legend in favour of fresh historical claims for their Arthur (Clive Owen) who is the product – we are told during the opening credits – of spanking new, but unrevealed, archaeological evidence. The film discards the usual Arthurian mood of courtly romance and instead celebrates the nitty-gritty of the Dark Ages: a time when the Roman army was withdrawing from Britain and Saxon warriors, led by a cowboy-like Stellan Skarsgård, were on the attack. Arthur himself is Romano-British, and, as such, is experiencing a crisis of identity while leading his knights in defence of his homeland and wallowing in the inherited values of Rome ('freedom' being his familiar catchword).

All this back-story is a confusing, over-long preamble to a series of quite exciting battles. Ultimately, though, Owen fails to muster enough charisma to carry the film, and an impish Keira Knightley as Guinevere is a little redundant, despite the unfulfilled, longing glances she exchanges repeatedly with Lancelot (Ioan Gruffudd). A simpler story would have suited the bombastic Bruckheimer style.

Source: *Time Out*, 28 July 2004: 65. Reprinted with permission. © 2004 Time Out Magazine Limited.

In this 275-word review, see how each phase is represented broadly by successive paragraphs. The first paragraph talks about the basis of the film and describes the context in which the film is offered. The second paragraph offers some information about the people involved in the film, thus continuing the descriptive phase, and then moves into an interpretive discussion of the film and a brief outlining of some of the plot. The third, evaluative paragraph gives the reviewer's opinion of the film and some information through which readers can gauge whether – despite the reviewer's own conclusion – they may want to see the film.

Some shared knowledge between reviewer and reader is required for full appreciation of the conclusion, notably that of the work of producer Jerry

Bruckheimer, but *Time Out*'s readers are generally thought to be interested in films and film-makers (short of being film buffs) and it is nevertheless possible to understand and appreciate the review without being a student of Bruckheimer.

Some more tips for reviewers

Building on the King Arthur copy we can highlight some other important elements of the reviewer's task.

- See how the opening par captures an important dimension of the film to draw in the reader – just as a striking news intro works. Here the writing is particularly colourful: notice, for instance, the deliberate alliteration in 'mine the mystery' and the un-newsy build-up of adjectives in 'ready-made, all-conquering medieval folk hero'.
- Preparation is essential. Here, details about the previous work of the director and producer and the historical background are fed into the review through extremely concise writing – to add context and factual density. If you are reviewing a novel, read the author's previous works, do a Google search on them, talk to your friends about them. Generally, immerse yourself in the task. Your enthusiasms and knowledge will then be conveyed through the review. But, as Harriett Gilbert stresses (1999: 105–6), the amount of research you can do will be dependent on the ambition of the review (a 700-word article on an Edward Hopper exhibition will need more preparation than a 250-word piece on Mike Leigh's latest film), on the amount of information available and on the amount of time you have.
- Always try to take notes. For a theatre review make them in the interval and immediately afterwards. For a television review compose them as you watch, concentrating on getting names and titles correct, highlighting some major facts or quotes. Accuracy is, of course, as important in reviews as in news and features.
- Try not to disclose a crucial final twist to any plot (though you may want to allude to it). This will spoil the element of suspense for anyone later consuming the work under review.
- Check the rhythm of your piece. Does it flow?
- Read reviews voraciously. Enjoy the different styles: Mark Kermode, passionate about films in the *Observer*; the anonymous reviewers drily ironic (bordering often on the contemptuous) in *Private Eye*; Jacqueline Rose, elegant in the *London Review of Books*.
- Regard the review essentially as a creative challenge. Develop your own style through constant practice.
- You may be bored by a classical concert, a book, an exhibition. So your challenge is to convey your boredom in an interesting way. Don't try to hide your feelings behind bland words of praise. Inauthenticity can always be spotted.
- And try to avoid the fate George Orwell highlighted in his *Confessions of a Book Reviewer* (1970: 215–218) of becoming a hack routinely bashing out the 'stale old phrases' typical, he grumbled, of so many newspaper reviews.

freebie range of services and entertainments (e.g. drinks, meals, trips abroad funded by organisations, concert tickets, etc.) provided free to journalists. Some journalists believe acceptance of freebies compromises 'objectivity' and refuse them.

To freebie – or not to freebie?

An important practical dimension of reviewing is represented by the need to be invited to openings and previews and to receive books, videos, etc., for the purpose of review. Publishers and broadcasters are generally appreciative of publicity for their output whether it is positive or negative, but they are intelligently aware of circulations and viewerships and before issuing invitations or sending out free copies they will want to be aware of the extent and nature of the audience to be reached by the reviewer.

Books are often sent out speculatively to a publication rather than an individual, and news desks often receive invitations to launch events and previews which they then allocate to individual reporters. As journalists build up their reputations as reviewers – particularly those in the freelance field – they will receive their own review copies and invitations, enabling them to offer reviews to a news desk (or a reviews editor) rather than having to wait to have jobs allocated to them.

It is important to understand the nature of the transaction in this context: public relations (PR) departments often arrange quite elaborate and expensive events to launch a show or a book. At the least a glass of decent wine will be offered; at the most a trip to an exotic location and a free luxury hotel room will be included in the package. For the producer, this is part of the price of obtaining publicity; there is no obligation to be positive about the product on the journalist. On the contrary, the journalist's obligation is to be honest about the product because their first duty is to the readers, who trust them for guidance about products or services.

Yet, interestingly, some journalist cultures ban all freebies. As Karen Sanders comments (2003: 121): 'Journalists' codes of conduct prohibit any activity which may be understood to establish an interest that conflicts with professional duties and undermines the reporter's credibility'. Certainly, ethical or political dilemmas confront the reviewer as much as any news or feature writer.

The work of the television reviewer

When television started, newspapers saw the new medium (with some justice) as competition and some of them refused to include any mention of it at all. As late as the mid-1950s the *Daily Express* declined to include programme listings, let alone reviews, in its pages. Others, such as the *Daily Telegraph*, saw television as a source of news in itself and engaged a radio and television reporter as early as 1935 (Leonard Marsland Gander, the first such reporter in the world, covered the opening of the BBC's public service from Alexandra Palace in 1936 and occupied the job until the 1970s).

In addition, the *Telegraph* printed programme listings, recognising that people would buy the paper for information about their evening's television. Because of the novelty of the medium, programmes – though mainly transmitted 'live' and not repeated – were reviewed, though in some cases the reviews were not unlike news stories. Even the opening night of BBC2 on 20 April 1964 became a front-page news story, because a massive power cut in the London area knocked it straight off the air as soon as it was launched.

Yet as television matured into the medium it is today, fewer and fewer disasters and hitches were seen as newsworthy. Television reviewing became a specialist form and a number of national reviewers used their positions to create a form of witty, elegant writing which transcended reviewing and turned it into an aspect of feature writing which was often displayed prominently and used as a means of promoting the paper. The progenitor of this form was Nancy Banks-Smith who still writes amusing and discursive television reviews in the *Guardian;* the writer who exploited the form most successfully was Clive James whose television reviews in the *Observer* gained him celebrity status (see James 1984).

James developed an acerbic, amusing style which made him immensely readable yet concentrated on the descriptive with almost no interpretive or evaluative dimension. Generally speaking, James liked almost nothing on television (apart, presumably, from his own prolific appearances on it), but said so each week with great style and entertainment. Today, the main champion of this style of television reviewing is Victor Lewis-Smith in the London *Evening Standard*, who is much more of an acquired taste than Clive James.

Nevertheless, television programmes continue to be reviewed after transmission by national and regional newspapers and magazines while TV companies continue to encourage such reviews by providing viewing copies or organising previews. Because much television is episodic, the hope is that viewers will be encouraged by a positive review of Episode 1 of a series to watched subsequent episodes. Reviews often shade into previews in any case, and most television listings are accompanied by longer previews of individual programmes which will have been seen by the reviewer or previewer in advance of transmission. Sometimes the listings themselves will incorporate quite detailed descriptions (and opinions) which will guide the viewer as to the potential enjoyability of the programme listed.

Listings reviews

Over the past twenty years or so the business of listings has developed way beyond the basic television- and radio-programme listings which appeared for many years in the broadcasters' house journals such as the *Radio Times* and the *TV Times*. The major breakthrough took place following the release of the restrictive copyright on television- and radio-programme listings in the 1980s. Until legislative change banned the practice, broadcasters used their copyright in programme listings to prevent weekly magazines from carrying details of programmes in advance, enabling them to publish their own magazines carrying only details of their own programmes and obliging viewers to buy separate magazines for BBC and ITV programmes. Permission was given to carry brief programme details in daily newspapers.

The main job of the listings journalist is to ensure accuracy and comprehensiveness. A thorough knowledge of the specialist area involved is required, and constant contact with the market is essential to make sure all venues and events are listed in the output. With areas such as television or West End theatre, there are efficient PR operations to make sure information is distributed to listings editors. But in fields such as jazz clubs, music festivals or comedy venues, where events and promoters are transient and often not well organised, it is much harder to obtain up-to-date and comprehensive information.

So constant contact with the field and a good deal of desk research among primary and secondary sources is required. But the other skill required of the listings journalist is the ability to make a coherent recommendation within the space of a dozen or so words accompanying the practical information about the venue or gig in the listing. An example:

Jazz – clubs
Ronnie Scott's, Tuesday: Gil Evans' trio continues to define state-of-the-art piano jazz. Shows 10:15, mdnt, ends Sat.

This listing is just twenty words long, but it consists of a clear sentence which incorporates a great deal of information as well as opinion. The heading covers a number of listings, of course, but it indicates that the entry is mainly of interest to those who like jazz. The name of the band is incorporated into the main sentence; the fact that it is Evans' trio and not his big band that is playing is communicated, and for those who don't know what he plays the fact that it is piano jazz is included without appearing patronising. And the critic's opinion – that Evans' jazz is of definitively high quality – is deftly inserted as part of the information included. Vital but tedious information is reserved until the end – two shows, late night and the whole enterprise continues until Saturday. Compressing vital information and expressing a coherent opinion within twenty words takes some practice, but it turns out to be easier the more you do it.

In this task the relationship with the reader becomes crucial. Journalists compiling club listings, for example, need to be confident there is a shared vocabulary allowing them to communicate quickly and efficiently with the audience: no time here to explain terms like 'old skool' or 'broken beats' because if the reader does not under-stand them he or she probably is not the customer for the gig. Moreover, speed is of the essence in the interests of the publisher, the journalist and the reader: these small items need to be written quickly and they are going to be read quickly and selectively. Readers are adept at picking out the parts of a listings column that are likely to interest them, and all listings sections are subdivided (sometimes quite minutely) into sections which appeal to different kinds of taste.

Meticulous, not to say obsessive, subbing is key to a successful listings operation; a well-planned copy-flow programme needs to exist alongside the skills of journalism on the listings desk and there are no deadlines as the calendar constantly changes and creates new challenges. Nevertheless, the content of the listings operation needs to reflect the needs and interest of the market and so listings editors end up making constant choices about what to include and what to leave out based, hopefully, on a view of their audience – but sometimes tempered by the flow of available information.

As everywhere in the newsroom, the choices listings journalists make are influenced by their own world view, their proprietors' assumptions about the audi-ence and shared assumptions about culture which lie deeply within the collective and individual unconscious. Journalists are consumers of culture just as much as their readers are, and decisions about what goes in and what stays out are as much subject to fashion and shifting ideology, not to mention social class, gender and ethnicity, as much as anything else that goes into the paper. An awareness of such assumptions and influences will help the listings writer.

References

Altschuler, G. and D. Grossvogel (1992) *Changing Channels: America in TV Guide.* Urbana, Ill.: University of Illinois Press.

Gilbert, H. (1999) 'Writing Reviews', in W. Hicks with S. Adams and H. Gilbert (eds) *Writing for Journalists*, London: Routledge: 99–123.

James, C. (1984) *Glued to the Box: Television Criticism from the Observer 1979–82*, London: Picador.

Lahr, J. (ed.) (2001) *The Diaries of Kenneth Tynan*, London: Bloomsbury.

Martin, F. and L. Jacobus (1997) *The Humanities through the Arts*, New York: McGraw-Hill.

McQuail, D. (1983) *Mass Communication Theory: An Introduction*, London: Sage.

Orwell, G. (1970) 'Confessions of a Book Reviewer', in S. Orwell and I. Angus (eds) *The Collected Essays, Journalism and Letters of George Orwell*, Vol. IV, Harmondsworth: Penguin.

Sanders, K. (2003) *Ethics and Journalism*, London and Thousand Oaks, Calif.: Sage.

Seiler, R. (2001) 'A Few Words on Reviewing by Nathan Cohen (Transcript of Speech)'. Available online at <http://www.acs.ucalgary.ca/~rseiler/cohen.htm>, accessed 28 July 2004.

Titchenor, C. (2001) *Reviewing the Arts*, Mahwah, NJ: Lawrence Erlbaum Associates.

Truffaut, F. (1980) *The Films in My Life*, London: Allen Lane.

Design for print media  17

Design for print media

Chris Frost

TARGETING THE TYPICAL READER

Today's modern magazines and newspapers are cleverly constructed mixes of information and design. They sit on the news stands enticing us to pick them up, buy them and then read them. So why do editorial departments design newspapers and magazines in the way that they do? Why spend so much money on designers and design software? Why not just run the stories one after another, as happens in books or on TV?

The answer is twofold. First, a publication needs to grab the reader's attention and invite him or her to buy the product. The design of the front page or cover is vital as a selling tool. Although many readers buy their newspaper or magazine regularly and get them delivered to their homes, many prefer to buy at the news stand and may well make a different choice from day to day depending on what catches their eye. This can be particularly true of consumer magazines where the reader may decide on which magazine to buy or, indeed, whether to buy at all, depending on what is displayed on the cover of each product. The second reason for designing the product as we do is to aid the reader's navigation through the publication. This is more about how the inside of the publication is structured rather than the front page, but watch any group of readers in a newsagents, and you will find that many check out the inside before they buy.

index listing of contents of publication.

Most publications have standard navigation aids that they change at their peril. Sport might be on the back. The **index** page of a magazine will be on the inside front cover and its problem pages may be at the back. These design traditions save the reader time and effort. Anyone who has been shopping in their favourite super-market following a major refit will understand this. Supermarkets used to regularly change where items were stocked in the hope of encouraging shoppers to buy things they might not normally purchase. Now they only do it because of necessity, as they have learnt that sales fall as frustrated shoppers fail to complete their shopping list or leave to go to another store where they know the layout better.

Newspapers and magazines are the same. The reader gains comfort from being able to find things easily and quickly and becomes frustrated if things are somewhere different. This desire to help the reader find things where they expect them does not mean that design should be dull, but it does mean that good design is about helping them identify where things are and what they are.

Good design is not only about navigation, of course. It is also an integral part of the character and identity of the publication. This needs to be a character with which the reader will identify. The publication should be saying something to them about the way they are and who they are and they should be happy identifying with the content and the design.

Newspapers and magazines compete in the marketplace. They are consumer items set out on the newsagent's shelves attempting to attract the attention of those prepared to part with their asking price in order to read them and be informed and entertained. To attract attention, the front pages that catch the casual glance of the potential purchaser must look as their would-be purchasers expect them to look. If their purchasers identify themselves as cool and fashion-conscious, then the front page must reflect this. If the reader prefers a more traditional style, then that is what the front page must confirm.

A well-designed publication will not only look the way its readers expect it to look, but will present the material in which they are interested in an appropriate way. The publication and each page within it will direct the reader to the stories in which they are interested and will present these in an easy-to-manage format. Design is there to help the reader, to act like a tour guide through the publication pointing out items of interest.

Designing publications is a two-stage process. A new publication is designed for its readers: styles are planned, **fonts** are chosen, design decisions are made. These choices are then reconfirmed with every edition but also evolve with time to ensure the publication stays up to date.

font family of type characters.

Setting a style for the publication

There are a huge number of decisions made when a new publication is being put together. All of them, however, are closely linked to the target audience and it is vital to keep this firmly in mind. How old are the readers? What sex? What is their shared cultural experience? A magazine aimed at holidaying for the over-sixties would be very different in look as well as content to a magazine aimed at sixteen- to twenty-five-year-old females interested in fashion. Any successful publication has a clear 'typical reader' in mind and you should be able to read a publication and get a clear picture of the type of person likely to be reading it both from the content and the design.

When most designers work day to day on a publication, they will be working to templates and patterns set out by the publication designer, but they should still bear that typical reader in mind and be prepared to evolve the design with time, in line with the original design concepts. The other limitation on design to consider along-side the target audience is budget. Newspapers are printed on cheap, thin, recycled paper with limited colour printing because they are designed to be disposable.

A newspaper is read on the day of purchase by three or four readers. It tends to look the worse for wear after that amount of handling, but that is not important since it will be in the recycle bin the next day. A textbook, however, is designed to be kept and accessed on a regular basis over a number of years. It must be able to withstand some fairly heavy use and so the pages are made of stronger paper and the covers are made of a card that will add further protection.

Most textbooks are full of printed copy so colour is an unnecessary expense. In a monthly magazine, the extra expense of full colour on every page is seen as essential.

No magazine, except the most specialist, is likely to survive in the modern consumer market without colour. The magazine also needs to stand up to firm handling over a period of a month or more so this also has thicker paper than a newspaper and a cover made of thin card. However, it does not need the kind of heavy-duty cover a book has since its lifespan is usually only a month.

Paper and size

So the first decision we need to take is how the reader will use the publication and, therefore, what we need to make it from. The second decision is how the reader will store the publication. A newspaper will be stored in a briefcase or a pocket or rolled up and held in the hand. The traditional tabloid or broadsheet sizes are at an advantage here. The newspaper's size makes it cheap and easy to print, easy to store and sell in a newsagent's or street-seller's stand and easy to handle, fold and store. When we are finished with it, it is easy to throw away. Of course, it is not easy to store and libraries find it easier to transfer newspapers onto microfilm. However, not many people buy newspapers to store them in libraries.

Magazines were designed to be read sitting down and stored in magazine racks or on table tops. For this reason an A4 size has long been the traditional choice. However recently, an A5 size has proved to be very popular with several magazines aimed at young women, presumably because they are easy to carry in a handbag. This size presents a new solution, but also new design challenges.

The exact size of the publication will be determined by the web size of the press about to print it, but its basic size (broadsheet, compact and so on) is determined by its market positioning.

Structure and look

The next stage in planning the new publication is to identify the structure and general look of it. The overall look of a publication becomes an important part of its character. Regular readers look for their publication on the news stands because they identify its look, not just the masthead.

typefaces full range of type of the same design.

The masthead is important but the shape of the front page, its style, **typefaces** and even colours all come together to make an identifiable product even though the actual stories or words on the front cover may be different in each edition.

This is not an unusual phenomenon in branding. Almost any product on the market changes its packaging carefully to ensure the brand image remains undisturbed because a buyer who does not recognise their favourite product on the supermarket shelves may easily end up buying a competitor. Coca-Cola would not suddenly decide to put out its product in green cans anymore than McDonald's would drop its twin golden arches.

Margins

Once the size of the publication has been decided then the presentation of the display on each page can be thought through. Margins are generally used in newspapers because this avoids the need to guillotine the edges, a more expensive and time-consuming activity. But quality colour magazines usually want to run their colour pictures right to the edge of the page. This involves printing slightly over the actual size and then trimming the pages neatly to size.

Margins take up space; however, large margins can add elegant white space that makes a publication look both more sophisticated and relaxed. Even though magazines run pictures to the edge of the page, you will often find the text has a substantial margin. Newspapers, on the other hand, try to use all available space so the margins tend to be reasonably narrow, broad enough only to ensure that the centrefold can accommodate occasionally inaccurate folding.

Fonts

The fonts used in a publication are vital to its appearance and need to be chosen extremely carefully. Heading fonts in particular say something about the publication even to a casual glance in a newsagent's. Plain and simple fonts will get their message over to the reader directly and will also emphasise the simple, straightforward message of the publication. Fancier types also have something to say about the publication.

Graphics

Pictures and graphics are used to illustrate stories, adding information, animation and emotion. We use our eyes more than any other sense to extract information and meaning from the world and so pictures allow us to extract information easily and add to our general understanding of the world. Whether the pictures are photographs, cartoons, drawings, maps or composite graphics, they should all add some extra information.

However, the quantity, size and use of pictures say something about the publication; its use of illustrations will change the face it presents to the world. A broadsheet newspaper, for instance, uses pictures with restraint whilst a tabloid will use them with much more enthusiasm. A fashion magazine will be largely pictures whilst a heavy, political magazine will be mainly text informing and analysing with only the occasional picture.

Imprint

Every publication in the country is obliged by law to identify the publisher and printer. This need not be too detailed, but it does need to be there. Most newspapers put the **imprint** on the bottom of the back page in very small type. But some magazines and an increasing number of newspapers are making a display item out of the imprint, including extra information not required by law such as editorial and advertising phone numbers or the names and titles of many of the more senior staff. This is a perfectly reasonable way of trying to build a more personal relationship with readers. In the same way, many magazines have a letter from the editor in each issue, which also tries to build a relationship with the reader.

imprint the printer's and publisher's details. Required by law.

Headers

Each page of a newspaper or magazine carries some basic information, and it is part of that publication's style to determine what this is. Most carry page numbers, many also carry the publication title. There may be additional information on each page, perhaps identifying the content as sport or fashion or reviews. The information carried above the top margin of a page is called the header. The information below the bottom margin is the **footer**. Additional style information may also be included in some pages. These might include the title piece (the publication's logo) or specific artwork identifying regular sections of the publication such as readers' letters, the advice page or gardening column.

footer bottom margin area of the page often used to insert the publication title, date or page number.

Advertisements

Advertisements are an unavoidable necessity in most publications. Very few publications are profitable through their sales alone and most rely more on advertising. Most broadsheet/compact newspapers, for instance, make the majority of their money from selling advertising space and so are not reliant on their relatively modest circulations. Tabloids are generally much more reliant on sales as they do not carry as much advertising and cannot charge as much for it – broadsheets/ compacts can access the lucrative ABC1 market: readers who are in high status jobs and have high earnings. Readers of the tabloids are more likely to be lower earners and, as such, are less attractive to advertisers.

Consumer magazines also tend to rely heavily on advertising so again the circulation of a specialist magazine may not be too significant. If an advertiser is selling computers, for instance, then a computer magazine is much more likely to net results than any other publication. The circulation may only be 50,000, but at least that's 50,000 people who are likely to buy a computer at some time in the future.

When a newspaper is being planned, the advertising department will usually produce some way of identifying which advert is where so that editorial staff know what space is left for them to fill. Of course, many publishing software systems will represent the pages with their advert spaces already listed and so a quick look at the individual pages, or **thumbnails** of all the pages, will soon show the editor what space there is.

Traditionally, though, there are two main ways of identifying space for use by editorial, and it may be that these continue on whatever publication you are working. The first is a **dummy** of the paper, a small-scale mock-up of the paper with ads marked on each page. This is useful, particularly for newspapers, as it gives the editor the chance to detail stories on the appropriate pages as well.

The second method is the **flat plan**. This is of more use to magazines as it allows the editor to view a large number of pages at once and see which are editorial and which advertising. Since most magazine adverts tend to be full page, this is easily done, even though the page size in a flat plan is very small. It is this flat plan which tends to be used in software systems and most allow you to view the range of pages on screen.

thumbnail substantially reduced image of page or graphic.

dummy newspaper mock-up to track the placing of adverts.

flat plan plan of publication showing all pages (see Figure 17.1).

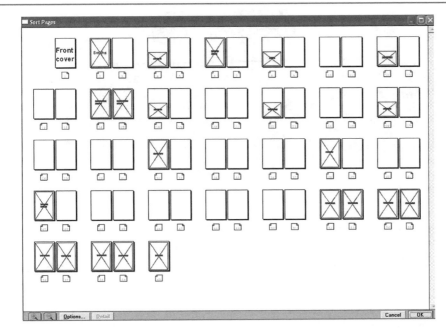

Figure 17.1 A flat plan shows which pages contain adverts and which are free for editorial

Importance of type

Type is essential to any published document. It is type that makes the imprint of characters and, therefore, puts words on the paper. In the days of hot-metal printing, type was cast from a lead amalgam into a shape that could press ink on to paper to print characters. Nowadays with much printing, particularly of newspapers and magazines, being done on web offset litho presses, the type is no longer anything other than a digital signature in a computer. The characters that make up the words we read are placed directly on to the plate used in the printing process to place ink on the paper in the appropriate patterns to represent a page. However, our understanding and descriptions of type still hark back to the days when type was something that could be seen and measured.

It has to be stressed that the printed word and the characters representing them are not a transparent medium. The way they are used has an effect on the message transmitted that needs to be considered. The reader will take different messages from the type depending on the font used, whether it is in lower or upper case, the colour of the ink, the amount and use of space around the type and the style of the font.

Only a moment's thought will show that writing a message of condolence to a friend calls for handwriting, using your best pen. Many people still use quality fountain pens to write personal messages of this sort. They would happily use a

Figure 17.2 Metal type, the precursor of modern fonts

computer and laser printer to send a business letter and would scribble a note to the milkman with a cheap ballpoint or pencil, but the extra care that comes through the use of the traditional pen and ink says something additional to the words they actually form with that pen.

Using type in design

The design of type is the skilled art of the typographer. There are thousands of fonts available although many look similar even under fairly close scrutiny. There are five main groups of type: old style, transitional, modern, Egyptian and contemporary (Craig 1980: 31). These broadly represent the development of type over the last 350 years or so of printing. From a design point of view, it is easier (and more helpful) to categorise type as old style, modern, slab serif, sans serif, script and decorative (Frost 2003: 92).

Old-style type follows the design of type of its day which was based on handwriting. The type has thick and thin strokes, providing an emphasis to certain parts of each character. The characters also had serifs, the small flicks at the end of each main stroke of the character. Modern type carried on much of this tradition but became blockier and squarer as the characters started to fit with the technology and the need to carve the new type meant that this took precedence over the more flowing style possible with a pen.

sans serif modern style font without (sans) the serif (the fine line finishing the main strokes of a letter such as at the foot of 'T').

Sans-serif faces took this to the limit with most of the types getting rid of the thick and thin strokes and having uniform thickness of stroke. All sans-serif fonts lost the serif, giving a much blockier appearance and making it more legible.

Scripts are designed to look like handwriting. These fonts are used on invitations and anywhere else where the aim is give a more personal feel.

Decorative fonts are hugely varied. The only common features of these are that you would be unlikely to use them for any length of type display because they are often difficult to read. However, they often add an extra message to the words set in the font and so are useful for headlines, logos or titles. A heading for a feature about fire safety written in a font that looks like flames conveys the fire message and so allows you to avoid that word in the heading. A feature about insulating the home could have a font that is covered in snow.

Clearly script and decorative fonts are only used occasionally in publications. Normally designers concentrate on modern serif fonts for body type and sans serif fonts for headlines. This is because serif fonts are generally believed to be easier to read and more legible whilst sans-serif fonts are seen as being more perceptible and, therefore, easier to read quickly and at a distance. A quick glance at any of the tabloids will show this choice in action. Heavy Gothic sans-serif fonts shout out the headlines, whilst the choice of a clear and easy to read modern serif font provides the body text. Sans-serif fonts are a bit like shouting: easier to hear but very wearing if continued for a long time.

Not all publications use sans-serif fonts for headlines, of course, and some like to use them for the body type. Try looking at various magazines and newspapers and spotting which uses which. Modern magazines will tend to use more sans-serif fonts on their pages whilst newspapers trying to present a traditional, authoritative and trustworthy image are more likely to use seriffed fonts, even in the headlines.

When a newspaper or magazine is first designed, the choice of fonts available to the page designer will have been set and those fonts purchased and loaded into the computer. The range of fonts available to an editor will, therefore, be limited. The choice of heading or body font will already have been made. However, each font is a family of type and within that family there is usually a wide variation. The type can be used **roman** (as the designer made it) bold, where the strokes are thicker than roman, italic, **condensed**, **expanded** or combinations of these.

roman not bold or italic.

condensed a version of a font that has been squeezed horizontally.

expanded a version of a font that has been expanded horizontally.

This means that the same font can be used for headlines on a news page, but each of the six or so headlines could look slightly different. This variety within the font means that the page designer can add a little variety without using different fonts. A range of different fonts on a page is a typical rookie error. The page will lack cohesion and may even appear to be a complete jumble of unrelated elements.

It is possible to insert one headline on a page from a different font (a device known as a kicker) as this will add extra emphasis to that story even though it may be hidden away down the page with only a small heading.

Structure

Because type started as physical pieces of metal used to press ink onto paper, much of the description of type is based on its appearance. But it has to be stressed that type and the space in which it lives are related. In the days of hot metal, the metal block from which the character design was carved or moulded provided the size of the type. The character had to be smaller than this. (If you don't believe this, try carving a character out of a potato or soap. It will be smaller than the body type. Incidentally, if you do try this, try inking the finished result and pressing it against paper to see how type used to work. Note how the image is reversed by the process.)

This means it is impossible to tell the size of type by measuring it once it has been printed. Nor can you measure the x-height (the height of letters without **descenders** or **ascenders**) because this is determined solely by the design of the type, not by its size. Just to further ensure that measuring characters printed in a newspaper is of little help in guiding on size, most printed material shrinks slightly after printing.

descenders the portion of a letter that descends below the x-height in the following: g, p, q, j, y.

ascender upright in the letters b, d, f, h, k, l.

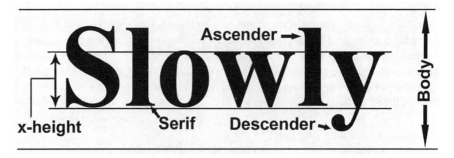

Figure 17.3 Type shape and description of its parts

Shape

The shape of the type will vary considerably depending on the design of the type. One of the most confusing aspects of type shape is the **x-height**. Some font designs have a very large x-height with small descenders and ascenders. These are often quite legible, unless the effect is extreme, in which case it can often be difficult to tell the letters, for instance 'n' and 'h', apart. At the other extreme, characters with small x-heights and long descenders and ascenders can look very elegant, but again, taken to extremes, can eventually become very difficult to read.

x-height element of typeface minus the ascender and descender (in effect, the size of the lower-case 'x').

Size

Type in the UK and USA is measured in points while in Continental Europe the Didot system is used where type is measured in ciceros. The point system is a measuring system in its own right and is not directly linked to any other system any more than the metric system is linked to the imperial system of measurement. However, it is possible to convert the measurements and there are approximately 72 points (pt) to the inch or 28.34 to the centimetre.

The point system was introduced when printers were able to pick up a block of type and measure the body. Most computer systems now make it easy to get a certain typesize and both word processors and desktop-publishing software allow you to choose a typesize anywhere from 4 pt up to 999 pt. In the old days of cast type, buying in a font at a particular size was quite an investment. Hundreds of cast characters needed to be bought and stored. Consequently, newspapers often limited the range of sizes available. Headline fonts would be available in perhaps 14 pt, 18 pt, 24 pt, 30 pt, 36 pt, 42 pt, 48 pt, 60 pt, 72 pt and 84 pt. Now any headline size is available at the click of a button.

The width of type is measured slightly differently. The square of a 12 pt line of text is called a **pica**-em. This is because 12 pt used to be called a pica (pronounced piker) and an em means the square of the body height. It is, of course, possible to get 10 pt ems, 8 pt ems and 36 pt ems and so on, but the standard measurement of width used nowadays is the 12 pt em. This means that a column of text is often referred to as being 12 ems wide. This would be 12 pica-ems, regardless of the height of the text the column is set in.

pica old name for 12 pt.

Most computer software allows the setting of column widths in ems – these will always be pica-ems or 12 pt ems. An old name of a 12 pt em is a **mutton**. A 12 pt-**en** (half an em) is known as a **nut**. An en (or nut) is the usual measurement used to indent a paragraph.

mutton slang name for an em.

en half an em.

nut slang name for an en.

White space

We have looked at type; now we need to look at the other side of the equation: the space in which it lives. When reading printed characters, one tends to concentrate on the printed character itself, but the space in which it lives is of equal importance. It is the contrast between the crisp black strokes of the character and the clean white of the page that gives definition and legibility to the character.

If the black character was printed in muddy grey paper or was cramped by surrounding characters, it would not be very readable. A good way to give emphasis to a message is to give it plenty of display space. There are two main ways to add space around a printed message. The first is **leading** (pronounced ledding) which is the space between lines; the second is the space inserted on the page between each block of type whether these are the column divides or the spaces above or below a story.

lead pronounced 'led'. The space between lines which is additional to the size of the body type. So called because it was originally strips of metal (lead) which spaced out lines of type.

leading pronounced 'ledding': as 'lead' above but also used to mean the actual space (as opposed to the body type) in which the type lives.

Leading

Leading is so called because when type was made up of physical blocks of metal and extra space between lines was required in addition to the type's body size, strips made of lead of the size required were inserted between the lines to pad out the gap. Nowadays, with computer setting, leading has come to mean the total space in which the type lives including the body size. So instead of saying 10 pt type with 2 pt of leading, we would now instruct the computer to provide 10 pt type with 12 pt of leading.

A quick look at Figure 17.4 will show the difference that leading can make. A crowded display with no additional leading looks rushed and busy. Of course, you can fit more words into the same space by reducing the leading to a minimum, but it is not so easy to read and long columns of close-spaced type is hard work. Tinker claims that adding a certain amount of space can aid legibility (1963: 93). However, packed, dense setting can be ideal for a tabloid with only short story runs. It allows for more to be put on the page, particularly as the pages are relatively small and they tend to be dominated by large pictures.

The closely packed type allows a fair bit of text to be published and adds a lively, busy feel. Broadsheets, on the other hand, tend to put some space between the lines. Extra space gives a feeling of authority and sophistication. Try looking at adverts to see how this works. The big electrical wholesalers cram their ads with small type squeezed into a small space, partly so they can gain space to put in all their 'bargains' but mainly to make it look as though the business is rush, rush, rush as customers sprint into the store to snap up the bargains on offer. This feeling of busyness and activity is all developed through the lack of space in the advert.

Banks and insurance companies want you to feel that their business is entirely trustworthy, that they have time for you and will discuss your needs in an unhurried

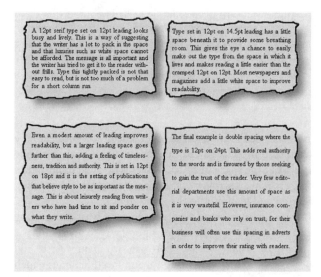

A 12pt serif type set on 12pt leading looks busy and lively. This is a way of suggesting that the writer has a lot to pack in the space and that luxuries such as white space cannot be afforded. The message is all important and the writer has tried to get it to the reader without frills. Type this tightly packed is not that easy to read, but is not too much of a problem for a short column run.

Type set in 12pt on 14.5pt leading has a little space beneath it to provide some breathing room. This gives the eye a chance to easily make out the type from the space in which it lives and makes reading a little easier than the cramped 12pt on 12pt. Most newspapers and magazines add a little white space to improve readability.

Even a modest amount of leading improves readability, but a larger leading space goes further than this, adding a feeling of timelessness, tradition and authority. This is set in 12pt on 18pt and it is the setting of publications that believe style to be as important as the message. This is about leisurely reading from writers who have had time to sit and ponder on what they write.

The final example is double spacing where the type is 12pt on 24pt. This adds real authority to the words and is favoured by those seeking to gain the trust of the reader. Very few editorial departments use this amount of space as it is very wasteful. However, insurance companies and banks who rely on trust, for their business will often use this spacing in adverts in order to improve their rating with readers.

Figure 17.4 The difference that leading can make

way. They want to put over a feeling of class and trust and they do this by putting plenty of space in the advert. Type is double- or even triple-spaced; there is often a huge amount of space around each block of type and it is unlikely to be cluttered by pictures or graphics.

Ink colour

The colour of the ink used is another important factor to consider after the type and space have been decided. Traditionally we print in black on white paper. The main reason for this is that this is the most legible type can be. The clear contrast between the type and the space has its maximum emphasis in this colour choice. However, this is not the only colour that works well. Dark blue ink or a heavy red are also perfectly readable.

However, once you move on to lighter colours, more care needs to be taken about choice. Whilst a light yellow, for instance, might suit perfectly what you are intending to do (perhaps it's Easter, or your heading says: 'Golden moments') you should be aware that yellow ink on white paper is very difficult to read. This can be helped by printing it on a grey or blue patch or by using an outline font where the yellow type is outlined in another, darker colour.

There are similar problems with the colour of the paper. White paper is best, with very pale colours not too far behind. However, care needs to be taken with coloured paper. A very pale yellow paper, for instance, printed in black can ring the changes from white paper without costing a lot. The *Financial Times*, for instance, has made it a trademark to print its pages a light, salmon pink. If you are printing in a mono colour, black or dark blue, a pale colour can add interest.

However, printing dark ink on dark coloured paper can make the type virtually unreadable, so if you are printing in full colour, then stick to white paper and make colour changes in the ink, not the paper. Take a look at the *Financial Times*. You will find that while its mono pages are pink stock (paper) overprinted with black, its colour pages are printed on white stock and that pink background is printed on.

Structuring text

Once decisions have been made about the font, the paper and the ink, then the type needs to be structured on the page. This is done in columns, even if there is only one column on the page. The column of type will be laid out in the chosen typesize with the chosen leading. Now there are other decisions that need to be taken in relation to the column of type itself.

Indents

The first choice to make is whether and where to indent. Adding an **indent** means putting a small space at the start of the line of type to move it away from the notional column edge. It is possible to indent a whole column, to move it away from the column edge to insert a **rule**. Or one can indent just the first line of type. It is normal, in setting type, to add an indent at the start of each paragraph so that each paragraph is clearly identified down the column of text. This helps break the column up into readable chunks and allows a return point for a reader who might break away from reading during a story.

indent   small space at start of line.

rule   a straight line.

Books, on the other hand, often do not indent paragraphs – it is a design choice. It is also possible to have a reverse indent where the first line of the paragraph is set '**full out**' and all the subsequent lines are indented. This can be useful for a sidebar, additional text set alongside the main story but separated from it by some design device, such as an indent.

full out   when text occupies the full measure of the column.

It is possible to indent both sides of a block of text and this would normally be done if a box was being put around the text to make room for the rules. Such indents are often added automatically by page make-up software, if the designer asks for a box around text.

Alignment

The look of the text in the column can also be altered by the way it is aligned. Text in newspapers is normally justified. This means that the text is lined up both with the left-hand margin of the column and the right-hand margin. The computer has to juggle the type by inserting extra space between characters and between words to ensure that each line of type is exactly the same length. If it is impossible to shorten a line sufficiently because the words used are quite long, the computer will hyphenate the last word on the line to keep the line the same length.

It will hyphenate according to a series of predetermined rules called 'hyphenation and **justification**' or 'H+J'. In the early days of computer setting, hyphenation needed to be checked to ensure the computer had not hyphenated in a way that changed the sense of what was written, but that happens rarely, these days. The classic example of words that should be hyphenated with care is the word 'therapist'.

justification   a way of setting type to ensure that all lines on both sides of the block of text are level.

Hyphenating after the 'the' gives 'the-rapist' which can easily be read as 'the rapist' as the reader's eye scans to the next line. The correct hyphenation is after the 'r' to give 'ther-apist'.

After justified alignment, the next favourite is left aligned. This is where the type aligns with the left-hand margin but is ragged on the right-hand side, in the way that anything handwritten tends to be. Right-aligned text, sometimes called ragged left, aligns with the right-hand margin and is ragged on the left. This can be useful to associate a piece of text with something to its right, drawing it away from the item on its left. Centre-aligned text, or ragged both, aligns to a notional centre point. This is useful for items such as film credits or football results.

Devices

Another way of making the block of text look different or stand out from the other blocks of text surrounding it is to add a 'device' to the text.

Drop letters

drop letter (also **drop cap**) printed version of the illuminated letters that started hand-scribed bibles and other manuscripts. The letter is large enough to run alongside two or three lines of text.

One of the first devices is the **drop letter**, sometimes called a **drop cap** because it is usually a capital letter since it comes at the start of the paragraph. This is similar to, although not as elaborate as, the illuminated letters that were put at the start of manuscripts by clerics of yore. The drop cap will normally be three lines deep and fits in an indent provided for it in the first three lines of text.

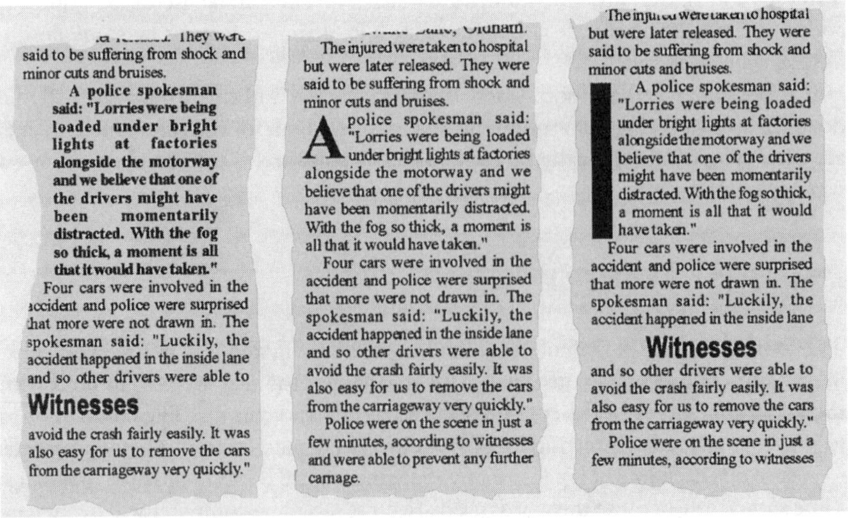
They were said to be suffering from shock and minor cuts and bruises.

A police spokesman said: "Lorries were being loaded under bright lights at factories alongside the motorway and we believe that one of the drivers might have been momentarily distracted. With the fog so thick, a moment is all that it would have taken."

Four cars were involved in the accident and police were surprised that more were not drawn in. The spokesman said: "Luckily, the accident happened in the inside lane and so other drivers were able to

Witnesses

avoid the crash fairly easily. It was also easy for us to remove the cars from the carriageway very quickly."

The injured were taken to hospital but were later released. They were said to be suffering from shock and minor cuts and bruises.

A police spokesman said: "Lorries were being loaded under bright lights at factories alongside the motorway and we believe that one of the drivers might have been momentarily distracted. With the fog so thick, a moment is all that it would have taken."

Four cars were involved in the accident and police were surprised that more were not drawn in. The spokesman said: "Luckily, the accident happened in the inside lane and so other drivers were able to avoid the crash fairly easily. It was also easy for us to remove the cars from the carriageway very quickly."

Police were on the scene in just a few minutes, according to witnesses and were able to prevent any further carnage.

The injured were taken to hospital but were later released. They were said to be suffering from shock and minor cuts and bruises.

A police spokesman said: "Lorries were being loaded under bright lights at factories alongside the motorway and we believe that one of the drivers might have been momentarily distracted. With the fog so thick, a moment is all that it would have taken."

Four cars were involved in the accident and police were surprised that more were not drawn in. The spokesman said: "Luckily, the accident happened in the inside lane

Witnesses

and so other drivers were able to avoid the crash fairly easily. It was also easy for us to remove the cars from the carriageway very quickly."

Police were on the scene in just a few minutes, according to witnesses

Figure 17.5 Different devices: bold par, drop cap and bold vertical rule – all ways to add emphasis and interest

Boxes

The text can be placed in a box made up from rules of an appropriate size. Rules are measured in point size, so a 2 pt or 3 pt rule would be fairly normal to surround a block of text. But other rules are available in thicker sizes or in specialised designs such as holly leaves for Christmas. A story about a party might have pictures of champagne bottles around it. You can also have a shadow box, when the text block is made to appear as though it has a shadow, or the whole block of type can be laid on a patch of colour.

Bold, italic, etc.

Another way of adding emphasis to the block of text or to parts of the block is to change the font. Normal setting is in roman but either the whole block, or a paragraph or sentence within it can be set to a different style. A bold paragraph, for instance, would give emphasis while a few words in italic would allow them to stand away from the rest of the text. This is often used to identify proper names of books, of films, and so on.

These are the two main methods of differentiating type but there are other styles such as expanding the text, condensing it or running it in capital letters. Capitals will add emphasis, particularly to a heading or caption, but need to be used sparingly. Using capital letters is a bit like shouting: it grabs the attention but it is wearing to listen to it for too long. A short sentence in **caps** can be useful but reading more than ten to fifteen words is hard work.

caps upper-case letters.

Another method of adding emphasis is to underscore a word or a series of words. Again, this should not be overused as it is more difficult to read but can draw a short sentence to the reader's attention. Another way of doing this for a piece of text longer than a sentence is vertical scoring. This is where a paragraph or two are indented and a vertical rule is placed in the space made. This vertical scoring can go either side of the column or on both sides. Again, it should not be overused but can add strong emphasis without making reading more difficult.

Bullet points

Text that is to be built into a list can be emphasised with bullet points. These can be either true bullets (small filled circles) or small shapes or designs. A list of phone numbers, for instance, might be listed against a small picture of a phone. Bullet points are useful because:

- they are easy to identify
- reduce space
- make listing easy to do and to follow.

Standfirsts

Another type device is the standfirst. This sits between the heading and the story intro acting as an explanation of the story. It often includes a byline. An example of a standfirst might read as follows: 'In our continuing series about the bridges of

Britain, Jane Fanshaw crosses the Forth rail bridge, a Scottish landmark best-known for its constant repainting.'

Bylines

Bylines are another type block device identifying the author of a story, although sometimes this is a very limited identification such as: 'By a staff reporter'. Usually these days the identification is more detailed. It might also contain a picture of the reporter and even some details. If the writer is a guest writer and their identity is significant, then the byline may also contain some biographical detail. The *Daily Mail*, for instance, runs a column called 'The Saturday Essay'. Academics, politicians and others in public life are invited to write this and a short biography is printed so that readers can know the author's background.

Using type

Type is the starting point of any publication and is formed into blocks of text. There are a number of different types of block in a modern newspaper or magazine. The first is the body text, the actual copy of the story that is to be read. This will be set in the body type, often a modern serif text designed to be highly readable, allowing the reader to take in the meaning easily and go on reading without effort for as long as they want.

The next kind of block of type used is the headline, or heading, and the subheading. These are designed to stand out from the page and draw the reader's attention into the article they lead. Headlines tend to be big and are often in a font that will grab attention, such as a sans serif.

Another type of block is the picture caption. This will normally sit under the picture explaining any detail that is not obvious to the reader. A picture containing a group of people, for instance, will need to give their names to the reader. A picture of a bridge over a river does not need a caption explaining this is a bridge over a river, but it may well need a caption explaining which bridge over which river and possibly why you are publishing a picture of it.

Captions are best set under the picture where convention tells the reader to look for it. Moving a caption to somewhere else risks annoying readers who cannot find it. It is possible to place the caption within the frame of the picture, up the side of the picture or in a block of captions referring to a series of pictures. A block caption should make it perfectly clear which caption refers to which picture. This is usually done by writing captions as follows: 'RIGHT: London's famous Tower Bridge. BELOW: The Humber Bridge. LEFT: The Severn Bridge'.

It is possible to put numbers or letters against each picture and then reference the captions in this way. So long as it is to house style and is easy for the reader to follow, how you caption pictures is up to you.

Pictures and graphics

Pictures are the other main component of news reporting and features. The days of text-only newspapers are long gone. Pictures started to appear in newspapers back in the 1800s with the invention of photography. By the early twentieth century, pictures were important to any newspaper, and the invention of television has only increased the importance of pictures.

Pictures add life and animation to a page. They can give us detail that no amount of descriptive writing can add. A picture of death and disaster from Iraq can tell more about the problems of violent solutions to intractable problems than any amount of writing. A picture of an overjoyed footballer in the World Cup can show us national pride and the triumph of victory in a flash of a camera shutter.

Good pictures or graphics provide an additional element that is difficult to obtain through text alone. A good picture should:

- illustrate the story
- underline the emotions in the story
- hint at action
- give the reader the chance to identify with the characters in the story.

Sometimes the picture is the story and it may be good enough to stand on its own with only scant caption details to give additional information. This is often the case for presentations and awards in local newspapers.

A good picture can dominate a page, drawing the reader in to flesh out the details behind the picture. Even when the picture is not award-winning, it should still add to the page and the story it supports. According to Harry Evans, the former *Sunday Times* editor and news-production guru, there are three tests for a publishable picture and a picture that fails any of these three should be rejected: animation, relevant context and depth of meaning (Evans 1978: 47).

Animation means that there should be signs of movement or emotion or activity. It could be a facial expression that tells us about the person or it could be evidence of movement. Relevant context means that the picture helps to explain what is happening. It adds detail about the event easily and without fuss. Depth of meaning adds emotion and feeling to the picture. The reader should feel as though they witnessed the events instead of just being told about them.

Choice of picture is vital. A good editor will never use a picture just because there is one. A dull, lifeless picture is just a waste of space that may have been put to better use by inserting another story or adding extra written information. Whilst a well-designed page probably needs a picture to give balance, a well-designed newspaper should only use copy and pictures that really tell a story and involve the reader in something that will interest them.

One of the hardest challenges for any designer or editor is to avoid the routine. It is vital to keep everything fresh, to be developing news ideas with lively, interesting copy supported by eye-catching and helpful pictures. One way of achieving this is to refuse to accept the standard 5:4 oblong picture. The classic shape for a photograph, whether portrait or landscape is 5 to 4 ratio. This is a shape that is pleasing to the eye and allows us to frame in a more interesting way than a square.

However, just because 5:4 pictures are a standard does not mean they have to be used all the time. Our eyes see things in landscape. Most people have vision that scans practically 180° in the horizontal plane. We cannot see so much in the vertical plane because our eyebrows and cheeks prevent it. After all, the ground immediately in front and the sky above rarely yield anything much worth looking at. So we can usually see as much as we need to, especially as a twist of the neck will actually allow us virtually 360° vision in the horizontal plane and 180° in the vertical.

This means we are used to seeing things as landscape. A move to a portrait shape, especially if it is particularly elongated, can make an unusual frame that will bring a picture to life. Try different frame sizes and shapes with any picture: it's amazing how a fairly ordinary picture can suddenly spring to life when the right shape is used.

Different angles can also add new life. A good photographer should be presenting the editor with a variety of shots with unusual shapes and angles. We are all used to seeing pictures from the point of view of someone standing up so pictures taken from a height of 5 to 6 ft are the norm. What about shooting from very low down or very high up? This is not to say any picture taken at eye-level should be rejected, but that pictures from high up or low down might bring a new look to a hackneyed picture idea. Photographers are much more likely to try new ideas if they know the editor is interested in using them.

Part of this shaping of the picture can be done during editing. By using unusual shapes, we often edit the picture in a way that concentrates the eye on the essentials, or at least what the editor considers to be the essentials for that particular story. Cropping the picture to remove unwanted parts can bring to life a section of the picture that until then had appeared staid. One of the advantages of photography is that it can take everyday scenes and then breathe new life into them by clever cropping and editing.

Figure 17.6 A picture should be cropped to show only the section that you require

If you are working on pictures on screen in a software package such as Photoshop, cropping experiments are relatively easy. Occasionally, however, you will want to look at a series of photographs to make a choice before scanning. When doing this, then two L-shaped pieces of card can be used as frames to try different shapes on the picture before sending the picture chosen for scanning.

Scaling

Once a picture shape and frame has been decided on, the picture will need to be scaled. This means choosing a size for it on the page. There are two elements involved in scaling the picture. The first is choosing the size and ensuring the picture is of sufficient quality to fit in the size chosen. For instance, a poor-quality picture, produced on the computer in low resolution may not take the kind of enlargement needed to make it a full-page picture.

The second element of picture scaling is ensuring that the ratio between the two dimensions of the picture remains the same. If, for instance, a picture is 25 cm wide and 10 cm deep, scaling the height down to fit a space 8 cm high means the width will reduce to 20 cm. You should always avoid squeezing or stretching a picture since this will alter the look and can distort the truth of a picture.

Pictures are printed in a publication using either black ink or the four coloured inks cyan, magenta, yellow and black. So how can we represent greys in single-ink pictures or a full range of tones in full-colour publications? The answer is known as half-tone. The picture is not produced as a painting would be by using a range of different pigments, but is represented as a series of dots of ink printed on to the

Figure 17.7 After cropping the section of picture you require, you need to scale it to fit available space on the page

white background. The larger the dot and the less space around it, the darker the area of the picture appears to be. Try looking at a published black-and-white photograph using a magnifying glass and you will see that each grey tone is represented by a collection of smaller or larger dots of ink.

Image ethics

There are many ethical considerations surrounding the use of images. Modern photographic software makes altering images extremely easy. Whether it is cropping the picture, altering the colour balance or removing something from or adding something to the picture the journalistic imperative of truth-telling needs to be constantly borne in mind.

Editing a picture to include the segment of the portrait that we want is inevitable. At some point, the photographer has to compose the picture, choosing what will appear and what will be excluded. The editor has to make similar decisions, perhaps cropping a picture to exclude even more than the photographer thought appropriate.

Consideration needs to be given at both these stages to the editorial decisions to be made in line with the story to be told and the element of truth-telling that is so important in journalism. The ease of adding or removing bits of pictures can lead editors to 'improve' the picture, some even claiming to improve the truth of it, by, in one famous case changing John Prescott's habitual pint of Newcastle Brown for a bottle of Champagne (Frost 2000: 137).

Special effects

As well as changing the truth of pictures, modern software allows easy access to a range of special effects that can be used to emphasise one element of a story or another. Pictures can be altered to appear to be underwater or be overlaid with clouds. It would be rare to use these effects in a news story but a magazine or newspaper feature might well find them useful. Overlaying pictures or piercing them with type or other pictures can also brighten the design and disguise a weak picture. A picture of a new building, with a large area of sky to one side could be made more useful by inserting a portrait of the architect over the sky, with the caption sitting below, but still within the main picture area.

Graphics

Graphics are another way of illustrating a story that might involve a photograph or a drawn picture or a combination of the two. Whenever a design is considered the illustration that should sit with the story should also be considered. It might be a map or an illustrated diagram of a machine or an artist's impression of a space vehicle, but they all help to illustrate the story. You should be held back only by your imagination and the time available to you when it comes to graphic illustrations.

LEFT and RIGHT: Two of the silver items found on the site. Archaeologists were surprised by the quality of the finds.

Figure 17.8 A graphic combining several pictures to produce one picture that gives much more information

DESIGNING A NEW PAGE

Designing a new page involves careful planning and a creative flair. Start with the entry point. This is the place where the reader's attention is first caught and drawn into the page. Locating it is best done by trying ideas on a visual. Sketching out a page so that the various stories are presented gives a sense of scale and also allows the designer to easily discard ideas that do not work well without a lot of extra work. A visual takes only seconds to produce and quickly shows whether the design is likely to work. Figure 17.9 shows an example of a visual and, although I have drawn my example fairly neatly, most visuals, in fact, are sketches in a notebook to allow a quick chance to see how a particular design may work.

First steps

The first step in designing a page is to list what stories are available and their comparative weight for inclusion on the page. Much of this information will have been decided by the editor or the chief sub-editor, or whoever is directly in charge of production. That person will have told the designer what the lead story is, which is second lead, what the picture stories are and so on.

Each publication has its own style relating to story count, shapes and sizes. Story count is an important decision to make on any publication. A low story count makes for a wordier publication with lengthy stories. A feature-based magazine, for instance, may carry only one story on a page; indeed, it may carry one story across

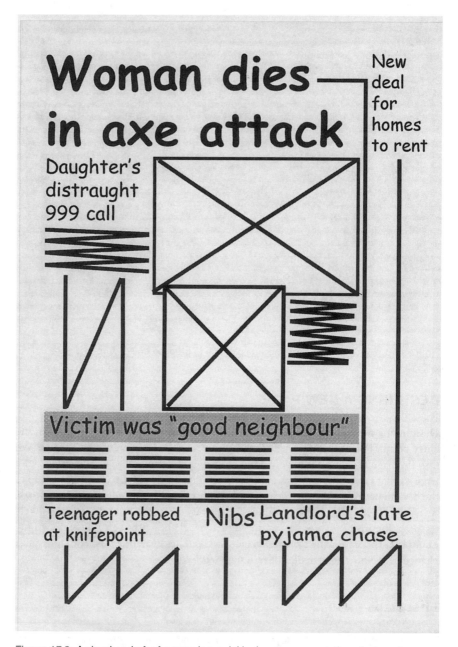

Figure 17.9 A visual or draft of a page is a quickly drawn representation of where the various stories might go and how the page will look

several pages. This is designed for leisurely reading where the reader has time to carry on reading over a number of pages at a time.

Newspapers, on the other hand, almost always carry a number of stories on the same page. A broadsheet regional newspaper will often try to maximise the benefits of a large page area to make its pages look busy and exciting by carrying up to ten stories on a page. An inside tabloid news page may follow a similar strategy, carrying six or seven stories on the page. This allows the reader to flick from story to story without turning the page, giving them ease of reading and a feeling of value for money.

Turning pages can be a problem on a crowded train, for instance, and a high story count can hold the interest of a reader who is not able to give their full attention to the page. A tabloid/compact front page, however, is there to attract the reader to buy the paper and it is rare to carry more than three stories. Many tabloid pages carry only one together with a large puff (adverts for the inside of the paper intended to entice the reader to buy without giving away the full story).

A lively page of a publication designed to be read at speed will have a high story count. This allows the reader to finish a short story quickly and then flick on to the next headline. A low story count suits a publication that specialises in longer articles intended to be read in comfort on a long train journey, for instance, or while relaxing at home. Take women's magazines, for instance. *Glamour* is a small, A5-sized magazine with a medium story count but this, combined with the small pages, is a magazine clearly designed for commuters or those with limited attention spans, which often includes young adults.

The more traditional women's magazine, such as *Bella* or *Prima*, remains in a traditional format with much longer features spread over several pages designed to be read during times of relaxation, whether on a train journey, in the evening or on holiday. The same is true with newspapers. The broadsheets/compacts assume the reader will invest the time required to read longer articles. Red-top tabloids need to grab the reader's attention, constantly telling the reader: 'No, look here, at me.'

Shaping the page

Once you know what your normal style is for the publication you work for, you can start to plan the page. Table 17.1 is a copy list for an inside page of a tabloid regional paper. The story count is fixed at five, but the lead is a good story and the chief sub-editor will have given instructions to give it a good show. This means that at least half the page, possibly more, should be allocated to this story. In fact, this story is so good it is a surprise it is not on the front. However, we can only assume the editor has an even better story for that position. This means the lead needs a lot of space and the other stories will then be fitted around it with the amount of display offered being varied according to what you think each is worth.

The first consideration when starting a page is the 'entry point' which catches the reader's attention as they flick through the pages and draws them in. Garcia and Stark tell us this is often a picture (Garcia and Stark 1991: 26). A secondary entry point next encourages the reading of the text. This is influenced largely by convention. In the UK, we read from left to right and down the text. So the starting point of any text is the top left-hand corner, and that is where the reader will look. Therefore, it is normal to run headlines from the top left-hand corner and to put the introduction to the body copy beneath that heading.

Running a banner heading across the top of the page and then putting the story on the right, with a different story on the left beneath the heading is going to leave

Table 17.1

Story	Length	Pix	Position
Murder – mother killed by axe murderer	450w lead; 150 sidebar	Holiday snap of woman; pic of home.	lead
Landlord story	193	None	base
L-driver and other nibs	272	None	S/c R/h
Knife-point robbery	167	None	Base
Pub landlord	223	None	Base

the reader confused. We need to identify clearly where they are supposed to go, and if this is not the conventional place, then we need to signpost where the reader can find the start of the story.

Headings of appropriate size should then direct them to the next most important story on the page and so on until the page is read. However, we need to remember that because of the reading convention, British readers tend to scan the page in a reversed 'C'. They start at left-hand top corner and then scan through to the right and down the page, ending at the bottom, towards the left.

There is a regular debate amongst editors and design journalists about the importance of the left-hand page versus the right-hand page. Standard wisdom tells us that the right-hand page has more impact on readers because they see that first as they open up the two pages. However, there is very little research to support that and Garcia and Stark suggest that the two pages are treated as one during the initial scan by the reader and the strongest entry point on either page is the one that draws the eye. Usually this initial entry point will be a picture, the most important entry point whether on a single page or two pages (Garcia and Stark 1991: 26).

Because the picture is the main entry point, this is the ideal starting point for a page. Our story listing above shows there is one lead story and this is the only story with pictures. We would make the entry point a block of these pictures in the centre top of the page, a heading would go above the pictures to draw the reader from the pictures to the text and the text would then drop from the headings on the left-hand side of the pictures.

Neither picture is very exciting, though. We have a picture of an ordinary town-centre home and a holiday snap of the woman obtained by a reporter. It will be worth checking whether we have permission to use the holiday snap. Taking such pictures from a home without permission is not only immoral but risks breaching copyright and may also be breaching the Press Complaints Commission's code of practice.

Can we do anything to brighten the picture up? Well it's possible we can. We could ask the artist to draw a plan of the building so that we could show where the woman was attacked. We could try to get a picture of her or members of her family. We will probably make the picture section a composite of several pictures.

The visual (see Figure 17.9) gives us the chance to try ideas, including blocking in a section of pictures in the centre of the page around which we can take the lead heading and subheadings and the story entry point. This will fill up the top and left-hand side of the page. There also is a sidebar story. As you can see in Figure 17.10, this has been run underneath the rest of the story to provide a clear break from the other stories. There are two pictures, one laid over the bottom of the other, with a small amount of white space surrounding it. The story is boxed off from those below but relies on the clear differentiation between the lead and the story in the right-hand column to separate them.

Looking at Figure 17.10, the final design makes the pictures reasonably large, even though they are not anything special, and the heading is strong and in two decks. There are some changes made between the visual and the final design – the visual is for guidance only and does not need to be followed slavishly.

You should not be afraid of using pictures and headings in generous sizes to give strength and life to the page. Calculating the amount of space taken by the headlines and pictures, you will find that these cover 39 per cent of the total page area. In other words, the pictures and heading on the lead story alone (not including the text) take two fifths of the total page area. The whole story takes up nearly two thirds of the page.

The next story laid in is the second lead about the landlords. It drops clearly down the right-hand column and stands well away from the others (see Figure 17.11). That means we can use the last three stories across the bottom of the page. There's a lot of crime on this page, but that's the nature of a lot of local (and often national) news.

This will give a nicely balanced page (see Figure 17.12), with the major story supported by three short stories running across the bottom of the page. The pictures will give strength to the centre of the page as well as drawing the eye into the page, and the strong intro paragraph on the lead will act as an entry point. Note how each story has an intro set in slightly larger type. This helps the reader easily identify where the story starts.

The centre story at the bottom of the page is indented both sides so that it can be set in a box, to set it slightly apart from the stories on either side. It is also run in a slightly greater width than is normal, but is not a full two columns. This is a change from the visual. The visual also anticipated that the second lead would fill the right-hand column to the bottom of the lead story but, in fact, it was somewhat short. The space left has been filled with a couple of nibs.

The second lead story could have been set in reverse indent to help stand it away from the rest of the stories but, in fact, I have not done that since the pictures act as enough of a break and nothing else is required. Note how the pictures are blocked together. One overlays the other, with a slight space cut around it, and they include the caption in space that is part of the natural shape of the entire block.

Running and shaping text

Text is run and shaped according to normal conventions once the entry point has been chosen. Newspaper text is traditionally run into fairly narrow columns. The width of text will vary according to the size of the type, with larger type needing

Woman dies in axe attack

Daughter's 999 call to save mum

A mother of two was killed last night in her own home after being attacked by an axeman.

Tracey Appleby suffered multiple injuries all over her body and was pronounced dead on arrival at hospital.

By Chris Frost

The 43-year-old mother of two teenaged daughters was at home when the attack happened. Her terrified 17-year-old daughter rang 999 to call police to the home, telling them that an axeman was attacking her mother in the kitchen.

Police arrived to restrain the man and paramedics gave emergency treatment to Mrs Appleby, but treatment arrived too late and despite an emergency dash to hospital the mother was pronounced dead from her wounds.

During the attack a gas pipe was nicked by the axe and the escaping gas forced the police to evacuate homes in the area. Neighbours were allowed to return after about a hour when emergency repairs had been made and the gas cleared.

Neighbours reported hearing a violent row late at night at the house in Smithson Road followed by blows. A front window was broken and glass was scattered in the front garden. A police officer was standing guard.

A forensic team was called in to conduct an investigation. A Spokeswoman for the police said: "Police received a call from a frightened young woman saying her mother was being attacked by a man with an axe. We responded promptly, but by the time officers arrived, they found a woman lying on the kitchen floor with multiple wounds across her body."

A hospital spokesman said: "By the time the ambulance crew were able to get the woman to hospital she had lost and enormous amount of blood and there was nothing we could do."

• A local 44-year-old man is due to appear before magistrates today in connection with the incident.

ABOVE: The house in Smithson Road where Tracey Appleby died following an attack by a man armed with an axe.

LEFT: Tracey Appleby in happier times, on holiday last year. Mrs Appleby was pronounced dead at the hospital after the attack.

'Good neighbour' shock to friends

Mrs Appleby had lived in Smithson road for several years. She had two children: the 17-year-old who rang the police and a 14-year-old daughter. Their whereabouts are unknown but neighbours say they are with family. Neighbours describe her as a quiet woman who never caused any trouble. She worked in a local supermarket.

Her boss, Mr John Herbert said: "She was a good and reliable worker who was never any bother. She was always on time and always cheerful and helpful. I can't believe this has happened to her, it sounds like something out of a horror movie."

A neighbour, Mrs Joan Harris said: "She was a friendly woman who would always stop to pass the time of day, but she wouldn't impose. She was a good neighbour. I can't believe that she's gone – the whole thing seems so incredible, I keep expecting to wake up and find that it's a nightmare."

A police spokesman refused to comment on the likely reasons behind the attack but said: "This is a very sad incident. Our thoughts are with the woman's family and particularly her daughters."

Figure 17.10 Early design (on screen)

more width, although this is not the only reason for varying column width. Giles and Hodgson (1996: 137) say that the publication's readership should also be considered.

A standard book, for instance, has that width because that is the optimum width for that size of type. The eye scans across the line quickly and takes in the words in three or four takes. This is fine for more relaxed reading. Many magazines with low story counts will have quite wide column widths since this makes for an easier read where the reader can concentrate on the text placement. But for reading in a crowded train, narrower columns, although more difficult to read in themselves, make it easier for the reader to hold their place after looking away at station sign, or whatever.

Figure 17.11 Middle design (on screen)

Narrower columns tend to be used for short news items for this reason and so newspapers will often have narrow columns in the news and wider columns for features.

The intro to the lead story is laid across two columns and is set in much larger type than the normal body, so a wider run of text is possible. However, once the text falls to standard body size, then a single column width is more acceptable. Designers are no longer limited to a standard width of text as used to be the case in the printing technology of hot metal. This means that what are known as bastard sizes (a non-standard column width) can be used. This is so much the norm now that it is rare to have a standard column width as such. Look at Figure 17.12 and you will see that one

Woman dies in axe attack

New deal over home rents

Daughter's 999 call to save mum

A mother of two was killed last night in her own home after being attacked by an axeman.

Tracey Appleby suffered multiple injuries all over her body and was pronounced dead on arrival at hospital.

The 43-year-old mother of two teenaged daughters was at home when the attack happened. Her terrified 17-year-old daughter rang 999 to call police to the home, telling them that an axeman was attacking her mother in the kitchen.

Police arrived to restrain the man and paramedics gave emergency treatment to Mrs Appleby, but treatment arrived too late and despite an emergency dash to hospital the mother was pronounced dead from her wounds.

During the attack a gas pipe was nicked by the axe and the escaping gas forced the police to evacuate homes in the area. Neighbours were allowed to return after about a hour when emergency repairs had been made and the gas cleared.

Neighbours reported hearing a violent row late at night at the house in Smithson Road followed by blows. A front

By Chris Frost

window was broken and glass was scattered in the front garden. A police officer was standing guard.

A forensic team was called in to conduct an investigation.

A spokeswoman for the police said: "Police received a call from a frightened young woman saying her mother was being attacked by a man with an axe. We responded promptly, but by the time officers arrived, they found a woman lying on the kitchen floor with multiple wounds across her body."

A hospital spokesman said: "By the time the ambulance crew were able to get the woman to hospital she had lost and enormous amount of blood and there was nothing we could do."

• A local 44-year-old man is due to appear before magistrates today in connection with the incident.

ABOVE: The house in Smithson Road where Tracey Appleby died following an attack by a man armed with an axe.

LEFT: Tracey Appleby in happier times, on holiday last year. Mrs Appleby was pronounced dead at the hospital after the attack.

A new accreditation scheme for landlords is set to uphold the rights of tenants in the town.

The new scheme is being planned by the town hall and is intended to help both landlords and tenants.

In exchange for providing homes to a standard laid down by the council, landlords will receive reductions in insurance rates and training and advice on tenant matters.

The scheme will also lay down guidelines to be followed by both landlord and tenant that should ensure fewer disagreements in future.

The scheme was welcomed at a meeting of local landlords held last night at the town hall.

After the housing chief had explained the new scheme to more than 50 local landlords, Hamish Smith of St Andrews St said: "This sounds a great scheme that will allow us to show we are legitimate business providing an essential service."

Mr Smith later became the first landlord to sign up for the new scheme.

Coun. James Pryde told the meeting: "This scheme is extremely good news for the town, its landlords and its private tenants. It should allow the council to help both landlords and tenants get a better deal."

Man dies in fall on stairs

A 69-year-old man died after falling down the stairs of his home, an inquest was told.

The body of Robert Deval was discovered by his wife and daughter in their St James Rd. home on their return from a Saturday afternoon shopping trip. Pathologist Dr Samuel Johnson told the inquest that Mr Deval had died of a broken neck.

Drama fest

An amateur drama festival is to be held at the town hall this Saturday at 7.30pm. The festival is open to all drama groups who want to stage a 20-minute production.

'Good neighbour' shock to friends

Mrs Appleby had lived in Smithson road for several years. She had two children: the 17-year-old who rang the police and a 14-year-old daughter. Their whereabouts are unknown but neighbours say they are with family. Neighbours describe her as a quiet woman who never caused any trouble. She worked in a local supermarket.

Her boss, Mr John Herbert said: "She was a good and reliable worker who was never any bother. She was always on time and always cheerful and helpful. I can't believe this has happened to her, it sounds like

something out of a horror movie."

A neighbour, Mrs Joan Harris said: "She was a friendly woman who would always stop to pass the time of day, but she wouldn't impose. She was a good neighbour. I can't believe that she's gone – the whole thing seems so incredible, I keep

expecting to wake up and find that it's a nightmare."

A police spokesman refused to comment on the likely reasons behind the attack but said: "This is a very sad incident. Our thoughts are with the woman's family and particularly her daughters."

Man robbed at knifepoint

A teenager was robbed at knife-point on his way home from a night out.

The 19-year-old was stopped by three men who asked for a light. As Mark Bayer, of Steeple Drive, put his hand in his pocket, two of the men grabbed his arms whilst the third threatened him with a knife.

The incident happened in St Aidms Road at about 11.30pm on Tuesday night. The victim was on his way home from Red Rover public house after an evening out with friends. Police say he had had a drink, but was not drunk.

Police are now hunting three men, all white and around 20 years old. The first was 5ft 9ins with dark brown hair and a Manchester United shirt. The second was 6ft 1in with blond hair and an Adidas top. The third man was 5ft 10in with brown hair.

The victim was said to be shaken but unhurt. The robbers took £80 and a mobile phone after searching his pockets. They then pushed him into a hedge before running away.

Police are appealing for any witnesses and have warned people to be careful walking home at night in the dark.

Learner driver over drink limit

A learner driver who was more than four times over the legal limit for drink driving crashed into a hedge and was then arrested by a concerned passerby as he tried to restart his engine.

Donald Watson admitted driving with excess alcohol, without insurance and without a licence. He was alone at the time of the incident.

The court heard that his car veered across the road before mounting the curve and driving into a hedge.

Watson got out of the car, staggered around and then climbed back in and try to restart his engine. A concerned passerby restrained him and took his keys until police arrived.

Watson was banned from driving for four years and fined £2,000.

Elderly flee blaze

Elderly residents of a nursing home were forced to flee a small blaze in the early hours of Tuesday night.

Alarms triggered in the Bide-a-wee nursing home in Cemetery Road after a small blaze took hold in a waste area near the kitchens. The fire brigade soon doused the flames and the elderly were able to return to their beds. No one was hurt.

Landlord's late pyjama chase

A pub landlord chased would-be burglars through the streets in his pyjamas after disturbing them on Tuesday night.

Pub landlord "Big" John Brophy heard a noise downstairs in the Winkley St pub at about 2am.

"I crept downstairs after picking up a baseball bat and spotted two men trying to climb over the bar," he said.

Mr Brophy then turned on the lights and yelled at them. Mr Brophy is almost seven foot tall and weighs more than 20 stone. The two burglars tumbled off the bar

Landlord John Brophy

and fled through the door they had broken open and ran up the street. Mr Brophy gave chase but soon lost them.

Police are now hunting the two men who are said to be in their early twenties. Both were of slim build and about

5ft 10in tall. They were dressed in sports clothes with peaked caps pulled low over their faces.

Despite this limited description, Mr Brophy is certain he would recognise them again. "They'd better not come back in here for a drink," he said. "They can take it from me that they are barred."

Pub regulars were surprised to hear Brophy had broken open and ran the raid. "They can't be local," said regular Mr John Carpenter. "I wouldn't want to be halfway through a robbery here and find Big John standing over me with a baseball bat."

Figure 17.12 Finished design (on screen)

of the stories is set in a different column width to all the others. This helps prevent the page looking like a series of fingers.

House style

Every newspaper and magazine has a house style and you will need to learn this and follow it. This will include the choice of fonts and how they should be used, but will also include indents, typesizes, how the pictures are used, where the captions go, whether there are column rules (lines between each column) and so on. A house style is an important element of any publication giving it its distinctiveness and allowing readers to identify it easily from look alone.

Some dos and don'ts of design

Do

- Choose your entry point with care and make it the focal point of the page.
- Break up long stories into easily manageable articles linked together by design.
- Use pictures and graphics wherever possible.
- Break type up to add interest.
- Consider using subheads and crossheads to add emphasis to sections of the text.
- Consider using bold paras, drop letters and bold pars to add emphasis.
- Keep things simple and easy to follow.
- Consider carefully how long each article should be, depending on your readership profile.
- Try to avoid clashing with adverts. Ads with large areas of half-tone should be cordoned off using text. Text-based adverts could be put next to pictures.
- Consider how best to get over the information. An annotated aerial picture may do more to describe the scene of an accident, for instance, than pages of text could hope to do. It will be the designer's job to arrange for the text and pictures to be turned into a diagram.
- Consider using just parts of a picture, cutting out the image or overlaying it with type.
- Ensure there is a suitable amount of white space around the headlines and any other elements.
- Ensure a caption always accompanies a picture clearly. Readers become irritated if they cannot find the caption to a picture.
- Emphasise your entry point with larger intro type, bold faces, drop letters and so on.•
- Make sure the strength of your stories is reflected in the design.
- Make it clear where the story goes to after it has ended in one column.
- Be imaginative in how you deal with the elements of a page.

---

continued

Don't

- Run headlines over adverts. Always break the space with text, pictures or whatever. If the space above a run of adverts is too small to be useful, don't be afraid to give it up and float the ads to the top or ask the advertising department to fill the space. Anything less than 6 cm is going to give you problems.
- Don't run a headline next to another headline unless the stories are connected or you have some way of ensuring they are not connected such as column rules or by using very different styles and sizes of font.
- Don't cover the page with lots of different typefaces. Too much variation will end up just looking a mess. Best to limit yourself to one font and its varieties.
- Don't use **cut-outs** on a picture just for the sake of it. Whether the picture is cut away from its background or a section is cut out, it will lose context and start to look isolated. A cut-out without any good reason usually looks ridiculous because it is clear you are trying to edit the picture and the reader will wonder why.
- Don't turn copy to another page. It's a great way of ensuring the reader loses interest in the story (Frost 2003: 7).

cut-outs when elements of a picture are cut away from the background (a simple device using an image editing program such as Photoshop).

Templates

template page on the computer screen providing a basic design pattern.

Increasingly newspapers and magazines are being made up to standard **templates**. This limits (often quite severely) your ability to design pages as the template will be a preset design pattern. On the other hand, a template ensures the house style for that magazine or newspaper is followed closely. It is also possible to set up master pages in some design software. Master pages hold all the standard elements of a page such as the headers and footers (usually the publication's title and page number) and other elements that sit on all the pages of a publication.

Templates are pages that are already predesigned and so the copy only needs to be fitted in and trimmed to fit the shape available. While these can speed up the operation and reduce the need for skilled designers, they can also bring a sameness to a publication and reduce the ability of the designer to play up a good story or play down a weak one, suggesting that all lead stories on a certain page, for instance, are of the same news value.

Another helpful tool for the designer is the style sheet. These predetermine the house style so that new stories do not need detailed setting instructions to be added. The style sheet required is selected and will then automatically apply this to the copy. Choosing caption style, for instance, would automatically apply whatever the font and style that had been decided for use in captions, no matter what style the copy had originally been written in.

Colour

Colour is a vital consideration for today's newspapers and magazines. Magazines have used full colour on all pages for a number of years, switching from older, less sophisticated mono-only publishing technology in the 1960s and 1970s. Newspapers did not start switching to full colour until the 1980s, with most newspapers working in full colour from the 1990s on. But even today, not every newspaper page is able to use full colour.

Newspaper pages are printed in blocks that are then cut up to make the newspaper. That means several pages are printed together on the same web. For instance, the front and back and two centre pages of a newspaper are printed together, so if colour is available on that web, then the front, back and two centre pages will all have colour. The number of colour pages in a newspaper will depend on the press and its configuration.

Colour is often used for rank or symbolism. For instance, crimson is the colour of cardinals in the Catholic Church, while the Pope wears white and bishops wear purple. We are less likely these days to identify colour with rank, but we certainly use it symbolically. Brides wear white while mourners wear black. We also use it as brand identification. Virgin uses red while McDonald's has its golden arches. Liverpool and Manchester United are famous for their red shirts while Everton favours blue. Colour is an important part of our lives and helps us identify and categorise items.

We can use colour in a newspaper or magazine to improve readability and navigation. For instance, many newspapers use colour on the television listings grids. Horizontal tone patches in different colours allow the reader to match up the programmes on different channels at the same time. If all the programmes at 10 p.m. are listed on a pale blue band running across the page, it is much easier to choose a programme.

Colour can be used in type or as a patch colour under the type. Generally speaking, only very dark colours should be used in type unless the type is very large. Pale colours become difficult to read against white paper as we look for the edge definition. Similarly, if one underlays type with a colour, then that colour should be very light and the type should be black to maximise the contrast. If the underlying colour is strong, then you should consider setting the type in white or a very pale complimentary colour.

Hue, saturation and value

We can measure colour using several systems, but the most usual is hue, saturation and value. Hue is the actual colour. In good light, we can identify about 500 different hues, the rainbow colours spanning from bright reds through greens to blues. However this is not the end of the story. Those hues are varied by the amount they are saturated (intensity) and by the value (lightness or brightness). The saturation of a colour is the amount of it available. A small amount of colour will look different to a full saturation. Saturation in printing is controlled by the amount of ink applied. 100 per cent saturation would give full colour, 0 per cent saturation would give no colour at all – it would be grey. The more of the ink, the more colour, the more saturation. The value of a colour is its brightness. A 100 per cent brightness would give white, while 0 per cent brightness would be black. Full colour is 50 per cent.

Colour interactions

Colours interact with each other in a way we need to bear in mind. Some combinations simply do not work and should not be used. Red on a blue background or vice versa, for instance, should always be avoided. The eye sees these at slightly different focal lengths and so cannot easily focus on the border between blue and red. Since we use these borders to determine the shape of characters, this lack of focus can be very disturbing. Few colour contrasts are quite so disconcerting, but many other colour selections do not work well.

In tests carried out by Karl Borggräfe (cited in Favre and November 1979: 50) to see which colours worked best together, the following taxonomy of colour mixes was discovered, starting with the most legible and working through to the least legible:

- black on yellow
- yellow on black
- green on white
- red on white
- black on white
- white on blue
- blue on yellow
- blue on white
- white on black
- green on yellow
- black on orange
- red on yellow
- orange on black
- yellow on blue
- white on green
- black on red
- blue on orange
- yellow on green
- blue on red
- yellow on red
- white on red
- red on black
- white on orange
- black on green
- orange on white
- orange on blue
- yellow on orange
- red on orange
- red on green
- green on orange.

Black on yellow, or vice versa, is the easiest to read and so is often used for signs that represent danger. Although yellow on black is the first choice, in practice this can be difficult to do well as both black and yellow need to be printed. Producing black on yellow paper might provide slightly better results, but would make pictures look odd. Black on white is still the easiest to produce and easiest to read.

Colour separation

Colour printing relies on a highly technical process that prints four colours one on top of the other. First the page and its colour pictures and type are photographically separated into four different plates, each picking out a different colour. This process is either done physically in the production camera or, more usually these days, it is done digitally by a computer. These separations are then output as different plates to mount on the press and print the four colours required for good quality colour printing.

The four different plates print in cyan, magenta, yellow and black (**CMYK**). Strictly speaking, the three colours, cyan, magenta and yellow should be able to produce black if correctly mixed in equal proportions but, in fact, the best that can usually be produced is a dark, muddy brown. Consequently, black is added to improve the contrast. In addition, the type can then also be set directly in black making the type image clearer than attempting to print in three colours.

Colour printing requires absolutely accurate **registration**. Registration is where the four plates all print in exactly the same place for each colour so that all the colours lie directly above each other to accurately represent the picture. If the colours are not placed accurately, then any colour pictures will look odd with, perhaps, a yellow band down one side and a cyan band down the other. When colour printing started, this kind of mis-registration was common, but it's a lot rarer to find now.

CMYK colours of ink used for four-colour printing: cyan, magenta, yellow and black.

registration exact alignment of the four plates used to print the four colours of ink used in four-colour printing.

Ethics of publication

Placement

There are a number of issues to keep in mind when designing a page. The first is the adverts on the page. It might well be entirely inappropriate to put a story about a particular person or company alongside an advert about them or their products. There may be other reasons why a particular story should not sit alongside a certain advert.

It can also be very tempting to run stories on a similar theme next to each other, even suggesting that they are linked in some way. However, you need to be certain there is no legal or ethical reason for not doing so. For instance, running the story of a town-centre car chase alongside a story about someone being arrested for speeding through town may well be seen by the courts as being prejudicial.

Copyright

Copyright is another important area. Copyright is there to protect intellectual property: the rights of creators. If you write something, take a picture, direct a film or produce a TV programme you have the right to exploit that intellectual property to your best advantage and the copyright laws give you some protection in doing that. You have the right to prevent someone using or amending your work and you have the right to ask for payment for the work to be used.

For an editor or designer, however, the obligation is reversed. It is your responsibility to ensure you have the right to use a particular story or picture. If the story is written by a staff reporter or a picture is taken by a staff photographer, then there is no problem. The publication has full rights to the material as a condition of employment. However, if the writer or photographer is a freelance and has either submitted the work on spec or has been commissioned, then they retain the rights and should be paid and their permission obtained for any changes. It's not usually difficult to arrange this when the material is first commissioned or submitted, but mistakes are often made when a picture is reused from the archive without checking whether rights have been properly identified.

Syndicating a story for which you do not have rights can also be a problem. Copyright can be a nightmare for television researchers who may well have to track down the rights holders for dozens of clips of films, background music or several writers, directors and producers. '100 top' television programmes' may be cheap television, but they are a lot of work for the rights department. Publishers do not usually have quite so much difficulty, but you must check that you have the rights or have approached the rights holder to use a picture or story again.

Good taste and decency

Printing offensive material, whether written or pictorial, can pose major ethical or legal problems for journalists. Nudity, violence, death and sexually explicit material all throw up potential problems. The first consideration is the audience. An adult readership known to be liberal and well educated is more likely to accept nudity and explicit copy about challenging, controversial subjects. Whilst tabloid readers seem to enjoy pictures of topless women, they are much less forgiving (or so the standard wisdom goes) of descriptions of explicit sex (particularly if it is of an unusual nature), death and violence.

Magazines, on the other hand, are more likely to carry sexually explicit material and it is now the norm for magazines aimed a eighteen to twenty-five age group, men or women, to carry several sexually explicit articles, often illustrated with pictures describing performance, technique or out-of-the-norm experiences. These are often flagged on the front cover. Even so, there are regular complaints about the sexually implicit material carried in magazines aimed at readers in the twelve to sixteen age group, particularly girls.

Web site

<http://www.poynter.org>

References and further reading

Ang, T. (1996) *Picture Editing*, Oxford: Focal Press.
Burnham, R.W., R.M. Hanes and J.C. Bartleson (1963) *Color: A Guide to Basic Facts and Concepts*, New York: John Wiley & Sons.
Cook, A. and R. Feury (1989) *Type and Color*, Rockport: Rockport Publishers.
Craig, J. (1980) *Designing with Type*, New York: Watson-Guptill.

De Grandis, L. (1986) *Theory and Use of Colour*, New York: Abrams.

Durrant, W.R. (1989) *Printing*, Oxford: Heinemann Professional Publishing.

Evans, H. (1978) *Pictures on a Page*, London: William Heinemann.

—— (1984a) *Newspaper Design*, London: William Heinemann.

—— (1984b) *Handling Newspaper Text*, London: William Heinemann.

Faver, J.-P. and A. November (1979) *Color and Communication*, Zurich: ABC Editions.

Frost, C. (2000) *Media Ethics and Self-Regulation*, London: Pearson.

—— (2001) *Reporting for Journalists*, London: Routledge.

—— (2003) *Designing for Newspapers and Magazines*, London: Routledge.

Garcia, M. and P. Stark (1991) *Eyes on the News*, St Petersburg: Poynter Institute.

Giles, V. and F.W. Hodgson (1996) *Creative Newspaper Design*, 2nd edn, Oxford: Focal Press.

Hodgson, F.W. (1993) *Subediting*, 2nd edn, Oxford: Focal Press.

Hutt, A. (1967) *Newspaper Design*, 2nd edn, London: Oxford University Press.

Kammermeier, A. and P. Kammermeier (1992) *Scanning and Printing*, Oxford: Focal Press.

Kress, G. and T. Van Leeuwen (2000) *Reading Images: The Grammar of Visual Design*, Blackwell: 186–219.

—— (2000) 'Front Pages: (The Critical) Analysis of Newpaper Layout', in A. Bell and P. Garret (eds) *Approaches to Media Discourse*, Oxford: Blackwell, pp. 186–219.

Quinn, S. (2001) *Digital Sub-Editing and Design*, Oxford: Focal Press.

Quinn T., M. Lindsay, D. Hewitt, K. Overbury and J. Ritson (1991) *The Key: A Guide to Best Practices for Thomson Regional Newspapers*, Belfast: TRN.

Sassoon, R. (1993) *Computers and Typography*, Oxford: Intellect.

Sellers L. (1968a) *Doing It in Style*, Oxford: Pergamon Press.

—— (1968b) *The Simple Subs Book*, Oxford: Pergamon Press.

Shipcott, G. (1994) *Typography for Desktop Publishers*, London: B.T. Batsford.

Smith, A. (ed) (1974) *The British Press Since the War*, Newton Abbott: David & Charles.

Steinberg, S.H. (1955) *Five Hundred Years of Printing*, Harmondsworth: Penguin.

Tinker, M. (1963) *The Legibility of Print*, Ames, Iowa: Iowa State University Press.

Twyman, M. (1970) *Printing 1770–1970: An Illustrated History of Its Development and Uses in England*, London: Eyre & Spottiswood.

Weinmann, E. (1998) *QuarkXpress 4 for Windows*, Berkeley, Calif.: Peachpit Press.

Williams, R. (1994) *The Non-Designers Design Book*, Berkeley, Calif.: Peachpit Press.

Zelanski, P. and M.P. Fisher (1989) *Colour for Designers and Artists*, London: The Herbert Press.

From blogrolls and wikis to big business

18

Going online

From blogrolls and wikis to big business

Going online

Neil Thurman

How online is different

Online journalism is different. Its screen-based nature changes readers' physical relationship with the textual surface. Its non-linear storage, retrieval and presentational capabilities change the narrative structure of stories and publications. Its global reach and reliance on expensive, partially adopted access technology changes the demographic and geographic profile of the readership. And finally, the ease and speed with which readers can interact with publications challenges the hierarchy inherent in traditional editorial processes.

The workflow in newsrooms is, however, not always compatible with individual journalists' desire to adapt their work to the characteristics of the medium. The complexity and sheer size of most online news operations means that almost all are run using content-management systems. (The *Telegraph*'s site contains more than one million pages.[1]) Whether developed in house (as with the *Independent* and *Belfast Telegraph*) or bought in (*The Times* and *Guardian* use Vignette), content-management systems standardise the production process creating efficiencies but distancing the journalist from the medium they are working with. Depending on their implementation, they can 'lock out' certain approaches journalists may wish to take to optimise their content for the web.

It is not just the mechanics of the publishing process, with its increasing automation, that can make it hard to distinguish between news providers' on and offline offerings. The economics of web publishing means that many sites simply do not have the staff or time to adapt or repurpose content for the peculiarities of the medium or the widely dispersed constituency of readers. Historically the direct financial returns from online newspaper publishing have been poor, making it hard for newspapers to justify large editorial staffs solely for online work. Indeed, according to Vin Crosbie (2003) no general newspaper web site with paid content secures online subscriptions equal to 2 per cent of its print circulation.

British newspapers: a decade online

In 1994 the *Telegraph* and *Guardian* became the first nationals to have a web presence followed two years later by *The Times*, *Independent* and *Scotsman*. Some of the tabloids (the *Mirror*, *Daily Star* and *Express-Sport*) launched online in 1997 but others, notably the *Daily Mail*, held off until much later. The *Daily Mail* finally began publishing on the Internet in 2004. Staffing at online operations has varied considerably, with the broadsheets committing more human resources.

In 1998–9 the *Independent* and *Times* employed about ten people, the *Guardian* and *Telegraph* around thirty. The tabloids had far fewer staff working exclusively online (the *Daily Star* had a head count of just three and a half in 1998). Staffing levels have risen considerably and by 2002 the *Guardian* was employing 120.[2] Opportunities for journalists employed on print editions to work on web-exclusive stories have increased. Until 2001 *The Times* took rather a dim view of print journalists working for its online edition. This is no longer the case and in 2004, 10 to 20 per cent of The Times On-line's content was being written exclusively for the web. Business, breaking news and sport (blogs and coverage of live events) are the focus as well as special reports in travel, health and entertainment.[3]

Over the past ten years virtually all British newspaper web sites have run at a loss. Eight years after launching their web site the *Guardian* admitted 'it's not that easy a business to run'.[4] One way in which online editions have sought to create a space for themselves is by shifting their strategic direction, postponing their break-even points and concentrating on other ways that they can add value to their print-parent's brand. For the *Telegraph* its web site became a way of allowing it to escape its 'old-fashioned, fuddy-duddy image'.[5] The *Guardian* saw an opportunity to build 'a community on-line',[6] and for the *Financial Times*, its dot.com operation acted as a 'marketing arm of the newspaper' reaching 'a whole new international audience who might not otherwise pick up a pink paper'.[7]

Despite losing money there has been substantial investment in the technology driving newspapers' online operations. In May 2002, FT.com overhauled and relaunched its site at a cost of £200 million. *The Times* invested in a content-management system costing several million pounds. Ongoing costs also can be substantial. BBC News On-line has an annual budget of £18 million a year[8] – one of the reasons it has become the most popular destination for online news in the UK (followed by the *Guardian*, CNN, Telegraph.co.uk and Yahoo in that order). There are signs that income is starting to match expenditure: the web sites of nationals such as the *Telegraph* are now making money.

In addition to more advertising income and better commercial partnerships, online newspapers have started to charge for content. The *Independent* charges for some exclusive content (Robert Fisk's articles, for instance), the *Telegraph* for crossword solutions, *The Times* for access to its general and law archive and crossword solutions,[9] the FT.com for some news and reports, financial data and archive access. Although the *Guardian* does not yet charge, registration has been introduced for access to popular sections (such as the Media Guardian).

The good news for journalists moving online is that the web is primarily a text-based medium and journalistic writing works well on the screen, not only because of its familiarity but also because many of its conventions suit the way people read online. News sites such as Swissinfo.org, Switzerland's publicly funded online news and information service, believe that online 'traditional journalist skills are paramount'.[10] BBC News On-line prefers its recruits to have several months' work experience on a local or national newspaper.[11]

To fully exploit the online medium it is necessary to have a good understanding of the technologies. The web is fundamentally different from print because digital technology is not just part of the production process but is fundamentally bound up with the content. Hypertext Markup Language (HTML), by definition, combines the copy to be published with the instructions about how to present it. In print, whatever the production technologies used, readers get their content in ink on paper. Online publications are dependent on complex and unpredictable combinations of technologies to encode, publish, deliver and present their work to readers. Understanding these technologies and their interrelationships can make journalists better writers online. Stories can be made more accessible, easier to find and bookmark and more comfortable to read.

This chapter focuses on the need for readers of online journalism to have relatively costly, globally connected, computing devices and how this changes the size and characteristics of the audience. Chapter 19 looks at how the experience of reading from paper and screen differs, what online journalists can do to adapt to these differences as well as those demanded by the hypertextual nature of the web. Chapter 20 examines the facilities the web offers readers for communication with journalists and for self-publication and the implications for the industry.

The audience for online journalism

letterpress printing method that presses raised, inked type against paper.

lithography printing method that relies on the inability of oily ink and water to mix.

Journalism has always been intimately bound up with technology. After all, without the invention of **letterpress** the industry would not exist. From linotype to photo-setting and offset **lithography**, and from full-colour editions to tabloid broadsheets, press barons have always sought to steal a march on their competitors by adopting novel technologies. For readers none of these innovations have changed the fundamental process of newspaper consumption: normally in exchange for a sum of money (though sometimes for free) the reader is furnished with a set of pages on which is printed information of a topical nature. Every copy of the same issue in any given location and at any given time is identical.

Putting journalism online blows this model, with us for more than 300 years, away. Suddenly technological change is not something that just takes place in the newsroom or shop floor but a process that directly affects every reader as their computer screen rather than the printing press becomes the location where the news is delivered, decoded and laid out. Online journalism relies on a complex mix of technology only some of which is under the publisher's control. The editor can oversee the creation of text, pictures, audio and video, their encoding using languages such as HTML and the publication of that material to a web server. That done, a whole series of technical processes must happen before the reader is able to view the online edition.

First the reader must request a page by entering a URL, such as <http://www.guardian.co.uk> into a User Agent (UA) such as Internet Explorer or Netscape. The UA sends a request to the server for a copy of that page. The server sends the page in several separate 'packets' over the Internet using a number of protocols HTTP (Hypertext Transfer Protocol), is one, RTSP (Real Time Streaming Protocol) is another. Once these 'packets' have been received and reassembled by the reader's device (usually a personal computer but increasingly a personal digital assistant or mobile phone) they are decoded by the UA and finally laid out on screen in a form that can be read.

In online publishing, large parts of the production process happen in the living room rather than the newsroom. For online journalists and editors this is a fundamental change. It is no longer possible to assume your readers will see what you expect them to see or even be technologically equipped to be able to read all or part of your publication at all. Online it is essential to understand the technologies used in the electronic publishing process and, furthermore, to understand something about the adoption processes (at a reader level) of those technologies. Only by doing this can online journalists and editors know the size and characteristics of their audience.

Internet take-up statistics

Significantly, the technologies required to access web sites are not familiar or quickly accessible to a large minority – possibly a majority – of the UK's population. In the UK almost half the female population go without using the Internet for months and just 20 per cent of those aged over sixty-five have used the Internet once or more. Only 12 per cent of homes in the bottom 10 per cent of gross household income have access to the Internet (Office of National Statistics 2003a and b, 2004). Longer established media such as radio and television are mature enough for the access technology to be almost ubiquitous with the result that the demographics of radio listeners and television viewers are the same as that of the general population.

According to the United Kingdom's Office of National Statistics, in 2002 some 99 per cent of UK households had access to a television while less than half that number (44 per cent) had access to the Internet at home (Rickards 2004). This discrepancy is, in part, due to the relative youth of the medium. Tim Berners-Lee only proposed the global hypertext system that became the World Wide Web in 1989 (Connolly 2000) and the first UK newspaper to go online – the Electronic Telegraph – did so as recently as November 1994.[12] The requirement to buy expensive hardware and to regularly update or patch software is also contributing to the lack of take-up. In June 2004 warnings were issued to Internet users to 'avoid using Internet Explorer until Microsoft patches a serious security hole'.[13] Warnings like this contribute to a wariness about the technology, with 38 per cent of non-Internet users staying away, in part, because they feel they do 'not have the confidence' to go online (Office of National Statistics 2003a).

The web and its contents have not yet become an essential part of the media diet for a significant minority of the UK population. Of the 41 per cent of the UK population who are not Internet users, 18 per cent do not see any reasons for going online (Rose 2003). Even if the web was as widely adopted as television or radio, the rapid pace of technological change that typifies the online medium means there is unlikely to be a lengthy period in which the technologies required to access news content online remain stable. Compare the rate of change in radio broadcasting and receiving technology with that of web technologies. The first regularly scheduled FM radio station (Columbia University's Radio Club) started broadcasting in 1941.[14] Digital radio was licensed for use in the United States by the Federal Communications Commission in October 2002.[15] That's sixty-one years in which radio listeners have not needed to upgrade their sets or adopt a new technology. Online the story is very different.

The need for regular updates

To view the full range of online news content, users need regularly to update their software and also their hardware, the latter less frequently. For example, as part of their coverage of the Euro 2004 soccer championships BBC Sport introduced Virtual Replay[16] animations to allow soccer fans to watch animated replays of key moments from matches. This innovative feature required users to install version 10 of Macromedia's Shockwave plug-in, a piece of software released for the first time on 25 March 2004,[17] less than three months before the championships began.

The partial penetration of web technologies and the rapid change in those technologies means that for online news publishers the patterns of consumer adoption of the software and hardware required to view online news sites are of particular interest as they can help to predict numbers of potential readers and give a broad indication of their characteristics.

Individuals do not adopt a new technology, product or idea at the same time. Instead they adopt in an over-time sequence, which means it is possible to classify individuals into adopter categories based on when they first begin to use a new product or idea (whatever that might be: the web or wifi, the car or condom). It turns out that in almost all cases where an innovation is widely adopted, the pattern of adoption is the same: the so-called S-shaped curve. If we plot a graph of the cumulative number of adopters it rises slowly at first, when there are few adopters, then accelerates to a maximum until half of the individuals have adopted. After this 50 per cent threshold has been reached, the rate of adoption slows as fewer and fewer of the remaining individuals adopt.

Adopting innovation: the five ideal types

The history of research into innovation adoption has proposed a number of categories of adopters. Everett Rogers (1995: 264–6) suggests the following useful model which provides a snapshot of five ideal types on the spectrum of innovativeness:

1. Innovators (2.5 per cent). These seek out others who share their near obsession with risk-taking – a process likely to bring them in contact with a relatively cosmopolitan and widely distributed social circle. Innovators are likely to have control of 'substantial financial resources' and to be able to 'apply complex technical knowledge'. They are prepared to accept the risk of a setback when 'a new idea proves unsuccessful' and lack of respect from others in the local system who do not share innovators' obsession with the new.
2. Early adopters (13.5 per cent). These are a 'more integrated part of the local social system than are innovators' which gives them a high degree of 'opinion leadership'. They often serve as role models for many other members of the social system with their 'successful, discrete use of new ideas'.
3. Early majority (34 per cent). Adopting 'new ideas just before the average member of a system', they 'interact frequently with their peers, but seldom hold positions of opinion leadership'. They are a significant group making up 'one third of the members of a system'. They 'follow with deliberate willingness in adopting innovations, but seldom lead'.

4. Late majority (34 per cent). Approaching innovation with 'a sceptical and cautious air', they do not 'adopt until most others in their system have done so'. They have relatively scarce resources meaning 'most of the uncertainty about a new idea must be removed before the late majority feel that it is safe to adopt' and that the 'pressure of peers is necessary to motivate adoption'.

5. Laggards (16 per cent). The 'last in a social system to adopt', these do not lead opinion and are relatively isolated in the 'social networks of their system'. Where they do interact it tends to be with others who prefer 'relatively traditional values'. The past is an important point of reference and informs their decision-making. It comes as no surprise to know that they are suspicious of innovations. If they do adopt an innovation it will be a long time after they become aware of that innovation. With limited resources they 'must be certain that a new idea will not fail before they can adopt'.

Making informed decisions about content

An understanding of these classifications constitutes an important part of the information required to make informed decisions about content planning for new media. This understanding can help in two ways. First if a publisher is intent on using a particular technology to deliver content, the groups of adopters that technology has reached will provide an indication of the characteristics of the potential audience and the content can be tailored accordingly. Second, if a publisher is aiming to reach a particular demographic, an understanding of diffusion rates will help the publisher select a technology that has been adopted by the target group.

The *Sun*'s web site, for example, requires the adoption of a number of technologies. The recommended requirements for Windows XP users who wish to access the site are:

- A personal computer with a 600 MHz Pentium III processor or above and 128 MB of RAM (256 MB recommended)
- Internet Explorer v6 or above
- Macromedia Flash player v7
- Internet connectivity.

We know that, in the UK, 44 per cent of people have access to the Internet at home (and, therefore, a personal computer). Internet Explorer v6 or above is used by 77 per cent of web users[18] while the Macromedia Flash player has been adopted by about 60 per cent[19] of Internet users.[20] This means that we could expect approximately 22 per cent of the UK population to be able to access the *Sun*'s web site at home. This level of adoption means that the content is only going to be immediately accessible by the 'innovators' and 'early adopters' and some in the 'early majority'. This example reinforces the fact that, online, it is not possible to assume that your readers will be technologically equipped to be able to read all or parts of your publication at all.

Diffusion is an ongoing process and editors and journalists can facilitate the adoption of technologies such as Flash by using some of the innovators' and early adopters' characteristics. Their 'cosmopolite social relationships', 'ability to understand and apply complex ideas' and 'greater exposure to interpersonal communication' (Rogers 1995: 263, 264, 274) means they can be harnessed to evangelise about a particular piece of content, driving adoption and increasing the potential readership. A major risk associated with technological adoption – loss of resources – is largely absent with web technologies as the software required to access online news content (web **browsers** and media players like RealMedia, QuickTime, Flash, Shockwave) are usually provided free of charge.

browser software program for navigating the Internet, in particular the World Wide Web.

Any piece of online journalism that makes use of a technology that has been incompletely adopted should encourage readers to recommend the feature and its means of delivery. Curiously, although, the *Guardian* allows readers to 'Send it (the story) to a friend' on their regular HTML pages, they do not extend this option to features that use non-standard, less widely adopted technologies such as their Flash-based feature 'Floods in Asia'.[21] Similarly BBC News On-line does not give innovators and early adopters a functional way to evangelise about their Flash-based features,[22] although, as with the *Guardian*, the BBC's HTML-formatted stories can be recommended to other readers by using an on-screen email tool.

Target for advertisers

Commercially, innovators and early adopters are attractive targets for advertisers. They have higher-than-average financial resources and lead opinion within their local social system. Interestingly, however, advertising seems to be less not more common in stories and features that require more than the default level of technological adoption for any given publication. For example, the *New York Times*'s multimedia feature 'A Land of Open Secrets' (Burns 2002) authored using Flash, carries no advertising, although advertising is carried on the *New York Times*'s regular pages. Similarly MSNBC.com, whose regular site is heavy with advertising, does not include adverts as part of its multimedia feature 'The Year in Pictures 2003'.[23] In both these cases the readers' short-term interests may be said to be served by the lack of advertising but, in the long term, the reader benefits if the publication has a strong financial base and not maximising advertising revenue by targeting innovators and early adopters seems an oversight.

Acknowledgement

The author is grateful to Wesley Johnson for his contribution to this chapter.

Notes

1. Felix Duckworth, Chief Sub, telegraph.co.uk, conversation with author, 15 July 2004.
2. Emily Bell, Editor, Guardian Unlimited, interview with Wesley Johnson, 18 March 2002.
3. Gareth Scurlock, The Times On-line, email with author, 14 July 2004.
4. Simon Waldman, Guardian Unlimited, interview with Wesley Johnson, 22 May 2002.

5. Derek Bishton, telegraph.co.uk, interview with Wesly Johnson, 21 May 2002.
6. Simon Waldman, Guardian Unlimited, interview with Wesley Johnson, 22 May 2002.
7. Clay Harris, ft.com, interview with Wesley Johnson, 19 March 2002.
8. Mike Smartt, conversation with author, June 2003.
9. Gareth Scurlock, The Times On-line, email with author, 14 July 2004.
10. Jonas Hughes, Head of English Department, swissinfo.org, email with author, 25 May 2004.
11. Mike Smartt, Ex-Editor BBC News On-line, conversation with author, 3 July 2003.
12. 'History of telegraph.co.uk'. Available online at <http://www.telegraph.co.uk/portal/main.jhtml?xml=/portal/aboutus/exclusions/history.xml>, accessed 25 June 2004.
13. 'Web Browser Flaw Prompts Warning', BBC News On-line, 26 June. Available online at <http://news.bbc.co.uk/1/hi/technology/3840101.stm>, accessed 25 June 2004.
14. 'The History of the Campus Broadcasting Network', WCBN.org, 10 October. Available online at <http://www.wcbn.org/history/wcbntime.html>, accessed 25 June 2004.
15. 'Digital Radio Debuts', CBSnews.com, 7 January. Available online at <http://www.cbsnews.com/stories/2004/01/07/tech/main591867.shtml>, accessed 25 June 2004.
16. 'Virtual Replay', bbc.co.uk. Available online at <http://www.bbc.co.uk/virtualreplay>, accessed 25 June 2004.
17. 'Shockwave Player Version History', macromedia.com, 1 June. Available online at <http://www.macromedia.com/support/director/ts/documents/sw_history.htm>, accessed 25 June 2004.
18. 'Browser Stats', thecounter.com. Available online at <http://www.thecounter.com/stats/2004/may/browser.php>, accessed 25 June 2004.
19. These figures are provided by Macromedia and may overstate the penetration rate.
20. 'Macromedia Shockwave Player Version Penetration', macromedia.com. Available online at <http://www.macromedia.com/software/player_census/shockwaveplayer/version_penetration.html>, accessed 25 June 2004.
21. 'South-East Asia Serious Flooding', Guardian Unlimited. Available online at <http://www.guardian.co.uk/flash/0,5860,1261181,00.html>, accessed 15 July 2004.
22. An example is 'Iraq After Saddam One Year On', BBC News On-line. Available online at <http://www.bbc.co.uk/iraqcons>, accessed 30 June 2004.
23. 'The Year in Pictures 2003', MSNBC.com. Available online at <http://www.msnbc.com/modules/yip03>, accessed 29 June 2004.

References

Burns, J. (2002) 'A Land of Open Secrets', *New York Times*. Available online at <http://www.nytimes.com/iraqjournal>, accessed 29 June 2004.

Connolly, D. (2000) 'A Little History of the World Wide Web: From 1945 to 1995', w3c.org. Available online at <http://www.w3.org/history.html>, accessed 25 June 2004.

Crosbie, V. (2003) 'Understanding the Economics of the Web', digitaldeliverance. com. Available online at <http://www.digitaldeliverance.com/speeches/economics_of_web.ppt>, accessed 26 May 2004.

Office of National Statistics (2003a) 'Households with Home Access to the Internet by Gross Income Decile Group (UK)', *Expenditure and Food Survey*. Available online at <http://www.statistics.gov.uk/statbase/expodata/spreadsheets/d6937. xls>, accessed 25 June 2004.

—— (2003b) 'Internet Access Individuals and Households', *National Statistics Omnibus Survey*, 8 July. Available online at <http://www.statistics.gov.uk/pdfdir/ int0703.pdf>, accessed 6 October 2003.

—— (2004) 'Adults Who Have Ever Used the Internet by Sex/Age', *National Statistics Omnibus Survey*. Available online at <http://www.statistics.gov.uk/ statbase/expodata/spreadsheets/d6928.xls>, accessed 25 June 2004.

Rickards, L. (2004) 'Living in Britain Results from the 2002 General Household Survey', Norwich: Office of National Statistics. Available online at <http:// www.statistics.gov.uk/cci/nugget.asp?id=823&pos=1&colrank=2&rank=704>, accessed 25 June 2004.

Rogers, E. (1995) *Diffusion of Innovations*, 4th edn, New York: Free Press.

Rose, R. (2003) *Oxford Internet Survey*, Oxford: Oxford Internet Institute. Available online at <http://users.ox.ac.uk/~oxis/index.html>, accessed 6 October 2003.

Journalism in a non-linear, screen-based environment

19

Practical online skills

Journalism in a non-linear, screen-based environment

Practical online skills

Neil Thurman

Ten years since the first British newspapers ventured online, the industry is exploiting some of what the web offers as a publishing medium, but there are significant blind spots and omissions. Their early reluctance to embrace the possibilities for multimedia, non-linear, near-instantaneous, capacious publishing that the web allows was understandable given the untested nature of the medium. The audience was small (as late as 1999, just 13 per cent of the population had access to the Internet at home) and unwilling to pay for an experience that was, and in many ways remains, inferior to print.

Newspapers seem unsure of how to respond to the fact that reading online is different. On the one hand they want their online versions to mirror the definitive reporting of their print editions: their web sites are electronic archives as well as publishing media in their own right. On the other hand they understand that, because reading online is uncomfortable and the web allows, theoretically, unlimited column inches as well as access to readers across the world, it is hard to justify uploading the paper as is. Nevertheless that is precisely what most have done and many continue to do.

These attitudes are starting to change. As web editions start to make money from readers who are increasingly willing to pay for premium content, respond to advertising and engage with commercial partners, online departments can employ more staff and reduce their dependence on print copy. The *Telegraph*'s site became profitable in 2003 and employs twenty editorial staff working exclusively on the online edition, supported by thirty working in technical, design and marketing. With these numbers they are generating their own stories which typically make up between 10 to 20 per cent of the content added to the web site in a typical day.[1]

This chapter begins by evaluating how and why the experience of reading from screen is inferior to reading from paper and suggests how journalists can adapt their work to compensate. It continues with an exploration of layout and design online and news providers' use of the non-linear nature of the web. I finish by looking at the implications of having a globally dispersed readership.

The problems of reading from screen

An important difference between newsprint and online journalism is the dependence the latter has on the screen for delivery. Most of the computer display monitors currently in use are significantly inferior to paper as a means of reading news and other text. Compared to cathode-ray tubes and liquid-crystal-display monitors, paper has better resolution, a higher contrast ratio and is more portable, making reading faster and more comfortable. However, technology is improving at such a rate that we are already seeing products (such Sony's e-book reader, the Librie) that equal or surpass paper in one important readability metric – contrast ratio. The Sony Librie uses electronic ink as its display technology. E-ink has a contrast ratio of about 9:1; in other words, whites appear nine times brighter than blacks on its screen. This compares favourably with newsprint which has a contrast ratio of about 6:1 (Patch 2001).

Reading from screen is slower and less comfortable than reading from paper. Compared to paper, screens have relatively low levels of resolution. Resolution is a loosely used term but here it refers to both the ability of a screen to reproduce fine detail (a function of its dot-pitch – the distance between individual pixel-elements) and the total resolution available on screen (as measured by the total number of pixels in the horizontal and vertical dimensions).

As an example of the difference in resolution between newsprint and the screen, let's compare the *Guardian* in its broadsheet form with the versions available for personal computers and mobile phones.[2] A single page of the *Guardian* measures approximately 54 × 38 cm. To reproduce that page digitally, without any loss of quality, would require a scanning resolution of at least 190 dpi.[3] The resulting scanned page would measure about 4040 × 2845 pixels. Currently no single desktop computer monitor could support an image of that size. Even if such a screen existed, its resolution would fall short of the 48,000 × 32,000 pixels Nielsen (1995a) believes are required for 'optimal user interface quality'.

The highest resolution monitor currently available, IBM's T220 can 'only' handle 3840 × 2400 pixels and carries a price tag of about £4,500. Currently the most popular monitor resolution is 1024 × 768 pixels;[4] a resolution about fourteen times smaller than that required to accurately reproduce the information contained on a single page of the *Guardian*. Mobile phones have much smaller screens. The Nokia 3650, which can be used to read a specially packaged version of the *Guardian* has a screen that measures 176 × 208 pixels, which could only display 0.3 per cent of the information contained on one page of a broadsheet newspaper.

It's not just their lack of resolution that makes reading from screens uncomfortable. Monitors have a fixed physical position that forces readers to adopt a static posture and they flicker as the image they display is refreshed. There is some evidence that this flicker causes small, involuntary movement in the muscles of the eye (the eye is attracted to movement and perceives flicker as movement). Recent advances in the design of computer monitors have begun to address this issue and refresh rates are getting higher, reducing fatigue and making it easier to read from the screen.[5]

Monitors emit rather than reflect light. Although emissive displays work well in situations where light is limited, they are less well suited to environments (such as the office and home) with ambient light sources. As the amount of ambient light increases, emissive displays can be washed out – light is reflected from the screen reducing the contrast between the dark and light areas. Contrast is one of the principal factors that determine readability for newsprint and electronic displays. In average conditions a newspaper has a contrast ratio of about 6:1 (the light areas are about six times brighter than the dark areas). By comparison, screens have a contrast ratio of about 4:1.

Taken together the poor resolution, low contrast ratio, flicker and immobility of current computer displays result in an actual drop in performance of about 25 per cent when compared to reading from paper (Nielsen 1995a).

Electronic ink to the rescue?

A number of technological solutions are being developed to overcome the problems inherent in conventional computer display monitors. One of the most promising comes from the Electronic Ink Corporation, <http://www.eink.com>. E-ink is a process that uses millions of tiny microcapsules to display text and graphics on a flat surface. Each microcapsule contains positively charged white particles and negatively charged black particles. When a negative electric field is applied, the white particles move to the top of the microcapsule where they become visible to the user. At the same time an opposite electric field pulls the black particles to the bottom of the microcapsules where they are hidden. Reversing this process causes the black particles to appear at the top. By applying electrical charges to various parts of a surface, letters and graphics can be made to appear.

E-ink has several advantages over traditional computer-monitor displays. Contrast ratios are higher (up to 11:1) a result of the fact that the technology relies on reflected light and is not washed out by ambient light sources. The resolution is higher 170–300 dpi (compared with 72 dpi for most CRT monitors). The fact that the pixels are made up of physical microcapsules means the display does not need to be refreshed during reading (thus eliminating flicker).

Although beneficial for reading text, this characteristic does mean that these screens, at their current stage of development, are not suitable for displaying video or animation – media that require high refresh rates. Finally the technology can be used to create portable displays: e-ink can be applied to thin, flexible surfaces. The resulting devices have low power consumption, on four AAA alkali batteries, the Sony Librie has enough power for around 10,000 pages of reading (Kharif 2004).

Adapting copy for the screen

Despite some promising developments such as e-ink, the current generation of computer monitors remain inferior to paper in terms of readability. It is, therefore, essential for online journalists and editors to ameliorate these problems by adapting the style, structure and presentation of their copy for the screen.

The good news for journalists is that in terms of structure and style the way that most journalism, particularly of the news variety, is written is close to the observed preferences of web readers. Research has shown that, on the web, readers prefer objective language. In a comparative study, text written in an 'objective' style was 27 per cent better than 'marketese' in terms of speed and accuracy of reading, recall and reader satisfaction (Nielsen 1997a).

The factual nature of journalism suits the web which is largely a cognitive medium: people use the web to get things done. Readers state that their most important use of the web is for 'collecting and comparing multiple pieces of information, usually [in order to] make a choice' Nielsen (2001). To make a choice users want concise, accurate and complete information.

Freedom from time and space?

The ability of the web to allowing publishing in near real time gives online newspapers some of the qualities of a broadcast operation. Visitors read multiple editions and return regularly, particularly on big news days. For the first time newspapers are able to publish one-line stories ('Sion Jenkins to face retrial. More soon') and publish articles in several parts.

When a story breaks, BBC News On-line, in common with most other online news providers, can have a one-line report on their news ticker as little as 20 seconds after the copy has been approved. **News tickers** (often written in Javascript) have an advantage over traditional HTML as they update without the reader having to refresh the page.

news ticker line of constantly breaking news headlines at top or near top of homepage.

After the one-liner, the BBC publish a four-paragraph story (also used on Ceefax, their teletext service) followed by the full story. Research shows that the frequency with which newspapers update their web sites varies greatly. In one study of thirty news sites, five 'made virtually no updates during the day, while thirteen added only a few breaking news stories'. Twelve newspapers updated their sites 'constantly' (Alves and Weiss 2004).

Online there is no theoretical limit to the amount of space available (BBC News On-line carries around 1.5 million stories). Newspapers are limited by the cost of newsprint and readers' preferences for a relatively portable, manageable product. Those limitations do not apply online. Whereas on paper a story on educational standards in UK state schools might be illustrated with a list of the top ten failing schools, on the web that list could be expanded to 100 or more.

The (inverted) pyramid style of writing, where the most important part of the story is contained in the first paragraph and incidental information relegated to the bottom of the story, has long been the standard form of news writing. Its development is, in part, a result of how printing technology evolved. Before computerised typesetting sub-editors had much less flexibility to change the layout and number of pages in a newspaper.

When late news broke or an advertisement needed to be included, stories were often shortened. Journalists learned to relegate the less crucial information to the bottom of their piece. If these paragraphs were not included because of last-minute changes, the story still made sense. This structure allows readers to scan stories before making a choice about which articles to read in depth and is highly appropriate in an online context where the fast and efficient communication of the essence of a story is essential if a publication is going to attract and retain readers. Whereas on the printed page stories compete with a dozen or so others for readers' attention, online the competition is much greater. Users are just a few clicks away from billions of web pages.

The importance of the intro

Because of the limited resolution of current computer monitors most news web sites can only show the first paragraph of a story on their front page. It is, therefore, vital for that paragraph to contain the essence of the story. Even when readers navigate to the full story, the limited resolution means that only a relatively small proportion of the copy (usually between 10 and 30 per cent) will be visible without scrolling. When the first newspapers went online in 1994/5 only about 10 per cent of users scrolled to 'below the fold' to view information that was not immediately visible in the browser window (Nielsen 2000). Although most readers now scroll, it is still essential to give them the essence of the story in the first paragraphs.

Keep it concise

A concise writing style where superfluous description is kept to a minimum is another attribute of journalistic writing that suits the screen. Nielsen (1997a) observed a 58 per cent improvement in speed and accuracy of reading, recall and reader satisfaction when on-screen text was deliberately made concise. He went on to show web pages using a scannable layout score higher (47 per cent) in speed and accuracy of reading, recall and reader satisfaction than sites not embracing scannability. This is defined as use of headings, large type, bold text, highlighted text, bulleted lists, graphics, captions, topic sentences and tables of contents.

Putting on the style

Design is a creative and intuitive action and, as Allen Hurlburt (1976: 42) says, 'many of the most successful designs [. . .] violate all rules of order and logic'. Nevertheless, typographic and design conventions reflect readers' expectations and provide a benchmark for producing legible publications. On the web, as in print, 'people read best what they read most' (Dooley 1998).

There is a long history of typographic rules and style guides in print. We are now starting to see design manuals that consider the web explicitly. One of the best is the *Web Style Guide* (Horton and Lynch 2002). It is still available in its entirety, free of charge at <http://www.webstyleguide.com>. Another web-specific style guide is *Homepage Usability* (Nielsen and Tahir 2001: 1) which sets down a set of guidelines which attempt to 'codify the best design practices for specific components of a web site'.

Although the codification of conventions and rules in web design is still in its infancy, authors such as Nielsen, Tahir, Horton and Lynch display a relatively high degree of agreement over some of the fundamental issues including the choice of fonts, layout and the width and height of pages.

Fonts

Until relatively recently *The Times* specified a seriffed font for its web pages, perhaps reluctant to move away from its distinguished typographic heritage (most web-browsing software uses Times or Times New Roman as their default serif font). On screen, the finishing strokes at the top and bottom of letters in seriffed fonts reproduce poorly. Until screen resolution improves, Nielsen and Tahir (2001: 53) recommend using sans-serif fonts for body text, something that *The Times*, in common with most British newspaper web sites, now does. Practice across the Atlantic is a little different. The web sites of the *New York Times*, *USA Today*, *Washington Post* and *Wall Street Journal* all use seriffed fonts for headlines and copy.

Line length

Journalists are used to seeing their work printed in narrow columns. A typical tabloid and broadsheet print layout uses twenty-five to thirty-five characters per line for a news story and up to fifty characters for a feature. Print's multi-column format is rarely used online – scrolling from the bottom of one column to the top of the next would be extremely frustrating. As a result wider single columns of text are preferred. Horton and Lynch (2002) recommend fixing columns to sixty to seventy characters per line. Most newspaper web sites use line lengths that fall in the fifty to seventy character range.

Layout

Fixing line lengths conflicts with recommendations for online publications to use flexible, 'liquid' layouts that expand or contract to fill the available browser space. Readers view web sites using screens set to a variety of pixel widths, the most popular is 1024 pixels (49 per cent) followed by 800 (37 per cent) and 1280 (6 per cent).[6] The actual space available within a maximised browser window at any of these pixel widths is slightly reduced by the presence of the scrollbar and default margins left and right. Nielsen and Tahir (2001: 52) recommend designing for 770 pixel width to accommodate the significant minority of readers running lower-resolution screens.

Page height

In print, newspaper readers are used to most stories being visible in their entirety. Online this is not the case. The limited resolution of the screen means that, without scrolling, most readers (49 per cent) view online newspapers through a 'letterbox' between 578 and 632 pixels deep. For 37 per cent of readers this letterbox is between 410 and 464 pixels high (Mulder 2002). Horton and Lynch (2002) recommend scrolling from the top to bottom of a story should be limited to between one and two screens. Nielsen and Tahir (2001) are more generous allowing up to three times the depth of the browser window.

For a newspaper such as the *Telegraph*, to follow this last recommendation would limit their web stories to between 270 to 430 words if they retained their current practice of not splitting articles over multiple pages. Most newspapers have taken the view that, online, readers expect full-length, unedited news and feature stories and those who find scrolling disruptive can always print the story to read offline. Some publications are experimenting with the presentation of text in shallower formats. The *Guardian*'s interactive guides, <http://www.guardian.co.uk/inter active>, are presented in a window fixed at 352 pixels in height. The Flash interface presents the text in a series of frames controlled by the reader.

Hypertext

As we have seen, the current disparity between the readability of news on paper and screen is likely to reduce as technologies such as e-ink allow screens to have levels of resolution and contrast ratios that match or even exceed paper. One characteristic of online journalism that paper will never be able to match is the speed and ease with which readers can navigate through a collection of information, following multiple pathways.

Non-linear reading patterns are not exclusive to digital media. Very few readers of traditional newspapers read in a truly linear manner (from front to back). Many readers invert the reading order and start with sport on the back pages or scan all or parts of the paper before returning to a story of particular interest. Nevertheless, the online medium is fundamentally different. The speed of access to content that digital, disk-based storage provides and the invention of widely adopted hypertext markup languages (in particular HTML) have made it easy for publishers to generate and readers to access multiple non-linear narrative paths.

Non-linear text is generally referred to as 'hypertext'. The term was first coined by Ted Nelson (1965: 96) who introduced the word 'to mean a body of written or pictorial material interconnected in such a complex way that it could not conveniently be presented or represented on paper'. The idea that hypertext adheres to no central structure or hierarchy has been central to the potential that many authors have seen in non-linear narrative structures.

The back cover of Landow's 'Hypertext the Convergence of Contemporary Critical Theory and Technology' (1992) proclaimed that with hypertext readers would gain 'unprecedented control of what – and how – they read'; that it would overthrow 'the author's usual pre-eminence, as the texts are atomized and the **lexias** are dispersed and reconfigured to serve the user's purpose'. Readers would 'choose their own paths along which to work and think non-sequentially', making 'all kinds of hierarchies of status and power' irrelevant. Of course, the paradox is that readers can only move freely through a text, following ideas in various directions and making spontaneous connections if someone has defined the content of the database and provided the hypertext links to facilitate those journeys in the first place.

lexia small fragments of text.

Hypertext in its pure, loosely structured form has not been as popular with readers or publishers as its early proponents predicted, although it is having something of a renaissance in new forms of online writing such as **wikis**. Before the popularisation of hypertext via the World Wide Web, the main format for hypertext was on disk: CD-ROMs and interactive videodiscs. An early entrant into the publication of hypertext and hypermedia content, Interactive Learning Productions (ILP), based two of their first CD-ROM publications *Inventors and Inventions* and *British Birds* on a pure hypertext model. It was the first and only time they did so. The company found that readers preferred their information more explicitly structured and that other navigation metaphors worked better. Hypertext continued to be used on ILP products only to access glossary definitions.

wikis site allowing users to add, edit and delete material.

One reason pure hypertext did not take off was that it forced users to constantly travel between a range of contexts. Readers are baffled by the large number of possible narrative paths and prefer a more explicitly structured interface, something closer to their familiar format of newspapers, magazines and books where the transitions between contexts are slower and more predictable.

Hypertext in online journalism

Although the support of hypertext linking between documents is fundamental to the World Wide Web, custom and practice varies a great deal. Readers can see examples ranging from the relatively unstructured, 'pure' hypertext of the Wikipedia, <http://en.wikipedia.org>, to highly structured documents with no links, or links that have been relegated to the margins of the document. Online journalism has tended towards the structured end of the spectrum but practice varies.

Hyperlinks in copy?

Traditionally hypertext has incorporated links in the body of the text. Although many if not most webpages continue this tradition, some commentators (Horton and Lynch 2002) recommend that authors should, 'put only the most salient links within the body of your text [grouping] all minor, illustrative, parenthetic, or footnote links at the bottom of the document where they are available but not distracting'. The idea that links distract the reader is a consequence of the fact that a link has to be distinguished from the rest of the text so that readers know to click it. The variations in text colour or formatting that links cause may interrupt reading. Horton and Lynch (2002) recommend that links are placed at the bottom of a document – a practice that has the additional benefit of allowing authors to categorise and rank links rather than have them appear chronologically in the story.

Most online newspaper web sites in the UK seem to be in agreement with Horton and Lynch and do not to put links into the body of stories (see Table 19.1). Although the placing of hypertext links outside the main text now seems to be standard practice, it is worth noting that, since 2002, ft.com and telegraph.co.uk have started to put links in their stories while thisislondon.co.uk has stopped!

Table 19.1   Do UK based news web sites place hypertext links in the body of stories? (Survey, July 2004).

news.bbc.co.uk	No
www.the-times.co.uk	No
www.guardian.co.uk	No
www.ft.com	Yes
www.thisislondon.co.uk	No
www.telegraph.co.uk	Yes
www.thesun.co.uk	No
www.mirror.co.uk	No

New browser windows

Good hypertext practice normally requires a 'consistent contextual space'. The text area should behave in a predictable way and be under the user's control. Readers, particularly those who are relatively new to the web, may be confused when a new browser window opens to display the destination of a link they have clicked. If the new browser window obscures the previous window some readers may not be aware that a new window has opened. New windows are commonly opened through the use of the target attribute of the HTML element <a>. In the example below, readers clicking on the link would find that the City University web site opens up in a new browser window.

```
<a href='http://www.city.ac.uk' target='newwin'>City
University </a>
```

Not using the target attribute maintains a consistent contextual space as the incoming HTML document replaces its predecessor in the same browser window. Some critics (Horton and Lynch 2002) take the opposite view believing that opening a new browser window can 'maintain context [. . .] allow[ing] your reader to access new material without losing visual contact with your site'. Nielsen (1999) argues that this strategy is 'self-defeating since it disables the *Back* button which is the normal way users return to previous sites. Users often do not notice that a new window has opened, especially if they are using a small monitor where the windows are maximised to fill up the screen. So a user who tries to return to the origin will be confused by a greyed out *Back* button.' Again practice amongst online newspapers in the UK varies, see Table 19.2 for more details.

Labelling links

Good hypertext practice provides readers with information about the destination of any link. Authors can make use of the title attribute of the <a>element in HTML to give additional information about the destination of links. Web browsers (such as Internet Explorer) display this information in a small box when the reader hovers their mouse over the link. The following example shows how to use this functionality in the HTML of a page.

```
<a href='http://www.city.ac.uk' title='The University
for business and the professions'>City University</a>
```

The take-up of this functionality has been poor with none of the newspaper web sites listed in Table 19.3 making use of link titles.

Headlines and hypertext

Until the resolution of the screens used to access journalism online improves, a concise writing style has been shown to be one way in which journalists can help

Table 19.2 Do UK-based news web sites open a new browser window when readers click on external and internal links? (survey, July 2004).

www.mirror.co.uk	Not for banner ads, internal links or links to external web sites referenced in stories.
News.bbc.co.uk	Not for links to other stories or sections within the BBC.co.uk domain or for links to external web sites referenced in stories. Yes for some internal links (e.g. their Broadband news service).
www.telegraph.co.uk	Yes for internal features such as picture galleries, adverts, links to other telegraph.co.uk sections and for links to external web sites referenced in stories.
www.guardian.co.uk	Yes for adverts. Not for links to other stories or sections within the guardian.co.uk domain nor for links to external web sites referenced in stories.
www.thesun.co.uk	Yes for adverts (including the *Sun*-branded but externally managed Sun Shop) and for links to some internal features such as Picture Galleries. Not for links to other stories nor sections within thesun.co.uk domain.
www.the-times.co.uk	Yes for adverts. Yes for some links to other Times On-line sections (such as Travel) but not for others (such as the bookshop). Not for most stories within the thetimes.co.uk domain.
www.ft.com	Yes for adverts, links to some internal sections (such as Special Reports and the Week in Pictures). Not for links to other internal sections nor internal links referenced in the body of the stories.
www.thisislondon.co.uk	Yes for adverts and some internal features including Picture Gallery. Not for links to most internal features and stories.

N.B. Between 2002–4: <thisislondon.co.uk> started to use pop-ups for some internal links (such as picture gallery). In the same period BBC News On-line stopped opening a new window for some internal features such as In Pictures.

Table 19.3 Do UK-based news web sites use link title text? (survey, July 2004).

news.bbc.co.uk	No
www.the-times.co.uk	No
www.guardian.co.uk	No
www.ft.com	No
www.thisislondon.co.uk	No
www.telegraph.co.uk	No
www.thesun.co.uk	No
www.mirror.co.uk	No

readers cope with the poor readability of computer-monitor displays. Counter-intuitively this principle does not apply to writing headlines, standfirsts or links for the web. The reason for this is that, online, these story elements are often seen out of context: on the front page as part of a list of articles, in a search-engine hit list, in web browsers' bookmarks or favourites file, or harvested and used as content on other pages (by content aggregators like Google News or Moreover.com).

The difficulty of reading online and the reduced amount of information presented on the screen compared with the printed page means there is little contextual information to support a headline. In print readers pick up information about a story, not from the headline alone but from the standfirst, photograph and caption, subheadings and the full body of the article – all visible in the reader's peripheral vision. Online the relatively limited space available means that a headline and brief standfirst are all the reader has to go on when making a decision about whether to read the full text of a story. For this reason headlines online tend to be fuller, use plainer language and avoid puns. Comparing the headlines used in the printed and web versions of *The Times* newspaper in October 2000 we can see that the subs had decided to modify the headlines for the web, making them clearer and less ambiguous (see Table 19.4).

Looking at *The Times* web site again in June 2004 showed a marked convergence between their print and online headlines as compared with three years earlier. The reason why, four year on, *The Times* is no longer adapting headlines for the web is unclear (see Table 19.5).

In the third example from July 2004, punning is used both in print and online (the 'Lord of the Rings' headline refers to the Cassini spacecraft's exploration of Saturn). Nielsen (1998) argues against the use of puns online saying:

> users have been burned too often on the web to have time to wait for a page to download unless they have clear expectations for what they will get. In print, curiosity can get people to turn the page or start reading an article. Online, it's simply too painful for people to do so.

Table 19.4 Comparing print and online headlines in *The Times*, October 2000.

Online	Print
Don't block Ken – Dobson asks Labour for a straight fight but he faces investigation for using membership lists	Allow Ken to Stand, Dobson tells Blair
Beef Thaw. New BSE tests to put British beef back on export menu	Move to new BSE tests
Jobs fear as Bank increases Loan rate	Rate rise blow for home owners
Hundreds of Boeing 767 aircraft could be flying with faulty tail bolts but company says this is not likely to pose safety threat	Faulty bolt fear for Boeings

Table 19.5   Comparing print and online headlines in *The Times*, July 2004.

Online	Offline
It's real love as Wimbledon falls for a fighter	It's real love as Wimbledon falls for a fighter
Adjani emerges to take her revenge on Jarre	Adjani emerges to take her revenge
Close encounters with Lord of the Rings	Close encounters with Lord of the Rings
Japan's hoteliers turn to Tarzan as passion wilts	Japan's hoteliers turn to Tarzan as passion wilts

A decision by BBC News On-line in 2003 seemed to support this view. For several years the BBC used **teaser** headlines on the front page (a selection is shown in Table 19.6). When they undertook an analysis of server statistics they found users were not sufficiently inclined to click on them to justify the amount of space they occupied on screen and they were abandoned as part of their relaunch in February 2003.[7]

> **teaser** a headline which only hints at the main angle of the story.

Table 19.6   A selection of teaser headlines used on BBC News On-line, October 2000.

Teaser Headline	Value of <a href> attribute 'title'
Sound and vision	Objects can be seen more clearly if they make a sound before they become visible, say scientists
Time to cull	Culling rats could actually worsen an outbreak of plague
Home boy returns	Former child start Macaulay Culkin says he's going back to acting but under his own terms
Hole in the sky	Chileans warned of dangers from the ozone hole.
Life after death	Scientists say they have evidence that the mind continues to function after the brain closes down
Green cure for pests	Scientists develop new anti-locust spray

Global readers

A defining characteristic of online journalism is its ability to reach beyond the traditional limitations of newspaper circulation. Overseas readers have always made up a large part of the readership of British newspaper web sites. The *Guardian's* site has more readers in the USA than in the UK (Mayes 2004). The Times On-line reports that 41 per cent of their unique users come from the US.[8] BBC News On-line estimates that 30 to 40 per cent of its readers come from overseas.[9] The *Telegraph* reports that 28 per cent of the hits on its web site are from North

America.[10] By contrast the *Telegraph* locates 95 per cent of its print readership within the United Kingdom and Northern Ireland.

Whether and how online journalists accommodate their overseas readers depends, to a large extent, on the commercial model of the publication they work for. Although BBC News On-line has a separate front page for readers from the rest of the world, (as opposed to the UK, England, Scotland, Wales or Northern Ireland), it receives no licence fee income from the vast majority of its overseas readers. In the run-up to the renewal of their Charter in 2006 the BBC may find it hard to justify expenditure on content that is not explicitly written for the UK licence payer. Commercial sites such as *The Times* do not try to interest advertisers in that part of their audience based outside the UK. The material *The Times* provides to advertisers considering their web site as a potential advertising vehicle focuses exclusively on their UK audience.[11]

This hard-nosed commercial approach has not always held sway. Back in 1999 The Times On-line had a distinctly broader news agenda with one foreign and one home story given equal prominence on the front page (see Table 19.7).

In the four years since the examples in Table 19.7 were gathered The Times On-line has moved closer to the print version in its news agenda with less prominence given to world news. In October 2004 *The Times* lifted subscription charges for readers who access the site from an overseas IP address. Whether this move will prompt a return to a more global news agenda remains to be seen.

Table 19.7 Comparing on print and online headlines in *The Times*, November 1999.

Date	The two most prominent stories on front page of the paper	The two most prominent stories on the front page of the web site
5 November 1999	Let me fight Livingstone says Dobson	Let me fight Livingstone says Dobson
	Belize picks Ashcroft for summit team	General Pervaiz Musharraf, Pakistan's military leader, says country's economy must come before democracy
8 November 1999	Brown to boost share ownership	Brown to boost share ownership
	Blair will allow me to run, says Livingstone	Chechnya accuses Russia of committing 'genocide' against its people, and appeals to West to force Kremlin to halt its three-month offensive
9 November 1999	Business Booms as City wins battle of euroland	Business Booms as City wins battle of euroland . . .
	Mandelson is back on Election Duty	Hundreds of Boeing 767 aircraft could be flying with faulty tail bolts but company says this is not likely to pose safety threat

Notes

1. Richard Burton, Editor, telegraph.co.uk, conversation with author, 16 July 2004.
2. Companies such as AvantGo <http://www.avantgo.com> package news content from providers such as the Guardian, The Times On-line, CNN.com and Reuters in a form that can be read on mobile phones such as the Nokia 3650.
3. Newspapers are printed at a resolution of approximately 85 lines per inch (lpi). The printer's rule of thumb for converting lpi to dpi is to multiply by at least two.
4. Resolution stats, thecounter.com. Available online at <http://www.thecounter. com/stats/2004/May/res.php>, accessed 30 June 2004.
5. Nielsen (1995a) claims we need a refresh rate of over 120Hz for 'perfect image quality'. Most of today's computer monitors refresh at a rate of between 50–100Hz although refresh rates of up to 260Hz are supported by some monitors.
6. Resolution stats, thecounter.com. Available online at <http://www.thecounter. com/stats/2004/July/res.php>, accessed 19 July 2004.
7. Mike Smartt, then-editor of BBC News On-line, conversation with author, June 2003.
8. Peter Bale, Times On-line, email with author, 14 February 2005.
9. Richard Deverell, News Interactive. Available online at <http://news.bbc.co.uk/ aboutbbcnews/hi/this_is_bbc_news/newsid_3280000/3280463.stm>, accessed 13 July 2004.
10. Sanjit Chudha, telegraph.co.uk, email with author, 22 February 2005.
11. User demographics, The Times On-line. Available at <http://www.timeson-line.co.uk/section/0,,462,00.html>, accessed 15 July 2004.

References

Alves, R. and A. Weiss (2004) 'Many Newspaper Sites Still Cling to Once-a-Day Publish Cycle', *On-line Journalism Review*, 21 July. Available online at <http:// ojr.org/ojr/workplace/1090395903.php>, accessed 23 August 2004.

Dooley, M. (1998) 'Critical Conditions: Zuzana Licko, Rudy Vanderlans, and the Émigré Spirit', *Graphic Design USA*, 18. Available online at <http://www.emigre. com/ArticleCriticalConditions/.php>, accessed 13 June 2005.

Grossman, J. (1993) *Chicago Manual of Style*, Chicago, Ill.: University of Chicago Press.

Horton, S. and P. Lynch (2002) *Web Style Guide: Basic Design Principles for Creating Web Sites*, 2nd edn, London: Yale University Press. Available online at <http:// www.webstyleguide.com>, accessed 10 June 2005.

Hurlburt, A. (1971) *Publication Design: A Guide to Page Layout, Typography, Format and Style*, New York: Van Nostrand Reinhold.

Kharif, O. (2004) 'Computing's New Screen Gems', *Business Week On-line*, 8 June. Available online at <http://www.businessweek.com/technology/content/jun 2004/tc2004068_1264_tc149.htm>, accessed 12 July 2004.

Landow, G. (1992) *Hypertext the Convergence of Contemporary Critical Theory and Technology*, London: Johns Hopkins University Press.

Mayes, I. (2004) 'A Girdle Round the Earth', *Guardian*, 10 July. Available online at <http://www.guardian.co.uk/comment/story/0,,1258030,00.html>, accessed 23 August.

Mulder, S. (2002) 'Sizing Up the Browsers', *Webmonkey*, 7 May. Available online at <http://webmonkey.wired.com/webmonkey/99/41/index3a.html?tw=design>, accessed 19 July 2004.

Nelson, T. (1965) 'A File Structure for the Complex, the Changing and the Indeterminate', Association for Computing Machinery, Proceedings of the National Conference. New York: ACM. Available online at <http://www.ischool.washington. edu/tabrooks/ 100/documents/nelsonbrief.pdf>, accessed 16 July 2004.

Nielsen, J. (1995a) 'How Much Bandwidth Is Enough? A Tbps!', Useit.Com, November. Available online at <http://www.useit.com/alertbox/9511.html>, accessed 12 July 2004.

—— (1995b) 'Be Succinct! (Writing for the Web)', useit.com, November. Available online at <http://www.useit.com/alertbox/9703b.html>, accessed 12 July 2004.

—— (1997a) 'How Users Read on the Web', useit.com, October. Available online at <http://www.useit.com/alertbox/9710a.html>, accessed 12 July 2004.

—— (1997b) 'Concise, Scannable, and Objective: How to Write for the Web', useit.com. n.d. Available online at <http://www.useit. com/papers/webwriting/writing.html>, accessed 12 July 2004.

—— (1998) 'Microcontent: How to Write Headlines, Page Titles, and Subject Lines', useit.com, September. Available online at <http://www.useit.com/alertbox/980906.html>, accessed 12 July 2004.

—— (1999) 'The Top Ten New Mistakes of Web Design', useit.com, May. Available online at <http://www.useit.com/alertbox/990530.html>, accessed 12 July 2004.

—— (2000) *Designing Web Usability*, Indianapolis, Ind.: New Riders.

—— (2001) 'The 3 Cs of Critical Web Use: Collect, Compare, Choose', useit. com, April. Available online at <http://www.useit.com/alertbox/20010415.html>, accessed 12 July 2004.

Nielsen, J. and M. Tahir (2001) *Homepage Usability: 50 Web Sites Deconstructed*, Indianapolis, Ind.: New Riders.

Patch, K. (2001) 'E-Paper Coming into View', *Technology Research News*, 12 December. Available online at <http://www.trnmag.com/stories/2001/121201/e-paper_coming_into_view_121201.html>, accessed 9 July 2004.

Ritter, R. (2003) *The Oxford Style Manual*, Oxford: Oxford University Press.

From Nexus to newslog

20

Online journalism from the grassroots

From Nexus to newslog

Online journalism from the grassroots

Neil Thurman and Susan Jones

The web has the great advantage of having network rather than broadcast architecture: there is a permanent two-way path connecting the readers at their 'client' computer and the publishers with their 'server' of digitised content. This model facilitates rapid and frequent communication between the two and, more interestingly, allows computers on the network to be the 'client', the 'server' or both at the same time, blurring the boundaries between consumer or reader and provider or publisher.

Anyone who has followed the development of the web will know that, even in its earliest days, readers were expected to want both to view and edit the material they accessed. In their 'WorldWideWeb: Proposal for a HyperText Project', Tim Berners-Lee and Robert Cailliau (1990) promised that what would become the first web browser would provide functionality to allow 'annotation by users of existing data' and 'collaborative authorship'. They felt that 'making it easy to change the web is [. . .] the key to avoiding obsolete information'. Their first web browser (initially called WorldWideWeb then renamed Nexus) was not just a browser but explicitly a browser/editor. The expectation that readers would edit continued as the web took off. The first commercial web browser (Netscape) included an option in its 'File' menu for users to 'Edit Page' using the built-in Composer editing software, functionality sadly now absent from the most widely used browser, Microsoft's Internet Explorer.

The publication and annotation of content by readers has always been a fundamental part of the history of the web, both technologically and conceptually. Unfortunately the idea that readers should be involved in the publication process and even become publishers themselves, has taken some time to find favour with established publishers, and even now there are relatively few examples of reader participation that go beyond the superficial. Not only has it taken publishers some time to begin to harness the potential of their distributed and knowledgeable readership, but the mainstream press has taken a long time to properly acknowledge the depth and breadth of information available online.

The emergence of 'We Media'

This is in part due to a natural suspicion of material published without the usual editorial processes, but also to the lack of a memorable name to give to grassroots publishing. Dan Gillmor (2003), one of the most vocal evangelists of making readers an integral part of the process of communication, calls it 'We Media'.

He recognises that 'journalism is evolving away from its lecture mode – here's the news, and you buy it or you don't – to include a conversation'. He continues with the observation that 'readers collectively know more than we do', seeing that fact as an opportunity rather than a threat: 'the evolution of We Media will oblige us all to adapt'.

Whilst Gillmor's concept of 'We Media' is not tied to a technology or set of conventions, the best-known form is the blog. 'Blog' is a contraction of 'weblog', a term that, according to the *Oxford English Dictionary*, first appeared in 1993 to refer to the file that stores a record of requests handled by a web server. In 1997 the term was being used in a manner that corresponds with its current widely accepted definition as a 'frequently updated web site consisting of personal observations, excerpts from other sources, etc., typically run by a single person, and usually with hyperlinks to other sites; an on-line journal or diary' (Simpson 2003). By the summer of 2004 Technorati, <http://www.technorati.com>, a search engine that indexes active content on the web (blogs and RSS feeds), reported it was watching 3,023,173 weblogs.

The birth – and spread – of blogs

One reason for the rapid establishment of blogging as a popular means of self-publication is that developments in technology have provided free, easy-to-use blogging tools such as those hosted by blogger.com. These developments have increased the supply of blogs while, at the same time, the demand for stories and opinions from the grassroots has grown, not least because of the events of 11 September 2001, which was something of a watershed in the use and recognition of blogs. On that day many of the major news web sites were unable cope with demand (BBC News On-line was unavailable for two hours, other online news providers and search engines for much longer). As a result, and because many of the most interesting stories were individual tales of survival or loss, many people found that chatrooms, emails, bulletin boards and blogs were the best way to fulfil their need for news, information and discussion. Comparing occurrences of the word 'blog' and its derivations in pages indexed by search engines reveals an eight- to tenfold increase in frequency of use in the year following 11 September 2001 compared with the year that preceded 9/11.[1]

The dramatic increase of information on blogs has provided a useful source of vox pops for the mainstream media, but blogs have also broken some big stories. One of the best-known examples involved a US Senator from Mississippi, Trent Lott. At a 100th birthday party for Senator Strom Thurmond, Lott appeared to praise Thurmond's past pro-segregationist views by saying 'we wouldn't of [*sic*] had all these problems' if Thurmond had won the presidency in 1948. The publicity that blogs gave the speech moved the story to the mainstream media and Lott's eventual resignation as leader of his party in the US Senate prompted the *New York Post* to describe the case as 'The Internet's First Scalp' (Podhoretz 2002).

Mainstream responds to blogs

More often than not, however, the mainstream media's coverage of the blogging phenomenon has had more to do with the medium than the message. 'Baghdad Blogger "Amazed" by Success',[2] 'The Blog from the Heart of Downing St' (Wilson 2004) and 'Teenagers Reach Out Via Weblogs' (Twist 2004) are three recent examples of where the blog has become the story. When the press have not been writing about blogs they have attempted to harness the buzz surrounding them by launching their own.

The Guardian's weblog was one of the first.[3] Since April 2000 it has provided excerpts from and links to news from a variety of other sources, although it does not have the personal character typical of most blogs. BBC News On-line's newslog (Robinson 2002), lacks the functionality that the blogging community has come to expect: the blogroll, permalinks, reader comments, trackback and syndication. Both of these examples, in common with other mainstream blogs, fail to conform to some of the social conventions of the blog.

Weblog conventions and blogspeak

As we have already noted, a blog is commonly expected to be a site consisting of a number of short pieces of writing. Although visually a blog is reminiscent of the front page of a news site such as news.yahoo.com or Guardian Unlimited, the stories (called 'posts' in **blogspeak**) are organised by time rather than with reference to a news agenda. The most recent entry appears at the top of the page and earlier entries below, eventually disappearing from the front page. Most blogs allow archived posts to be accessed through permanent links (known as permalinks). Permalinks are probably the most widely applied blogging convention on mainstream blogs.

blogspeak esoteric jargon of blogs.

Originally, blogs acted as online diaries where people described their lives for their friends and highlighted links to other sites that the writer had discovered and wanted to point out. More recently, blogs have also been used for activities more journalistic in nature:

- A 'broadcast' from a live event. 'Downing Street Says' is an unofficial weblog that publishes summaries of the British Prime Minster's official spokesman's daily **lobby** briefings and allows readers to add their own comments.[4]

lobby specialist group of correspondents reporting on the House of Commons.

- Regular opinion columns. Most of the best known are written by bloggers outside the traditional journalistic establishment. Dave Winer,[5] the founder and original Chief Executive of Userland Software,[6] (itself a supplier of blogging software), was one of the earliest regular, high-profile bloggers. Although he was not at the time a professional journalist, in 2003, the *Online Journalism Review* (Glaser 2003) rated his blog as one of the most influential. Professional journalists who run influential blogs, sanctioned and hosted by their employer, have included Dan Gillmor at the *San Francisco Mercury News*.[7]
- Niche or micro-journalism. Given the relative youth of the form and its dependence on evolving software, technology is a major theme. Influential blogs in this category include Many 2 Many,[8] a group blog on social software.

Many 2 Many's collaborative nature is the exception rather than the rule. Typically, blogs are written by one person and, even where collaboration takes place, there is a real sense of common idiosyncratic interests and opinions.

Blogs support writing in relatively small chunks, so a post may contain something as simple as a link and an 'I agree' comment, or an aphorism, or a list of notes. The genre is tolerant of this style; it is seen as an acceptable way to communicate unlike newspaper, journal or book publishing where even a small idea must be expanded into an something larger to be publishable. Blogs are often cited as examples of 'micro-content'. They allow ideas to be disseminated quickly, even in comparison with web sites based on more traditional formats. However, different blogs operate on different time scales. Some specialise in many short items a day; others in fewer, longer, well-considered items, appearing less frequently.

Blog technology

Blogs can be hand-coded in HTML using a text editor, but the technical expertise required may not encourage frequent posting, especially from less technical writers. So special software is often used to enable quick and easy publication. It manages a database of posts, giving users an easy way to add new items and supporting additional facilities for searching and linking. It can be found in three main forms:

1. A hosted service (e.g. blogger, typepad, diaryland, livejournal, aol). An external organisation maintains a server which manages multiple blogs. Users get an account and access their blog remotely through a browser. Some free services are available, or one can pay for enhanced accounts with extra features.
2. A software package for hosting blogs on a standard server (e.g. movable type, wordpress, bloxsom). This software is often open-source or free for non-commercial use. It can be installed on users' own servers, or on an ISP with facilities to run server-side scripts. The blog is again updated via a normal browser.
3. A desktop client and server, a.k.a. 'micro-content client' (e.g. Radio Userland).[9] This software sits on a desktop like a word-processor and allows users to write and organise their posts locally. It can either act as a webserver on its own (viable on a PC with a permanent IP or LAN address) or periodically *synchronise* itself with a publicly available server.

Each method has advantages and disadvantages. Desktop clients offer more convenient interfaces for writing and organising posts, but blogs on central servers can be read and updated from anywhere.

Individual weblogs provide a simple form of publishing, but the real significance and excitement comes from the interaction between them. Bloggers have developed modes of dialogue which involve both software functionality and, equally important, *social conventions*.

How to begin blogging

The quickest and least demanding way to start blogging is to use a hosted service. Blogger.com, now owned by Google, is one of the best known. Their service is free and can be accessed entirely through a web browser. Once you have opened up an account you will need to think of a name for your blog. Blogs hosted by Blogger follow this naming convention <http://yourblogsname.blogspot.com> where [yourblogsname] is the name of your blog. As with domain names and email addresses many common names have already been taken but you should not find it too difficult to find a memorable name that is still available.

Every post requires a title (think of it as the headline) and some content. Simple formatting can be applied to the content of each post (bold, italics and an indented quote) and hyperlinks can be added.

Preview then publish your post. Once you have got to grips with posting from the Blogger web site you can explore the more advanced features of the service. It is possible to publish posts via email and even by a phone (the post appears on your blog as an MP3 audio file).

Blogs are usually personal so bloggers often provide detailed biographical information. On the Blogger service you can provide information about your identity, (including a photograph) and where you live and work.

You can define the look and feel of your blog. Blogger provides a dozen or so pre-programmed templates. Seasoned bloggers can create their own custom template design.

Flyblogging and the crucial role of comments

Most weblogs allow readers to add comments at the bottom of a post. This adds value to the material; for example if a news story contains an error, a reader may be able to correct it. Or if the situation has changed since the story was posted, other readers may be able to update it so that the story remains relevant as new events occur. If the weblog is focused on opinion, there are likely to be strong arguments in the comments section. The writer can gain an insight into those who disagree and learn about other points of view. Blogs hosted by mainstream broadcasters and publishers have been wary about allowing unmoderated comments to be posted and some do not allow comments at all. Comments are an important social convention in the blogging community, but those blogs that post comments automatically may start to reconsider now that flyblogging, a.k.a. comment spam, has emerged as a phenomena. Flybloggers use automated software to post comments advertising a web site they are seeking to promote (Thompson 2003).

The blogroll

The 'blogroll' is a column at the side of the page containing a list of links to other blogs. It has several functions. First, it's a convenient bookmark list for the blogger – an index page to other weblogs which are regularly read. For readers, it acts like a citation list at the end of an academic paper — a way to find other relevant material. If X finds Y's blog interesting and Y find's Z's blog interesting, then maybe X will find Z's blog interesting as well. It may also allow a reader to make a judgment about the *person* behind a blog and become familiar with his or her technical or political or musical interests and allegiances so as to decide whether to revisit it on a regular basis. Blog search engines like Technorati rank blogs according to how many inbound links they have on other blogs' blogrolls.

Trackback and the conventions of multi-blog discourse

A conversation started by one post can potentially spread across multiple posts on other weblogs. In my weblog I might say that university top-up fees are a necessary evil. You may want to disagree strongly so you post a counter-argument. How are readers to know that these posts are connected? When you write your post, you can link to mine, explaining that you are answering me. But how does a reader of *my* weblog know that a counter-argument is waiting on *yours?* One technical solution is 'trackback': a communications protocol that allows your weblog to inform mine that you have commented on one of my posts. The existence of your comment is automatically signalled as a trackback link under my post and can be followed up by my readers.

Topic exchange and 'pinging'

The trackback mechanism has another application. The Topic Exchange site[10] provides a number of channels (essentially empty posts) whose content is provided entirely by trackbacks from other blogs. For example, if I am interested in Turkmenistan, whenever I post a new story in my weblog, I 'ping' Topic Exchange's Turkmenistan channel as if I were commenting on it via trackback. The channel then shows a link to my new story. If a channel is well supported it forms a useful hub or specialist publication on a particular subject. Popular channels on the Topic Exchange site include 'Mars', 'Google' and 'Seinfeld'.

Syndication

Weblogs provide a world of dynamic information that is always changing. Syndication allows their contents to be delivered directly to the desktop of sub-scribing users. RSS stands for 'Rich Site Summary' or 'Really Simple Syndication'. It is an XML file format for lists of story titles and summaries. Several popular weblog systems make posts available in this form because it allows them to be found and presented by special aggregating software. Examples of aggregators are Amphetadesk, Netnewswire and Radio Userland. These can be installed on a local machine, allowing their user to subscribe to RSS 'feeds' from different weblogs (or news sites). When executed, the aggregator program fetches the most recent contents from these feeds and combines them into a single page, so items coming in from many sources can be conveniently read together.

The social network

A weblog is a mechanism for publishing on the Internet and operates as a genre of writing with its own conventions. But weblogs are about people. To use weblogs effectively, readers and writers do not need to think about which buttons to click or how to configure a server. They need to think about the social world, trust and reliability. Whose weblog do you invest time in reading each day? Whose news is likely to be right? Whose opinions and speculations are valuable? How do you find the people who know the things you want to know? 'Social network analysis' tries to extract useful information about the social network. For example, the search engine Technorati uses a technique similar to Google's Page Rank to analyse weblogs and the links between them. It can monitor:

● which blogs have the most links from other blogs, that is, who is well read and respected;
● which news stories are most often referenced;
● which are the most recent topics for discussion. This is done by identifying 'word bursts' – words whose frequency of occurrence in stories has suddenly increased.

The 'flow' Internet

The conventional view of the web is a collection of static documents with unique addresses, but a relationship with a weblog is more like a relationship with a radio or television station. Its URL does not correspond to a static page but to a channel generating a regular supply of new material. There is a change of perspective – instead of having to go to a site for information, we expect the information to come to us via the aggregator.

As a story percolates through the flow Internet, some information is gained and some is lost. Errors are both introduced and corrected. It might seem intuitive that the information will degrade. People are more likely to misunderstand and corrupt the information as they pass it from one to another. After all, weblogs have no formal editorial or fact-checking process to pick up on mistakes. And no one stops malicious bloggers publishing lies.

But it also seems that most people aren't stupid or malicious. A stupid weblog will lose trust and other bloggers won't read it or link to it. So self-correction occurs too within the system as a whole. The phenomenon of warblogging (blogging by supporters and opponents of the 2003 US invasion of Iraq) demonstrated the presence of 'echo chambers'. These are partisan groupings of bloggers who read, link to and quote each other obsessively, often ignoring those with alternative opinions and so reinforcing their own beliefs and world views. Each group highlighted certain facts and myths, either culled from the conventional media or gained directly from residents of Iraq, military personnel or others on the ground.

Echo chambers work against error-correction and help sustain lies and mistakes. But it remains an open question whether problems here are greater than those due to comparable biases and blindspots in other media. The hope is that as weblogs extend the population of those who write, comment, criticise and offer their evidence, the larger number will allow the good to outweigh the bad and correct more falsities than are introduced.

Among the warbloggers, deliberate ignorance of alternative viewpoints is balanced by those who 'fisk' or deliberately and aggressively criticise and pull apart the arguments of their opponents. So although the option of remaining within a particular camp is open, a reader who chooses to read both sides will find a thorough survey of all the relevant evidence and counter-arguments.

Wikis: an alternative model of collaborative publishing

A less reported form of grassroots publishing is the wiki. Unlike most blogs, wikis give all users the freedom to edit and even delete material. The name 'wiki' derives from Hawaiian for 'quick', and the wiki principle emphasises informality, simplicity and speed of interaction. Unlike a blog where material is organised by time, the most recent post appearing at the top of the page, a wiki is more like a newspaper, magazine or book, based around pages and containing longer, more considered articles.

In many ways, however, wikis are radically different from traditional journalism since in principle *anyone* can read, add or delete text from pages. Layout and presentation tends to be very simple, with the emphasis on the storage and exchange of ideas rather than visual sophistication or branding. Wikis emphasise the convenience of writers (contributors) over readers. They are intended for participation rather than passive viewing. Both content *and* structure exist in a state of flux and, unlike other web sites or publications, it is acceptable for them to have loose ends.

As a form the wiki has, thus far, tended to be used for reference works (Wikipedia being the best-known example containing more than 300,000 articles),[11] but the speed with which information can be added and organised means there is no reason why a journalist should not use a wiki as an electronic notebook, drafting tool or ideas processor. In the research for a story, the pure form of hypertext that wikis support make them ideal for planning or analysing and recording interactions between characters and incidents; and as a collaborative tool the wiki provides an excellent mechanism for collecting and linking large quantities of factual information. On 2 December 2004 the Wikimedia Foundation launched Wikinews.

Wiki software

The basic unit of information in a wiki is the page. Each page has a unique name which is used as the basis for linkage. Normally, wikis are hosted on a public site and use a content-management system to store and index pages and links. A number of wiki systems are available: Usemod and PHPWiki are two of the better known. They allow pages to be created, edited and viewed; they accept text input using simple mark-up conventions and convert it into HTML for display. In addition, they are able to show, on demand:

- a list of recent changes;
- a history for each page, listing successive versions, plus the time, date and author of the changes;
- highlighted differences between any two successive versions;
- details of links to any given page from other pages.

The last point effectively turns all wiki links into two-way connections, an idea which was implicit in classical hypertext theory but lost in standard WWW navigation.

As already stated, a basic wiki need not impose any security constraints but current wiki software can implement restrictions on reading and writing if the wiki administrator wishes to activate them. Even where no restrictions are applied, wiki software normally stores a copy of every page before any change is made to it and so provides an easy way to roll back to earlier versions. So damaged pages can be restored, either by the wiki administrator or by any conscientious user. To deal with more serious vandalism, such as 'denial of service' attacks, the software should allow IP blocking to stop edits coming from, say, a hostile robot.

How to write for a wiki

To read the contents of a wiki, enter the URL of its home page and follow any links of interest to other pages. The name of each page acts as its link address and should provide some indication of its subject. Many link/page names take the form of 'WikiWords', i.e. two or more real words with initial capitals, run together as one. This is the basic wiki linkage convention though other methods are possible; for example, enclosing a word or phrase in square brackets. It is usually possible to view page histories and changes and to find all the inbound links from other pages.

An 'Edit' button will normally appear on each page viewed. In response to a click, the browser presents a text-area showing the current page contents which can be changed by insertion and deletion. A simple set of formatting rules can be used, which map on to some underlying html tags. They may vary slightly according to the particular software implementation but they generally support paragraphing, headings, lists and bold and italic fonts. Pages can be previewed before the new version is saved and, to economise on storage space, it is possible to specify that a change is only a minor edit.

To create a new page it is necessary first to set a link to it from an existing page:

- in edit mode, enter a WikiWord, or a word or phrase in square brackets, to form the name of the new page;
- save the edit and view the result: the new page name will appear often followed by a question mark acting as an html link;
- click the question mark to go to the skeleton new page, go into edit mode and add the new page contents.

Using wikis: the social conventions

Wikis work when a community of contributors cooperate. Its members are expected not only to add new material but, as time goes by, to improve what is there by correcting errors, repairing damaged pages, adding and assigning useful categories and *refactoring* page content to make it more coherent. For example, over time a single page might acquire a number of contributions on different topics which would be better reordered or even distributed amongst several new pages. Likewise, material spread over separate pages might with advantage be summarised and brought together. In this context, a wiki can be viewed as a single large draft document in a continual state of flux which represents the current thinking of a group of people.

Provided it succeeds in carrying forward that group's objective, it need not matter that there is never a final version. Unlike blogs, wikis make no logical distinctions between original posts and comments, nor do they present the kind of hierarchical structures seen in a typical threaded discussion list. In practice, however, many page edits are actually comments on what has gone before and groups may need to adopt some formatting conventions (such as paragraphing, font selection, horizontal rules) for distinguishing between separate entries of this kind. It is good etiquette to sign one's name to any substantial new contribution, though being aware that its individual identity may be lost after refactoring. Wikis are not the ideal platform for egotists!

Early wikis were based on private **intranets** where users knew and trusted each other. Later, wikis appeared on the public Internet and have been found to work surprisingly well there too, despite the lack of conventional security measures. In essence, a wiki is like any public space; it can be vandalised but, if its users care enough to repair damage, the vandals will not win. Because it is so easy to revert to earlier versions, it normally takes less effort to fix a piece of damage than to cause it in the first place.

intranet a privately maintained computer network that can be accessed only by authorised persons.

Unlike a normal discussion forum where readers' comments are immutable, until recently, wikis have been fairly resistant to commercial vandalism (spamming) for the same reason. If an unwanted advert appeared in the wiki, the first person to see it could remove it. For the mischievous hacker, damaging a wiki was no challenge nor any demonstration of skill in outwitting security provisions. Now the appearance of automatic spamming (seemingly designed to increase Google page rank) is causing the wiki community to rethink these issues.

Nevertheless, wikis are not a suitable solution for every application or organisation. They are designed for the convenience of writers rather than readers. Structure and organisation are the responsibility of the contributors: the software does not enforce it. Each page must be given a unique name comprising a meaningful word or phrase, which may be difficult to achieve in large-scale document collections. And the requirement to keep back-up copies of every version of every page means that they involve greater overheads than other content-management software.

Why blogs are history – wikis are geography

Both wikis and blogs as forms of writing allow the publication of relatively small chunks of information directly and make communicating and sharing information quick and easy. Both are based on active cultures, groups of people who are experimenting with and developing new technologies and new social practices. There have been attempts to synthesise them, to produce 'wikiweblogs' or 'blikis' which include elements of both. But dedicated bloggers are not necessarily good wiki-citizens. They would rather write complaints about things being disorganised than reorganise them themselves, or move discussions away from the 'confusing' wiki pages and into their own weblogs.

The main difference between the two genres is that weblogs are focused on individuals and their voice. Understanding the social network and finding informed people you like is an important way to use the world of weblogs. By contrast, wikis are often about the submersion of the individual in an anonymous group where it is not always obvious who said what. Most importantly, weblogs are organised around *time* whereas wikis are organised around related topics in an information *space*. In other words, blogs are history – wikis are geography.

Acknowledgement

The authors are grateful to Philip Jones for his contributions to this chapter. His wiki can be accessed at <http://www.nooranch.com/synaesmedia/wiki/wiki.cgi>.

Notes

1. On 8 July 2004, the Alltheweb search engine (http: //www.alltheweb.com) listed 22,905 occurrences of the words 'blog OR weblog OR blogs OR weblogs' between 11 September 2000 and 10 September 2001 compared with 184, 133 in the period from 12 September 2001 to 11 September 2002. Altavista (http://www.altavista.com) listed 63,400 occurrences for the same period pre-9/11 and 667,000 occurrences in the year following.
2. Anonymous (2003) 'Baghdad Blogger "Amazed" by Success', BBC News On-line, 9 September. Available online at <http://news.bbc.co.uk/1/hi/world/middle_east/3092646.stm>, accessed 9 July 2004.
3. <http://www.guardian.co.uk/weblogindex/0,6799,340346,00.html>.
4. <http://www.downingstreetsays.org>.
5. <http://www.scripting.com>.
6. <http://www.userland.com>.
7. <http://weblog.siliconvalley.com/column/dangillmor>.
8. <http://www.corante.com/many>.
9. <http://radio.userland.com>.
10. <http://topicexchange.com>.
11. <http://en.wikipedia.org>.

References

Berners-Lee, T. and R. Cailliau (1990) 'WorldWideWeb: Proposal for a HyperText Project', W3.org, 12 November. Available online at <http://www.w3.org/proposal.html>, accessed 5 July 2004.

Gillmore, D. (2003) 'We Media', *Columbia Journalism Review*, January/February 2003. Available online at <http://www.cjr.org/issues/2003/1/wemedia-gillmor.asp>, accessed 9 July 2004.

Glaser, M. (2003) 'Bloggers Rate the Most Influential Blogs', *Online Journalism*

Review, 23 June. Available online at <http://www.ojr.org/ojr/glaser/1056050270 .php>, accessed 9 July 2004.

Podhoretz, J. (2002) 'The Internet's First Scalp', *New York Post*, 13 December: 41.

Robinson, N. (2002) 'Newslog', BBC News On-line, 29 May. Available online at <http://news.bbc.co.uk/1/hi/in_depth/uk_politics/2001/newslog/2013240.stm>, accessed 13 July 2004.

Simpson, J. (ed.) (2003) *OED On-line*. Available online at <http://www.oed.com>, accessed 9 July 2004.

Thompson, B. (2003) 'How Spammers Are Targeting Blogs', BBC News On-line, 24 October. Available online at <http://news.bbc.co.uk/1/hi/technology/ 3210623.stm>, accessed 9 July 2004.

Twist, J. (2004) 'Teenagers Reach Out Via Weblogs', BBC News On-line, 6 June. Available online at <http://news.bbc.co.uk/1/hi/technology/3774389.stm>, accessed 9 July 2004.

Wilson, G. (2004) 'The Blog from the Heart of Downing St', BBC News On-line, 1 March. Available online at <http://news.bbc.co.uk/1/hi/magazine/3523629 .stm>, accessed 9 July 2004

Part III
More key areas

Ethics, law, copyright and politics

Is virtuous journalism possible?

21

A critical overview of ethical dilemmas

Is virtuous journalism possible?

A critical overview of ethical dilemmas

Richard Keeble

The questioning approach

Let's begin with a simple and clear ethical principle: journalists should be accurate and report the truth. As Bill Kovach and Tom Rosenstiel argue in *The Elements of Journalism* (2001), 'journalism's first obligation is to the truth'. And they report that 100 per cent of journalists interviewed for a survey by the US-based Pew Research Centre for the People and the Press and the Committee of Concerned Journalists said 'getting the facts right' was journalists' major responsibility.

If only ethics were that simple! In fact, there are no simple answers in ethics. That's what makes it such a fascinating, challenging and potentially subversive subject. Ethics is essentially concerned, as the Greek philosopher Socrates stressed, with answering the question: 'What ought to be done?' In other words, while it can deal with profoundly significant abstract concerns (for instance, about objectivity and 'the public interest'), at root ethics is concerned with basic practical dilemmas.

According to theorist Valerie Alia (2004), media ethics is inextricably linked to strategies for social change. It deals in questions rather than answers and prefers doubt and sceptical laughter to the dullness of dogma. Returning to our first principle, for example, is there an absolute truth? Is there an objective reality out there? Or is 'reality' a highly contested territory – with many different definitions of 'realities' competing for prominence? On a more basic level, you may report someone's views faithfully, but what if they are lying or ignorant of the issues? Truth will then, inevitably, be compromised.

Journalism's ethical diversity

There are many journalisms. To simplify matters, print media can be divided into three basic sectors. There are the mainstream publications (such as *The Times*, *People*, *Marie Claire*) owned by major, profit-based companies. The alternative print and online media (*Socialist Worker*, *Peace News*, *Eastern Eye*, *Muslim News*, coldtype.net) are outside the control of major companies, targeted at specific audiences according to religion, political bias and so on, and often collectively organised and non-profit oriented.

Between these sectors are hybrid and, consequently, fascinating publications such as the satirical and investigative *Private Eye* and the *Big Issue* (campaigning for the homeless) which mix elements of both mainstream and alternative media. Journalists in the various sectors face very different ethical challenges. And reporters, sub-editors, photographers, columnists and cartoonists in each sector will face dilemmas specific to their journalistic roles. In other words, beyond the dominant consensus over news values in mainstream print publications lies an extraordinarily diverse and complex range of approaches across a number of sectors.

Ethics tends to draw on universal values such as accuracy, honesty, fairness, respect for privacy, the avoidance of discrimination and conflicts of interest (Grevisse 1999). But cultures and political systems around the globe throw up very different ethical challenges for journalists. For instance, in Russia and Colombia where dozens of critical reporters have been killed in recent years, ethics inevitably becomes enmeshed in questions about personal survival, not normally confronted by journalists in advanced Western capitalist countries. Yet, is it possible to consider journalism ethics in Britain and its relative cultural and political freedoms without referring to the suppression of human rights and the appalling impoverishment of millions in Second and Third World countries – on which those freedoms are based?

Ethics and the political economy of the media

Ethics is often associated with matters of personal conscience. Karen Sanders (2003) highlights a range of day-to-day ethical dilemmas for reporters, such as over-deception, reconstructions, the reporting of terrorism, racism and homophobia, invasions of privacy, whistle-blowers and chequebook journalism. And part of her strategy for making 'good' journalism focuses on the individual: their need to be socially responsible, accurate, accountable to colleagues, sources, the public and to themselves. The BBC's veteran war correspondent John Simpson is quoted approvingly (Sanders 2003: 163): 'All you can do is make sure your conscience is as clear as a profession full of compromise and uncertainty will allow it to be.'

This dominant approach, however, significantly fails to root the personal in the political. Since the political economy of the mainstream media (based on monopoly ownership and hyper-competition) is so central in determining the standards of journalism can any debate about mainstream journalism ethics avoid confronting these basic political, structural issues (McChesney 1999, Golding and Murdock 2000, Kamenka 1969)?

Ethics implies choice (between 'good' or 'bad' or a set of messy compromises between the two) and an understanding of the political and historic contexts in which the choice is being made. And ethics implies the ability to effect change. But in hierarchically organised institutions, such as news organisations and magazines, what power has the individual alone (and in particular young recruits) to bring about change?

On primary and secondary dilemmas

Ethical dilemmas can be usefully divided into two kinds. First there are the primary questions related to your choice of sector in which to work (whether as full-time or part-time staffer or as a freelance). Implicit in your choice are a range of ethical and political decisions (though you may not necessarily be consciously aware of them).

For instance, you may aim to work for a local evening newspaper, a national tabloid or a **campaigning** leftist journal. Or, like reporters such as John Pilger and the late Paul Foot, you may choose to work for both mainstream and alternative media. In each case the ethical challenges (and salaries) along with the inevitable compromises you will have to make will be very different. Once the primary decision has been made, the secondary decisions (over such issues as taste, bias, anti-sexism and militarism) will follow – all of them determined in some way by the primary decision.

George Orwell, for instance, was one of the finest journalists of the past century who knew the significance of the primary ethical decision. For him, the mainstream media were nothing less than the propaganda sheets of their wealthy proprietors. Thus his primary decision was to direct his main journalistic output (though not all of it) at obscure, largely leftist journals such as *Adelphi*, *New English Weekly*, *Fortnightly Review*, *Tribune*, *Left News*, *Polemic*, *Progressive*, *Persuasion* (Keeble 2001a). In this way he was engaging in the crucial political debate with the committed people of the left who mattered to him. They were an authentic audience compared with what Stuart Allan (1999: 131) calls the 'implied reader or imagined community of readers' of the mainstream media (see Hunter 1984: 133–60).

Some important secondary dilemmas

Many journalists are striving, while confronting various secondary dilemmas, to challenge damaging stereotypes and discrimination based on gender, sexual orientation, disability, age, mental health, race and so on. Yet the dominant culture often tends to view sceptically lobby groups linked to anti-racism, anti-sexism and anti-militarism issues, criticising them as PC (politically correct) fanatics. Within such a highly charged context, protest and defensiveness result, but also lots of ideas for creative solutions.

Anti-racism

A report by the European Monitoring Centre on Racism and Xenophobia, in May 2002, accused the British mainstream media of using damaging stereotypes of Muslims and portraying asylum seekers as 'terrorists' and the 'enemy within' after 9/11. A lot of media racism, then, is overt. But much is more subtly institutionalised and 'naturalised', impacting on overall news values (such as in the marginalising of Africa and demonising of foreign leaders) and employment practices (Allan 1999: 158–72). For instance, a Journalism Training Forum study in 2002 showed only 4 per cent of journalists were from African or Asian backgrounds (Hargreaves 2002). Would the appointment of more ethnic minority journalists reduce the level of racism in the press?

How important is it to focus on the 'right language' when rooting out racism? Most magazines' and newspapers' style books cover not only editorial matters, such as spelling and the use of capital letters and italics, but also ethical issues. On race, the style of Reuters, the international news agency, is typical (MacDowall 1992: 125) when it says: 'Mention a person's race, colour or ethnic or religious affiliation only if relevant to the story.' The NUJ's *Guidelines on Race Reporting* stresses 'immigrant'

campaigning
journalism overtly
partisan journalism
promoting particular
cause. US: advocacy
journalism.

is often used as a term of abuse and should only be used when someone is strictly an immigrant. Most black people were born here and most immigrants are white. Is special care needed when using the word 'riot'? Simon Cottle (1993: 164) suggests it can be used to de-politicise an event with the media ignoring the deeper structural causes of conflict such as the acute levels of social and cultural deprivation.

Anti-sexism

The stereotyping of women in the print media has long been a concern of feminist critics. To what extent would the employment of more women improve the situation? The percentage of women on national dailies is, certainly, low at 22, though magazines often include more women than men and, of the 70,000 professional journalists in the country, half are women (Hargreaves 2002). Linda Christmas (1997) argues that the employment of women has had a dramatic effect of 'humanising' the news, leading to a 'huge increase in human interest stories'. But these views do not go unchallenged. Women journalists often deny they have a distinct news and 'softer' feature agenda (e.g. Stephen 1997) while Ros Coward has expressed concern over rising anti-male rhetoric in the media (1999).

Feminists have directed their critique particularly at sports coverage. According to Valerie Alia (2004: 132–3): 'Sports teams remain gender segregated and except for tennis and Olympic sports such as figure skating, women's events are almost never given the newspaper space, television or radio time of equivalent men's events.' When women tennis players (such as Gabriela Sabatini, Mary Pearce, Anna Kornikovo and Maria Sharapova) feature in the sports pages their presence is often sexualised. But the issues are far from black and white. As David Rowe comments (1999: 128), 'Such debates are especially intense when sportswomen explicitly play the role of soft pornographic subject on the covers of sports magazines, in calendars, posters and publicity shots.'

In countering sexism, are separate women's sections in newspapers part of a solution? Or do they tend to perpetuate the stereotypes focusing on sex, health, domestic issues and lifestyles? And should more importance be given to the use of non-sexist language in the media? (See Doyle 1995).

The historic origins of the objectivity ideology

Many journalists, in the face of all these competing secondary dilemmas, will say their major responsibility is to be objective and 'get the facts right'. According to the first clause of the Press Complaints Commission's Code of Practice: 'The press, whilst free to be partisan, must distinguish clearly between comment, conjecture and fact.' Clause 3 of the National Union of Journalists' Code of Conduct similarly stresses, 'A journalist shall strive to ensure that the information he/she disseminates is fair and accurate, avoid the expression of comment and conjecture as established fact and falsification by distortion, selection or misrepresentation.' This notion of objective 'fact' has significant historic origins.

In the early 1800s, a radical press committed to working-class solidarity and workers' rights captured the revolutionary spirit following the American and French revolutions and began to challenge the mainstream press for supremacy (Williams

1987: 28–47, Curran and Seaton 2003: 6–23, Conboy 2004: 88–108). Many radical journalists were fined and jailed for their pains.

By the mid-century, the campaigning working-class press had faded. Advertising and stamp duties were introduced in the late eighteenth century as an instrument of social control, limiting ownership and access to the press to 'men of some respectability and property' (Curran and Seaton 2003: 8). In 1855 the stamp duty was removed; paper duty was scrapped in 1861. As mainstream newspapers shifted to a reliance on advertising a new consensual ideology emerged on the left that stressed capital and labour could operate together (Williams 1987: 45), the radical left was forced on to the margins. The market (rather than the state), in effect, served to censor radicalism from the public sphere. In place of a media based on a close political and cultural identification between journalist and reader, a new mass-selling media emerged in which the professional's link with their audience was cut.

Questioning the objective/subjective dualism

It could, then, be argued that objectivity, which emerged as the dominant ideology in Britain and the USA in the late nineteenth century, was part of a strategic ritual to legitimise the activities of the mainstream media. At root, beyond the rhetoric of 'public interest', 'democracy' and 'press freedom', the 'objectivity' myth promotes the interests of the economic and political elites (see Allan 1999: 7–26). Explicitly partisan, alternative journalists, such as those on indymedia.org and schnews.org.uk, significantly reject all notions of objectivity and 'balanced reporting' (Atton 2002, 2003).

Moreover, in response to the advocates of objectivity, some mainstream journalists advance the values of subjectivity. James Cameron (1997: 172), the legendary peace-campaigning journalist who was the first Western journalist to visit Hanoi during the Vietnam War, commented: 'It never occurred to me, in such a situation, to be other than subjective. I have always tended to argue that objectivity was of less importance than the truth.' Myra Macdonald, in her seminal text, *Exploring Media Discourse*, also stresses the values of subjectivity to the journalist (2003: 74–8). Focusing on the war reporting of Maggie O'Kane and Lindsey Hilsum, she argues that journalistic reflexivity and the personalising of news can serve to highlight problematics within dominant routines and values.

In contrast Nick Stevenson (1995: 30–1) argues for a sense of reality based on 'communicatively held inter-subjective values [. . .] Even if it is recognised that claims to balance, impartiality and objectivity are shaped linguistically, this does not necessarily mean that they are not values worth defending.' A stress on subjectivity would automatically circumvent any possibility of rational dialogue and discussion on the public issues raised. 'But if truth claims are seen as communicatively held inter-subjective values that refer to states in the real world, this would allow for an open discussion of the issues at hand.' How does your stance on this intriguing debate reflect and affect your response to the media and journalism?

Dumbing down – or up?

Most periods witness moral panics over the mainstream press. And many elite commentators have, over the ages, lambasted newspapers and magazines for their outrageous standards. 'Grub Street' and 'Street of Shame' have inevitably become associated with the press. Thus, is it most useful to view today's frenzy over falling standards as part of a historic continuum which began with the first newsbooks and newspapers? (Keeble 2001b: 3–12). Particular concerns focus on the alleged **'dumbing down'** of standards with a growing emphasis throughout all the print media on sex, lies, scandal, smear, celebrities and ruthless invasions of privacy (Greenslade 2004). According to Tessa Mayes (2000: 30), 'Emotional indulgence and sentimentalism are replacing informative, fact-based news reporting. Today, reporters are providing therapy news.'

> **dumbing down** claim that media standards, in general, are falling, with increasing emphasis on sensationalism, celebrities, 'human interest' stories, sexual titillation, scandal and sleaze.

As the competition between the leading magazine and newspaper titles intensifies, so the demand for profit dominates all other considerations. Accordingly, trashy tabloid 'values' infect the whole of the press. Ian Hargreaves (2003: 104) sums up this way:

> Journalism has always entertained as well as informed. Had it not done so, it would not have reached a mass audience. But today, say critics, the instinct to amuse is driving out the will, and depleting the resource, to report and analyse in any depth. Obsessed with a world of celebrity and trivia, the news media are rotting our brains and undermining our civic life.

There are problems with this stance. Some journalists, such as the editor of the *Guardian*, Alan Rusbridger, and the former editor of the *Observer*, Will Hutton, argue the media have, instead, 'dumbed up', opening up quality journalism to a broader public. Similarly, academic Brian McNair (2003: 224) comments: 'We inhabit not a dumbed down news culture but one becoming steadily more sophisticated and literate.' Yet, more significantly, the attention of the 'dumbing-down' critique is directed entirely at the mainstream media, and thus the alternative media are subtly eliminated from the debate. And the stance prioritises moral outrage while rational, political analysis and action are more needed if media standards in general are to be lifted.

Codes and the professionalisation problematic

Much of the current debate over print-media standards revolves around the decisions of the Press Complaints Commission (PCC <http://www.pcc.org.uk>) and its Code of Practice (see Frost 2000). Set up in 1991, so replacing a discredited Press Council, the PCC represents a major attempt by journalists at self-regulation. It promotes ethical standards through its rulings on complaints and advisory notices to journalists (on chequebook journalism, royal coverage and privacy issues, for instance) and, most significantly, wards off legislation that could threaten press freedom. Or, depending on your point of view, it is a toothless watchdog, crucial in the construction of the professionalisation myth and a PR stunt for the print industry. As Julian Petley argues (1999: 155),

> to read its code's high-flown rhetoric about 'accuracy', 'opportunity to reply', 'privacy', 'harassment', 'intrusion into grief or shock', 'discrimination' and so on

and then to immerse oneself in the daily debased reality of so much of the British press, which quite clearly cares not a jot for such self-deluding nonsense, is all that is needed to understand why the PCC cannot be seriously regarded as a regulatory body.

The National Union of Journalists' Code of Conduct, first adopted in 1936, now incorporates thirteen general principles (<http://www.nuj.org.uk>). Clause 4, for instance, states: 'A journalist shall rectify promptly any harmful inaccuracies, ensure that correction and apologies receive due prominence and afford the right of reply to persons criticised when the issue is of such importance.' Most recently, a clause was inserted (Clause 11) on photographic manipulation: 'No journalist shall knowingly cause or allow the publication or broadcast of a photograph that has been manipulated unless that photograph is clearly labelled as such. Manipulation does not include normal **dodging**, **burning**, **colour balancing**, **spotting**, **contrast adjustment**, **cropping** and obvious **masking** for legal and safety reasons'. Can you envisage any problems in enforcing this clause?

In contrast, the PCC's code currently has sixteen detailed clauses which have been subject to constant revision since 1991. Many journalists cynically argue that codes are there only to be broken. As Harris pointed out (1992: 67): 'One of the consequences of bringing out detailed sets of regulations is that it fosters a loophole-seeking attitude of mind. The result could be that journalists will come to treat as permissible anything that does not fit the precise specifications of unethical behaviour.' But in contrast, Claude-Jean Bertrand (2001) highlights the fact that there are now more than seventy press councils around the world and 250 codes in operation (see <http://www.presscouncils.org>) making the media more accountable and open to public criticism.

The NUJ stopped using its code to discipline members in the 1980s because it was found to demoralise journalists. The PCC can force editors to publish adjudications. But until it acquires powers to fine publications for breaching the code, many argue it will fail to have any major impact on press standards. When so many journalists are ignorant of the content of codes and clearly breach them daily (with the constant stream of racist and sexist coverage, for instance) then why bother with them? And is not journalists' professionalism (and accompanying claims of specialised skills) under increasing threat from the explosion of the Internet which allows anyone, in effect, with a computer/laptop to become a self-styled journalist?

dodging, burning, colour balancing, spotting, contrast adjustment, cropping and masking special facilities in image-making programs such as Photoshop.

Privacy issues and the secret state

Fleet Street is bursting with scandals over intrusions into privacy and grief. Hardly a week passes by but another controversy erupts. Mostly they concern celebrities, politicians, randy royals, sports stars, TV personalities and the like (Keeble 1998, 2001: 47–60). A range of royal commissions on the press, official inquiries, PCC rulings and parliamentary pronouncements have all focused on privacy issues but their overall impact on press behaviour appears minimal. Sleaze, editors argue, guarantees sales so its constant presence is inevitable.

Yet since 1998, when the Human Rights Act incorporated the European Convention of Human Rights into British law, the privacy row has reached fever pitch. Significantly, Article 8 of the Convention (note the sexist language) states: 'Everyone has the right to respect for his private and family life, his home and his correspondence.' Supposedly balancing this privacy right, Article 10 states: 'Everyone has a right to freedom of expression. This right shall include freedom to hold opinions and to receive and impart information without interference by public authority and regardless of frontiers. This article shall not prevent states from requiring the licensing of broadcasting, television or cinema enterprises.' Many journalists claim the (somewhat confusing) operations of the Act mean that press freedom is, in effect, being undermined 'by the back door' (see Mayes 2002).

Supermodel Naomi Campbell, footballers Gary Flitcroft and David Beckham, television newsreader Anna Ford, Hollywood superstars Catherine Zeta-Jones and Michael Douglas, actress Amanda Holden, Home Secretary David Blunkett and radio DJ Sara Cox have been amongst the celebrities recently caught up in privacy controversies with the media.

Beyond the celebrity spectacle, it could be argued that far more serious threats to privacy, marginalised in the media, come from the expanding Big Brother state – with the moves by the police, security services and businesses to monitor and intercept emails and mobile-phone conversations and the increasing presence of CCTVs in our everyday lives. In particular, radical critics have expressed concerns over the impact of the Regulation of Investigatory Powers Act (2000) and the Anti-Terrorism, Crime and Security Act 2001 which provides a statutory basis for the authorisation and use by the security and intelligence agencies, law enforcement and other public authorities of covert surveillance, agents, informants and undercover officers (see <http//www.privacyinternational.org>, Todd and Bloch 2003).

Go on: name some good journalists

I want to end by encouraging you to identify the journalists you consider 'good'. Take a look at those highlighted by Fred Inglis in his fascinating history of journalists in the twentieth century, *People's Witness* (2002). For me, they are the thousands all around the world (and across the ages) who display a profound moral commitment for progressive social change, working in many small ways (often for appalling salaries and in the face of serious dangers) to improve media standards against pressures from proprietors, advertisers, politicians and, in many countries, gangsters and the military. Take a look at *Index on Censorship* for reports on journalists around the world oppressed for speaking out.

Then there's Tariq Ali, John Berger, Tom Bower, Yasmin Alibhai-Brown, Fenner Brockway, Wilfred Burchett, James Cameron, Albert Camus, Noam Chomsky, coldtype.net, Robert Fisk, Paul Foot, Martha Gellhorn, Roy Greenslade, Germaine Greer, Bonnie Greer, C.L.R. James, Mark Kermode, Naomi Klein, Phillip Knightley, *Lobster, London Review of Books*, Media Lens, Linda Melvern, George Monbiot, *New Internationalist* (<http://www.newint.org>), George Orwell, Gregory Palast, *Peace News*, John Pilger, Anna Politkovskaya, *Private Eye*, Arundhati Roy, Edward Said, Sebastiao Salgado, Anthony Sampson. Saira Shah, Mark Steel, I.F. Stone, Mary Stott, Kenneth Tynan, Natasha Walter, Günter Wallraff, Donald Woods. How does your list compare? Why not send it to me at rkeeble @lincoln.ac.uk?

References

Alia, V. (2004) *Media Ethics and Social Change*, Edinburgh: Edinburgh University Press.

Allan, S. (1999) *News Culture*, Buckingham: Open University Press.

Atton, C. (2002) *Alternative Media*, London: Sage.

—— (2003) 'Ethical Issues in Alternative Journalism', *Ethical Space: The International Journal of Communication Ethics*, 1(1): 26–31.

Bertrand, C.-J. (2001) *Arsenal for Democracy*, Creskill, NJ: Hampton Books.

Cameron, J. (1997) 'Journalism: A Trade', in M. Bromley and T. O'Malley (eds), *Journalism: A Reader*, London: Routledge: 170–3.

Christmas, L. (1997) *Chaps of Both Sexes? Women Decision-Makers in Newspapers: Do They Make a Difference?* Wiltshire: Women in Journalism in association with BT.

Conboy, M. (2004) *Journalism: A Critical History*, London: Sage.

Cottle, S. (1993) *TV News, Urban Conflict and the Inner City*, Leicester: Leicester University Press.

Coward, R. (1999) 'Women Are the New Men', *Guardian*, 1 July.

Curran, J. and J. Seaton (2003) *Power Without Responsibility: The Press, Broadcasting and New Media in Britain*, 6th edn, London: Routledge.

Doyle, M. (1995) *The A–Z of Non-Sexist Language*, London: The Women's Press.

Frost, C. (2000) *Media Ethics and Self-Regulation*, Harlow: Pearson Education.

Golding, P. and G. Murdock (2000) 'Culture, Communication and Political Economy', in J. Curran and M. Gurevitch (eds) *Mass Media and Society*, 3rd edn, London: Hodder Headline: 70–92.

Greenslade, R. (2004) 'Do These People Have a Right to Privacy?', *Guardian*, 26 January.

Grevisse, B. (1999) 'Chartres et codes de deontologie journalistique: une approche internationale comparée', in C.-J. Bertrand (ed.) *L'Arsenal de la democratie: media, deontologie et MARS*, Paris: Economica: 54–70.

Hargreaves, I. (2002) 'Young, Graduated and White', *Press Gazette*, 12 July.

—— (2003) *Journalism: Truth or Dare?* Oxford: Oxford University Press.

Harris, N. (1992) 'Codes of Conducts for Journalists', in A. Belsey and R. Chadwick (eds) *Ethical Issues in Journalism and the Media*, London: Routledge: 62–76.

Hunter, L. (1984) *George Orwell: The Search for a Voice*, Milton Keynes: Open University Press.

Inglis, Fred (2002) *People's Witness: The Journalist in Modern Politics*, London and New Haven, Conn.: Yale University Press.

Kamenka, E. (1969) *Marxism and Ethics*, London and New York: Macmillan and St. Martin's Press.

Keeble, R. (1998) 'The Politics of Sleaze Reporting: A Critical Overview of the Ethical Debate in the British Press of the 1990s', *Recherches en Communication*, 9: 71–81.

—— (2001a) 'Orwell as War Correspondent: A Reassessment', *Journalism Studies* 2 (3): 393–406.

—— (2001b) *Ethics for Journalists*, London: Routledge.

Kovach, B. and T. Rosenstiel (2001) *The Elements of Journalism*, London: Guardian Books.

McChesney, R. (2000) *Rich Media, Poor Democracy: Communication Politics in Dubious Times*, New York: New Press.

Macdonald, M. (2003) *Exploring Media Discourse*, London: Hodder & Stoughton Educational.

MacDowall, I. (1992) *Reuters Handbook for Journalists*, Oxford: Butterworth.

McNair, B. (2003) *News and Journalism in the UK*, 4th edn, London: Routledge.

Mayes, T. (2000) 'Submerging in "Therapy News"', *British Journalism Review*, 11 (4): 30–6.

—— (2002) *Restraint or Revelation? Free Speech and Privacy in a Confessional Age*, London: Spiked.

Petley, J. (1999) 'The Regulation of Media Content', in J. Stokes and A. Reading (eds), *The Media in Britain: Current Debates and Developments*, Basingstoke: Macmillan: 143–57.

Rowe, D. (1999) *Sport, Culture and the Media*, Buckingham: Open University Press.

Sanders, K. (2003) *Ethics and Journalism*, London: Sage.

Stephen, J. (1997) 'The Trouble with Women', *Guardian*, 7 July.

Stevenson, N. (1995) *Understanding Media Cultures: Social Theory and Mass Communication*, London: Sage.

Todd, P. and J. Bloch (2003) *Global Intelligence: The World's Secret Services Today*, London: Zed Books.

Williams, K. (1998) *Get Me a Murder a Day! A History of Mass Communication in Britain*, London: Hodder Headline.

Courting controversies

Law and the journalist

22

Courting controversies

Law and the journalist

Richard Orange

Journalists who are unfamiliar with the law or are careless in its application are liabilities to themselves and to their employers whether they are senior reporters or trainees. The prospect of litigation arises once the reporter commits purported facts or opinions, criticisms and allegations to print. Journalists also come under the legal spotlight as soon as they write about victims of crime, suspects and offenders and the judicial system. This chapter, in focusing on the law, covers some of the major areas all journalists (from local cub reporter to top investigative reporter) should be aware of, highlighting crucial cases and the views of various experts. It also offers some hypothetical scenarios as a way of exploring the kinds of legal questions you will need to ask when handling tricky stories.

LIBEL (A.K.A. DEFAMATION)

First, let's look at libel. In simple terms, this is an untrue statement or inference published to a third party, damaging a person's good name. Defamation also applies to businesses, particularly in relation to commercial products. Councils and police authorities cannot sue as corporate bodies but can assist in actions brought by individual officers and members.[1]

Criminal prosecutions for libel are rare and concern the deliberate publication of material known by the author to be false and harmful. Inaccurate and damaging statements concerning candidates during election campaigns (e.g. falsely stating he or she has withdrawn from a contest or wrongly implying dishonesty) risk falling into this category.

Most defamation cases are civil actions and deal with a claimant's desire for redress. It is for the journalist to prove the truth of the statement in question. The claimant needs to show that he or she is the subject of the statement, that it is damaging to his or her reputation and that it has been read by someone else. The jury will decide, without an interpretation from the judge, what the words mean and whether the statement is defamatory. If the finding is for the claimant, then the jury will consider the level of compensation.

Reporters should expect their motives and intentions in wording the statement to be examined during a libel trial. But it is no defence for the journalist to assert that he or she did not mean the article to have the interpretation placed on it by the claimant.

AN EXPERT VIEW: GLENN DEL MEDICO

Too often, defamation actions are commenced due to a failure by the journalist or lawyers to establish the meaning they wish to draw. If there is a possibility of readers confusing who did what and to whom, then resort to the phrase: 'There is no suggestion that . . . '. The importance of clearly stating the identities of those against whom allegations are made cannot be overstated. We have to block out all innocent parties.[2]

Something of a fad has grown up around the deployment of the word 'allegedly'. It is not an all-purpose judicial equivalent of a flu jab. Libel concerns the meaning behind a phrase, which can be a statement of fact, a comment, opinion, inference or a malicious allegation. The word 'allegedly' highlights the fact that the truth is unclear. Sometimes it is important to use the word, especially in police and court reports. The level of protection afforded by the phrase 'is alleged to have' will depend on the degree of privilege derived from the source of the story.

It can be hazardous to leave names out of stories in the hope of avoiding a libel action. Journalists run the risk of defaming the anonymous person plus all of his or her innocent associates.

ANOTHER EXPERT VIEW: TONY JAFFA

It is a recurring problem with stories about the medical profession. A mother takes a child to the surgery and the doctor says there is nothing wrong. Both return home but the youngster's condition deteriorates. Eventually the mother takes the child to hospital where it dies of meningitis. This sort of thing happens every year and the newspaper is faced with the dilemma of whether to name the surgery or doctor. If there is a risk of libelling other doctors, I tend to advise the newspaper to identify the particular GP.[3]

Justification

If you can show that an offending statement in your report is true and that the public had a genuine right to be informed, then you should cite justification as a defence. Be aware that the claimant (formerly plaintiff) has certain advantages.

AN EXPERT VIEW: LORD JUSTICE BROOKE

In *Polly Peck (Holdings) plc* v. *Trelford* (1986) the court held that where a publication contains two or more separate and distinct defamatory statements, the plaintiff is entitled to select one of them for complaint, and the defendant is not entitled to assert the truth of the other(s) by way of justification.[4]

---

continued

Note that the case of *Bonnick* v. *The Gleaner* provides journalists with some protection regarding the meaning of words. See also the section on the Reynolds Defence on pp. 286–7.

Offer of amends, accord and satisfaction

A correction and apology agreed between the publisher and the complainant can be used to avoid legal action or limit damages. Negotiations are generally left to the editor or publisher and often involve lawyers. *McNae's Essential Law for Journalists* reminds reporters to be careful about what they say to people who complain about articles, to avoid accepting liability.[5] Matters are made worse if a reporter makes a careless admission or neglects to furnish the editor with full details of a complaint.

Fair comment

For 'fair', do not assume 'respectful' or 'balanced'. Unpleasant, discourteous, insulting, biased and rude remarks about celebrities, politicians, journalists, artists, musicians and football referees can be protected. The comments must be the writer's honest opinion, must be based on facts that are true or are privileged and must be made in the public interest.[6]

In *Hunt* v. *Star Newspaper Co. Ltd* (1908), the court stressed that comment must 'not be so mixed up with the facts' that the reader could not separate the two.[7] In *Adams* v. *Guardian Newspapers* (2003), the Scottish Court of Session considered a defamation claim brought by an MP. The newspaper said its story was protected by 'fair comment on the surrounding facts'. The court disagreed. Lord Reed: 'Counsel for the defenders was unable to point to any statement in the article which might be construed merely as an expression of opinion.'[8]

The court will also look at the overall treatment of the article and balance between comment and fact.

AN EXPERT VIEW: LORD NICHOLLS

The comment must explicitly or implicitly indicate, at least in general terms, what are the facts on which the comment is being made. The reader should be in a position to judge . . . how far the comment was well founded.[9]

The journalist should make sure that the comment does not carry or infer an untrue statement. To insert the word 'allegedly' into the offending part of the piece rather points to the notion that an unproven reality must be lurking behind an opinion.

Reviews of commercial products are particularly troublesome. The phrase: 'I reckon the firm's new car is ugly and I found it a brute to handle on the narrow country lanes,' is unflattering. But it is the writer's view. The sentence 'I like the car but the manufacturers have to sort out the problem with the suspension' blurs comment and fact.

Malice

Fair comment and privilege (see below) are lost if the court concludes that publication was malicious. This has a number of meanings, beyond hatred or a desire to injure. Many judges have cited *Horrocks* v. *Lowe* (1975) which described malice as a genuine indifference to the truth. However, this judgment contained an important rider.

AN EXPERT VIEW: LORD DIPLOCK

If he publishes untrue defamatory material recklessly, without considering or caring whether it be true or not, he is . . . treated as if he knew it to be false. But indifference to the truth [. . .] is not to be equated with carelessness, impulsiveness or irrationality in arriving at a positive belief that it is true [. . .] despite the imperfection of the mental process by which the belief is arrived at it may still be 'honest,' that is, a positive belief that the conclusions [. . .] reached are true. The law demands no more.[10]

In writing the defamatory article, the reporter may have failed to appreciate the relevance of certain facts or statements helpful to the claimant. Lord Diplock's view was that so long as the journalist could show that he or she had been motivated by a desire to get to the truth and that he or she honestly believed that he or she had, malice would not apply. This is akin to the fair comment test where the opinion (however unorthodox) must be genuine.

In *Cheng and Wah* v. *Paul* (2001), Lord Nicholls concluded that a writer's ulterior motive or intent to damage someone might not matter. He gave the example of a journalist who genuinely believed that a minister was untrustworthy. The journalist held a grudge against the minister and wrote a story based on spite. The judge said the law would protect the journalist as long as facts existed that would lead an honest person to form the same view.[11]

Absolute privilege and statutory qualified privilege

Journalists cannot be sued for fair, accurate and contemporaneous reports of court proceedings. These are protected by absolute privilege. Articles must comply with injunctions and usual reporting restrictions.[12]

Care must be taken with other types of stories. Outside of a courtroom, any statement or allegation that slights an individual's actions and behaviour and undermines his or her standing in society can be actionable. However, the law recognises that, in a democracy, the public is entitled to hear informed criticisms of individuals, politicians, organisations, charities and companies and so on. Qualified privilege concerns the forum or context in which the questionable words were spoken or written and the degree of public interest in the topic.

The Defamation Act (1996) lists the occasions where journalists can report statements, allegations or comments that risk or result in a complaint or legal action. Typical events include parliamentary debates, local-authority meetings, statutory and local inquiries, tribunals, press conferences and meetings called to discuss matters of legitimate public concern (at the international, national and local level). Reports are only protected if the proceedings are open to the press or the public or both.[13]

Qualified privilege also applies to articles generated by official documents intended for public consumption. These include statements issued on behalf of any government, the minutes and agendas of local authorities, public registers, audit reports, press releases from authoritative sources, selected reports from UK public companies and notices issued by a host of charitable, trade, recreational and intellectual/artistic bodies.[14]

Take the example of a press release issued on behalf of a senior police officer, rebutting a complaint filed by a solicitor. In denying the allegation, the press release described the complaint as 'malicious'.

AN EXPERT VIEW: TONY JAFFA

If the press release is an official response that has been issued for the attention of the public, then it will be covered by statutory qualified privilege. There is no requirement to get a response from the solicitor before publication.[15]

If stories are challenged on matters of fact or interpretation, qualified privilege is lost if newspapers decline to print reasonable clarifications or explanations.[16] The only exceptions are reports of defined governmental, parliamentary, judicial and international proceedings involving government representatives (and related documents), along with records that are required by law to be available for public inspection. In all cases, journalists' reports must be fair and accurate.[17] Articles shown to be motivated by malice lose protection.[18]

Once defamatory material is published using privileged sources, people may want to repeat or expand on the issues. The journalist should treat each contribution as a new but unqualified allegation. The journalist can be sued for these statements. The protection does not migrate from source to source.

AN EXPERT VIEW: LORD MAY

Newspapers published a report of a select committee of parliament containing material defamatory of the plaintiff. Another newspaper published an article relating to the same matter which was not privileged. The question was whether the fact of the privileged publications was available to reduce the plaintiff's damages for the unprivileged defamatory publication. It was held that they could not.[19]

Press releases issued at press conferences or public meetings are privileged so long as the text relates to the subject matter, even if they are not read aloud or if the spoken versions differ from the script.

ANOTHER EXPERT VIEW: LORD BINGHAM

A meeting is public if those who organise it or arrange to open it to the public or [. . .] manifest an intention or desire that the proceedings of the meeting should be communicated to a wider public. The test is whether, assuming the meeting to have been public, the contents of the written press release formed part of the materials communicated at the meeting to those attending.[20]

A note of caution

People making defamatory statements are protected by qualified privilege only if they are under a legal, moral or social duty to communicate the information.

Where qualified privilege is subject to explanation or contradiction, the situation is not as clear cut where the organisation or representative quoted was premature or not in a position to make the allegation in the first place. The journalist faces the choice of contesting an action or opting for an out-of-court settlement. Best practice when compiling an article is to seek and include a response from the person criticised (see next section on the Reynolds Defence) and consider how you can justify any subsequent articles that head into new territory.

Two nursery nurses were cleared of child-abuse charges by a court. Newcastle City Council commissioned an independent review team to produce a report. It was published by the team and presented at a press conference which was advertised and staged by the council. The report accused the two nurses of abuse. The allegations were printed in the *Newcastle Evening Chronicle* and the two nurses went into hiding. The newspaper subsequently ran more than 100 articles about the issue. The two nurses sued the council, the review team and the newspaper.[21]

At the trial, the newspaper advanced the defences of justification and statutory qualified privilege. As the evidence from the review team drew near to completion, lawyers for the newspaper and the two nurses agreed to settle out of court without any admissions of liability. The review team's defence of qualified privilege was undermined when the judge concluded that malice had played a part in the report. One problem was that there had been a failure to distinguish between 'gossip and fact'.[22]

AN EXPERT VIEW: MR JUSTICE EADY

Even though the publishers withdrew from the case, those articles cannot be excluded from consideration. The main thrust of their attack derives from the report. The review team [. . .] must bear responsibility in law for such re-publication. They are not, however, responsible in law to the extent that newspapers went off on a frolic of their own and published matter not deriving from the content of the report.

The review team proceeded on the footing that whatever they published would be protected by qualified privilege. In so far as their original publication may be vitiated by malice, then they become exposed to liability correspondingly for the re-publications.[23]

The judge's comment about newspapers going 'on a frolic' is important when reporters come to tackle follow-up stories or to compile reaction pieces. The problem is that no journalist can be expected to know the detailed history of any official report or be sure that a qualified privilege defence will succeed.

Hypothetical example

A council agenda contains a report of a routine visit by a lay member (councillor) to a care home, for the purpose of informing colleagues. The report comprises notes of observations during the visit, including suggestions to the management of the care home. The report is critical of certain practices, including hygiene in the kitchen, unsuitable allocations of rooms on upper floors to clients who should be on the ground floor and concerns that smoking has been permitted in non-smoking areas. The report also praises staff and management over other aspects of their work.

These are the kinds of questions you should be considering:

- Is the report an official document that forms part of the agenda?
- Has the report been issued to the press and the public, or is it marked as confidential or exempt under local-government legislation?
- Is the report to be received or discussed in the public part of the meeting?
- Is this report mentioned elsewhere in the agenda?
- If so, what is said and who has said it?
- Does anything in the agenda undermine or contradict the report?
- Is there a response from the care-home management?

Your article needs to make the context clear to the reader. As a lay person, the councillor is unlikely to be qualified in this field of work. Legal responsibility for monitoring standards in the care industry lies with professional inspectors. It would be wise to highlight this point. How much time has elapsed since the councillor's visit? Have circumstances, the management or staff changed in the meantime? Previously, what has been said about this home? It would be sensible to contact the management of the care home and the official inspection service to invite a response to the councillor's report.

The Reynolds Defence

Privilege has existed at common law level for many years but in a somewhat nebulous form. The case of *Reynolds* v. *Times Newspapers* (1999) established modern parameters for the media. Former Irish taoiseach Albert Reynolds sued over a story about his conduct in government in 1994. Rulings by the Court of Appeal and the House of Lords held that a story containing defamatory material may be protected under common-law privilege if the journalist can establish it was important for the public to be informed about the allegations at the time.

The Reynolds Defence is more likely to succeed if the journalist has raised matters of legitimate, public concern, if the journalist has taken responsible steps to check allegations and to seek a comment from any person criticised and if previous statements helpful to that party have been included in the absence of a response to allegations.[24] Inaccurate and defamatory opinions or comments should not be presented as statements of fact.

The case of *Bonnick* v. *The Gleaner* (2002) held that where there are words which are capable of more than one meaning and the journalist honestly chose the wrong meaning, it does not mean the reporter was motivated by malice. Reynolds privilege can apply.[25]

AN EXPERT VIEW: ANDREW CALDECOTT QC

There are two quite distinctive species of Reynolds. There is the reportage case where the newspaper is neutrally reporting a bust-up between two politicians, where the paper is informing the public. If you are in a reportage case, you can rely on others. Your duty of verification is reduced. But you have to be satisfied that there is a genuine dispute. The other is the investigative Reynolds Defence, where the newspaper is exposing what it suspects or believes is misconduct.

What about putting the view of the party criticised? It is simply not enough to go through the motions. If you talk to a secretary, get their name. If you have a deadline, tell them when they have to ring back by. Have regard to any other statement on the record and put this in, even if you can't get a comment. Press for a comment the following day. If someone comes back late, then get it in the next edition. You should put the main story and the main evidence to them. I have had two cases where documents were forged. The fact and existence of the documents were not put, so there wasn't a chance for the party to say: 'We don't have those documents.'[26]

Another hypothetical example

A reporter is contacted by the parents of a child who was knocked over by a cyclist on a pavement outside a school. The youngster appeared to have suffered no injury and a teacher apparently decided the child was all right. An ambulance was not called. The parents want a story published. The school and local education authority decline to comment. Some important follow-up questions:

- Should an ambulance have been called?
- Do staff appreciate that accident victims may have serious internal injuries not visible to the eye?
- Will the local education authority review advice to schools?
- On the other hand, what ulterior motive may the parents or the child have for exaggerating or not telling the truth?

continued

If the purpose of publishing this story is to raise a matter of public concern, then this must be evident at the newsgathering and writing stage. Otherwise, the court may conclude that the motive was just about getting 'a big splash'.

An editorial decision to identify the teacher in this case could be interpreted as 'naming and shaming'. The court would look at what the reporter knew or suspected to be true at the time. The journalist should have understood that the allegations could be false and should have appreciated the potential for damage to the teacher's reputation.

AN EXPERT VIEW: TONY JAFFA

I would be inclined not to name the teacher. That is because there could be an issue about mistaken identity. There is no dispute about the identity of the school. If everybody has been given the opportunity of commenting, then the article should attract Reynolds qualified privilege. That being the case, the other teachers would not be able to sue.'[27]

REPORTING CRIMINAL COURTS

Now let's look at the coverage of criminal courts. Always make sure your reports are fair and accurate to either side. Adult defendants should be identified by their full name, street address, age and occupation to avoid any confusion with innocent persons. Magistrates and judges occasionally order details to be withheld. The court does not have to give reasons but should cite relevant legislation. These orders can be challenged but remain in force until lifted.

Charges, pleas, verdicts and sentences must be included. Prosecution and defence solicitors and barristers should be identified. Claims and allegations reported in the course of a trial or a full hearing must be substantiated and attributed.

If the accused pleads 'guilty' to a charge and evidence is heard, journalists can report what is said about the matter to the magistrates or to a jury. After hearing the evidence, the court may adjourn the hearing for pre-sentencing reports or adjourn sentencing to another day. Magistrates can send the offender to the Crown Court for sentencing. You can still report the evidence and the guilty plea.

Magistrates and judges will hear mitigation on behalf of the accused before sentence is passed. The Criminal Procedure and Investigations Act (1996) allows courts to ban the press from reporting any 'derogatory assertion' concerning another person. An order must relate to a false or irrelevant comment, made in mitigation, which damages someone's character. An order cannot be made where the comment reiterates something previously heard in evidence or in other proceedings.[28]

If an adult defendant pleads 'not guilty' to a charge and the case is adjourned, journalists can only report:

- the defendant's name
- the defendant's age
- the defendant's address
- the defendant's occupation

- the wording of the charge (and dates)
- the names of lawyers
- the date of the next hearing
- the location of the court
- the 'not guilty' plea
- conditional bail terms
- remand in custody.

No other statements or evidence heard in court, including details of previous convictions or reasons for bail being refused, can be reported. These restrictions apply at all adjournment hearings held prior to a trial or a full hearing.

At a trial, journalists can only report what the magistrates or the jury hear for themselves. Previous convictions cannot be disclosed until magistrates or jurors have returned verdicts on all charges. Never include anything that casts doubt on a 'not guilty' verdict.

Blackmail, sexual assault and rape victims have lifetime anonymity. Schools should not be identified, directly or indirectly, in cases involving pupils. Reporters must not identify defendants, victims or witnesses aged under eighteen unless the court lifts reporting restrictions. In *Todd* v. *DPP* (2003) the Court of Appeal established that juveniles should be named if their conviction followed their eighteenth birthday.[29]

Youth courts

Hearings are not open to the public but bona-fide journalists have a right to attend under Section 47 of the Children and Young Persons Act (1933). Reporting restrictions banning the identification of juvenile defendants, victims, witnesses are automatic. Schools should not be named. When working outside adult courts, press photographers should be careful not to include juveniles in pictures by mistake.

Anti-social behaviour orders (ASBOs)

The police, local authorities and social landlords can apply to the courts for ASBO decisions against adults and juveniles under Section 1 of the Crime and Disorder Act (1998). These are civil actions, and a juvenile can be named unless the court makes an order under Section 39 of the Children and Young Persons Act (1933).

As far as criminal matters are concerned, the law is complex. If an application is made to the court at the time of conviction (before sentencing) there is no automatic identification ban. But the court can impose a general Section 39 restriction. If it does not, then you can report only those matters relating to the making of the application. Details of the criminal offence cannot be published together with a name unless the court directs otherwise.[30]

If a juvenile appears in court charged with breaching an ASBO, automatic Section 49 restrictions from the 1933 Act apply. Courts have discretionary powers to lift reporting restrictions, and in all events journalists are entitled to make representations at hearings. The Home Office has encouraged magistrates and judges to lift anonymity orders where it is in the public interest, particularly in cases involving persistent young offenders.[31]

Other tribunals

A court martial will be heard by a jury panel of senior military officers. A judge advocate, independent of the panel, will make decisions on admissibility of evidence points and law in the absence of the panel. The judge will also sum up the case to the panel. Matters heard in its absence must not be reported until the end of the trial. Courts martial are open to the press and public, and Ministry of Defence establishments must provide escorted access to hearings. The judge will make directions on any reporting restrictions involving sensitive or secret evidence. Gilbert Blades, a Lincoln-based lawyer specialising in courts martial hearings, advises journalists:

> The rights of access for the public are the same as the crown courts, but one problem is that these are not standing courts sitting regularly. Increasingly, cases are heard at dedicated centres such as Colchester, Aldershot, Plymouth and Portsmouth. But cases are still held on camps and stations all over the country and abroad. The regulations state that a public notice must be posted in the guardroom, 24 hours before a hearing starts. It is necessary for the journalist to make an arrangement with someone to tip him or her off that something is coming up. Many cases are not covered in the media.[32]

REPORTING CIVIL COURTS

Now let's focus on civil courts. Civil actions can be heard by judges sitting alone, as in the breach of confidence application brought by Catherine Zeta-Jones and Michael Douglas in *Douglas* v. *Hello!* (2003). Defamation cases are heard by juries. As with criminal courts, matters heard in the absence of jurors must not be reported until the case has concluded.

In family courts, reports of divorce proceedings are restricted by the Judicial Proceedings (Regulation of Reports) Act (1926). Articles must not go beyond the detail of the names, addresses and occupations of the parties, a 'concise statement' of the charges, defences and countercharges, submissions on points of law and decisions and of the judge's summing-up and judgment.[33]

Employment tribunals

Hearings are open to the press and public and are considered by a panel led by a qualified lawyer. Applications usually deal with claims of wrongful or unfair dismissal, discrimination on racial, sexual or disability grounds, breach of contract and victimisation for religious beliefs or trade-union activities. In general, you are free to report comments and statements from employees, employers, their legal representatives, witnesses and the panel. The rules are different with cases involving sexual conduct.

The Industrial Tribunals (Constitution of Rules of Procedure) Regulations (1993) empower tribunals to issue restricted reporting orders. These are reserved for cases involving allegations of sexual misconduct. Journalists do not have a statutory right to address the tribunal when applications are considered but may be allowed to speak at the chairman's discretion. The order is effective until the tribunal issues its decision.

A notice of the order must be posted at the entrance to the room. It must specify who should not be identified, either directly or indirectly. The order covers any description of the individual affected by the alleged behaviour and information likely to enable readers to identify an individual. In practice this can mean that virtually no one involved in the case may be named until the outcome of the hearing. The regulations also give tribunals the power to instruct journalists what evidence can and cannot be published in cases where a sexual offence is alleged.[34]

Inquests

Coroners courts inquire into the circumstances of deaths, such as fatal industrial accidents, traffic accidents, apparent suicides, unexplained or suspicious deaths, employment-related illnesses and cases referred by the medical profession. The verdicts available to the court are 'death by natural causes', 'misadventure', 'accidental death', 'suicide', 'by unlawful cause' and 'an open verdict'.

It is contempt of a coroner's court to speculate about the cause of death ahead of the verdict. In your reporting you should not imply that a person took their own life, even if the police, relatives, friends or eyewitnesses say so. The word 'suicide' must not appear in the article or headline.

Inquests are typically opened for identification of the victim to be confirmed and are then adjourned. At full hearings, the coroner will call witnesses, relatives and experts (for example, pathologists, medical practitioners, police, paramedics) and pose questions. If the hearing is attended by legal representatives of parties involved, then the coroner will decide how and what questions can be put.

It is not the purpose of an inquest to apportion blame. Witnesses have the right to decline to answer questions that might implicate them in criminal proceedings. Journalists must ensure that their reporting does not suggest someone has committed an offence. To do so would risk litigation or prosecution for contempt of court.

Witnesses can give conflicting and contradictory accounts. Your report must explain what happened in a clear, logical, uncomplicated and newsworthy fashion. The reporter is also expected to have an eye on the wider story, such as the consequences for family, friends and colleagues, and on any unanswered questions. But guilt or innocence must be left for the criminal courts to decide.

Contempt of court

Journalists must not influence court proceedings or interfere with the administration of justice. The provisions of the Contempt of Court Act 1981 come into play once a person is arrested on a criminal charge or after a warrant for arrest or a summons is issued. The rules become 'inactive' from the time of a release without charge or a verdict. In terms of injunctions, orders specify the nature of the information not to be published. Contempt at either common or statutory law level can lead to a heavy fine or imprisonment.

Thus, in 2001, the editor of *Punch* magazine was fined £5,000 for publishing revelations made by former MI5 officer David Shayler. The House of Lords upheld a ruling that the magazine had committed common-law contempt by breaching an injunction that restricted disclosures by the ex-agent. Lord Nicholls said contempt was evident because the editor, although an unnamed third party to the injunction, 'must have appreciated that by publishing the article he was doing precisely what the order was intended to prevent'.[35]

The Law Lord defined contempt as 'wrongful conduct which consists of interference with the administration of justice',[36] such as ignoring or frustrating a court order or corrupting a trial by exposing the jury to extraneous, prejudicial information. A number of other major cases have highlighted the rules on contempt.

- In 1949, the editor of the *Daily Mirror* was sent to prison after being found guilty of contempt of court for pre-trial coverage of a notorious murder case. A front-page article, reporting the arrest, read: 'The Vampire Killer will never strike again. He is safely behind bars, powerless to lure victims to a hideous death.' A subheading read: 'Made to sign alibi notes, says brother'. The article printed details of the suspect's confession. The newspaper was fined £10,000.[37]
- In 1991, several newspapers were called to account for articles published while a jury considered multiple verdicts in the trial of Grantham nurse Beverly Allitt. Jurors had found her guilty of two counts of murder and had re-retired to consider eighteen remaining matters. The judge gave a direction to the media to confine any coverage to the evidence heard in court. The following day, an editorial comment in a national newspaper referred to the offender as 'a psychopath'. It prompted a further warning from the judge to news desks. Despite this, several national newspapers, a regional newspaper and a regional broadcaster continued to publish and broadcast material that could have influenced jurors while they considered their remaining verdicts.
- In 2001, a trial of two Premiership footballers was halted after the *Sunday Mirror* published a background article concerning the case. It was an interview with a relative of a witness, and the judge concluded that it posed a substantial risk of influencing the jury. A re-trial was ordered and the newspaper was fined £75,000.[38]
- In 2001, the *Manchester Evening News* was fined £30,000 and ordered to pay £123,000 costs for an article on its web site that stated the distance between two secure units where the killers of toddler Jamie Bulger were being held before their release. The article breached an injunction relating to the whereabouts and new identities of the two offenders.[39]

AN EXPERT VIEW: LORD GOLDSMITH

The Attorney General is responsible for referring contempt cases to the courts. In 2003, he briefed journalists on the common pitfalls.

Perhaps the most common problem is reporting that assumes or suggests the guilt of the defendant. It might be a detail of the case, influenced by biased commentary.

---

continued

Law books are full of cases that appeared to be open and shut, but turned out not to be.

There is reporting that suggests some issue would be determined in a particular way, such as the fitness of the defendant to stand trial. There are also reports that may prejudice the police investigation, such as the publication of a photograph before it is clear that identity is not an issue. My actions [. . .] in seeking to prevent the identity of Premiership footballers being disclosed were not taken to protect their reputations. They were taken because their identity was an issue.

Other examples would be publishing a police appeal after an arrest or a charge. There are reports that have a detailed account of charges in question, sometimes presented as statements of fact. It may be [. . .] immaterial to a criminal case but would be retained by a jury member.

A rape case went ahead and the jury could not reach a verdict. Over the weekend a local radio station said the defendant had been charged with a second rape. Up to that point, the jury would not have been told he was facing a separate charge. The judge asked members of the jury about it. One juror said she believed that the defendant had already committed a rape.[40]

It's good to talk: to a lawyer

To conclude, newsroom bosses may be fond of reminding reporters of the mantras 'Get it right first time', or 'If in doubt, leave it out', or 'If in doubt, find out'. Perhaps the one to remember is: 'When in doubt, talk to the media lawyer.'

Notes

These relate to the British and Irish Legal Information Institute's web-site archive of appeal decisions at <http://www.bailii.org/>.

1. Bailii: *Reynolds* v. *Times Newspapers* (1999), House of Lords, Lord Nicholls on privilege and publication to the world at large, in reference to *Derbyshire County Council* v. *Times Newspapers*.
2. Glenn Del Medico, Head of Programme Legal Advice, BBC, Law for Journalists Conference, Royal Society of the Arts, London, 28 November, 2003.
3. In conversation with the author, 28 July 2003.
4. Bailii: *Cruise and Anor* v. *Express Newspapers and Anor* (1998), Court of Appeal, Section 9.
5. T. Welsh and W. Greenwood (2001) *McNae's Essential Law for Journalists*, 16th edn, London: Butterworths: 239.
6. Bailii: *Cheng and Wah* v. *Paul* (2000), Hong Kong Court of Final Appeal, judgment of Lord Nicholls.
7. Bailii: *Adams* v. *Guardian Newspapers* (2003), Scottish Court of Session, Paragraph 28.
8. ibid. Paragraph 30.

9. Bailii: *Cheng and Wah* v. *Paul* (2000), section on fair comment, the objective limits.
10. Bailii: *Loutchansky* v. *Times Newspapers and Ors* (2002), Court of Appeal, Paragraph 37.
11. Bailii: *Cheng and Wah* v. *Paul* (2000), section on spiteful comments.
12. Defamation Act (1996) Chapter 31, Paragraph 14 (1).
13. ibid. Schedules I and II.
14. ibid.
15. As note 4.
16. Defamation Act (1996) Chapter 31, Paragraph 15 (2).
17. ibid. Paragraph 14 (1).
18. ibid. Paragraph 15 (1).
19. Bailii: *Burstein* v. *Times Newspapers* (2000), Court of Appeal, Paragraph 36.
20. Bailii: *Turkington and Ors* v. *Times Newspapers* (2000), House of Lords, Conclusions, Paragraph 4.
21. Bailii: *Lillie and Anor* v. *Newcastle City Council and Ors* (2002), High Court.
22. ibid.
23. ibid. Paragraphs 1542–3.
24. Bailii: *Reynolds* v. *Times Newspapers* (1999), House of Lords, Conclusion of Lord Nicholls.
25. Bailii: *Bonnick* v. *Morris and Ors* (2002), Privy Council, Paragraph 24.
26. Andrew Caldecott QC, Law for Journalists Conference, Royal Society of the Arts, London 28 November 2003.
27. See note 4.
28. Criminal Procedure and Investigations Act (1996) Chapter 25, Sections 58 and 59.
29. Richard Shilitto, Farrer and Co., Law for Journalists Conference, Royal Society of the Arts, London, 28 November 2003.
30. ibid.
31. ibid.
32. Gilbert Blades, in conversation with the author, 28 July 2004.
33. Bailii: *Nicol* v. *Caledonian Newspapers* (2002) Scottish Court of Session, outline of case.
34. Tony Jaffa, Foot Anstey Sarjent Solicitors, Plymouth.
35. Bailii: *HM Attorney General* v. *Punch Ltd and Anor* (2002) House of Lords, Paragraph 52.
36. ibid. Paragraph 2.
37. *Daily Mirror*, 4 March 1949.
38. *Press Gazette*, 25 April 2002.
39. *Press Gazette*, 6 December 2001.
40. Lord Goldsmith, Attorney General, Law for Journalists Conference, Royal Society of the Arts, London, 28 November 2003.

Getting it right

Copyright and the journalist

23

Getting it right

Copyright and the journalist

Iain Stevenson

The words 'intellectual property', like 'final salary pension', 'value-added tax' or 'public liability insurance', tend to induce a state of boredom in the average journalist. Many normally only engage with them in a state of panic once a situation has arisen requiring immediate attention or, more usually, when it is far too late to take any remedial action. But it is important for journalists to understand enough about intellectual property law as it affects their day-to-day activities so they can protect themselves from costly, potentially seriously unlawful action. It's also useful to know in protecting against the actions of others who ignorantly, maliciously or callously breach your own intellectual property rights.

What is intellectual property?

The concept of intellectual property (or 'IP' as it is referred to in legal circles) is that the products of the mind – literature, art, drama and performance, music, inventions, scientific discovery, broadcasting and so on – once put into concrete form (not necessarily communicated) have ownership rights attached to them that are as real as the rights existing in other classes of property such as houses, cars and clothes. 'Intellectual' does not imply any judgment of value or quality. If a person can think of something and then express it in concrete form then that expressed thought may qualify for legal protection as 'intellectual property'. IP rights normally originate (though not always) with the creator of the property, but like all other property rights they can be sold, transferred, inherited and gifted.

Most everyday thoughts are, of course, not worth protecting although some of them may enjoy protection, for example if they are confidential. But clearly some items of intellectual property, even if small, are of immense value. The formula for a new cancer-beating drug or the lyrics and music of a chart-topping song are worth millions and, indeed, tend to be protected by special classes of IP law such as patents and trademarks. For writers and broadcasters who use words as their daily currency, copyright is the crucial branch of IP law. But if you work in a specialist field such as health, scientific or financial journalism you should make yourself familiar with patent and trademark (TM) law by reading some of the references given at the end of this chapter. The penalties for breach can be enormous and ignorance, of course, is no defence in law.

What is copyright?

Copyright is the branch of IP law protecting original text or indeed anything original, in the colourful words of the Act, 'that can be written, spoken or sung'. It is literally 'the right to copy', that is, the owner of the copyright material has the absolute right to determine how, where, how much and for what reward it can be reproduced subject to a limited range of exceptions (for example critical or educational use). This reproduction takes place under a 'licence' usually written from the owner to the user under a strictly controlled and defined set of conditions. This is where IP law differs importantly from other property law. If you sell a house, you can generally do it only once and to only one person. If you grant a copyright licence, you still own the underlying copyright and you are only licensing a specific type of usage. Once the licence expires or is revoked, you can license that same right again. Moreover, you can make a licence exclusive or non-exclusive. This is an important concept for journalists (and particularly freelances) because it means they can sell their material in many forms and at different levels provided they know what rights they control and what licences they are able to grant.

The idea that writers should be paid for work they write is surprisingly recent. For most of history, writers were just badly paid hacks to whom publishers and printers felt they owed nothing more than a basic pittance. John Milton was famously paid only £5 for his epic poem *Paradise Lost* by his publisher and received nothing more when it went on to become a best-seller. As writing became a profession and newspapers emerged, it became recognised that people who wrote for a living needed protection from exploitation and some means of being fairly paid for their work. The 'Statute of Anne' (1709, coming into force in 1710) gave Great Britain the world's first copyright legislation, but it was limited since it only covered 'literary works' and the period protected was short.

As the media expanded, laws were introduced and their coverage extended to sculpture, engravings, music, recordings, cinema, television programmes and computer programs throughout the eighteenth, nineteenth and twentieth centuries. Other countries introduced copyright laws but those in the 'Roman law' tradition (such as France and Italy) had a noticeably more author-friendly system (*droits d'auteur*) than 'common law' countries (such as Britain and the USA). As communication improved, international protection was needed for copyright work so in 1886 came the first global copyright agreement, the Berne Convention, its signatories guaranteeing the same copyright protection for foreigners published in their countries as their own nationals. It is still in force. Piracy (where copyright material is published without permission and payment) remains a major issue and is currently policed by the World Trade Organisation (WTO) under the TRIPS (Trade-Related Intellectual Property Agreement). Generally copyright is supervised by WIPO (World Intellectual Property Organisation), a branch of the United Nations.

Copyright in Britain is governed by the Copyright, Designs and Patents Act (1988) and a number of more recent amendments which have modified it in various ways (mainly to harmonise with our European Union partners). But many experts believe that the Act will need replacement before long. It did not envisage the Internet, for example, and it has not much to say about digital publishing in general. Various directives from the European Commission on software protection and e-commerce have improved electronic copyright protection but there still remain loopholes and problems. Nevertheless, it is the best legislation available and while a new law will probably come around sooner or later, your career will for the next several years be influenced by its provisions.

What can't I do as a journalist with copyright material?

Every day journalists deal with copyright material and thus must be aware of what is legal and avoid committing what the law defines as an 'infringing act'. All journalistic research involves reading, copying, interviewing and patching together bits and pieces from published and unpublished sources. And while no honest journalist would consciously wish to infringe anyone else's rights, you need to be constantly vigilant to ensure you do not do so inadvertently.

The first principle is that it is perfectly acceptable to make a transcript by hand of anyone else's written or printed work provided it is for your own private use as the basis of your own research and in a single copy. It is not permissible to photocopy large chunks or to record or store it electronically for a commercial purpose without a licence. That would be a clear 'infringing act'. You may quote a small amount of another's copyright text in your own writing – this is called 'fair dealing'. It is generally said that you may quote up to 400 words in total from a whole work, but this is only an accepted guideline. The Act contains no quantitative definition of 'fair dealing' and it would be up to a judge to decide how much quotation was fair depending on the context or the type of use. You may only quote a reasonable proportion of copyright poetry or song lyrics, perhaps as little as one line without a formal licence.

There is much misunderstanding about how long copyright lasts. The law is unequivocal: the duration of copyright harmonised throughout the European Union is seventy years from the 1 January of the year following the death of the author. If the work was published posthumously, the duration is calculated from the date of the first publication but otherwise the actual date does not matter. At the end of the duration, copyright expires (apart from a few trivial exceptions) and enters the public domain when you can do what you like with it. Beware, however, that durations and rules for use of public domain material are different in other countries, particularly the USA.

Since 1989 (the date of the Act coming into force) authors in the UK have had moral rights in their work. Deriving from Berne, this gives authors rights of integrity and paternity. This means authors have a right not to have their work given derogatory treatment (a complicated concept, but think of it as not being messed about with) and for it to be clearly identified as theirs, generally through a byline and a copyright line – the © symbol. In the UK, the right of paternity has to be asserted to the publisher by the author. This accounts for the statement seen at the beginning of many books that the author asserts the right to be recognised as the author. If you breach moral rights, the way the law is drafted a smart and expensive lawyer could probably get you off, but it is good practice to observe paternity and integrity.

It is also bad manners and may be an 'infringing act' to pass off anyone else's writing as your own or to misquote or invent an attributed statement. Matters become even more complicated if you deal with anything else copyrighted other than straight text. Photographs, drawings, cartoons and any graphic symbol are all copyright objects and you need the permission of the owner, usually the photographer or artist – but not always. Sometimes they belong to the person who commissioned them. Anything with the symbol ® or ™ attached should not be quoted without the symbol attached. Spoken words, music, dramatic performances and anything else capable of being recorded, stored or reproduced is copyright and you must remember this if you are a broadcast or Internet journalist using archival footage or databases created by someone else.

The general rule should be that journalists may make use of copyright material to base and support their work indirectly – paraphrasing in your own words without copying a substantial part of the original work is perfectly fine – but anything direct is likely to require a licence which can be costly or may be refused. Copyright owners have an absolute right to deny the use of their work and do not need to explain why. There is no copyright in ideas – only in the expression of those ideas. Using your own words is a perfect defence against copyright infringement.

How does copyright protect the journalist?

At the same time, copyright provides journalists with powerful and comprehensive protection to their creative work. Copyright does not need to be registered in the UK (although it may need to be in some other countries). Anyone who writes, paints, draws, sings, acts, performs, broadcasts, photographs, films, videos, programs or does any other act resulting in an original physically expressed communication (even posting a letter or sending an email) automatically gets their work protected by copyright. Copyright owners receive worldwide protection under international treaties like the Berne Convention which places formal requirements on member states (even Russia and China) to respect the copyright in works of other member countries. However, this does not mean that piracy may not sometimes occur in those countries. You can grant licences and receive payment. You can sell your work over and over again and the rights remain yours. You can refuse permission to use your work and sue anyone who infringes.

This is unless, of course, you have not waived, transferred or conveyed your rights to someone else, in which case none (or very little) of the above applies. If you are employed as a salaried journalist by a newspaper, magazine, web site or broadcaster, then it is likely your contract of employment specifies that the copyright in all you produce while in the course of employment belongs to your employer. By signing a standard employment contract it will usually be assumed that you have agreed that the copyright in your work will be owned by your employer, at least if you do it during the day job.

Matters are (or should be) very different for freelances. As a condition of acceptance, many publishers seek to oblige freelances to convey their copyright to them. Some publications have even sought to do this retrospectively, i.e. after the work was published. This is bad practice (although doubtless good for shareholders) and freelances should try to resist it. At the most, they should sell a limited-term licence in their work so that they retain control and, once it has been made use of by the publisher, so the writer can use it again.

You should make it clear when you sell a freelance article that you are selling First British Serial Rights only and that you reserve all other rights. Generally this licence will have to be exclusive (you can't sell it again) but you can sell other licences (for example, second serial rights, broadcast rights and particularly electronic-publishing rights which may be subdivided into Internet rights, database rights). You should also insist that, in addition to a byline, a copyright notice in the form © (alongside your name and year of publication) should appear at the end of your piece – or on screen if broadcast or online.

Your success in this area will depend on how much the publisher wants to publish and how much you need the fee (starving is generally a good antidote to a high moral stance). But as the media carrying journalists' work become ever more interconnected and diverse, by signing a copyright conveyance for an article you could find it being reused without your permission and without payment in many different ways and forms. This is particularly important for publishers who operate print and online titles where the latter is much more widely read than the former. If you retain the copyright, you can (and probably should) refuse to have your print article transferred and archived to the digital publication without further payment or at least your permission.

Acknowledgement

I am extremely grateful to Hugh Jones and Lynette Owen for reading over a draft of this section and for their most helpful comments.

Further reading

Crone, T. (2001) *Law and the Media*, 4th edn, Oxford: Focal Press.
Jones, H. and C. Benson (2002) *Publishing Law*, 2nd edn, London: Routledge.
Owen, L. (2001) *Selling Rights*, 4th edn, London: Routledge.

Beyond the parish pump

24

Reporting local and national politics

Beyond the parish pump

Reporting local and national politics

Richard Orange

In the satirical BBC TV series *Yes, Prime Minister*, writers Jonathan Lynn and Antony Jay suggested that the problem with local government was that too few people voted in local elections, too many treated it as an opinion poll on the national government, even fewer voters knew the names of their councillors and the system lacked proper democratic accountability.[1]

In terms of national and local politics, it falls to journalists to act as the public's watchdog. The territory stretches beyond simple party politics. It encompasses campaign and pressure groups, business, trade unions, the European Union, statutory bodies such as the Audit Commission, Highways Agency and the national offices responsible for investigating the conduct of councillors. In addition it takes in the Standards Board for England,[2] the Standards Commission for Scotland[3] and the Local Government Ombudsman in the case of Wales.[4]

Local authorities include parish, town, district, borough, county and unitary councils, together with police authorities. It is the reporter's job to explain what politicians do in the taxpayer's name. The landscape is changing. Devolution in Scotland and Wales has respectively delivered a parliament and a national assembly with specific powers. Regional government is on the cards for parts of England.

But there is no uniform model for local government in the UK. Parish, town, district, borough, London borough and county councils are in place. Some above town and parish level are unitary authorities. That means they run all municipal services for the area, such as education, social services, fire services, council housing, planning and development control, highways and local tax collection. Elsewhere, responsibility for these services is shared by different tiers of councils that serve the same communities.

Some councils are run by a mayor, directly elected by the voters, working with a council manager or a cabinet of hand-picked councillors. Other authorities have an internal vote for a leader who, in turn, selects members of a decision-making cabinet. Remaining back-bench councillors call the mayor, leader and cabinet members to account for actions, priorities and decisions. Local authorities employ more than 2 million staff and spend £70 billion a year on services.[5] Decisions about how this money should be spent have an impact on individuals, families and communities. Local politics is a busy area for the journalist.

Reporting local authorities

The majority of local-authority meetings take place in public. Electors must be given advance notice of the venue, together with a brief description of the business to be discussed. Councillors are not allowed to convene a meeting at whim. For similar reasons, there are restrictions on what can be raised under an agenda heading of 'Any Other Business'.[6]

Many councils are divided along party political lines. Others, notably parish councils, are not. The former are required to provide representatives with seats on committees. This must be in proportion to the number of councillors elected under each political banner.[7] The only exception is the ruling cabinet/executive committee, appointed by the leader of the council or the directly elected mayor.[8] It is usually drawn from the majority party. Each member will hold a portfolio and can take urgent decisions on behalf of the council. A standards committee, charged with upholding the authority's code of conduct for councillors, will include a third of members who are independent of the authority.

A third of the members of police authorities are councillors, appointed by the local council in proportion to the political balance. Another third are drawn from the local magistrates committee and remaining independent members are selected from a list approved by the Home Secretary. All have the same speaking and voting rights and receive assistance from a clerk, treasurer and monitoring officer.

Councillors and certain officials have speaking rights at meetings. Procedures will be outlined in the authority's standing orders and written constitution, both of which are public documents. Some authorities allow the public or interested persons to make presentations or to ask questions at meetings. This is not a universal practice, but where it happens it does form part of the formal meeting and can be reported as such.

Most meetings fall into three categories:

1. discussion (and/or decision) regarding a report prepared and presented by officials, cabinet portfolio holders or individual members
2. debate or discussion (and/or vote) conducted by councillors
3. scrutiny by councillors of actions or decisions of executive members and/or officials (or representatives of outside bodies).

The journalist is likely to encounter:

- a debate at a meeting of an authority involving councillors from all parties represented on the council
- a scrutiny or policy working group meeting, involving a cross-party section of the authority, calling evidence on a specific topic or issue, or questioning actions or decisions taken by senior members or officials
- a committee meeting.

The committee meeting may be:

- the council's decision-making cabinet/executive
- a committee with delegated and statutory powers to make decisions on behalf of the authority (for example, planning, standards panel, personnel)

- a committee shadowing a departmental or executive responsibility (for example, highways, housing, social services, fire service)
- an ad-hoc committee established to investigate or advise on a particular matter or issue.

Statements made in meetings open to the press and public can be reported and journalists can claim qualified privilege for fair, accurate and contemporaneous reports.[9] This is subject to the usual caveats regarding defamation (statements subject to contradiction or explanation) and to contempt of court (discussion of public affairs). Journalists have a right to quote from documents tabled at meetings unless material is classed as confidential (see below). Details about how councillors vote, any declarations they make about personal or prejudicial interests, and their general conduct are not subject to any reporting restrictions.

Journalists' rights

Journalists are entitled to receive agendas and reports ahead of a meeting. These should include the minutes of previous, relevant meetings. The first port of call should be the official account of any business that was discussed in closed (secret) session. There is nothing to stop a reporter from running an advance, speculative piece based on the minutes and on reactions to the issues. The journalist should bear in mind that the accuracy of the minutes might be challenged at the meeting. Best practice is to attend, both for a follow-up article and in case the record needs to be set straight.

Checklist on news reports

News reports of local-authority meetings may include (in no particular order):

- the background to the issue under discussion, including options outlined to the members
- names and titles of speakers (councillors and officials)
- comments made by councillors and officials who are held responsible for the issues
- comments made by councillors during the debate
- comments from the political party in control and (balanced) comments from opposition parties
- contributions from people or organisations involved in the issue
- financial details (for example, how much will it cost the council and taxpayers?)
- timings (for example, when is it going to happen?)
- decisions taken
- the likely impact (for example, who is going to be affected?)
- ongoing or unresolved issues (of public interest)
- contact details (of the people in charge).

As with a sports match, the reporter usually starts the story with the result ('What has been decided' or 'What is going to happen'). Check whether decisions are final or subject to approval at a later meeting. It is important that stories are balanced and fair. There may not be any opposition councillors in the meeting or even on the council. Reporters should seek comments from external sources afterwards.

Best practice

Best practice is to look outside the confines of the council debate. What impact does this issue or decision have on the general public? What does it mean for the ordinary person in the street?

Avoid falling into the trap of using council jargon. Officials often use complicated and unwieldy language. Translate it for the reader. Avoid being tied to the sequence of events in the council chamber. Get the keynote quotes in the copy early on. If some aspect of the issue or debate needs to be explained then the reporter must spell it out.

Much local authority business appears mundane on the surface. But behind most agenda papers, there is a story waiting to get out.

Exercising your rights

Local government legislation places councils under an obligation to make minutes and agendas of meetings available to the public in advance and requires authorities to publicise decisions and other statutory reports.[10] Local authorities must make background papers, used for the preparation of agenda reports, available to the public at specified locations.[11]

Councils have powers under the Local Government Act (1972)[12] and the Local Government (Access to Information) Act (1985)[13] to exclude the press and the public from meetings for the discussion of business classed as confidential. The authority is required to cite the relevant section of the Act, which defines what information is confidential.

Examples include details of contractual matters, pending legal matters, information relating to the personnel records of employees, information relating to children in care, information relating to other clients of the authority and confidential matters involving general staffing issues.

The law does not entitle local authorities to exclude the press and public from meetings for reasons of political convenience or to prevent potentially embarrassing matters being disclosed to the public.

Parish councils retain powers to exclude the press and public from meetings under the Public Bodies (Admissions to Meetings) Act 1960.[14] The terms are defined more loosely. Journalists can be excluded if publicity might prejudice the public interest if the business is confidential by its nature, or for a reason specified in a resolution. However, in *Peachey Property Corporation Ltd* v. *Paddington Borough Council* (1964), Lord Denning ruled that 'an authority must consider whether publicity would be prejudicial to the public interest, not just the confidential nature of the matter'.[15]

Challenging parish councils

Parish councils are liable to challenge if they vote to exclude the press and public from a meeting to discuss a matter such as a planning application. The reasons are that:

- The law recognises planning applications as matters of public interest.
- The local planning authority is obliged to consider applications in public.
- Parish-council observations on planning applications are taken into account when members of local authorities make decisions.

The law requires the process to be transparent and journalists should question any attempt by a parish council to consider such business in closed session.[16]

Authorities, officials or councillors have no powers to order the press not to report statements made during meetings open to the public. Sometimes a councillor will be required to 'withdraw' a remark. The journalist is entitled to record what was said. Authorities, officials or councillors have no powers to order the press not to report statements in official documents and papers released by the council to the public.

'You're not supposed to know this, but . . . '

Legal protection for statements made in meetings is outlined in the media law section on qualified privilege. Interviews with people outside a meeting (such as demonstrators, trade-union representatives, spectators or politicians not involved in the meeting) do not attract statutory qualified privilege. But these occasions may be privileged under common law, depending on what was said, the context and the element of public interest in the issue. Publishing a photograph of a protestor's banner (containing defamatory material) could land a newspaper in trouble.

Journalists must be careful with any confidential documents. The leaking of exempt information is treated as a serious matter by local authorities and is a breach of both the model code of conduct for councillors and the code of conduct for employees.[17] The unauthorised disclosure of certain information (such as details of children in care) can result in criminal proceedings.

Unsanctioned, off-the-record statements made by officials or councillors are not privileged. Unattributed statements authorised on behalf of the authority are protected. Most political correspondents at national and local level have off-the-record briefings with contacts and the Press Complaints Commission's code of practice demands that journalists protect confidential sources.[18]

Anything to declare?

Apart from meetings, journalists should study records required to be kept on public display. Planning files usually contain correspondence between applicants, architects, agents and council officials. Files may include reports from organisations such as English Heritage, the Environment Agency, technical and business appraisals and letters of objection from neighbours and interested parties. These records provide a means of verifying information about individuals, companies and their contact details and are a useful source for stories. A seemingly mundane file can unearth a gem. In one case, an application for an extension to a derelict city-centre restaurant contained an architect's report that revealed part of a Roman wall had collapsed because of persistent rainfall. Note that authors of such submissions may assert that the content is 'confidential' or copyrighted. In reality, these are public records.

Councils are compelled to keep a public register of councillors' pecuniary and non-pecuniary interests. Members must give details of all employment, property, contractual, political, charitable (including freemasonry) and certain financial commitments that could be seen to influence their council activities.[19] Parish councillors are under the same obligations. Reporters should keep a check on registers. My own routine inquiry of a council's register in 2001 unearthed a story that resulted in the prosecution, conviction and imprisonment of a councillor for misconduct in public office.[20]

Who's spending our money?

Electors have a legal right to peruse local authority accounts. For twenty days every year, electors of a borough can inspect and make copies of contracts, bills, deeds, payments, invoices and receipts. Councils and police authorities must publish details of these inspection exercises. The main restriction applies to payments to employees. It is a criminal offence for an authority not to comply with a legitimate request to inspect and make copies of the accounts. The elector must live in the borough.[21]

The reporter can present himself or herself at the council offices and request sight of the relevant material. Prior research is advisable. A general, haphazard trawl may turn up material useful for a story. It is more likely to be unproductive.

The local government financial year runs from 1 April to 31 March, but it might not be possible to view parts of the February or March accounts until the following year's inspection is held. This usually happens when the council is invoiced for work after the 31 March cut-off point. The bill goes into the following year's accounts, even though the job was done in March, February, or earlier.

Journalists are entitled to inspect records relating to payments and contracts left over from the previous year's inspection of accounts. But it can be frustrating to be told that you must wait another twelve months to see a document concerning work carried out more recently and during the period under review.

One way to find out some basic information is to request sight of a 'credit of reserve' note. This is a report by a director or treasurer that specifies outstanding debts and payments, following the closure of the accounts. If this note is dated before the end of March, then it forms part of the report of that year's accounts and the journalist should be entitled to view it.

Journalists may wish to challenge local authorities that cite the Data Protection Act (1998) as a reason to withhold material. Section 34 says that 'personal data' are exempt from the 'non-disclosure provisions' if other legislation requires the information to be made available for public inspection.

The Audit Commission Act (1998) says that councils are obliged to withhold 'personal information' about a member of staff. Section 15 says that the information must relate to a specific individual and must be 'available to the body for reasons connected with the fact' that the person holds an office or employment. This includes payments and benefits relating to the individual's salary and pension arrangements.

There is an important point here. This clause should not entitle councils to censor or withhold parts of contracts, bills or invoices containing information which is incidental to the employment of a member of staff (i.e. the material is available to the authority for another reason such as the provision of goods or services to the council). Journalists should also note that references to 'personal information' in the Audit Commission Act relate to employees and not to councillors who hold political office.

The Local Authorities (Members Allowances) (England) Regulations 2003 require councils to keep a public register, detailing each and every allowance, expense or payment made to council members. Section 15 entitles a local elector to inspect this register, free of charge, throughout the year.

Pursuing the paper trail

Best practice is to have a specific topic in mind and see where the paper trail leads. Take an example of a reporter wanting to find out how much money was spent by the chief executive's department during the financial year. This would involve hundreds of receipts and invoices. It is far better to request a general breakdown of figures and hone in on one aspect, such as the amount spent on entertainment and alcohol in the council chairman's office. Receipts may give details of guests attending civic receptions. Who knows? The reporter could be on to a scoop about links between these civic 'jollies' and contracts awarded to outside businesses.

Alternatively, questions can be put in writing. This may save time and effort, but there are disadvantages. The authority may take some time to provide the answers. The reporter has no control over the format of the reply. If the purpose is to examine original invoices or receipts, then a letter requesting photocopies of paperwork will not suffice.

Whether verbal or written, the wording of the question matters. The request: 'I wish to inspect records relating to expenditure on entertainment provided on behalf of the council chairman' pins the authority down. Once a query is raised, the elector can pursue the matter by posing additional questions. The elector cannot open up different topics. The council can refuse a later request for information about entertainments provided by, for instance, the public relations department. Ensure the question leaves room for manoeuvre. Try: 'I wish to inspect records relating to expenditure on entertainment provided by the council on behalf of elected members and officials.'

Be aware that councils provide information only in the format in which it is collected. It may seem sensible to check how much money was spent on a particular project. Officers may have devoted considerable time and effort to a problem or issue. But will there be a record of how many hours staff clocked up on a certain topic? Likewise, the amount of money spent gritting a particular road may not be available. A council official may give advice on the wording of a question.

Freedom of information

Journalists' rights of access to documents and records have been strengthened by the Freedom of Information Act (2000). In force from January 2005, the provisions enable anyone to request specific information held by a local authority. There is a fee to pay and the authority must respond to requests within twenty days. It should provide the information, give a timescale if disclosure will take longer or explain why the information must be withheld.[22]

However, there are restrictions ('exemptions') to the material that councils and police authorities may release to applicants. The list includes:

- advice (such as legal advice)
- information 'likely to prejudice the effective conduct of public affairs'
- information likely to 'endanger the physical or mental health or safety' of an individual
- confidential personal data about the applicant
- disclosure of information that would result in a breach of confidence.[23]

With the Act in its infancy, journalists are advised to keep up to speed with developments through the columns of *Media Guardian*, *Press Gazette* and *Media Lawyer*.

Reporting national government affairs

Having spent the 1990s as a political specialist for a regional newspaper, I have interviewed prime ministers, leaders of parliamentary political parties, dozens of senior ministers, MPs and MEPs and countless civil-service press officers. From experience, many alluded to 'government' as a singular entity (e.g. 'the government will do x, y or z'). But the operations of government are complex – and all journalists need to be aware of them.

Here in Britain, the prime minister appoints MPs to run Whitehall departments. Their powers to take day-to-day decisions 'in the interests of the country' are derived from the royal prerogative which technically makes them accountable to the monarch rather than to the prime minister or to parliament. They swear loyalty to the head of state, can gain privileged access to information as privy counsellors and are known as ministers of the crown.

Nevertheless, ministers are hired and fired by the prime minister and are put in place to see that the government's political programme is implemented. But ministers are also advocates for their respective departments. They owe political patronage to the prime minister as employer and leader of their party and constitutional loyalty to the monarch. They are also aware of the interests of the political party and of their own constituencies. In these circumstances, the scope for tension within cabinet over the allocation of funding for ministries is considerable, especially if the cabinet comes under pressure over an issue in the House of Commons or from the public at large.

To counter the threat of ministerial discipline evaporating amid the rough and tumble of national debate, cabinet members are required to sign up to the principle of collective responsibility. This approach – akin to 'we all stand together or hang together' – reinforces the notion that the government 'speaks with one voice' in the political sense. Ministers who disagree with decisions (e.g. Robin Cook over the Iraq invasion in 2003 and Michael Heseltine over Westland Helicopters in the mid-1980s) resign rather than accept the outcome. Likewise, the Queen's speech outlines a commonly agreed legislative programme on behalf of the government to which all ministers are expected to subscribe. The chancellor of the exchequer delivers a budget on behalf of all ministers. Backbench MPs are subject to disciplinary action if they do not support the leader in speeches or votes in the House of Commons.

However, the politics of government are much more than the theatre of prime minister's question time in the House of Commons, intrigue between cabinet colleagues and occasional rebellions by backbench MPs. The government also operates at arm's length from the politicians. A ministerial example is provided by the attorney general. In representing the government's legal interests, the post-holder is obliged to divorce himself or herself from the raw considerations of cabinet and party politics.

Therefore, you will need to understand that the British political system operates on several distinct levels: the executive (cabinet), judiciary (courts and constitutional affairs) and the legislature (parliament). All three must take account of national obligations under international treaties and law, such as the decisions of the institutions of the European Union. At the same time the political parties exert influence over the executive, the legislature, the European parliament and (indirectly through the prime minister and other EU heads of government) the Council of Ministers.

What does this mean for the provincial journo?

What does this mean for the provincial journalist whose daily dealings with government are limited to frequent contacts with the local MP, the occasional ministerial visit and more regular contacts with regional and national press officers working for various government departments?

Journalists become adept at the political interview through experience and practice. It is exceedingly rare for a skilled media interrogator to wrong-foot an MP or minister. Therefore, an aggressive approach with a visiting politician or the local MP is likely to be counterproductive.

A VIP visit by the prime minister or a cabinet member may afford the journalist an opportunity to ask a question about a matter of local concern. The reporter should expect the politician to have been briefed by national and regional press officers and to have a prepared response. However, senior politicians have the upper hand. In one-to-one situations, they can and do insist on being told the question in advance. They are understandably conscious of the need not to appear unbriefed or unfamiliar with an answer to an unexpected question. The situation is different during election campaigns, when politicians actively encourage media exposure.

Aside from interviewing politicians, journalists on provincial newspapers must understand what MPs and ministers do. This is not just a matter of familiarising oneself with terminology (for example, when the chancellor of the exchequer talks about 'GDP' during a budget statement). The journalist needs to know how parliament goes about formulating laws. Local authorities, charities, churches, companies, schools, trade unions, sports clubs, the editor, other journalists and readers will expect nothing less.

- What is a 'green paper'?
- What is a 'select committee'?
- What is a 'by-law'?
- What is meant by a 'three-line whip'?
- What happens if the House of Lords amends a bill submitted by the House of Commons?
- What is an 'early day motion'?
- What powers does the parliamentary commissioner for standards enjoy?
- How are laws repealed?
- Is an MP allowed to take up an issue on behalf of a voter living in a different constituency?

These questions demand answers, but not on a plate. Talk to an MP, or to the chairperson of the constituency party or its press officer. After all, the active acquisition of knowledge is an ideal aid to understanding. Or, as one of my former editors put it: 'You don't know? You're the journalist. Go and find out!'

The relationship between national and local politics

The relationship between local and national government is complex. Generally speaking, councils' legal powers and responsibilities derive from parliamentary statute and Whitehall decree. Local authorities are supposed to represent their communities, but sometimes councillors must override local wishes in deference to national policies.

This is evident in the area of planning. Contentious development applications may arouse widespread hostility from residents, organisations and councillors. But proposals must be tested against rules and guidelines set in Whitehall. A comment from the local MP and a statement from the press office of the respective government department may be required.

The Government Information and Communications Service (a.k.a. Central Office of Information) operates in Whitehall and at regional centres such as Nottingham, Cardiff and Bristol. Its many press officers provide a proactive and reactive service – organising conferences, handling the media during ministerial visits, issuing press releases and responding to journalists' enquiries. Press officers also monitor media coverage of issues and arrange for journalists to be briefed by civil servants on particular matters.

As with all individual contacts, the relationship between the newspaper, the journalist and the local MP often depends on personalities and agendas. It is rare for the professional politician to give the press a wide berth, particularly during election campaigns. For day-to-day stories about MPs, ministers and Whitehall officialdom, editors rely on their head-office specialist political reporters and on their parliamentary correspondents. Most national titles and leading provincial newspaper groups have dedicated reporters working at the House of Commons. The next section looks at their work in detail, through the eyes of seasoned lobby journalist Mike Ambrose.[24]

A day in the life of a parliamentary correspondent

The first job of the day is to read the national newspapers and listen to BBC Radio 4's *Today* programme, which sets the political agenda of the day. Correspondents for the London and regional evening newspapers will start as early as 6 a.m. They will have stories to complete from the previous night and will chase contacts and talk to their news desks. They will be checking out potential stories for the day and will write about what the newspapers' local MPs have been saying and doing.

The first Downing Street briefing of the day is at 11 a.m. It normally opens with a run through of the Prime Minister's day and an outline of other ministers' activities. There may be an indication of what the Prime Minister will say in the Commons later on. The civil service spokesperson will then provide responses to prominent issues and breaking stories. It is a sophisticated operation and there is a 'pecking order' for questions from the media. Priority tends to be with the BBC, ITN, Sky, the Press Association and the national press.

Political correspondents from the regional press seldom attend the daily conferences and have their own Number Ten briefing at the start of the week.

The 11 a.m. briefing gives the national press an opportunity to find out what the 'opposition' is working on. The questions from a rival newspaper can be more illuminating than the answers given by the civil servant. Journalists will analyse the nuances of the reply or measure the silences of the official spokesperson. It can be indicative of how near the knuckle the questioner has got, or of how careful the civil servant needs to be with the response. The 11 a.m. briefing is tailored for the broadcast media, and reporters working on morning newspapers must wait to see how stories develop during the day.

Correspondents rarely venture into the House of Commons press gallery, even for prime minister's questions or major debates. One reason is that television cameras provide live coverage of the chamber. Regional correspondents must watch out for what their local MPs are saying, but events can be viewed on the television screen from the comfort of a desk. Reporters can file copy and make telephone calls at the same time.

Accredited lobby correspondents have privileged access to the lobby area next to the Commons chamber where MPs gather out of the public glare. The correspondent will look at making afternoon visits as MPs arrive for the start of the day's proceedings, before an important statement or after a key vote. There are conventions and rules. One is that journalists should not approach MPs. It is for politicians to speak to correspondents. Another maxim is that anything said or done in the lobby area is off the record. Comments made in the reporter's earshot are off limits. To keep within the rules, the experienced lobby correspondent will preface his or her story with: 'Eyewitnesses report that.'

Proceedings in select committees tend to be covered by specialist reporters such as defence, agricultural or science journalists, rather than the political or lobby correspondents. The regional parliamentary writers need to keep their news desks supplied with regular copy about local MPs and national developments on important local issues.

Thus, it is important to forge relationships with the press offices of the respective government departments. Reporters must keep a regular check on the internal post for deliveries of press releases from political parties and Whitehall departments. Correspondents will spend a good part of their day dealing with the civil service and ministers. The long-term position of a department on a particular issue may be at variance with the minister's stance, and journalists can gain the confidence of senior civil servants. However, the correspondents on national newspapers often have more time to cultivate these contacts than their regional counterparts.

Downing Street hosts its second press briefing of the day at 4 p.m., geared to the evening news bulletins and the national morning papers. It gives the Number Ten spokesperson a chance to highlight the government's line on running stories and to respond to the lunchtime broadcasts. Once stories are filed, correspondents will work on a news list for the following day. They will also head for the various Commons tea rooms and Westminster bars to seek out talkative MPs.

Party conferences

The experienced journalist will decide what he or she wants from the conference before the event. Editors will demand coverage of breaking stories, but there is so much happening that it is not possible to be everywhere. Regional journalists will need to keep a check on any local delegates called to speak in the conference hall. The experienced reporter will connect national debates and statements with issues that matter locally. Party conferences feature various fringe events which may have a bearing on local issues. A basic rule is to stand at the back of the room, making it easier to come and go. The seasoned conference hack will find out where delegates are staying and will make connections early on.

In conclusion, you should remember that you are not writing for politicians or officials. Whether reporting local or national government, your articles should be purged of technical and unwieldy language. Put the reader first, in terms of what has been decided. The story must explain how the debate or decision will impact on the reader.

Notes

1. J. Lynn and A. Jay (1989) *The Complete Yes Minister*, London: BBC Books: 382.
2. <http://www.standardsboard.co.uk/about_us/index.php>.
3. <http://www.standardscommissionscotland.org.uk/about_us.html>.
4. <http://www.ombudsman-wales.org/english/code.html>.
5. Local Government Association report on local-authority services, Paragraph 1. Available online at <http://www.lga.gov.uk/lga/the_lga/laservices.pdf>.
6. Devon Association of Parish Councils, Factsheet 6. Available online at <http://www.devon.gov.uk/dapc/pdfdocs/6_meetings-procedure_and_record_keeping.pdf>.
7. Local Government and Housing Act (1989), Section 15. Local Government (Committees and Political Groups) Regulations (1990), regulation 13.
8. HMSO.gov.uk: Local Government Act (2000), Chapter 22, Part II, Paragraph 24.

9. HMSO.gov.uk: Defamation Act (1996), Chapter 31, Part II, Section 11(a).

10. HMSO.gov.uk: Local Government Act (2000), Chapter 22, Part V, Paragraphs 97–8.

11. Local Government Act (1972), Section 100D.

12. Local Government Act (1972), Schedule 12A, Part I.

13. A. Maidment and J. Steele, DTLR, Local Government Research Unit report on public access to information about local government. Available online at <http://www.local.dtlr.gov.uk/research/public.htm>.

14. See note 4.

15. John Davidson, local government law specialist, Andrew and Co Solicitors, Lincoln, in conversation with the author, 28 July 2004.

16. ibid.

17. HMSO.gov.uk: The Local Authorities (Model Code of Conduct) (England) Order (2001), Schedules 1 and 2, Part I, Paragraph 3(a).

18. T. Welsh and W. Greenwood (2001) *McNae's Essential Law for Journalists*, 16th edn, London: Butterworths: 385.

19. HMSO.gov.uk: The Local Authorities (Model Code of Conduct) (England) Order (2001), Schedules 1 and 2, Part III, Sections 14–17.

20. Orchard News Bureau coverage of *R* v. *Speechley*, Sheffield Crown Court, 2004. Online at <http://www.orchardnews.com>.

21. HMSO.gov.uk: Legislation in England and Wales: Audit Commission Act (1998) Chapter 18, Part II, Section 15 (in England amended by the Accounts and Audit Regulations (2003), statutory instrument 533). Legislation in Scotland: Local Authority Accounts (Scotland) Regulations (1985), Section 6 (2) as amended.

22. HMSO.gov.uk: Freedom of Information Act (2000), Chapter 36, Sections 1, 3, 9, 10, Part II (exemptions) and Schedule 1, Part II (local authorities).

23. ibid.

24. Ambrose M., *Morning Star* industrial correspondent (1969–84), parliamentary correspondent (1984–2003), in conversation with the author, 20 July 2004.

Part IV
And finally

An education overview

Preparing reflective practitioners

 **25**

Preparing reflective practitioners

Rod Allen

Until about thirty years ago, practically the only way into newspaper journalism was to start on a local weekly, and practically the only way to learn about journalism was to sit at the feet of (or, more likely, to sit at a desk near) an older journalist. If you were lucky, he (it was invariably a 'he') would teach you the rudiments of the job, take you on an assignment or two and help you learn to pay for your round in the local pub. It was called 'sitting by Nellie' (even though in most newspaper offices 'Nellie' was unlikely to be a woman), and it was a primitive combination of informal apprenticeship and experiential learning – or 'learning by doing'.

Here, I will outline the way in which journalism education has developed since the days of 'sitting by Nellie', describe the minimum training required of a journalist starting out, and the broad scope of the courses in higher education. Finally, I will discuss some of the theoretical issues surrounding journalism education at the university level.

A brief history of journalism education

Some formal education was available in the period immediately following the Second World War. The National Council for the Training of Journalists (NCTJ) was founded in 1951 and it provided post-entry examinations which could be taken by young journalists wishing to improve their career prospects. Some institutions of higher and further education offered HND (Higher National Diploma) or certificated courses in journalism which, in some cases, linked up with the NCTJ syllabus and provided a means of pre-entry training.

It is worth noting that Britain was some way behind the rest of the world. Journalism education in institutions of higher education had been available in the USA since about 1870. There, the University of Iowa was the first to offer undergraduate courses, and by the end of the nineteenth century, a number of other courses were available at several American universities, often in combination with a discipline known as 'public rhetoric' (see, for example, Boylan 2004, Holtz-Bacha and Frolich 2003). In China, the first higher education institutions to offer journalism courses did so in 1921. During the 1930s, the London School of Economics offered a form of journalism studies at postgraduate level, but the experiment was short-lived.

National and local newspaper publishers launched formal in-house training schemes, and a much sought-after route for graduates in the 1960s took the form of six months at the Thomson Foundation Training College in Cardiff (or, for broad-casters, the Thomson Foundation Television College in Newton Mearns, Glasgow), followed by paid work at a Thomson regional weekly such as the *Reading Evening Post* or the Thomson-owned Scottish Television in Glasgow. Even so, many editors remained sceptical of journalists who had not received their training wholly on the job and, of these, most rejected the idea of graduates becoming journalists. In the 1960s, a university education remained the domain of a privileged few and most regional newspaper editors themselves did not have degrees.

The Thomson newspaper-training operations eventually linked with the University of Cardiff under the distinguished direction of Tom Hopkinson, a former editor of *Picture Post*, and this led to the introduction of practical postgraduate training within the university itself. This was followed by the launch, in 1976, of the Graduate Centre for Journalism at City University, London, under the guidance of Tom Welsh. These pioneering courses were relatively quickly followed by others in universities and colleges of further education to the extent that, by 2004, the Universities and Colleges Admissions Service (UCAS) handbook listed more than 600 undergraduate courses with 'journalism' in their titles. In addition, twenty-eight higher education institutions were listed as offering postgraduate courses in journalism and related subjects.

Gaining those crucial qualifications

Obtaining a pre-entry qualification is thought of as one of the more effective ways of getting a job in journalism, though the number of undergraduate degrees in journalism currently being awarded each year probably outweighs the number of journalistic vacancies available in the market. But there are other routes as well. Since the wages paid to beginners on regional weeklies are such that it would be difficult to justify the kind of student debt that needs to be incurred for a first or second degree, there is still in the regional weeklies a substantial market for *ab-initio* training followed by qualification through the National Certificate Examination (NCE) administered by the NCTJ.

Other routes include abbreviated commercial courses – private institutions such as the London College of Journalism and the strangely named NoSweat Training offer intensive courses that can provide some of the required underpinning for a journalism career. Unlike in the USA, where there is a long tradition of high-school journalism, the topic is not generally taught in British or European secondary schools, so it is difficult to acquire the necessary knowledge to start a job in jour-nalism straight from school. (City University, in association with Islington Council, recently started a series of summer schools for gifted school leavers and similar schemes are being run elsewhere.)

Whereas unqualified juniors represented the majority of entrants into the industry thirty years ago, today a substantial number of entrants have a university degree of one kind or another, though only a minority of new journalists have a formal journalism qualification (Delano and Henningham 1995). Again, whereas thirty years ago newspaper and magazine publishers and broadcasters saw it as their duty to provide a training of one kind or another to their new employees, today potential new journalists are, on the whole, expected to arrange and pay for their own basic training, though employers still provide conversion training to their own house styles, techniques and systems.

What does a new journalist need to know?

It was asserted at an industry meeting, organised in 1997 by the then Guild of Editors to discuss journalism training, that what employers really needed in new journalists was 'the right attitude'. Actually, the basic NCTJ syllabus is more modest. The council sets preliminary examinations in five areas:

handout   story sent to media outlets by press relations office of organisation or PR company.

- **Handout,** in which candidates are asked to rewrite and provide follow-up ideas for a new story from a press release.
- Newspaper journalism, which is tested by one writing question and two short rewrite questions.
- Public affairs, with questions on both local and central government structures and procedures.
- Law, in which court reporting, defamation, contempt, crime terminology, the PCC code and confidentiality are covered.
- Shorthand, in which a minimum of 100 words per minute in any of Gregg, Pitman, New Era or Teeline must be achieved.

The basic NCTJ syllabus has not changed for many years, though it is currently being critically examined by a new management team determined to reform the overall procedures of the council. Much of the criticism levelled at this syllabus over the years has focused on the fact that it is most suitable for new entrants to regional weekly newspapers, and although this route is still an important one, many people now enter journalism through other routes. There are now first jobs in national newspapers and broadcasting, in regional dailies, in business-to-business and business-to-consumer magazines and, most importantly, in the wide range of online operations which make more or less use of the skills of journalists.

To be fair to the NCTJ, there are other training councils – notably the Broadcast Journalism Training Council (BCTJ) and the Periodicals Training Council (PTC) – which accredit courses provided in their fields, but none of them fully cover the routes into journalism which have become available over the past few years.

Shorthand: the big issue

Shorthand is not a specific requirement of the broadcast- or periodicals-training councils, yet the NCTJ insists on proficiency in shorthand. For news reporting, it is difficult to say that the aspiring journalist should not learn shorthand, even though in many ways the idea of it seems old-fashioned. For feature interviewing, for instance, there is no reason why the journalist should not depend on a tape or digital recorder; but in news reporting, shorthand provides a reporter with the best way of taking the accurate, contemporaneous note that would be required in the event of a challenge to her or his accuracy.

The puzzle of public affairs

The role of public affairs (PA) is also a puzzle to many journalism students. As a new local newspaper journalist you will spend much of your time at council meetings, yet the ways in which local government works and the way in which it relates to central government are not immediately obvious without some guidance. A problem increasingly seen on journalism courses is that students frequently present themselves with a surprising lack of knowledge of current events, and it cannot be assumed they know about structures of government, the European Union and so forth. Yet employers would rather new recruits had some command of such matters than the ability to deconstruct texts.

Perfecting press-release skills

In the NCTJ syllabus, the news reporting and handout assignments place a considerable emphasis on the skills of rewriting and expanding on a press release; it is true that much of today's regional and local journalism consists of just that. With the growth of the Internet, employers prefer their journalists to do their primary and secondary research in front of a screen rather than in the pub or on the **doorstep**, so as a beginner you will need to have the skills of making a press release sound unique and fresh.

doorstepping journalists pursuing sources by standing outside their front doors. Now journalists often wait in cars.

Getting it right: law and ethics

Finally, the NCTJ syllabus addresses law, which is increasingly encroaching on the world of journalists. Editors need to know their employees are familiar with the defamation, confidentiality and other relevant laws because a lack of such knowledge is likely to be costly if damages are awarded against a newspaper, magazine or broadcaster for their breach. Proprietors, of course, have in-house lawyers, but as a reporter you are expected to know how to avoid the basic legal problems and should not need a pricey lawyer to spend time inserting 'alleged' and 'the trial continues tomorrow' where necessary. The law syllabus also covers the journalist's ethical codes, most notably those of the Press Complaints Commission (PCC) and the National Union of Journalists.

Developing the critical approach

The NCTJ syllabus, created largely by employers rather than by educators, only goes so far in providing the critical thinking that is vital to journalists and journalism students. At university level, both undergraduate and postgraduate courses add a great deal of value to the basic skills taught in NCTJ courses, and there is a lively debate in the journalism-education community about the value of the NCTJ syllabus in the twenty-first century. All university courses take the NCTJ syllabus and its companion, the NVQ (National Vocational Qualification) post-entry syllabus as a baseline from which they add and improve. Many courses add specialisms, such as investigative reporting in one respect all journalism involves investigation. But investigative journalism tends to reveal something of social or political significance which someone powerful or famous wants hidden. US: muckraking.

crime, arts, health, science and sports reporting; others concentrate on **investigative reporting** or international coverage.

Some higher-education institutions link journalism with other courses such as politics, psychology and English in joint degrees. All courses also take in ethics units: looking not just at the PCC's Code of Practice and freebies but also complex dilemmas such as those involving racism, sexism, the coverage of wars and censorship. And most programmes these days recognise that journalists will have to be at least somewhat multi-skilled: magazine journalists are taught the elements of broadcasting; print journalists are exposed to photography; broadcast journalists are taught some linear print; and everyone gets to have a go at web journalism.

Most postgraduate courses are one-year diplomas which mix a strong practical element with theory and usually incorporate a substantial investigative project. But increasingly higher education institutions are offering Journalism MAs which are practice-oriented with the theoretical component culminating in a substantial, academically rigorous dissertation. At the highest level, some universities offer opportunities to take journalism PhDs.

Making your way in magazines

You may be aiming for magazines rather than newspapers. In this sector, the accrediting body, the PTC, enjoys a high reputation for its sensitive approach to enhancing standards. Rather than set examinations and training, it merely monitors, on behalf of the periodicals publishing industry, the courses (including those at private institutions) on offer. Those currently accredited include Bournemouth University, Cardiff University, City University, Goldsmith's College, Harlow College, Highbury College, London College of Communication, Southampton Institute and Surrey Institute of Art and Design University College. But this does not mean that other courses are not worth exploring.

As Jenny McKay stresses (2000: 16):

> Students aiming at careers in magazines will probably try to choose the periodicals courses in universities but a newspaper training will almost certainly contain many of the same elements (with perhaps less emphasis on production). Career paths are not tightly fenced into one medium and so if money dictates that you study at the nearest college and that offers only newspaper journalism, if you take a place there, it does not mean you can't expect to work in magazines.

Most journalism students will aim to do some work experience on a publication. But there are dangers of such trainees being exploited as 'free labour' by managers. Significantly, the PTC has also drawn up some commendable guidelines on attachments covering such areas as selection, learning agreement, preparation, payment and post-attachment evaluation. On the learning agreement it says (<http://www.ppa.co.uk/cgi-bin/wms.pl/173>):

- Once a placement has been confirmed it is recommended that a learning agreement is drawn up between the student and editor responsible for the placement.

- Students should consider carefully their aims and objectives for work placement, and these should be formulated into the learning agreement. This should include areas of interest, aims, objectives and what it is hoped will be achieved during the placement. This will also act as a valuable evaluation tool after the placement has taken place.
- It is recommended that, where possible, a placement should last a minimum of two weeks to enable students to understand the publication in some depth and complete the tasks they are set.

Theoretical issues in journalism education

By anticipating the needs of employers, journalism educators provide employers with appropriately equipped people at the right time. But if you are considering the bewildering number of courses on offer, it will be important for you to appreciate the differences between university journalism education and commercial or vocational journalism training.

In universities, the pressures on journalism education are to develop more critical, reflective practitioners. At the same time educators need to tackle the growing problems of practical teaching posed by the increasing rapidity of technological change. Many university journalism educators pride themselves on the fact that they teach journalism in a thoroughly practical fashion. Students write stories, produce newspapers, television and radio programmes and work in an environment which is intended to seem more like a workplace than a university. The practical dimension of many journalism programmes, at both undergraduate and postgraduate levels, is what sets them apart from the media-studies courses which derive from critical theory developed in social-science and literary studies and which do not claim to prepare students for professional work in journalism.

At the same time, journalism teachers aim to promote reflective practice and most courses incorporate theory units on, say, history, human rights, globalisation or postmodernism.

Promoting the reflective practitioner

Herbert Simon, who as Dean of Carnegie-Mellon's school of business administration in the 1960s addressed some of the issues faced by business schools, which also affect journalism and other professional schools, wrote of the danger that: 'the "practical" segment of the faculty becomes dependent on the world of business as its sole source of knowledge inputs. Instead of an innovator, it becomes a slightly out-of-date purveyor of almost-current business practice' (Simon 1969: 350).

Simon goes on to argue for 'practical' and 'academic' staff in institutions to come together to formulate science and theory to underpin their teaching. But Schön suggests a strategy for placing what he calls a 'reflective practicum' at the centre of the work of the professional school, creating a bridge between the worlds of practice and the academy (Schön 1987: 309). In this way, Schön argues, it is possible to move towards resolving some of the conflicts between the academic and vocational dimensions of the professional school.

Increasing the emphasis on the reflective dimension of journalism education can be helped by exploring the research in the field of adult learning which has focused on the value of learners' experience. Five key propositions about learning from experience are outlined by Boud, Cohen and Walker (1993). Summarised, they are:

1. Experience is the foundation of, and stimulus for, learning.
2. Learners actively construct their own experience.
3. Learning is holistic.
4. Learning is socially and culturally constructed.
5. Learning is influenced by the socio-emotional context in which it occurs.

In other words, learning from experience takes place through a number of filters that ensure that each learner's perception of a given experience is, as might be expected, different from another's. As Boud and Miller argue (1996: 9):

> Each experience is influenced by the unique past of the learner as well as the current context. Each individual is attuned to some aspects of the world and not to others, and this affects his or her focus and response. Learners attach their own meanings to events even though others may attempt to impose their definitions on them. The meaning of experience is not given; it is subject to interpretation. The major influence on the way learners construct their experience is the cumulative effect of their personal and cultural history.

Understanding the variables which act on the different ways individuals react to a common experience helps explain why relying exclusively on providing common experiences can be problematic in terms of learning. For example, sending students out to cover events, even events in which there are definably common experiences, such as press conferences, and then assessing the stories they write in terms of external criteria satisfactorily replicates the workplace environment.

But the question that then needs to be asked is about the extent to which a student's learning is improved by the process. Most journalism educators provide class feedback or 'copy clinics' in which students' work is analysed, but the danger is that this can often take the form of instruction, perhaps based on the way the teacher would have written the story, rather than structured reflection on the experience itself.

The experiential learning cycle

The experiential learning cycle, in which reflection is seen as an explicit and necessary dimension of learning from experience, is generally attributed to Kolb (Kolb et al. 1971; Kolb 1981; Kolb 1984). He wrote that the experiential learning cycle is: 'a model of the learning process that is consistent with the structure of human cognition and the stages of human growth and development. It conceptualises the learning process in such a way that differences in individual learning styles and corresponding learning environments can be identified' (Kolb 1981: 235).

The experiential learning cycle consists of discrete activities that take place in order. Concrete experience is followed by reflective observation that, in its turn, is followed by abstract conceptualisation or, in some models, theory-building. This is followed by active experimentation and then again by concrete experience. Thus the cycle is continuous and, although the concrete experience will not take exactly the same form every time, it is valuable if learners can return to a similar experience after having reflected on what they have learned from it.

An example of experiential learning at work in journalism education can be seen in the way students familiarise themselves with techniques of covering a press conference. You may be sent out to cover a press conference and come back and write a story about it, within a word limit and by a deadline (concrete experience). You will then:

- reflect on the whole experience of covering the event and writing the story (reflective observation);
- derive some principles from the experience, which might be as complex as how best to sort out facts from hype at a press conference or as simple as learning that it is better to ask a question after the opening statements (abstract conceptualisation);
- work on some strategies and plans for the next similar experience (active experimentation);
- go out to cover another press conference.

In terms of applying the experiential learning cycle to teaching, it becomes clear it is important for students to have a number of opportunities to undergo similar activities; in this example, sending them out to a press conference only once would never do.

Stressing the emotional dimension

It is easy to underestimate the emotional dimension of the reflective process, and acknowledging the existence of other than intellectual components to education can sometimes run counter to an established academic or professional ethos. Yet, as Boud and Miller argue, 'Emotions and feelings are key pointers both to possibilities for, and barriers to, learning. Denial of feelings is denial of learning. It is through emotions that some of the tensions and contradictions between our own interests and those of the external context manifest themselves' (1996: 10).

Journalistic work often stimulates intense emotional reactions. Whether you cover the carnage of a civil war or deal with unhelpful telephonists and receptionists, you will have to develop ways of dealing with your emotional reactions before you can start writing about whatever it is you have been asked to write about. Similarly, in the institutional environment, the process itself sometimes generates fierce reactions, which can be provoked by problems ranging from the inadequacy of a school or department's computer systems to the boring repetitiveness of the shorthand class.

Without adequate structures for reflection which enable learners to express their emotional responses as well as their intellectual or practical reactions, it will always be hard to deal with the barriers to learning that emotional differences erect; it will equally be hard to grasp the positive opportunities that learners' emotional make-ups offer.

Building confidence

However, in all of these reflective processes, you need to have the confidence to know you will not be made to feel foolish or be embarrassed by your participation. This means the journalism educator has to be aware of a number of issues about power and control which can affect the usefulness of structured reflection. In the institutional setting, teachers inevitably occupy a position of power over learners; it is important for teachers to be self-reflexive 'in accepting that they are also part of the culture and context and may act in ways which are oppressive and reinforce power, thus closing possibilities for learning' (Boud and Miller 1996: 10).

The most powerful influence of context is often language, and it can be hard to be aware of the effect of language in the relationship between teachers and learners. Sometimes the issue is of cultural difference, but more often it can be to do with carelessness in expression. Journalism is club-like as a profession and it is easy, for instance, to dismiss important issues with excluding language. People often do not recognise ways in which they exercise power – or engage in oppression – in education, and self-reflexivity should not be underestimated as part of the teacher's repertoire. Those involved in learning from experience, whether in an institutional context or not, should be careful to try to avoid seeming to be judgmental during structured reflection, which also means trying to remove judgmental dimensions from their general relationships with learners. As Schön suggests, 'A reflective practitioner must be attentive to patterns of phenomena, skilled at describing what he [*sic*] observes, inclined to put forward bold and sometimes radically simplified models of experience, and ingenious in devising tests of them compatible with the constraints of an action setting' (1987: 322).

By enabling you to reflect in a structured way on the practical activities that form the bulk of your journalism education, the need, as expressed particularly by Meyer (1996), to develop graduates who understand the processes and effects of mass communication is being met without compromising the acknowledged success of practically based vocational journalism education.

References and further reading

Boud, D. and N. Miller (1996) 'Animating Learning from Experience', in D. Boud and N. Miller (eds) *Working with Experience: Animating Learning*, London: Routledge: 197–211.

Boud, D., R. Cohen and D. Walker (eds) (1993) *Using Experience for Learning*, Buckingham: SRHE and Open University Press.

Boud, D., R. Keogh and D. Walker (1985) *Reflection: Turning Experience into Learning*, London: Kogan Page.

Boydell, T. (1976) *Experiential Learning*, Manchester: Manchester Monographs.

Boylan, J. (2004) *Pulitzer's School: Columbia University's School of Journalism, 1903–2003*, New York: Columbia University Press.

Delano, A. and J. Henningham (1995) *The News Breed: British Journalists in the 1990s*, London: The London Institute.

Gunaratne, S. and B. Lee (1996) 'Integration of Internet Resources into Curriculum and Instruction', *Journalism and Mass Communications Educator*, 51 (2) (summer): 25–35.

Holtz-Bacha, C. and R. Frolich (2003) *Journalism Education in Europe and North America: An International Comparison*, Cresskill, NJ: Hampton Press.

Kolb, D., I. Rubin and J. McIntyre (1971) *Organisational Psychology*, New York, Prentice-Hall.

Kolb, D. (1981) 'Learning Styles and Disciplinary Differences in Today's Students and their Needs', in A. Chickering and R. Havinghurst (eds) *The Modern American College*, San Francisco, Calif.: Jossey-Bass: 232–55. Available online at <http://www.asne.org/kiosk/editor/september/meyer.htm>, accessed 28 July 2004.

—— (1984) *Experiential Learning: Experience As the Source of Learning and Development*, Englewood Cliffs, NJ: Prentice-Hall.

Lemmon, S. (1996) *Wake Up and Kick Your Classmate: Teaching is About to Change*, University of Indiana School of Journalism. Available online at <http://www.journalism. indiana.edu/j200/curriclm.html>, accessed 28 July 2004.

McKane, A. (2004) *Journalism: A Career Handbook*, London: A & C Black.

McKay, J. (2000) *The Magazines Handbook*, London: Routledge.

Meyer, P. (1996) 'Why Journalism Needs PhDs', *American Editor*, September.

Schön, D. (1987) *Educating the Reflective Practitioner: Toward a New Design for Teaching and Learning in the Professions*, San Francisco, Calif.: Jossey-Bass.

Simon, H. (1969) *Administrative Behaviour*, 2nd edn, New York: Macmillan.

Useful addresses

The National Council for the Training of Journalists, Latton Bush Centre, Southern Way, Harlow, Essex CM18 7BL. Web site: <http//www.nctj.com>.

The Periodicals Training Council, Queens House, 28 Kingsway, London WC2B 6JR. Web site: <http//www.ppa.co.uk>.

The Association for Journalism Education, c/o Department of Journalism, Liverpool John Moores University, Dean Walters Building, Upper Duke Street, Liverpool L1 7BR. Web site: <http//www.ajeuk.org>.

Association for Education in Journalism and Mass Communication, 234 Outlet Pointe Blvd, Columbia, SC 29210–5667, USA. Web site: <http//www. aejmc.org>.

Useful web sites

A number of web sites provide useful data on training opportunities:
<http//www. journalism.co.uk>
<http//www.newsdesk-uk.com>
<http//www.holdthefrontpage.co.uk>
<http//www.nuj.org.uk>.

Glossary

ABC Audit Bureau of Circulations: organisation providing official figures for newspaper circulation.

access provider a company that sells Internet connections (also known as an internet access provider or internet service provider).

ad abbreviation for advertisement.

add additional copy as when the Press Association (*PA*) follows lead of major story with new paragraphs.

advance statement or speech issued in advance to the media.

advertising feature editorial feature produced to support an advertisement or series of advertisements.

advertorial where distinction between editorial and advertising becomes blurred.

agency main news agencies are PA, Reuters, Agence France Presse, Itar-Tass, Associated Press. Also a large number of smaller agencies serving specialist and general fields. Copy known as wire copy. See also **snap**.

agony aunt woman offering advice to people who write to newspapers with personal or emotional problems. Agony uncle is the male equivalent, but not many of these around.

alternative press loose term incorporating wide variety of non-mainstream newspapers. Can include leftist, religious, municipal, trade-union publications.

ampersand character (&) representing the word 'and'.

anchorpiece story placed across the bottom of a page.

angle main point stressed in story usually in intro. Also known as 'hook'. US: peg.

anti-aliasing process to smooth the edges of digital pictures to minimise pixelation.

ascender upright in the letters b, d, f, h, k, l.

attribution linking information or quote to original source.

backbench group of top-level journalists who meet to decide the overall shape and emphases in newspaper.

background section of news or feature story carrying information which serves to contextualise main elements. Also in computer jargon, indicates hyphenation and justification system is operating while copy is being input.

backgrounder feature exploring the background to main story in the news.

bleed picture printed beyond the area to be trimmed on page.

blogspeak esoteric jargon of blogs.

blurb words describing a story within the paper or magazine.

body copy following intro.

bold more heavily defined version of a roman font.

broadsheet large format newspaper (e.g. the *Financial Times*) in which four pages fit across the width of the press; usually considered to be of a more serious quality than a tabloid. Some former broadsheets (such as *The Times* and the *Independent*) have recently gone tabloid (though they call this format 'compact').

browser software program for navigating the Internet, in particular the World Wide Web.

byline gives name of journalist who has written article. Otherwise known as 'credit line'. Subs sometimes call it 'blame line'. When appears at end of story known as 'sign-off'.

calls, check calls routine telephone calls (or sometimes face-to-face visits) by reporters to bodies such as police, ambulance, hospitals, fire brigade (usually supplying information on tapes) to check if any news is breaking.

campaigning journalism overtly partisan journalism promoting particular cause. US: advocacy journalism.

caps upper-case letters.

caption words accompanying picture or graphic.

casting off estimating the length of copy.

casual journalist employed by newspaper/magazine on a temporary basis. Since it is cheaper for employers, numbers are growing.

catchline usually single word identifying story which is typed in right-hand corner of every page. Now more likely to be called the filename. Sub-editor will tend to use this word to identify story on layout. US: slug.

centre spread two facing pages in the centre of a newspaper or magazine.

classified ad a short advertisement in a newspaper or magazine (usually in small print).

CMYK colours of ink used for four-colour printing: cyan, magenta, yellow and black.

colour section of newspaper copy focusing on descriptions or impressions. Thus a colour *feature* is one which puts emphasis on description and the subjective response of the journalist though the news element may still be strong.

column vertical section of article appearing on page. Also known as 'leg'.

columnist journalist who provides comment in regular series of articles.

compact tabloid version of former broadsheet newspaper e.g. the *Independent*, *The Times*.

condensed a version of a font that has been squeezed horizontally.

conference meeting of editorial staff to discuss previous issues and plan future ones.

contact journalist's source.

contacts book pocket-sized booklet carried by reporter listing contact details of sources.

copy editorial material. Hard copy refers to editorial material typed on paper.

copy approval person allowed to see and approve copy before publication.

correspondent usually refers to journalist working in specialist area – e.g. defence, transport – or abroad, e.g. Cairo correspondent.

credit byline of photographer or illustrator.

crop to select an area of a picture for publication.

cross head a heading placed within the body of a story; *see side-head*.

cut-outs when elements of a picture are cut away from the background (a simple device using an image editing program such as Photoshop).

cuttings stories cut from newspapers or magazines; 'cuttings job' is an article based on cuttings; also known as 'clips' or 'clippings'.

database storage of electronically accessible data.

dateline place from which story was *filed* usually applied to stories from abroad.

day in the life of profile *feature* focusing on particular day of subject. Not to be confused with 'life in the day of' profile, which covers subject's life but in context of talking about currently typical day.

deadline time by which copy is expected to be submitted.

death knock when a journalist breaks news of a death to a member of the public.

deck often used to mean the number of lines in a heading is, strictly, the number of headings.

delete to cut or remove.

demographics specific characteristics.

descenders the portion of a letter that descends below the x-height in the following: g, p, q, j, y.

desks departments of newspapers: thus news desk, features desk.

diary day-by-day listing of events to cover.

diary column gossip column, also a day-to-day personal account.

diary piece article derived from routine sources (press conferences, press releases, council meetings, parliament) listed in diary (originally in written form but increasingly on screens) which helps news desk organise news-gathering activities. Off-diary stories come from reporter's initiative and from non-routine sources.

dig to do deep research.

direct entry entry to journalism through publication which runs its own training programme.

display ads large advertisements usually containing illustrations and appearing on editorial pages. Advertising department will organise distribution of ads throughout the newspaper which is usually indicated on a dummy handed to subs before layout begins.

district office any office away from newspaper's main one.

doorstepping journalists pursuing sources by standing outside their front doors. Now journalists often wait in cars.

dots per inch a way of measuring printing and scanning resolution.

double page spread facing pages used for the same story.

downpage story appearing in bottom half of newspaper page.

downtable subs other than the chief and deputy chief subs (who often used to sit at the top table of the subs room).

drop letter (also **drop cap**) printed version of the illuminated letters that started hand-scribed bibles and other manuscripts. The letter is large enough to run alongside two or three lines of text.

Drudge Report US gossip web site run by Matt Drudge which controversially first exposed the President Clinton/Monica Lewinsky scandal in January 1998.

dumbing-down claim that media standards, in general, are falling with increasing emphasis on sensationalism, celebrities, 'human interest' stories, sexual titillation, scandal and sleaze. See also **tabloidisation**.

dummy newspaper mock-up to track the placing of adverts.

edition specific version of a publication. Editions can be published for a specific day or a specific time of day or place.

editionalising publishing more than one edition on any day to take in breaking news.

ellipses three dots (. . .) usually indicating a pause or that some copy is missing.

em the square of the body height of the typesize. *See* **mutton**.

embargo time (often found on press release) before which information should not be published.

em-dash a dash the size of an em.

em-quad the square of the body type. Usually assumed to be a pica-em or a 12 pt.

en half an em.

entry point the place the page designer intends to draw the reader to on starting the page.

EPS encapsulated postscript: a digital graphics format.

exclusive story supposedly unique carried by newspaper. System becomes devalued when attached to stories too frequently or when the same story is carried in other newspapers (as often happens).

expanded a version of a font that has been expanded horizontally.

eyewitness reporting presence of reporter at news event can provide unique opportunities for descriptive writing.

face typeface.

fact box listing of facts (often boxed) relating to story. Useful way of creating visual and copy variety on page.

feature as distinct from news story, tends to be longer, carry more background information, colour, wider range of sources and journalist's opinion can be prominent.

filler short story, usually of one or two pars, filling in space when a longer story runs short (also known as 'brief').

fireman person sent from newspaper's headquarters to cover major story (either at home or abroad). (Notice gender bias in word.)

flat plan plan of publication showing all pages (see Figure 17.1).

font family of type characters.

footer bottom margin area of the page often used to insert the publication title, date or page number.

Fourth Estate the supposed position of the press as the fourth most powerful institution after Lords Spiritual, Lords Temporal and Commons. (Lord Macaulay: 'The gallery in which reporters sit has become a fourth estate of the realm.')

freebie range of services and entertainments (e.g. drinks, meals, trips abroad funded by organisations, concert tickets, etc.) provided free to journalists. Some journalists believe acceptance of freebies compromises 'objectivity' and refuse them.

freelance journalist contributing to several media outlets and not on permanent staff of any one organisation. See also **stringer**. US: freelancer.

full out when text occupies the full measure of the column.

full point full stop.

generalist non-specialist reporter. News teams tend to be mixes of generalists and specialists.

gonzo journalism a highly subjective genre of journalism, sometimes drug induced, pioneered by the American, Thompson (1937–2005) in the 1960s and 1970s.

gutter space between pages.

half-tone any rasterised picture where shades of grey are represented by different-sized dots.

handout story sent to media outlets by press relations office of organisation or PR company.

hanging indent the first line of a paragraph is full out while the rest is indented, usually by one em.

hard copy copy typed on sheets of paper (usually A4 size). Each page is known as a folio.

hard news news focusing on who, what, where, when, why based on factual detail and quotes and containing little description, journalist comment or analysis. See **soft news**.

heavies broadsheet 'serious' papers such as *Guardian, The Times, Financial Times*.

house media organisation. Thus in-house (meaning within particular media organisation). House organ is company's own newspaper or magazine. See also **style**.

human-interest story story focusing on success, failures, tragedies, emotional or sexual histories of people, eliminating or marginalising more abstract and deeper cultural, economic, political, class-based factors.

imprint the printer's and publisher's details. Required by law.

indent small space at start of line.

index listing of contents of publication.

intranet a privately maintained computer network that can be accessed only by authorised persons.

intro opening of news or feature story usually containing main angle. Not necessarily just single par. Also known as 'lead'. US: nose.

inverted pyramid traditional representation of news stories (with main point at start and information declining in news value thereafter and ending with short background). Tends to oversimplify structure of news story. Better to imagine series of inverted pyramids within an overall large pyramid.

investigative reporting in one respect all journalism involves investigation. But investigative journalism tends to reveal something of social or political significance which someone powerful or famous wants hidden. US: muckraking.

issue all copies of the day's paper and its editions.

justification a way of setting type to ensure that all lines on both sides of the block of text are level.

lead pronounced 'led'. The space between lines which is additional to the size of the body type. So called because it was originally strips of metal (lead) which spaced out lines of type.

lead pronounced 'leed'. The main story on the page. Could also mean the story's intro.

leader the editorial comment.

leaders line of dots, dashes or other devices to lead the eye across the page especially in a table.

leading pronounced 'ledding': as 'lead' above but also used to mean the actual space (as opposed to the body type) in which the type lives.

letterpress printing method that presses raised, inked type against paper.

lexia small fragments of text.

lift to use whole or section of story from one edition to the next; also to pinch story from other media outlet changing and adding only a little. When barest minimum is changed known as 'straight lift'.

linage   payment to freelances based on number of lines of copy used.

listings   lists usually of entertainment events giving basic information: times, venue, phone numbers and so on.

lithography   printing method that relies on the inability of oily ink and water to mix.

lobby   specialist group of correspondents reporting on the House of Commons.

masthead   paper's title piece.

measure   width of a block of text measured in 12 pt ems.

middle-market   newspapers such as *Mail* and *Express* which lie (in overall style and appearance) between *heavies* and the *red-tops*.

mutton   slang name for an em.

narrowcasting   targeting publication to specific groups of people such as property owners or clubbers.

negs   photographic negatives.

nibs   short news stories.

nut   slang name for an en.

off the record   when statements are made not for publication but for background only. Information derived from comments should in no way be traceable back to source.

off-beat   unusual story often with a humorous twist.

on spec   uncommissioned article submitted voluntarily to media.

on the record   when there are no restrictions on reporting what is said.

op ed   abbreviation of opposite editorial, being the page opposite one on which editorial/leader comment falls. Usually contains important features and commentary by prestigious columnists.

opinion piece   article in which journalist expresses overt opinion.

orphan   short line left at foot of column.

outro   final section of a feature.

pagination   arrangement and number of pages in publication.

par, para   abbreviation for paragraph.

patch   geographic area of special interest.

pay-off   last par with twist or flourish.

pica   old name for 12 pt.

pick-up   journalist attending function might pick up or take away a photograph supplied by the organisers, known as a pick-up job; also journalists following up an event after it has happened is 'picking up' news.

pierce   cutting a shape into a picture to insert type or another picture.

pitching   proposing story idea to newspaper/magazine.

pix   journalese for pictures/photographs (singular: pic).

poached   when a staff member is lured to a rival publication (usually with the bait of a higher salary and/or fancier title).

point   unit of typographical measurement. Approximately 72 pt to the inch or 0.01383'.

pool   privileged, small group of journalists with special access to event or source. Their reports and findings are distributed to those news organisations outside the pool.

popbitch   www.popbitch.com web site focusing on satirical celebrity gossip.

pops/populars mass-selling national tabloids; now known as red-tops because their mastheads are in red.

press release announcement made by organisation specially for use by media (not necessarily just press).

probe investigation.

process colour another name for four-colour printing using four different coloured inks. Also known as CMYK.

profile picture in words which usually focuses on an individual but organisations, cars, horses, a building, and so on can be profiled.

proof to mark editorial changes/corrections on draft copy of text/graphic.

puff advert for editorial material inside a publication.

pull quote short extract from news or feature set in larger type as part of page design.

punchline main point of story. Thus 'punchy' means story has a strong news *angle*.

qualities see **broadsheets**.

quote abbreviation for quotation; also when a reporter files copy over phone 'quote' then means first inverted commas. End quote marks are often known as 'unquote'.

raster dot dot of ink in a screened picture that allows shades of grey to be represented with black ink.

readership number of people who read paper as opposed the number of copies sold.

red-tops tabloid newspapers such as the *Mirror*, *Sun* and *People*, so-called because their mastheads are red.

register exact alignment of the four plates used to print the four colours of ink used in four-colour printing.

rejig/rehash rearrangement of copy provided by reporter usually by sub-editor to produce a better structured piece.

renose to change the angle of a story.

replate unplanned change of plate on the press to produce a new page to include urgent news or correct a major mistake.

retrospective feature looking back on event.

revamp change story or page in light of new material.

revise see **proof**.

rewrite to use information provided in story but compose it in completely new language. Known as 'rewrite job'.

ring-around story based on series of telephone calls.

roman not bold or italic.

round-up gathering together of various strands of story either under the same heading (otherwise known as umbrella story) or under variety of headings.

roving reporter reporter who travels around a lot.

RSI abbreviation for 'repetitive strain injury' which journalists can suffer through their use of a keyboard and mouse.

rule a straight line.

run period of printing edition.

running story story which runs or develops over a number of editions or days.

sans serif modern style font without (sans) the serif (the fine line finishing the main strokes of a letter such as at the foot of 'T').

scoop   exclusive.

sexy story   story with popular appeal. But many 'sexy stories' give sex a bad name.

sidebars   short stories printed alongside longer article providing additional, contrasting or late-breaking items.

side-head   heading within a block of text.

sign-off   byline at foot of story.

silly season   supposedly a time (usually in the summer holiday period) when little hard news is around and the press is reduced to covering trivia. For some newspapers silly season can last a long time. Wars and invasions often happen in silly seasons, too.

sister paper   when company owns more than one paper each is described as sister. Thus *The Times* is the *Sun*'s sister since both are owned by Rupert Murdoch.

sketch   light, often witty article describing event. Most commonly used with reference to reporting House of Commons.

slip   special edition for particular area or event.

snap   brief information given by news agency before main story is sent.

snapper   photographer.

soft news   light news story that can be more colourful, witty and commenty than hard news.

soundbite   short, pithy quote used by journalists. First coined by US radio and television journalists in the late 1960s.

spike   to reject copy or other information (e.g. press release). Derived from old metal spike which stood on wooden base on which subs would stick unwanted material. Had advantage over 'binning' since material was accessible so long as it remained on spike.

spin doctors   people who attempt to influence news or political agenda (the 'spin' in the jargon) such as press officers, communications specialists and other propagandists.

splash   lead news story on front page.

spot colour   additional colour added to a black-and-white publication.

standfirst   text intended to be read between headline and story which can elaborate on point made in headline, add new one or raise questions which will be answered in story (a teaser). Sometimes contains byline. Helps provide reader with a 'guiding hand' into reading large slice of copy – thus mainly used for features and occasionally long news stories. Also known as the 'sell'.

strapline   heading placed over another heading or headings.

streamer   heading covering the full width of the page.

stringer   freelance, in provinces, in London or overseas, who has come to arrangement with news organisation to supply copy on agreed basis. Super-stringer will contract to devote most of working for one organisation but still be free to freelance for other media outlets for rest of time.

style   special rules adopted by newspaper relating to spellings, punctuation and abbreviation. Often contained within style book though increasingly carried on screen. Many newspapers somehow survive without them.

sub-editor/sub   responsible for editing reporters' copy, writing headlines, captions, laying out pages etc. Stone sub makes final corrections and cuts on page proofs. US: copy editor.

tabloid   newspaper whose pages are roughly half the size of broadsheet. All pops or popular papers are tabloids as are sections of some of the heavies. Serious tabloids exist in France (*Le Monde*, for instance) and in the USA (*Los Angeles Times*).

tabloidese shoddy, over-sensational, cliché-ridden copy most commonly associated with the tabloids.

tabloidisation claim that media in general are following tabloid values prioritising entertainment, sensationalism and scandal above 'hard facts'.

taxonomy breakdown of an issue into groups, categories or listings.

teaser a headline which only hints at the main angle of the story.

template page on the computer screen providing a basic design pattern.

think piece analytical article.

thumbnail substantially reduced image of a page or graphic.

tip-off information supplied to media by member of the public.

titlepiece publication's name and logo.

to legal to send copy to lawyer to be checked for libel, contempt etc.

tots abbreviation for 'triumph over tragedy story', particularly popular human interest genre.

trim cut a report.

two-way broadcast discussion between studio anchor/newsreader and reporter.

typefaces full range of type of the same design.

umbrella story see *round-up*.

underline to carry a line or rule under headline or *crosshead*.

upper case capital letters when used alongside small (*lower case*) letters. When just capital letters are used (as in headlines) they are known as *caps*.

URL uniform resource location: a string of characters identifying internet resource and its location; the most common ones begin http://.

web browser software for viewing web sites, such as Internet Explorer and Netscape Navigator.

whistleblower person revealing newsworthy and previously secret information to media.

widow short line left at top of column.

x-height element of the typeface minus the ascender and descender (in effect, the size of the lower-case 'x').

zeitgeist spirit of the age.

A list of useful web sites

<http://www.192.com>, electoral register, directory enquiries.
<http://www.abc.org.uk>, Audit Bureau of Circulations.
<http://www.africa-confidential.com>, for in-depth Africa news.
<http://www.amnesty.org>, Amnesty International.
<http://www.anti-spin.com>, campaigning site.
<http://www.ananova.com>, breaking news.
<http://www.bjr.org.uk>, British Journalism Review.
<http://www.bl.uk/collections/newspapers.html>, British Library newspaper collection.
<http://www.cjr.org>, Columbia Journal Review.
<http://www.corporatewatch.org.uk>, critical analysis of News Corporation etc.
<http://www.cpbf.org.uk>, Campaign for Press and Broadcasting Freedom.
<http://www.cpj.org>, US-based Committee to Protect Journalists.
<http://www.companieshouse.gov.uk>, information on companies.
<http://www.dictionary.com>
<http://www.disinfo.com>, US-based site focusing on surveillance, counterculture.
<http://www.hrw.org>, Human Rights Watch.
<http://www.holdthefrontpage.co.uk>, massive local newspapers database.
<http://www.indexon-line.org>, *Index on Censorship*, opposing censorship worldwide.
<http://www.indymedia.org>, alternative, radical politics.
<http://www.johnpilger.com>, site of the celebrated investigative reporter.
<http://www.journalismuk.co.uk>, journalism links.
<http://www.medialens.org>, media monitoring.
<http://www.minorityrights.org>, Minority Rights Group.
<http://www.muncipalyearbook.co.uk>, online searching on councils.
<http://www.newsdesk-uk.com>, site for journalists.
<http://www.nujtraining.org.uk>, training organised by the union.
<http://www.ofcom.gov.uk>, site of new media regulator, Office of Communications.
<http://www.ojr.org>
<http://www.parliament.uk>, includes Hansard reports of debates.
<http://www.polis.parliament.uk>, massive parliament database.
<http://www.presswise.org.uk>, campaigning over media ethics.
<http://www.presscouncils.org>, press councils across the world.
<http://www.quoteland.com>, a quotation search engine.
<http://www.rsf.org>, Reporters sans frontières, Reporters without borders.

<http://www.schnews.org.uk>, alternative news.
<http://www.spinwatch.org>, monitoring spin with radical fervour.
<http://www.statistics.gov.uk>, statistics from government departments.
<http://www.thesaurus.com>, *Roget's Thesaurus.*
<http://www.upmystreet.com>, local information and maps.
<http://www.un.org/womenwatch/index.html>, campaigning for women.

Index